Gratitude for Power Wishing

"Anne Louise is a very intuitive teacher who is able to communicate in a way that resonates so clearly for each person on a different level, awakening their Soul. After learning Power Wishing techniques, I have tools to be present and stay awake. My emotions support me, creating a life that is happy. I am living experiences that are no longer challenges." – Jamie

"*Power Wishing* has been an invaluable tool in my life because it allowed me to become a happier version of me. I have awareness of the things I want to shift in my life and take emotional steps, instead of staying in my head." – Alina

"*Power Wishing* is an extremely important book of tools and strategies to enhance your life in a positive and healthy way. It has helped me tremendously on an ongoing basis in every area of my life. As if I woke up to more possibilities that are realized and more joy in areas that I wished to enhance." – Meagan

"*Power Wishing* gave me the emotional base when I sold my house. I went through the steps Anne Louise describes and I sold my house just like that. I recommend *Power Wishing* to others because these tools are life skills and go beyond regular techniques of visualizing what you want in your life. It is a system that is now my lifestyle." – Dan

"The most useful tool I have received from *Power Wishing* is to be able to organize my feelings and thoughts so I know the direction of where I am going and I am in control of what I am creating. I began to use Anne Louise's *Stage Your Day Technique* and I quickly realized how my imagination creates my experiences and I design here first. Anne Louise is a special gift to the world." – Joyce

"Anne Louise's techniques are truly encapsulated in *Power Wishing*. Her work has a profound transformative effect on my life. It has helped me visualize and manifest realities so quickly and with such ease. Her work is full of Light and Love. This book will influence immense positive change on any reader." – Isa

"Anne Louise's *Power Wishing* has changed my life for the better. I was not sure how to get my dreams out of my head and actualize them. With these tools I was surprised how easy it was. Everyone deserves this gift of her work, she is full of insight and knowing." – Ingrid

POWER WISHING®

VISUALIZATION TECHNOLOGY® FOR MANIFESTING
Master Your Vibrational Language® To Enhance Your Life

www.PowerWishing.com

November 2017

Dear Sam,

Thank you for being so cool!
So real and wonderful to share with.
Many Blessings of Joy
and
adventure

ISBN: 978-0-9911822-0-6
First Edition: July 2014

POWER WISHING

VISUALIZATION TECHNOLOGY FOR MANIFESTING
Master Your Vibrational Language To Enhance Your Life

Anne Louise Carricarte
www.PowerWishing.com

Simple Results©
Inspiration. Enhancement. Success.

My belief is that we are all enlightened
Whether you choose to be awake or asleep
with your enlightened self is a choice...
The choice is called free will.

— Anne Louise Carricarte

To my children Sophia & Andrew –
With both of you in my life,
every moment is a wish granted.

Contents

The Gift

Anne Louise Carricarte is a unique and profound teacher whose playful and powerful work comes from the heart. Her mission in life is truly to share her intuition and insight with others on this magical journey we call life. Anne Louise, known as "Missy" to many, has a deep knowing and wisdom that amazes and delights those fortunate to be touched by her gift.

I have been honored to closely support her in the past five years as she expanded her extensive body of work to share with a broader audience. I have had the privilege to witness the results of her private consultations with various clients, from top Fortune 500 CEOs to her neighbor's grandmother, as well as the effect her work has had on the thousands of participants who attend her workshops and seminars. In this time, I have personally journeyed through my own life and manifested results both small and substantial using the effective principles and tools of *Power Wishing®*. I have witnessed the potency and true magic of her work on a personal level and through all of the touched souls who receive the empowering awareness and capacity to consistently create the authentic life they desire.

Anne Louise's work truly awakens renewed self-awareness in others and creates clarity for manifesting the goals and desires you dream of. Often called a "Soul Catalyst," she inspires and is able to break through emotional barriers to allow your authentic spirit to move forward with joy and ease. Her teachings cut through the self-created chaos and unnecessary drama to see the cause and effect of a situation clearly. Her inspiring messages bring out an emotional mindfulness and her valuable formulas deepen your knowledge of how to form the certainty of achieving success and prosperity without struggle.

Anne Louise has a layered perspective and understanding of the psychology of human behavior and relationships, religion, spirituality and metaphysics. She truly is a visionary powerhouse of intelligence and imagination. Refreshing, candid, and compassionate, Anne Louise's writings pose insightful questions, share informative case studies from her years of private consultations and workshops, and offer efficient tools to support stimulation of your aspired potential. Able to merge ancient universal laws, spiritual teachings and other knowledge into modern day living, she provides a powerful and supportive safe space for self-reflection of the potential paths you desire to create in your life.

At any point, when Anne Louise discusses Universal Energy, Creator, God, Spirit, etc., please know, as she often shares, that it is not her intention to define God for anyone. She strongly supports your own definition and relationship with God and sincerely respects that we all have different religions, beliefs, backgrounds and experiences. The beauty of her teachings is that they awaken emotions on a deep level differently for everyone and they personally resonate in their own profound way for each one of us.

Anne Louise offers you an opportunity to claim your wellbeing, create more joy and abundance, and steer your life in the direction of dreams. As you journey through *Power Wishing* and experience the gift of Anne Louise, you will be blessed in experiencing a wonderful journey of heightened awareness, a strengthened spiritual connection and an enhanced life that you create by simply visioning, believing what you expect and Power Wishing.

—   Christina Nicodemou, Director of Simple Results

A Message From Anne Louise

So often we have wishes that we think about all day long. I remember when I was a young girl I would love to visit wishing wells. I cherished my opportunity to throw a penny in and make a wish. This simple act made me feel that my wish had the possibility to be true. With this action, my hopes felt reinforced by my belief that the wishing well gave some magical care to my wish and I was not alone, as if a messenger took my wish somewhere special to come true. I still smile as I remember this hopeful feeling of wishing and feeling so certain my wish would be granted.

I developed Power Wishing® based on a playful way to integrate a solid foundation of Universal Law and proven formulas for manifesting. My work has a playful approach: I use wishing as a way to have lightness with creating your world and to bring playfulness to the seriousness of life. Though a wish may feel as though it does not have real form, it does. This body of work is a vehicle to bring awareness to what you expect from your feelings of hopes, dreams and wishes. This body of work is powerful and proactive. You will consciously transform your feelings to beliefs that manifest your life, and at the same time release creating experiences that do not serve you. You will create clarity of what you desire. What you believe is possible is what you believe you can expect; Power Wishing gives you the tools to enhance your awareness and identify your beliefs to accomplish this.

If something is worth having, then it is worth asking for. When you wish, you are asking – this is the start that creates the possibility of a wish being granted to you in your physical experience.

I believe we are all Amazing Souls that are given Divine gifts by Loving Energy that many name God, G-d, Source Energy, Creator or Spirit, among others. How you define this Energy is personal to you. I am not here to define God, and I sincerely respect your personal relationship and definition. What I know to be true through my own personal connection with Source Energy, and what I will share, is my belief that we are all connected to this Universal Source Energy of Love. I believe this "Source

Energy" is a pool of Love waiting for us to consciously access it. In accessing this love, you remember your true Self and activate the gifts that are Divinely yours to manifest your Soul's calling as your physical reality. I wholeheartedly believe in this Love that has given us the tools to be the deliberate creator of our lives. My intention for this work is that you wake up every day feeling empowered, knowing how to activate your life as a wish granted.

Love is personal, as is everyone's individual journey and Soul. Your dreams and how you believe to live them is distinctive for you. I would like to reiterate and be clear that I do not define what love is for you or advocate any spiritual doctrine within this writing. I simply wish to bring awareness for you to explore your Divinity.

I am not separate from my teachings; they are a part of me. Through my own personal connection with Source Energy, and with years of studies and experience working with formulas to create and manifest, I believe we are absolutely connected and co-creating with this Source Energy. I am not separate from this Universal Source Energy of Love; it is within me and surrounds me.

Love is a special gift; life is a gift of love.
Your Soul is here to experience the experience of love – yes!
It really is all about love.

As far back as I can remember, it fascinated me as I observed that all human behavior was motivated by the desire to be loved or give love, and this created our beliefs about ourselves and what we believe we can expect from the world that surrounds us.

With this awareness, I became passionate about asking why people live their lives embracing love or actively pushing it away. Why do they say they wish they could do this or that and then do not? It seemed at some point that many forgot they are Amazing Souls and instead felt trapped in this "world."

In my eyes, the world is a magical playground for creation. Having a fine sense of intuition since I can remember, I observed the world with this sixth sense, which gave me an opportunity to witness from a place of multiple perspectives. I can feel the energies of others, and can also feel unseen energies all around me. As a child, I assumed everyone could see and feel the same way. I just presumed that everyone processed the same and then I realized that I processed my surroundings differently than most. I also have the gift of dyslexia, and this is another layer that influenced my way of processing. At times this created a feeling of solitude. I remember sharing with my grandmother about my differences and discussing my insecurity about wearing bifocal glasses on top of all this and she said, "There is nothing wrong with you, you just see differently." At the time, I was fortunate enough to avoid being labeled as dyslexic or extrasensory, etc., as these labels were not as popular or mainstream. Besides these differences in my perception, I was often told I was overly sensitive so I naturally was placed in a position to just figure things out for myself. In order to keep up in school and personal studies of interest, I had to learn another way. Because my processing was not conventional, I became aware of how I could depict patterns and simplify concepts. I became very observant of this and grew my trust in the fact that I filtered my surroundings differently; therefore, I was able to receive different information.

Though it may seem like a wonderful gift to be able to "see" and feel in a more complex multi-dimensional way, more often than not, as I got older this gift added to me feeling like an outsider. I witnessed all that I "saw" and attempted to process human behaviors that were painful to feel with my heightened sensitivity. It took me some time to learn how to language the empathy of what I was witnessing. This often caused me to retreat to the consolation of Spirit as I did as a child and continued as an adult and to learn from that perspective. Nevertheless, as a child I trusted my relationship with Source Energy and my gift of partnering with this energy, and I found comfort and wellbeing in this Love. To this day, this is where I find my comfort, understanding and knowing. For me, there is no loneliness in this place.

I began to quickly realize that this language of *emotions* was one that few paid attention to. I found myself asking, "Is it possible to feel love for others and ourselves as a core emotion and utilize this to manifest differently no matter what our life circumstances are?" "Why do so many people treat emotions like a liability?" "Is it possible to formulate our emotions to systematically work for us as an asset and stay aware as Conscious Creators?"

As I grew older, I was more and more aware of my ability to connect with Spirit, read energy and interpret people's emotions on a deeper level with my gift of sense. From the early age of 14, I began to fine-tune my intuition and learn other healing practices with spiritual teachers and mentors. It took me many years to perfect how to language the understanding of this skill and balance my sensitivity of witnessing and interpreting the energy of feelings to support others. I am able to "see" patterns, life plans, and the "Movie" of a Soul through the DNA of a person and through that person connect to ones close to them and their family DNA in the seen and unseen. This definitely can be complex at times, but there is also a simple beauty of love when reading a Soul and sharing as I witness others awaken with knowing of their true Self. This is beautiful because it has served as a gracious and life-altering gift to activate this in their life. I use the information from these energetic readings to support them to shift beliefs for themselves, as well as past and future generations.

Through these interpretations, I am able to deliver compassionate understanding, self-empowered healing and enhanced awareness of the connection to your Soul as it relates to your partnership with the Universe we live in. My work is always about empowering you to be your number one resource and know that you are Divine beyond your imagination. I will remind you of your gifts and capabilities with tools to reinforce the power you have to activate your life as you wish; no person, no thing, no circumstance has power over you. They only possess the power you give them. You are the power of your creation, you have already been provided with all that is necessary to create the life you wish for, and it is your discovery of this that activates these opportunities to achieve your wishes granted.

Everyone desires to both give and receive love in their lives, but all too often our emotional behaviors do not serve the love our rational Self may define. And these behaviors create beliefs of what we can expect and greatly shape our life experiences. How do we shift our life experiences? How do we stay connected to ourselves and have healthy boundaries of love with beliefs that honor that which we genuinely are? Can we do so even when it feels the world around us seems to be falling apart? How do we utilize our emotions to drive our great potential as our physical reality?

All these questions and more created a passionate drive for me to find a simple formula to manifest our dreams. Like many of you, through my own personal life challenges, I desired to heal emotionally and physically at different crossroads in my life. I have seen great abuse, loss, betrayal and sickness. Through all of this, I have continued to persevere through my conscious connection to Source Energy, and ultimately, to live a life that I love that is a constant expansion of whom I am. I witness my external world as a reflection of what I love. Even when I find myself in moments of chaos, there is tranquility in my Soul that navigates my direction. Through my work, I offer you a safe space to allow your perception of possibilities to expand creatively and for your connection to Absolute Love to strengthen.

I feel fortunate to be able to explore my passion and empower results for so many to experience being the "Amazing Soul" that they are and feel a heightened sense of love. There is so much to explore in life and there is far more Divinity to explore within ourselves. *What is seen with our naked eye is limiting in relation to all that is unseen within us.*

I believe that we all have the opportunity to create our lives as our design and to live a life feeling free and joyful. I also understand that we can benefit from a type of structure to support ourselves emotionally to achieve our dreams. Power Wishing gives you the framework where you can easily structure your life as you wish it to be and become a true master of your emotions and experiences. This work supports you with awareness of your Soul's voice by harmonizing this with your personality to create dreams as reality here in the physical.

I have dedicated my studies, my gifts and my time to supporting others to resolve emotional conflicts, illness and pain. Many of us experience anxiety and chaos with loving ourselves, maintaining physical and emotional health, sustaining loving relationships, and achieving joy and success. We often carry beliefs that sabotage these goals and push love away.

The gift of Power Wishing is to support you with harmony in all areas of your life as you shift your emotions, solidifying your beliefs for life experiences that bring you inner peace, happiness and abundance with ease. This is an organized system of emotion-based formulas to support you in enhancing or shifting patterns in your life. Tried and tested, the body of work I present to you is not theory; it is based on proven results. I began teaching and writing my work over 30 years ago, as I gave my first formal workshop of *self-awareness* at the age of eighteen.

This has been my life's work, which is based of my life creations, whether it is in relationships, my family, my children or business. The emotional structure of a human being fascinates me. Everyone has their story and it amazes me to see what people choose to do with the experiences of their lives. I have developed successful workshops and courses such as Power Wishing, Language Your Life®, Visualization Technology®, and Character Legacy among others, which are based on strengthening one's emotional intelligence and foundation.

I am passionate about witnessing others awaken to having a greater appreciation for themselves with more love, and therefore love others in a way that they could not have previously imagined. I love the smiles that reflect the empowerment they feel to create their world and the joy they feel when they become deliberate creators. In my view, it is not about right or wrong, it is about fine-tuning your definition of life that is authentic. It is really about witnessing, examining and choosing your emotional experience. I deeply appreciate how this work resonates with people from all walks of life and how they begin to live a fuller, healthier life experience after they begin to use Power Wishing. They quickly take accountability for their own emotional wellbeing and enhance their best Self to be the reflection of their actions. Experiencing miracles soon becomes a normal way of life.

I often say "Your Soul Will Win." By this, I mean that your Soul will always desire to be aligned toward fulfilling its purpose. When you are off track and not living a life genuine to your Soul's purpose, I believe your Soul will give you signs to redirect you; those signs are guided by your emotions. Your emotions are an extraordinary asset to lead you, like a GPS would, to support you in navigating your driving route.

Our life experience is a journey, and each of our paths is unique and ever changing. I believe our experiences provide the emotional growth we wish to explore in our life. The foundational purpose of my work is to proactively awaken the expansion of one's definition of Love, Joy and Divine Love – an experience where you feel this as your connection to your Self and the world around you.

No matter what the circumstances are …
We can always choose love.
And no matter what the circumstances are …
It is always our choice.

Define your life with your definition; your life is a definition of YOU! Connect every bit of your being with the power of love, kindness and gratitude, expecting the best! It has been my wish for many years to translate this beloved body of work into a book and share the understanding that we are to experience life full of love, wellbeing and joy. I thank you for sharing with me what is so dear to my heart and Soul.

With love and blessings for your continued wishes granted,

Anne Louise – "Missy"

Amazing Soul

Life is a continuous journey, an ever-evolving story full of unique experiences that define who you are. It's not about being perfect; it is about being a reflection of how you define yourself as the Amazing Soul you are.

You Are An Amazing Soul

I truly believe we are all Amazing Souls and *we are having an emotional experience of our Soul in the physical.*[1] We activate this experience by utilizing our emotions and our imagination. As we play out our emotions as the expression of what we believe we deserve, our life reality unfolds.

Life = Your Definition

Our imagination plays out these emotions as scenes, possibilities to the "Movie" we wish to have as the reality we create outside of ourselves which is called life. Playing out your emotional scenes as a "Movie" in your imagination allows you to play with possibilities so you may have clarity about your choices and what you expect. This is more efficient than playing out several of these possibilities in your day-to-day experiences. In your imagination, you can figure out what you really wish for and therefore accelerate the process of manifesting[2] by attracting your expectation into your reality.

My philosophy is that there is nothing to fix in you. No matter what has happened, no matter what you are feeling right now, I assure you that you are not broken, damaged or incomplete. Sometimes circumstances in your life are not what you would like to have experienced I understand that this can be hurtful, sad and challenging.

---

[1] When I use the word physical, I am referring to our physical bodies and our physical existence here on Earth – to the physical world.
[2] By manifesting, I mean bringing something you desire into your physical life. Whether it is love, health, a new home or different career.

This does not mean you need fixing or you are broken. We often focus too much energy on what we define as "broken" or on what "needs fixing" in our life. Instead of thinking you need to fix things about your Self or your life, I like to think of it as simply desiring a different experience that feels better and is a more defined match of who you truly are.

We Attract More Of What We Say

It is best to avoid constantly talking about what we say we do not want because then we naturally focus on what needs "fixing," which is comical when we wish to attract the opposite. With this as your focus, your mental "to-do" list keeps growing with what you think needs changing. You likely continue another list about what needs to be fixed in others and in the world. Your energy focuses on what you don't want, which only attracts more of it, so I say, "Forget that list!"

The feeling that you or others need fixing will get resolved when you focus on what you love about your Self and others. When you focus on what you love, then whatever you believe needs fixing will resolve itself because what you love has taken the place of lack or drama.

Your World Is Your Quantum Leap

Power Wishing® utilizes Universal Law and the principles of quantum physics in its formula. The beauty of Power Wishing is it provides you quantum physics in a digestible format, sharing basic formulas based on key principles that will greatly enhance your awareness.

These formulas enable you to build a solid foundation of awareness, so you can construct your world and experience your life consciously and purposefully in a way that you desire. Remember, your conscious and intentional thoughts, as well as your unconscious and unintentional thoughts, all contribute to what you manifest.

Why is quantum physics at the base of Power Wishing? Quantum physics investigates the nature of reality from an unseen level. All humans, animals, objects, events, experiences, circumstances stem from somewhere. Quantum physics examines this and breaks it all down to the most basic form, just as Power Wishing does with your emotions. Quantum physics attempts to reveal where all physical things are derived from and demystifies the process of creation.

Whether you realize it or not, quantum physics, your spirituality, your ideas, feelings and accomplishments or lack of accomplishments in life are all very closely intertwined and interconnected. Quantum physics determines what happens in your life, your environment and even all the Universal Energy and matter that we cannot see with the human eye. Power Wishing uses this concept as it relates to your emotions, which translates to the Vibrational Language[3] that you manifest with.

My studies of quantum physics enabled me to fine-tune the Power Wishing formula to create clear results for manifesting. Although many of my diverse studies guided me in creating these formulas, it is through a deeper understanding of quantum physics that I developed a stronger belief in my own personal ability to consciously create the experiences I desired to have in life.

With my gift of multi-dimensional sight, I am able to see what goes unseen by so many. There are many unanswerable questions pertaining to life and death in our society and I wish to share what I know and have been privileged to witness. I desire to share this information so that even the questions and concerns we have about our loved ones passing on or our own struggle with disease and death can be met with ease.

For you as an Amazing Soul to be able to live in harmony with whom you truly are and feel complete with your expression of love in your physical experience. All is Divinely within you. Love brings the answers to all your questions and peace at the moment answers cannot be found.

What I know to be true is that the nature of human behavior, our experiences, the Earth's natural system, science, spirituality, as well as everything else, is all intricately tied together.

As you discover Power Wishing, you will experience the benefits of quantum physics as a system to easily manifest miraculous life changes that are activated by you.

Even if your life right now may be challenging, if all you did was recognize the good in you and acknowledge the *good will* that surrounds you, a shift would already begin.

---

[3] Throughout *Power Wishing*, you will develop a deeper understanding of the term Vibrational Language, as well as the "Ask," prayer, Source Energy, Emotional Imagination, Universal Computer, Authentic Self and your Emotional GPS.

You Always Find What You Are Looking For

Look for the good and the good will follow. I created my Power Wishing courses to give structure to the practice of manifesting your genuine desires and enhancing what you love as your life experience. The Power Wishing formula and tools support you to release repeating experiences that no longer serve you and shift habits to serve the experiences that do. This method truly supports you to enhance what you love and magnify that as your life experience.

What if you left behind shame, guilt and "fixing" by resolving what no longer serves you for the future you wish to have?

What if you released completely the notion you are punished or have "bad" consequences for being your Self?

What if you are able to bring forward from those experiences an acknowledgement of what will support you now?

What if the expansion of these experiences is the recognition of growth from your past to build into your future? What would that look like?

How different would your future look if you released regret and the idea of needing to fix the past or another?

What if you consciously brought the talents and gifts from your past experiences to the next part of your journey?

How would your life feel if you expressed and trusted more of your unique Authentic Self as your experience in your daily life?

Bringing forth this knowing, pulling forth this growth from your past, is utilizing your past as strength. With this strength, your journey continues as an experience of wholeness that honors the YOU that you truly are.

Different Choice = Different Opportunity

From time to time we may make choices that are not in our best interest; this does not make anyone a bad person. Although these choices may not make us feel good, it is nevertheless valuable to be accountable and aware so you can shift to better choices. If you have made an unhealthy choice, it does not mean you are an unhealthy person. You can always reflect on the choices you have made and create clarity on the different choice you would make now with your new understanding.

Using shame or judgment, especially with a child as a way to reprimand, only blocks them from being open towards making better choices. Some may feel that the emotions of guilt, shame, blame and judgment motivate us to make better choices, but how can you find better choices when you feel so bad about your Self? Imagine making a choice based on a foundation of guilt, shame or in the defense of feeling judged. Now imagine the choices that come from that. It is a choice that comes from a place of disempowerment.

Imagine knowing that you are always an Amazing Soul and you are here to have experiences and these are all opportunities for you to make choices, develop your vision and expand your emotional capacity. Things that we may call *bad* or *unhealthy* are experiences that have offered us contrast to know better what we wish to choose going forward. Heighten your human experience as a choice, and open your Self up to all that this world has to offer you, the Amazing Soul.

It's Your "Movie!"

"All the world's a stage
and all the men and women merely players:
they have their exits and their entrances;
and one man in his time plays many parts,
his acts being seven ages." – Shakespeare

I believe we are all here for an emotional experience. Each moment in your life is a part of your story, which I will often refer to in this book as your "Movie," and you are the "Director." By witnessing your life as a "Movie," you are able to make choices and build a life that is happening *for* you, not *to* you.

Through Power Wishing, you will start to observe your life as if you are witnessing a movie. You will witness your "Movie" with clarity and therefore respond to the scenes around you versus reacting to them. You will make choices that create scenes that serve the emotional experiences you wish to have. By having awareness that you are the director of your "Movie," there is a feeling of empowerment where you become an active participant in writing your script.

You can shift your experiences or "scenes" to create new ones, and you can even edit your perception of past scenes or performances. Acknowledge what has already been done and clarify how you desire to feel now. This is an empowering place from which to make healthy decisions. There is nothing to prove or defend. This is your "Movie!" You have the starring role on your stage.

Own The Rights To Your Script

Remember you are the lead star, the writer and the academy-award-winning director. You also choose the characters for your "Movie." Take full rights and ownership of your script or allow someone else to write it for you – the choice is yours.

- Do you feel as if you have signed away the rights to your script? Why would you allow another to write the "Movie" of your life? The experiences in your life support you to strengthen your lead role as YOU.
- Make choices to build with your experiences without the struggle of trying to fix what is already done, and view your past as an experience to strengthen your choices.
- You created one scene; therefore, you can create another one. You have the capability to write how you wish to experience your life circumstances and write new experiences into your life as you wish.

I know there are experiences that happen in life that have no real explanation and sometimes these are hard to process. When bad things happen to good people, how does one find any good in this? Sometimes we have no real understanding that can alleviate a painful experience, but we can choose how we wish to write this into the script of our "Movie."

How you choose to move forward in your life always remains your choice. Understanding how to observe your experiences and how you would like to feel are two important components of Power Wishing. Using the emotion-based formula of Power Wishing, you will build from the experiences you have had and shift or enhance them.

In one way or another, I believe that certain experiences or habits that may no longer serve us now have served us at one point in our lives.

You can use what you have learned and grow from these experiences. You can pull the positive aspects from these experiences into your present and allow your Self to release the pain and move forward with the healing. This is very different than distorting the truth of what happened or being in denial so you can attempt to move forward.

Using the past positively is about having a system to support what you wish to feel as you go through your current or future experience; you are making a choice. It is not what happens to you but how you choose to move forward that make the difference.

When bad things happen, we hear comments about how this was expected. Or you often hear, "You cannot always expect things to run so smoothly" or, "Sooner or later it had to go bad." When bad things happen, you may feel it was expected and not even question this.

What about all those unexpected good things that happen to good people? Really, more good happens than bad. But, where is your focus? I am always surprised when good things happen and people say, "This is too good to be true!" Great way to let the Universe know that when life feels good you would prefer to question it from a place where you lack trust in knowing that you are deserving.

How are you expecting to receive what you have asked for – with ease or with struggle?

Again, this is your choice.

Feel Good And *Good Will* Follow

What are you asking to find when you start your day?
What do you expect your experience to be?
Your expectation is what you anticipate and will therefore be your experience.
How are you expecting to receive what you have asked for?
You get what you are looking for.
Look for the good and you will find it.
Expect it.
You always get what you expect.
Expect it quickly, easily and with joy!
You always find what you are looking for.
Inherently, I believe that we all desire the same things: to be loved and visible to those we love.

Energy Meets Energy

Since my experience with my first formal teacher of self-awareness when I was 14 years old, and in my continuation of spiritual and other studies and teachings, what I know to be true is the Universe has an energetic frequency that is here to support us in creation of the experiences that we desire. We also have an energetic system that translates to a Vibrational Language®. This language is our "vibe" and encompasses our emotions, beliefs, thoughts, actions and words as a form of energetic communication. Our Vibrational Language is the form of communication used with this Universal energetic frequency, often called God or Divine Love.

Many times, the Vibrational Language that we carry is overlooked and not given the importance that it deserves. This is why mastering your Vibrational Language is essential to enhancing your life.

In Earthly terms, we have the controlling interest over our lives. We have the majority vote with our free will to make our choices. Sometimes we may feel that others or other forces are in control and affect our ownership of our life choices. I believe we all have free will, and this is what gives us the final vote.

What "If"

What I find extraordinary and exciting is that we as Amazing Souls have the power to create possibilities: our emotional experiences do translate into our life experiences because they define our expectations. We also have the opportunity to create our world by making choices through our Emotional Imagination®.

Because we have the ability to master our emotions, we have the ability to master our lives. With emotions, you can shape and shift your life into one that reflects what you love about yourself. When we feel self-love, we reflect this love with others, which naturally brings peace to our relationships.

Let's play! What if? Let's play with a story of you as an Amazing Soul, playfully thinking about different possibilities. Playing in your imagination with "What If" gives you another way to look at something, to open up possibilities with imagination and stories that lead you to another way of feeling.

So let's play with a story:

What if you as an Amazing Soul believe with total certainty that you chose to come to this Earth?

What if you planned which emotions you wish to explore as an expansion of your Soul and which experiences you could have as possibilities that would support this expansion?

What if you chose this because you desire to the opportunity to experience your Soul, an infinite energy of Love, made manifested human form?

What if your plan included the possibilities of other Souls to experience this with?

What if your Soul is conscious of this plan that was created together in harmony with Source Energy/God/Divine Love?

What if it is not a God or some outside force that asked you to have this plan but God reminding you that you are Divine and knowing?

What if YOU created this plan with Source Energy, being fully aware this connection supports you to accomplish what you desire?

What if prayer or meditation is a method to activate your Divine magnificent Soul to reveal your Authentic Self as a physical experience?

YOU have the opportunity to create and witness in action all your Soul desires here on Earth. How you choose to experience your Self emotionally is the formula that creates your world.

Your Soul has the whole "Movie" based on what experiences you ask to receive, along with the possibilities of different future stories. It is all there inside of you. Add to that the talents you wish to discover and emotions you wish to explore with other Souls you would like to share with. What if your destiny is not completely mapped out, but rather you have possibilities of destinies to choose that you placed in your path as spiritual Selves to experience your emotions in physical form?

What if you knew that once you arrived on Planet Earth that you would forget the details of your plan for the expansion of growth you said you wish to experience? At the time you created your plan, you understood this and it did not worry you because you knew that the re-discovery of your Self would be the excitement in your life. I feel this is why when we do discover something in ourselves that is a match to our plan, our Authentic Self, we get excited; it feels "right" as a reaffirming of this knowing.

What if you trust that your heart is so full of love that no matter what happens it is an act of grace, an act of love for the possibility to realign your Self authentically? What if at times you have forgotten this, and feel your life with fear and doubt? What if you know you are always loved, and can do no wrong for this love to be taken away from you? As an Amazing Soul, you know with total certainty that you are always in the hands of the Divine Love, that you are always seen and always matter with so much love. With this knowing, you are conscious and recognize that everything that happens is a part of your greater plan.

Of course, you are not left without a support system to discover what you wrote for your Self. You have a support system that aligns your physical experience with your Soul and this is done through your own emotions anchored in Divine Love. Your emotions bring you back home to your authentic magnificent Self.

Your Internal GPS: Emotions

Your Emotions are your "Internal GPS." We have an amazing emotional support system, and I designed Power Wishing to strengthen the knowing and activation of this system according to you as an individual.

We are all amazing and unique Souls that yearn for different life experiences. Because of this, not everyone's Emotional GPS will lead him or her to the same place. We are all different and we all emotionally awaken in our own way for different reasons, at different times. Not all feelings are the same or defined alike for everyone, even though we may have some feelings in common.

Respecting others on their journey is important. This is why it is valuable to listen to your own GPS as a guide to awakening your DNA and allow others to do the same.

Your emotions guide you to stay on track and make sure you stay in check with your Authentic Self. This is why when you stay connected to your Emotional GPS; you are being true to your Self. I will remind you time and time again that you are an Amazing Soul. Emotions are what awaken us.

Our emotions are so vital in driving us to a direction of peace, even when there is no logical understanding about our decisions. How many times have you heard about beautiful love stories that defy logic? You hear stories of people who randomly meet on a plane and then develop a loving life together forever as partners. Or you hear about someone moving across the country for no real reason besides a feeling that they should and then they discover a life where all their dreams are coming true. I have witnessed this in my own life and in the lives of so many. It never ceases to amaze me how we receive so many unexpected gifts when we stay connected to our internal Emotional GPS.

There are all these amazing rewards waiting for us if we just follow our intuition and simply listen to ourselves. Your intuition confirms when you are in alignment; it supports the discoveries you wish to find. When you feel good emotionally, it's because it is good. You have uncovered a discovery that is good for you. Feeling good is good! When you feel bad, you are simply off course and it should not be more complicated than that.

One of the blocks I observe with others to feeling *good* is the fear of making a wrong decision. I ask, "What is the worst that could happen?" Then I remind people that they can make other decisions. In Power Wishing, you break down your fear to an understanding so it is no longer an unknown energy that has much power over you.

Hello! Your Soul Is "Checking In!"

What if pain and feelings that do not feel good are a way for your Soul to remind you to check in with your Self? Pain is there for a reason! How loud or how painful does it have to be for you to listen to your Self?

If you could look in a mirror and see an image when you feel pain, it would be an image that shows you that you are misaligned somewhere within your Emotional Self. Do not ignore your pain; it is your Emotional GPS alerting you to a major detour. View this as an opportunity to check in with your Self. What if there are no "tests" or a *God* testing you? What if feeling tested is just an opportunity for you to reflect? This "feeling" is about taking a moment to reflect if you are aligned with your Soul's voice.

Let's imagine that in this experience here on Earth, the Universe has got our back. As with any new adventure in a new land, it is essential to learn the law of the land and how the system works. Some things are just what they are. Like gravity, it just is. You can challenge gravity, but it will not change. You can learn to work with gravity so it serves you.

As with the example of gravity, some things are what they are.

- We have emotions.
- We are emotional beings.
- There is an energetic system, a vibration that mirrors back the signals we send through our Vibrational Language.

The System Works For You

You can spend your life challenging these systems that are here to support you or you can choose to educate your Self to know how they work for you. Power Wishing supports you to be aware of an energetic system that you are connected to along with offering you powerful tools on how to use them to co-create a genuine life of loving choice.

Power Wishing is a technology[4] that supports you in your day-to-day life by acknowledging the knowing that you do indeed make choices on how to live your life. This is your "Movie!" Knowing how to manifest what you wish for through the discovery of your Self is made clear by using This Visualization Technology® is a systematic awareness tool for the discovery of your Self and the know-how to manifest what you wish through this discovery.

I know that at times life can seem challenging and we want "the quick fix," "the answer" or "the pill." We want the perfect method to secure our outcome, so we know what to expect. Life is not designed that way; there is no sure way to do anything. I developed this work because I truly believe that knowing your Self from a place where you master your emotions with trust creates inner security and stability. Being your authentic Emotional Self always gives you the best opportunity for the outcome you desire. From this emotional base, you are empowered to drive the direction of your life with ease as you master your life experiences. Life is not just about being inquisitive and asking questions; it's also about discovering the untapped resources within your Self that bring you the answers. We are not here to survive a life; we are here to have one worth living. Living your life as your Authentic Self is having a life where you acknowledge your Self as an Amazing Soul with blessings.

---

[4] I use the word technology because Power Wishing is an organic process that transforms into a system of programming.

Life As A Conscious Choice

As you lay this foundation of beliefs, play with the concepts of "What If?" "What Ifs" are those possibilities created using your Emotional Imagination to create thoughts, which support actions for the experience of Heaven-on-Earth as your life reality. With Power Wishing and through this imaginative play, you create life as a Conscious Choice and your "What Ifs" become "What Is!" There is no escape from your feelings. Your feelings are yours and there is no escape from your Self. This is a good thing, if you accept who you are.

Why would you avoid paying attention to your life? Avoiding the awareness and acknowledgment of how you feel is like having a long, long, long commercial in your "Movie" that keeps repeating itself.

Creating or enhancing from the perspective of your present circumstances of "What Is" when you wish for a different reality is not a very effective way to manifest. It is limiting. How can you believe in what you would like to be possible based on the present circumstances that you wish to shift?

When I speak of "What Is" versus "What If," I am also referring to how you feel – *How you feel now* versus *how you wish to feel.*

By acknowledging your awareness, which here I refer to as "What Is," you embrace and accept what is happening now without avoiding your feelings. This plays a vital role in moving to another scene in your "Movie" that you wish to choose now, which I refer to as "What If." If you could feel differently, what would the scene that you wish to choose for your life feel like now? By acknowledging this awareness, you create movement of energy from one place to another by anchoring to the "What If" possibility as an expectation. If you are not aware of "What Is," it is challenging to move to creating "What If."

Why have the commercials when you can use that essential space to have your "Movie," your way. That commercial space can be used to plug in your life choices instead of repeatedly showing advertisements that do not serve you.

When you are aware of "What Is" as a feeling, not circumstances, you can move towards the "What If" and how that would feel. Again, if you focus on your circumstances, you are limited. When you focus on the feelings to match the possibility you desire, then so be it, it will be done. Now that you have acknowledged "What Is," you have announced it to your core Self. It is like saying, "OK, I know where I am, I know how this feels ... Next! I am moving on towards the possibilities of asking from the place of "What If." When you are in the space of what could be, you play with stories as possibilities of your choices.

Playfully, we move forward with the knowing that you are a wonderful Amazing Soul expecting an amazing emotional experience here on Earth. I use the word "play," but in no way does this take away from how I value life and the seriousness of our choices.

Your Soul has the job of supporting the purpose you chose for your life experience; therefore, your Soul has a mission to keep you on track. Now that we have shared about the Amazing Soul that you are, we will explore Power Wishing as the Visualization Technology that it is, but it is also a way of life ... a lifestyle.

I invite you to embark on your journey of discovering the best aspects of your Self and others. Connect with emotions that feel good using tools that are designed to set you up for success.

Divine Connection

Throughout the book, I will be discussing spirituality[5] and Divine Connection, sharing thoughts about prayer and spirituality. I would like to take this moment to create clarity. As you read what I am sharing, I ask that you feel my sincerity in honoring your definition of God, prayer and your religion, if you identify with one. If you do not belong to any religion or do not believe in "God," I also honor this.

As you explore this journey, I ask that you please be open to the possibility that there is a connection between you and the Universe that is co-creating with you. I may call this Source Energy but I define this as Pure Divine Love that we have access to as if one is swimming into an infinite sea of Love. A sea of Love that is so complete and has infinite resources to complement all that we are and all that we wish for.

I share this information from a loving place wishing to offer a positive way to complement what you believe. I have my beliefs and you have yours. I feel the beliefs that we have towards spirituality; religion and God are very personal and complex. I am fascinated with the conversations I have with people from all walks of life and religions. No matter how differently we define God, we can always find common ground and learn from each other.

---

[5] When I use the word spiritual or spirituality I am referring to the relation of your Soul.

For me, I focus on how this Divine Love is expressed in our everyday lives and how one lives the expression of this.

About two months after the death of my children's father, my son in his early teens announced to me that he no longer believed in God. He made this announcement one night when we were at dinner in a beautiful restaurant in Paris. He was so gentle as he said, "Mom, I know you lecture about spirituality and God, but I have to tell you I do not believe in God." I said, "OK. Share with me what you do believe."

Then, with my daughter present, we had a conversation about God and beliefs. I asked him if he believed in himself. He replied that he did. I asked him if he believed that there is an energy of Love that he is connected to that supports him with love and he replied, "Yes." I said, "Do you feel you are always connected to this Loving Energy to support you and can consciously connect when you focus." He replied, "Yes." I continued, "Wonderful, to me what you believe is one of the main reasons why people believe in God. You just bypassed the formality of a religious system. You believe in Divine Love and your Self, and know the connection of Divine Love in your life."

I shared with him that the great loss and trauma of his father passing awakened him to more of himself. Then he clarified that he did not believe in a religious God, he did not believe in an organized religion, as he defined, "a *God* where you turn over your power like a puppet." I said, "Do you feel that some definitions of God feel disempowering and does not empower who you are?" He agreed. I continued, "As long as you believe in your Self and you feel supported and connected to a Loving Energy that expands and enhances your life, this is what I believe is important."

Everyone defines God and religion differently, along with some having no belief in this at all. Some even use the same wording, but the definitions can be different. What is true for me is that kindness, love, honor, truth and integrity without righteousness are what the great religions wish to express. Anyone who chooses to express these qualities is of greatness and love; as they are of "God" and for "God."

Basically, the bottom line of the conversation with my son was that it is not as important for two people to agree on how they have come to their beliefs as it is for you to have clarity on what your beliefs are and where you have common positive beliefs with others. With your clarity, you can listen to others and share with the possibility of a wonderful conversation that brings growth, awareness and unity … even amongst differences.

The Common Thread

We are all Amazing Souls with our own individual journey and each of us is very unique. We were not designed to be alike; we can complement each other with our differences and acceptance with love as the energy base that supports this.

Because we are all so different with various perspectives, with influences of backgrounds and cultures, what is the real truth about God or religions? Since I was 14 and in Catholic school this was a quest for me, and I have continued my studies since.

I was fortunate that the different resources I studied encouraged that I question everything, and not take anything for granted because they said so, to come to my conclusions with the information at hand. This is similar to the Socratic Method, which is my style of teaching and the format of this book.

There are many truths that have common threads. Religions and beliefs serve many purposes; they create communities, support, comfort, and an opportunity to discover your Self. As with anything in your life, question what is being told to you. If something feels good and is a match to your beliefs, then this is wonderful. If there is something that is said to be a *truth* and does not settle this way for you, question it before you accept it as your belief. Question *truths* in a positive way to know more of your Divine Self.

I feel that as your life experiences change, so do your beliefs and understanding of the world that surrounds you, along with how you may define God. We all deserve tolerance. There is such an unsettling of peace in our world, and we know that peace begins with us. Taking the opportunity to find the common thread in those that surround you, whether with God or issues of life, creates peace. Those truths for you, which may not have a common thread with others, can be respected. Discover ways to have peace within your Self amidst another's differences.

What if this is an opportunity for us to know how to be peaceful even amongst truths that are not ours? We do not have to accept them but we can grow within ourselves, as we stay open to new ways of believing. We are all so blessed that we can make choices because of our freedom to choose; in a way, being tolerant is a small way to have gratitude towards this.

Existence Of Love In The Physical World

When I share words about the sensitive subject of God and spirituality, I do so with tremendous love and respect for you and how you define this in your life. The information I share with you is to stimulate you to ponder your thoughts and feelings, and to inspire openness that will support you to feel an enhanced sense of peace and joy by living a life that is authentic to you.

As I share with you different perspectives that enhance your awareness, this is not solely an intellectual conversation but one that is spiritual. I am a teacher who expands self-awareness, and it is your choice to journey through these explorative conversations with me in a way that supports you to embody and define the Amazing Soul that you are.

You Are Always Plugged Into "Source Energy"

When we feel ourselves as solely physical without spiritual connection or connection to Love Energy, we feel limited or alone in our existence no matter who is around us. I believe that you are NEVER separated from this Universal Love Energy, Source Energy, God, Holy Spirit, Love, however you honor this Energy. You are always connected.

Your free will and your choice to be aware of this energy are what direct the conscious activation of this partnership, which then energizes the reality you wish to choose. With your conscious awareness you connect to tremendous abundance releasing consciousness of lack.

One way I see this partnership is as if it is electricity:

You = Electrical Cord
(Your cord carries the prayer you are asking for)
Universal Love Energy = Electricity
(This Energy ignites your "Ask" – It is the booster)

Without the electrical cord, the electricity would have nothing to ignite. Universal Love Energy does not tell you where to plug in your electrical cord, but if we choose to plug into Universal Love Energy, it is positive and electrifying. We may define this energy similarly or differently, but no matter what your definition is, you are likely on a journey of life that feels Spiritual.

You are Spiritual. Spirituality is not about survival but about feelings awakening more of your journey. Spirituality is a consistent feeling that is part of your everyday life as you accept yourself as a spiritual being having a physical experience. Spirituality is not about being perfect; it is about you having an experience of YOU.

There are no secrets to spirituality; there is the unfolding of the treasure of who you are.

Spirituality is a connection to the All-Of-You with the energy of your Soul connected to the All-Of-Everything. You cannot separate from this. Thinking that you can separate spirituality or your Spirit from your day-to-day life is like trying to separate your blood from your body and still be healthy and alive.

I invite you to explore yourself as a physical being, knowing the God within you, feeling connected to a Loving Energy that is consistently there for you as a partner to expand your creation. This resource of energy is so powerful at activating our "Godness" within us.

When we pray or "Ask," we are connecting to this Source Energy to also awaken within us what we have possibly forgotten about ourselves. The resources within us are our gifts. This Energy empowers you and loves sharing all with you.

Source Energy Is The Fuel

Let's go back to the story of the Amazing Soul who chooses to come here to have an emotional experience. The opportunities to have these experiences may not always be pleasant and can even be painful beyond what we can comprehend at times. But then again, we also have spectacular and beautiful experiences. If, on some level, we believe that we have chosen what emotions we would like to explore as an Amazing Soul, then we will have experiences of certain emotions to match this.

Let's say we wish to experience the feelings of love for a child that is so deep and pure, or we wish to experience love without judgment – it may show up as a painful experience for us to transcend in love without conditions. And, if one of the emotions we wish to experience is forgiveness, then how would we be able to play with the experience of forgiveness if there is not an experience to forgive? Would it be possible to have this experience if, for example, our father or mother were not conditional with the way they loved us, or if a loved one did not betray us or some other similar situation?

As I share examples or ask questions, I am in no way making anyone wrong or justifying the wrongdoings of others. I am simply pointing out that you have choices on how you can respond to these experiences and use them as opportunities to expand your best Self.

So now I will continue this story with the understanding that your Soul is the holder of the experiences you choose, not Source Energy.

This Loving Energy is a partner to you and does not love with conditions; therefore, it does not choose your life for you.

It is as if this Source Energy is the fuel and the Soul is the motor with all the components. The fuel given does not question the motor; it just provides the energy for the motor to run. Now you are the driver and the one that questions the motor and determines the drive – the capacity of whether the motor has enough fuel or is running well and what direction it wishes to go. Neither the fuel nor the motor makes these determinations. The driver does.

Free Will Is Your Will

You have the free will to choose, as there is no higher power controlling your destiny. With this gift of free will, you have been given power to make choices.

Would you feel more peaceful if your life was already planned out for you and there was nothing you could do to change your destiny? Would that feel like you were a puppet on a string being run by some unseen force that is controlling your destiny? You have free will and you command your life. You change your fate by your beliefs regardless of your circumstances.

The use of your words is a way to use this free will and it is your choice on how you wish to direct your free will to create.

There are two main emotions: fear and love. Love creates and fear dissipates. You are free to choose which emotional foundation you live your life from. Our beliefs are ours; they cannot be taken away from us. No matter how many mistakes you believe you have made, you have many opportunities to correct them.

There is only Love and the freedom to choose because you are loved without conditions. If you choose your free will in a way that does not serve you best, I believe that this is not about a *God* testing or punishing us. We create our cause and effect.

My belief is that we are all enlightened. Whether you choose to be awake or asleep with your enlightened Self is a choice.

This choice is called free will. The good news is that you have the final vote on your life reality. You can choose, create and have the freedom to be the best YOU with Source Energy always expanding your creation. You are loved and love is the base of who you are.

Feeling Good Is A Powerful Force

"Life is not a business to be managed, it is a mystery to be lived." – Osho

We all have longings, whether they are conscious or unconscious, spoken or unspoken. Many of us live out our decades busy with the tasks at hand without much thought given to how we are making choices or being aware of what choices are really available to us. What about having the awareness of how you are feeling about your choices and what you feel you can expect from them?

Your life is a reflection of what you believe is possible with your choices. You cannot receive what you do not believe is possible. Do not use your emotions to deny your Self what you truly wish to receive.

Live your dreams that you hold precious and dear while you have the strength and vitality to experience them. Create the possibilities to expect to receive what you truly wish for. Feeling good is a powerful force that brings ease to your world. Because when it *feels* good, *it is good*!

Many times I hear people say, "Later ... I will get to that later," "Later I will do this or that," or "When this happens, then I can do what I wish." Later is now! This is not about life being "too short." This is about your life being too precious and your dreams being too valuable.

Live Your Definition Of Your Life Today

Living from a place of knowing that life is precious and valuable releases a resistance of going against your Authentic Self. Going against your beliefs that are connected to your Authentic Self is like swimming against a current. Exhausting! Now imagine swimming with the current, being connected with the flow of who you are and living a joyful life attracting all you wish for.

You cannot escape the truth of that which you are or the desires that burn in your Soul. Why would you? Why would you miss an opportunity to have a joyful life and share your Self in this way with the ones you love?

Do not fool your Self into thinking that you can bypass who you really are. *I assure you that it is much easier to be your Self than someone else's definition of you.*

Later is NOW!

What is your bucket list? What beliefs do you hold of the possibilities that this list can be your life experience? When? Tomorrow? Later?

Later is NOW! Tomorrow will take care of itself based on your care of today. Imagine if you were more willing to be conscious of the power of your imagination to create and use it fully. For a moment, step back and imagine how things would be in your world if you believed what you wish for truly has the possibility of being the reality of your life. Would you take more care of your feelings? Value yourself as the magical Amazing Soul that you are. Honor your Self as a creator.

You have everything to gain by dreaming big. The only things you will lose are beliefs that no longer serve you and experiences you do not wish to repeat in your life. Sounds like a win-win experience to me.

Dream the dreams you may have put aside! Awaken your dreams, allowing your Self to dream every possibility as your reality. Go for it!

Who else is going to dream for you and who else can make them your life? Only you.

You Are Love – You Are Loved

As you awaken your dreams with Power Wishing, know with total certainty that there is so much love for you everywhere. Love is the base of all creation; it is the energy we are creating with and it has also created you. Love is inside of you and all around you. With this knowing, all you create is harmonious.

Love can be defined in many ways. Love is defined differently for every Amazing Soul, for love is always evolving and expanding as we evolve and expand our Selves. I believe we use life experiences as a way to define and redefine the beauty of exploring love within our Selves and with others.

Live your definition of love; be your definition of love and this magnifies all you love in your life.

With this as the expression of who you are, dreams are realized and miracles become your life experience. Life as a reflection of your Authentic Self is a life experienced as a constant miracle of love.

Power Thoughts

Amazing Soul

- I am an Amazing Soul, having an emotional experience of my Soul in the physical.

- I always find what I am looking for; I look for goodness and more follows.

- My life is a Conscious Choice.

- Later is NOW! Tomorrow will take care of itself based on my care of today.

- My emotions are what awaken me.

- I get what I expect.

- I am the best example of what I believe.

- My present circumstances do not own my future.

- My life is a reflection of how I define my Self.

- I have everything to gain by dreaming big.

Foundation of Power Wishing

Our emotions attract *everything* in our world; they are the alchemy of our creations.

You Are An Emotional Being

Your feelings are the architect that designs your world. Your emotions construct the reality of your life, your beliefs and your thoughts; habits and words structure what I refer to as your Vibrational Language®.

The tools of Power Wishing® awaken you to be present with your feelings, identify them and choose how you wish to direct them. Your emotions are the base of creation.

Power Wishing is an awareness vehicle that empowers you to effectively use your emotional intelligence and, in doing so, to eliminate self-created chaos and unnecessary drama. By taking this opportunity, you are inviting your Self to consciously live your life proactively: you are taking ownership of your world, being your creation and building experiences that are exciting to wake up to every day.

I was motivated to develop these formulas because I was convinced there had to be a better, quicker way to manifest results in my life without all the chaos to get there. I believe wholeheartedly that I create my world and I am conscious of this. So if this is my truth, why were things happening differently than the way I believed they should? I read everything I could, from the bible to new age books, to find a practical formula.

I enjoy researching different sources and through my gift of dyslexia I am able to recognize patterns and find the common pattern. In my search for the key to successful manifesting, I sought to uncover an underlying pattern. What I found in common among most of these writings was in regards to the value of one's Self: being authentic and living truthfully provides the freedom to a glorious life. All this sounds wonderful if you believe that living this way does indeed provide freedom.

To me the key was how one defines authenticity, freedom, truth, etc., according to one's beliefs; this is what does or does not create the glorious life. I was open to a new way of organizing my life, but how?

Because I like to have a clear, practical understanding that is not complicated, I continued to play with different concepts.

Understanding the complexity of emotions and knowing that life is not so black and white, I was determined to find a formula for manifesting clearly and understanding the major cause that was creating the effects in my life. So first, I processed things through the mind, but I was left exhausted and felt this could be a bit controlling and manipulative. It did not feel authentic. When I focused on the heart, I felt too vulnerable and confused about how to create boundaries that were both noble and fair. Since I was having emotional responses or reactions to my life, I determined that my emotions were the key component.

So I played with my experiences from the prospective of my feelings and beliefs. I realized that the more I accepted my feelings and myself, the easier my hopes were manifested. When this was not the case, I knew that I was not using my emotional energy efficiently and chaos would be a part of my manifesting.

Master Your Emotions

There were two main areas in my life that I knew I had to shift. The first was accepting who I am and building from this place versus being at odds with my natural Self. I had to have discernment between finding things to fix in me versus enhancing or improving certain aspects. The second was to correlate my feelings as the factor that creates my life. I knew that if I mastered my emotions to reflect the way I expected to receive, I would be mastering my reality. My goal of mastering my emotions was not to be robotic. So how was I to create a system to know my best Emotional Self in a world that I felt was unpredictable?

I decided first to focus on these two areas, accepting myself and understanding my feelings, since I believe they basically controlled the outcomes of my life. I chose to learn where I needed to make a few skillful adjustments to these areas in order to create a positive shift. Since I viewed this as alchemy of energy, it was clear to me that using my energy to break myself down was not an effective way of creating better results in my life. Identifying my strengths and focusing on building my foundation from here was a far better use of my energy. I also focused on shifting the habit of denying my feelings or making them wrong. Instead, I embraced them as a fuel that propelled and directed my expectation. I focused on accepting myself, building on my positive attributes as my strength, and creating my life using my feelings as a GPS towards solidifying the beliefs to match the possibilities I aspired.

As I experimented with these as the focus of my formula, I began to create great results quickly. Sometimes, even with my conscious focus, I would get off track and could feel myself falling into the trap of feeling bad or as if I was not enough. At times I questioned my Self and compared my Self against images and expectations I felt I needed to be. Our non-verbal society projects so many messages that train us unconsciously to think there must be something wrong if we are different.

There are many so-called "life rules" that we think we need to follow to be successful. There is this collective consciousness that if we go outside of the norm, we will fail or be left behind or we may even disappoint God. We can also consciously or unconsciously interpret our feelings based on others' reactions and spend time changing our feelings so we can receive a different reaction from another. All this mental chatter used the energy that took me away from living my life. To avoid this, I realized I had to create an internal support system for myself to build from until I felt I had an external support system that I could collaborate with.

Many times we focus on trying to mold our lives to what we think will create our success rather than focusing our attention on knowing what is our definition of success. How can we expect ourselves to follow a set standard of rules or a certain mold when we are all born different? I believe we are all supposed to be ourselves and embrace our individual desires and feelings.

Why be someone you are not? It is unnatural to go against your Self and your heart. As an intuitive healer, I have witnessed so many people living a life that was not a genuine reflection of who they are, what they feel or what they desire. I witnessed the lack of positive results of this, along with the confusion and illness that often follow this life choice. Why do so many people forget who they are?

I asked myself why do so many people seem to attempt to sway from their beliefs and sway others to believe as they do instead of supporting each other to live according to the truth of who they are? Instead of focusing on why people do what they do, I paid attention to why I do what I do and how I could perfect a formula to support and enhance being my Authentic Self. With this as my goal, along with my tremendous life passion to support others in awakening to their true Self, I studied and experienced the formula firsthand. I then established seminars and a clientele of Power Wishers, and I created my life according to my belief that we are here to design our life as a joyful one.

When I visualize this belief I see "the Light at the end of the tunnel," and no matter what is happening in the moment that may not feel joyful, my anchor is always towards that Light.

When you begin to fully accept your Self and acknowledge that things are the way they are, you are free. You give your Self a chance to decide to live a life of your possibilities. There is a fear that is released when you are sincere with your Self; there is an inner security and certainty that fills you even in uncertain times.

Your Authentic Self = Abundance

We witness many in our environments investing their time and energy in being their false Self. Logically, this may seem like it is not a big deal and easier than the risk of making other choices that seem too challenging. Leaving a job you totally dislike to do something that may bring you joy may have the risk of income loss, or rejection, I understand that change can seem disruptive. The same goes for relationships; altering them may feel overwhelming as fears of being alone, financial concerns, or worried about of other people's perspectives that lead you to feel anxious or rejected. It may seem ironic that investing in being your Authentic Self will create much more abundance.

Even if your mind wishes to challenge this, the mathematics of energy supports this: if you choose to focus on enhancing your Self versus fighting against your Self, your energy has a united and direct focus. It is like running a marathon: would you get there faster and without injury with half your body going in one direction while the other half goes somewhere else or with your whole body going in same direction? You are a reflection of what you focus on. It is a far safer return on the investment of being authentically YOU. You gain more than you expect.

Life experienced with your best Emotional Self as the architect is an exploration, an adventure of your choices. Being your Authentic Self is the key that discovers the Divinity within you and a calmness of your Soul is felt. This creates a harmony where you experience life in a peaceful and balanced way and miracles become a normal way of life.

There are a few key components that create the foundation of Power Wishing. The main component is that everything is related to your Emotional Self. It all goes back to how you feel, and this creates the belief of what you expect to receive. The emotion-based formula of Power Wishing will give you structure to support you in manifesting your wishes, which are rooted in feelings that are fertilized with self-worth.

Basics Of Power Wishing

The formula of Power Wishing is designed to always take you back to your feelings as the cause that creates the effect in your life. Therefore, you create the skill of activating your feelings to construct a life that is happening *for* you. Meaning, the chase to *make* things happen will be in the past and feeling your life is happening *for* you will become your present experience.

There have been numerous studies showing the negative effects of stress in one's life, and one major factor is when people feel they are not in control of their life. By absorbing this material, you will understand how to be a master of your destiny. This will release tremendous stress from your life and replace it with peace. Every opportunity is for you to build your life.

Power Wishing is based on these principles:

- You are asking for your wishes consciously and subconsciously all the time.
- Through this emotion-based formula, you will consciously be aware of how to utilize your "Ask" through prayer or Emotional Imagination®.
- Your wish is communicated as your Vibrational Language, which is the energetic dialogue used for attracting and expanding your co-creation with Source Energy/God and with others in your surroundings.
- Feelings are your Emotional GPS – They are the base of your creation and are the guide that signals you to know if you are on course with the life you say you wish.

When You Shift Your Emotions, You Shift Your Outcome

Envision yourself as a chemist playing with formulas, and as you experiment with different formulas or different emotions, you come up with different experiences. If there is an aspect that you love about your life, you can "pump up the volume" and enhance the feeling of this. If there is an aspect of your life that is not a wish you would like to have, you will have the ability to formulate it to another wish or prayer.

The journey you will explore with Power Wishing as your guide is emotionally safe and private. It is your own internal journey. It is a playful way of exploring your Emotional Self to strengthen your definition of who you are *at your core*.

I invite you to move out of your comfort zone of asking your Self the same questions or thinking that you know what the outcome will be. I invite you to ask questions that you would not normally ask your Self and hear your genuine answers.

You have everything to gain by being your definition of your Self. You create your emotions and design your life as your reality.

No matter what is happening in your life right now, good, bad or indifferent, no matter what you expect can happen tomorrow, give yourself the freedom to go on this journey *knowing* that all can shift for the better, in your favor. You can take ownership of your Emotional Self. Right now, let go of whatever you feel is possible because of your present circumstances and anchor positive emotions towards the possibilities you wish for. *Right now this is all that matters; the rest will follow.* Tomorrow will take care of itself, based on your care of today. The details will work themselves out, not as a mysterious appearance but because you systematically attracted all that you desire with the beliefs that serve this.

Yes, It's Really All About Your Feelings

We have feelings about ourselves, relationships, business, life, death, etc. Whether we are aware of our feelings or not, whether we embrace them or not, how we feel about our emotions gives energy to the creation within and around us.

We have so many feelings through all our moments each day. Feelings are the force that changes our lives and creates the beliefs of what we believe we can expect from our life and with the lives of others we connect with. The alchemy of creating your world is through your feelings. Everything we do and create goes back to a feeling as the starting point of our beliefs.

Everything we manifest is based on our emotions; how we feel connected to an experience is what creates it. This is the specific reason why Power Wishing is developed as an emotion-based system. Through my years of experimenting with formulas to create the Power Wishing system, I have discovered that the most productive way to manifest is by adjusting the feeling of expectation towards what we believe is possible.

At times, when I wished to create a different experience from a past situation, I would catch my Self focused on the same feelings that created what I said I did not wish for. How could I create a new situation if my focus was on repetitive feelings of the past situation I was wishing to change? Those repetitive feelings were only re-creating the same experience. It made practical and efficient sense to use my energy to shift my current feelings about the past experience in order to produce a positive expectation of my desired outcome in a similar situation.

Since your experiences are the results of your feelings, my rationale was that it made sense to focus on the feelings attached to the desired experience as alchemy to shift or create. Shifting the feeling will create the flow to the end result you wish for in the physical. When we only focus on shifting an experience by concentrating on a physical goal as an end result, without being conscious of the beliefs we have connected to this, it is like throwing lots of money to the wind hoping it will land in your bank account.

As you progress with Power Wishing, pay attention as you reflect and connect with your authentic emotions. Be aware of how you wish to feel with the experience you desire, as this is how you will receive. The evolution of your feelings is a natural progression of life as your feelings activate you to awaken more to your genuine Self. This powerful formula has proven successful to efficiently manifest based on your feelings of what you expect to receive. You are what you feel! What you "see" in your reality is based on what your belief is of what you can expect as a possibility.

Embrace your emotions; enjoy them and do not run from them or numb them. Have your feelings guide you to love, be loved and transform your life with love as the base of all that you create. Value the importance of feeling them and know you are mastering them as an asset to claim the life that you wish to be possible.

Live In A State Of Conscious Wishes Granted

Your emotions are your gauge to clarify what you desire, and they are also the indicator of what you expect to receive. Take time to be aware of how you wish to feel.

Reflect for a moment on how often you say to yourself or out loud, "I wish I could have this," "I wish this would happen," "I wish things were different," "I wish the weather was sunny," "I wish my job was closer," "I wish my true love would appear," "I wish I could buy those shoes," "I wish gas was not so expensive," "I wish I felt better," "I wish that I could go on vacation," and so many more phrases like this. You get the picture.

As you create awareness around you, take inventory: Do you remember how you felt about the possibility of receiving what you have presently created? What were your expectations before receiving what you presently have in your life? Do you believe that the aspects of your life can shift easily? What emotion would you choose that would totally empower the possibility you aspire to be your reality?

I will consistently remind you that you have created your life and your feelings have led to the beliefs you have about what is possible. Do not let your emotions unconsciously run you, know your Self emotionally. You created one experience; therefore, you can consciously create another one. Through Power Wishing, you will skillfully master this.

Our Dreams Are Real

Feelings are not right or wrong; they are simply your feelings. Feelings are defined based on the beholder. All feelings are good, because each emotion tells you something.

Many times we underestimate the power of emotions as our ally to heal and create miracles. Feelings are vibrational frequencies that have a powerful charge like an electric current charging and igniting your "Ask" of what you desire.

Our Dreams are as real as our ability to feel them being true. Feelings are the connection to your core truth; they are your wisdom and your guide as a powerful source that creates.

Our Emotional Choices Create Our Life

We are an emotional society that has been asked to control or suppress our emotions and create outcomes based on our logical thinking. As a society, we are generally taught to use our thoughts for problem solving and dealing with life situations. Many of us come to believe that the logical and practical side of ourselves is the ticket to our success.

Because we are not an emotionally educated society, many times we create expectations of what emotions should feel like through the brain. We attempt to think through our feelings instead of feeling our emotions. We tend to have our intellect replace our emotions. When you are so driven by your intellectual thoughts and repress your emotions, you begin to process your feelings through your brain. Creating outcomes based on your intellectual thoughts can be great if you have not bypassed your emotional self-awareness; otherwise, this can be limiting.

But what happens when you use logic to understand and direct your life, yet this does not bring peace to your Soul? What happens when you have a desire that is burning in your Soul and you feel compelled to make a decision that is not based on logic? Are you fulfilling your Soul's request by choices made from your heart or your logic?

We have all been at this place at different times in our lives, where logic did not fulfill us and following our heart felt illogical. But then again, think of the times you knew your heart had all the logic and lived that experience.

A Prayer Says It All

Many, many times all I had was a prayer, a prayer with my heart and Soul's desire for better possibilities. This work is a creation based on my life experience of wishing for possibilities and hoping for my desires when there wasn't necessarily clear logic from my brain's perspective but there was a strong connection and pull from my heart's perspective.

When I was formulating Power Wishing, I realized that the way I felt about what I was asking for affected what I believed was possible; my expectations were based on what I was feeling. Many times I thought I was asking in a way that matched the way I wished to receive, but when life did not fulfill my "Ask," I had to look further to understand why. The answer always had to do with me. Sometimes I was disappointed, but I would still playfully formulate as if I was researching the cause like a scientist to come up with answers. I also would pay more attention to the many times that things did go as I wished and times they even went beyond my expectation. It was clear that my feelings and underlying beliefs made the difference, along with my surroundings.

Now that I had this understanding, what could be done about it? Instead of praying for a manifestation of a specific result, I wished for an emotional base that would be the foundation to support what I desired to receive. For example, if at the time I was wishing to increase sales in my business and this was not happening, I reflected on how I was feeling about what was happening.

At one time in my business, I did not feel I knew where to go for the sales or I felt uncomfortable cold calling on new sales. So instead of asking for new sales, I prayed for what I felt I was lacking or wished to have as support emotionally: trust in my awareness to recognize opportunities and for courage to take action towards the possibilities I prayed for.

With this emotional awareness, answers and direction started to present themselves. I continued to utilize this information as I witnessed myself using my emotions actively in my imagination; I refer to this as Emotional Imagination. As if I was playing out a movie, I played out scenes with feelings of trusting my awareness and stepping into the experience with courage. This led me to have other memories of feeling this way, and I played with those scenes in my imagination too.

I released focusing on the details and used my imagination to support me by strengthening the feelings I desired to have so I could expect to receive what I had asked for – more sales. Nevertheless, more sales was not my main focus. Why? Because having the emotion that supports more sales as my base made the expectation of these sales inevitable, along with other expectations attached to that same emotion.

I had clarity on how to use my emotions to navigate with action towards the hope I wished for. In my imagination with my emotions, I witnessed my Self as if I was in a movie. I played with how I wished to feel and if I felt some resistance, I explored this. In this case I realized I needed to release the defense mechanism of waiting to be disappointed if my dreams did not come true. This was something I was not aware of until I played out these scenes like a movie in my imagination. Expecting to be disappointed was obviously sabotaging my end result. Imagine sending out a prayer with the expectation to be disappointed! What kind of results would this create?

I shifted my emotions towards encouraging what I believe, the possibilities as my answered prayers. Sooner than later they appeared as my reality. Not only did the increase in sales appear but also other areas shifted where I was previously asking with the expectation of being disappointed. Shifting my emotional base in one area simultaneously shifted other areas of my life. This is another reason why in creating Power Wishing I focused on emotions, because shifting emotionally can cover far more ground than focusing on one wish at a time.

Your Emotional Self Awakens Your Reality

Feelings. It's all about feelings. Yes again, I will remind you that it really goes back to feelings. I will continue to emphasize and repeat this in different ways; this is the oxygen to the creation of your life.

The instant that you have a feeling to desire something, you have just created an energetic "Ask." This creates an image as an energy that will soon manifest in the physical realm.

With the philosophy of Power Wishing, your feelings create what you expect to receive even before you actually verbalize your "Ask." You imagine everything and you attach your emotions to this in your Emotional Imagination. You go over your vision in your imagination, consciously or not, and imagine emotionally what it would be like to receive something. This emotion dictates the expectation of what you expect will happen.

When we choose to deliberately use our Emotional Imagination to give us images, this is a powerful focus that directs our personal "Movie" to appear as our life. Our imagination and our feelings construct our prayer with clarity. It fine-tunes our belief of what is possible for our experience. What an opportunity it is to combine your emotions with your imagination to design the creation of your vision knowing this will become your reality.

The more you collaborate with the Power Wishing system, the more you will instantaneously be aware of your emotions as signals, as something that works with you. You will witness which ones you wish to enhance, shift or maybe just be aware of and do nothing. No different than a mathematic equation. This will be the way you begin to process throughout your day-to-day life with little effort, utilizing the support of your emotional awareness to guide you in a flow.

How wonderful and exciting to have a system where you are able to make adjustments to your outcomes in your life based on your own personal desires and emotions.

Emotions Are Digestible

The formulas of Power Wishing enable you to break down the complexity of your emotions so that they are digestible. I understand how intense and overwhelming the feelings of loss, pain, anger and resentment can feel. As I share this work with you, and as you reflect on your experiences and feelings, in no way do I undervalue your emotions, nor should you. So many of us have experienced deep pain and this creates its challenges for us, *but in no way should this prevent us from having the life we dream of.*

Now, I am fully aware that we all have our own lives to live. In no way am I saying that every emotion has to be a process. We would never have time to have a life if we were always processing our emotions. The idea here is to have your emotions feel integrated in supporting you.

As we continue on this journey and go more in depth with Power Wishing, you will recognize more and more the gift of your feelings as your guide, what I call your Emotional GPS. Listening to this inner guide will enhance your trust in your possibilities to be given to you and in knowing that you are Divinely Loved for this to be so.

As an Amazing Soul, you were not left alone with the discovery of your Divine Self. Your Emotional GPS is a gift to help you assemble this exciting adventure, a support system much like our bodies have internal support systems that keep us functioning whether we are aware of it or not. Your Emotional GPS has a mission to keep you on course with awakening the life experiences you have dreamed of.

Your Feelings Know

As you continue to move forward, have confidence and trust that if you are feeling something, there is a reason for this. Trust that you will know what to do with your feelings. Know with every core of your cellular body that you are lovingly supported with how you wish to feel. Stop questioning yourself about what you know is your truth. Really, you can just stop it!

If an emotion feels like it has a charge, it is valuable to pay attention to this. You are confirming what you expect through these emotions. This is your Emotional GPS giving you heightened awareness of what you are activating in your Emotional Imagination to appear as your reality. Therefore, when you make an "Ask" and hold this as true even if it is not in your physical appearance as of yet, it will be. This is also natural law: "As So Above, So Below." Meaning, if you are asking and feeling your expectation as true, you are claiming this to be so in your physical reality.

Using your emotions as your GPS on a consistent basis allows you to be grounded within yourself, which translates to peace even when chaos may surround you. Training yourself to process consciously may feel a little bit overwhelming in the beginning. This will pass as you recognize more and more that your prayers are being answered. Your beliefs become your answers and this shapes your habits ... and you know the rest of the story ... it's a good one!

In time, as you wake up more and more to the Amazing Soul that you are, you will expand what you love about your Self. As you continue to embrace loving and nurturing your Emotional Self, you will reduce the need for experiences that no longer serve you, and you will share this perspective with others.

By deepening your skill of these techniques, you will recognize the cause of a situation and be able to create the outcome you choose.

Power Wishing goes beyond asking for your desires; it gives you an opportunity to grow emotionally and acquire the realization of why certain emotional experiences show up in your life. Taking full accountability for creating your world gives you access to a universal support system to partner with that is in synergy with what you expect with your "Ask."

You will have this knowledge that you are never alone in your creation of life; there is consistent reinforcement reaffirming your spiritual connection. This provides you added inner security to step into your life with trust. Your imagination and beliefs become your strength, and positive emotions become your guide to fulfilling your Soul's voice, easily.

Fundamental Values of Emotion-Based Wishing:

- You honor your Self by valuing your feelings.
- Your feelings matter and they activate your world to materialize.
- You are always experiencing emotions even if you are not conscious of them.
- Your feelings are the main anchor in what you expect to receive from your "Ask" or prayer, which is essentially an energetic message signaling a point of reference for your attraction.
- You are the creator of your world; therefore, you create one experience and are capable of creating another.
- You are always asking and you always receive what you expect, based on what you believe is possible.
- Your beliefs are a reflection of the reality you live in.
- The conditioning of your beliefs fuels all your actions and behaviors.
- You are the boss of you; therefore, no one has control over your ability to create.
- It is the awareness of your asking that shifts how you receive; if you shift the emotional base of your "Ask," you shift your beliefs and trust what you expect to receive.

As you awaken more and more to the Amazing Soul you are, your focus will shift to recognize more in your world that is already present. Your life is a reflection of what you *believe* is possible and what you believe you can expect from the world around you. This is being a Conscious Creator.

The "Ask"

An essential component to receiving is that we first must ask. We are actually asking all the time, through our feelings and with a belief system that we may or may not even be conscious of. The moment you ask, you are sending out energy of what you expect to receive. Even though nothing has happened yet in your physical reality, the energy has been set forth to manifest as your physical reality. The most efficient way to ask is consciously through focused feelings, which I define as prayer.

A prayer is a conscious "Ask." Prayer is personal. The actual definition of prayer is: *Earnest or urgent request.* The word *ask* is an English translation for an Aramaic word that also means "prayer." Synonyms for prayer are: *appeal, plea, request, desire or wish.*

Prayer is a tool that energetically asks for the possibility of your desire to be your reality. Asking is a form of prayer – a request that is asked with a connection or partnership with loving supportive Energy that I define as Source Energy and many define as God. To me, prayer is not a religious request, although some may choose to pray feeling connected to their religious beliefs of God or the Universe. For me personally, I connect my prayer to what I define as God – Source Energy, Divine Love.

Regarding prayer, if you are present in your feelings, thoughts or desires, I believe this is a prayer or what I call an "Ask." In being present in our prayer, we are focusing our energy of creation. Even if you are saying thank you, it is a prayer of gratitude. You are in a prayer of appreciation, acknowledging the goodness in your life and this is a focused prayer that has asked for more.

Because you are asking, feeling and thinking all the time, let's say that you are in a constant state of asking or in a constant state of prayer. I am using the word prayer versus ask or desire at this moment so that you are able to feel that your thoughts and your feelings are sacred. When the word prayer is used, many correlate this with the sense of sacredness. I would like you to correlate that your feelings, thoughts and actions are sacred.

Imagine Living As A Sacred Walking Prayer

Imagine feeling that we honor one another as sacred beings having a physical experience, wishing the best for each other. Take a moment to feel the peace and harmony of this. What would the world look like? How would you feel if you started to treat yourself as sacred?

What if your thoughts and feelings towards your Self and others are sacred? We are constantly asking all the time through these feelings and thoughts. Since we are doing this anyway I believe that *YOU are a "walking prayer"* and therefore *YOU are a sacred prayer.* We are all sacred prayers. As you expand your understanding of Power Wishing and Vibrational Language, you will begin to consciously hold your thoughts, feelings, words and actions as sacred.

If this were so, would you speak to your Self differently? Would you choose to feel thoughts of anger or peace, knowing the sacred being that you are? Would you trust your Self or others differently? Would you ask differently? Would you honor your Self?

"Ask And It Shall Be Given To You"

You receive a match that is a reflection of what you expect. The clearer your "Ask," the clearer the response for Source Energy to co-create your expectation. It is as if you are placing an order at Starbucks and you ask them for what you want: "Latte, tall, skinny, 130 degrees, fill only ¾." They do not question you or make comments like, "Are you sure?" or "Is this because you are having a bad day?" or "What you really meant to ask for is a cappuccino." The cashier is not judging you and does not limit you by saying, "You have had too many lattes today and maybe you should not have another one." They simply repeat your order to confirm what you have asked for and deliver it. No drama, no opinion.

This is natural Universal Law. It is a law that has been constructed to empower us to create. When we ask, we command the creation we expect, accessing our free will, which opens the gate for the expansion of co-creation with Source Energy and all that surrounds us. Since there is free will, this loving Energy does not interfere with how you define reality or make decisions for you. Universal Energy is here to serve you. It loves without conditions towards loving you and serving you. I do not believe there is ever a "No" response from this Loving Energy when answering our prayer or our "Ask." This would be contradictory to unconditional love. The belief that there would be a "No" as an answer from God is a belief, a lack of trust to believe in the "Yes" to possibilities we have asked for.

This Loving Energy does not processed in the same way that humans process information. When this Loving Energy receives what you are asking for, it does not process with comments like, "What I think she really means is …" or "What I really think he is feeling is …" or "What she meant to ask for was …" The Universe does not have its own emotions and the Universe does not control you or have a control over you. Its purpose is not to define your feelings. Its purpose is not to challenge or judge you or decide what is best for you. No! This is a belief and if it did, then why would we have free will?

This loving Source Energy has no issues in giving to you with ease. The solid factor of fulfilling what we have asked for is our belief. I believe that with our will we activate this Energy to provide for us. It is not a question about providing for us, it is about what you believe will be provided for you.

You Are A Creator

Reflect how this statement holds true for you:
You are the creator of your life and you have all you could possibly imagine to create. The more you create, the more possibilities you have to be realized. It is your belief that makes the difference in your creations. In essence, you are always creating, and Source Energy is your loving partner enhancing all that you expect to receive. Trust with certainty that this powerful partnership of Love will manifest your wishes as your life experiences with joy and ease.

Vibrational Language

Your Vibrational Language is the energetic dialogue that gives direction vibrationally for your creation. This language is comprised of your emotions, heart, mind, beliefs and Soul's desires, along with your faith and beliefs of how you define God. It also carries the belief of what you believe is possible in the world. This may seem like a lot to pull together and have in synergy, but in reality you are already using this energetic dialogue. When these are not in sync and the *vibe* that you send is chaotic and unclear, you receive results that are chaotic and unclear. You will fine-tune the synchronicity of this to be in tune with the core of who you are. When this is all in sync, well, just imagine the amazing results. We always receive what we ask for and every wish is always granted.

Assume that you are a "walking prayer" and all your feelings, thoughts and imagination are a vibration that creates energy around you. This is what we call your Vibrational Language. This is a signal that creates points of reference for your reality creation. These signals verbalize your "Ask" and are felt as prayer by the Universe. This energetic system literally gives you what YOU expect to receive, no questions asked. I used to share with my children when they were little that God made the world round as an empowering reminder to always remember that what we send out with our heart and thoughts bounces right back to us. We create based on how we give out what we say we desire, and how we feel about this comes back to us. Just like throwing a ball against the wall and it comes back to us based on the force and direction with which we threw it.

Before you even step into a room physically, your energy has already dictated the expectation. Your Vibrational Language goes ahead of your physical presence. The base or the seed of your experience is a feeling and the Universe responds to your emotional frequency, your Vibrational Language. What you put out is what you will receive. This is why I place such importance on having the awareness of your genuine raw emotions and beliefs, as this is the dominant current that drives your manifestations.

When you use your Emotional Imagination proactively, this also fine-tunes your Vibrational Language propelling your communication with the qualities of attracting what feels good to you and the Universe takes these vibrational signals literally.

The art of asking in Power Wishing terms is asking with the energy of the belief of how you wish to receive your "Ask." Whether your "Ask" is through words, thoughts or feelings, this emotionally charged energy is the command that takes your "Ask" to being answered. In other words, this is the synergy contained in your Vibrational Language.

As you use my coursework to clean up your "Ask," the signaling or dialogue for your attraction that we call Vibrational Language, your ability to attract your desires, will become more precise. This is what I mean when I say, "Your life is happening *for* you." You do not feel like you are chasing your dreams, you know you are attracting them. You naturally begin to receive with feelings that feel good with beliefs that match how you wish to feel, and accelerating your manifestations easily will become a lifestyle.

Universal Computer

In Power Wishing, we define our "Ask" as an energetic action, whether through focused Emotional Imagination or not. Where do you think your energetic "Ask" goes? I play with this imaginary thought of your "Ask" physically shooting off to the Universe to the likes of a computer with your feelings as the programming of what you expect to receive. Your "Ask" is received by a Universal Computer that is commanded by its programming to deliver a match to what you have asked for. Your "Ask" is a program, a command. It works in the same way we prepare our computers to give us information through the way we program what we expect of it.

The Universal Computer is a mechanism designed to serve you. Similar to a computer, the Universe only does what it is programmed to do. Bad programming is not the computer's fault; it is that of the programmer. A computer with good programming creates amazing things. And many times great programs for computers have come from the growth of bad programming. You get the picture. The Universe, or loving Source Energy, is supporting you and has a clear message for you: *Your wish as you believe is the command for your expectations.*

When we ask, pray or have a focused emotional thought, we are not asking for permission to obtain what we are asking for, we are stating it. Universal Law does *not* state, "Ask and you shall wait to see if you are *approved* to receive." We receive based on what we anticipate we can receive. I feel that it is important to clarify this. For example, let's say that I have a financial certificate deposit (CD) at a bank. It has been there for years, and every few months I add money to this CD and it continues to accumulate interest. I am really not sure how much interest has been gained, but I know it is building up. It feels good to have these financial savings.

One day I decide that I would like to take a vacation and so I go to the bank and take money out of my CD to pay for my trip. Since I am the owner of my own bank account, I do not ask the bank teller how she feels about my withdrawal or vacation. I do not ask for permission to withdraw my funds nor do I wait to see if she approves of me taking my own money out of my own account for my own vacation. The transaction is non-dramatic; I walk in and simply state that I want to receive my money by giving her a withdrawal slip and use my free will to take out my money.

Let's play with this analogy. When you make an "Ask," whether consciously or not through focused feelings, prayer, imagination or spontaneous feelings, you are not asking for permission from a *God* force. You are not waiting to see if this Energy will approve or disapprove of your "Ask." This *God* or Energy does not interfere with your "Ask"; it only wishes to give to you. What you have in your "spiritual bank account" is what you have accumulated based on your actions of your choices of who you are and your beliefs and this is what you shall receive.

You cannot manipulate the authentic feelings of your "Ask." Energy is energy and there is no way of getting around this. Source Energy is your resource to access by "asking." When I wish to access from this energetic resource, I feel as if I am swimming in a pool of vibrant positive energy that supports me and I feel myself pulling from it what I am asking for. This ocean of Love embodies me, answers my prayers and reminds me that loving support is here to expand any possibility that I believe. This Source Energy can also be a support to ask for more clarity and to expand possibilities in ways we may not be aware of.

Your Emotional Imagination Fuels Your Prayer

"Our imagination is the most important faculty we possess. It can be our greatest resource or our most formidable adversary. It is through our imagination that we discern possibilities and options. Yet imagination is no mere a blank slate on which we simply inscribe our will. Rather, imagination is the deepest voice of the Soul and can be heard clearly only through cultivation and careful attention. A relationship with our imagination is a relationship with our deepest self." – Pat B. Allen

I am passionate about the fact that I can retreat into my imagination and know with total certainty that I am creating my physical reality, as did so many great visionaries in history. The ancient Hebrews called the imagination the workshop of God. Before we go into the conversation of imagination, I would like to invite you to reflect on some of my favorite quotes.

"Imagination is the eye of the Soul." – Joseph Joubert

"Imagination has given us the steam engine, the telephone, the talking-machine, and the automobile, for these things had to be dreamed of before they became realities." – L. Frank Baum

"We do not need magic to change the world. We carry all the power we need inside ourselves already: we have the power to imagine better."
– J. K. Rowling

"Your imagination is your preview of life's coming attractions."
– Albert Einstein

"If everyone is thinking alike, then somebody isn't thinking."
– George S. Patton

"What is now proved was once only imagined." – William Blake

"You can't depend on your eyes when your imagination is out of focus." – Mark Twain

"To invent, you need a good imagination and a pile of junk." – Thomas A. Edison

"I only hope that we don't lose sight of one thing – that it was all started by a mouse." – Walt Disney

"I paint objects as I think them, not as I see them." – Pablo Picasso

"Live out of your imagination, not your history." – Stephen Covey

"A rock pile ceases to be a rock pile the moment a single man contemplates it, bearing within him the image of a cathedral." – Antoine de Saint-Exupery

"Imagine for yourself a character, a model personality, whose example you determine to follow, in private as well as in public." – Epictetus

"I cannot imagine a God who rewards and punishes the objects of his creation and is but a reflection of human frailty." – Albert Einstein

"Here in your mind you have complete privacy. Here there's no difference between what is and what could be." – Chuck Palahniuk

"Imagination is the voice of daring. If there is anything Godlike about God it is that He dared to imagine everything." – Henry Miller

"All our other faculties seem to have the brown touch of earth upon them, but the imagination carries the very livery of heaven, and is God's self in the Soul." – Henry Ward Beecher

"Hate is a lack of imagination." – Graham Greene

"Imagination means nothing without doing." – Charles Chaplin

"Imagination rules the world." – Napoleon Bonaparte

"They who dream by day are cognizant of many things which escape those who dream only by night." – Edgar Allan Poe

"Imagination, that magic glass that colors all the pictures of the brain." – C. B. Langston

"Reality can be beaten with enough imagination." – Mark Twain

"To know is nothing at all; to imagine is everything." – Anatole France

Your Imagination Is Your Tool For Creation

Imagine a sculptor who designs from a piece of marble. Out of that marble, through divine imagination and the ability to ask for what he believes is possible, the sculptor goes on a journey of experiencing the creation of any image. The image is created as he chiseled and chipped away all the parts necessary with his imagination to reveal the image in physical form.

"I saw the angel in the marble and carved until I set him free." – Michelangelo

You create the masterpiece of your life by sculpting your feelings in your imagination. For a moment, let's say you are a sculptor and the chisel in your hand is your imagination.

What life experience would you be sculpting if you stay in a job you dislike because it pays well even though you complain about it every day? What are you creating through your experiences in your imagination with these complaints about your work? Do you think you are sculpting a life of more complaints? What piece of art or life experience is created from this? Since you are already using your imagination to create one experience, shifting the way you utilize this tool to envision your possibilities will simply create another experience that serves you better. You would create far greater life experiences using your imagination to design possibilities of opportunities for work that you love.

This excitement would not only bring more positive work opportunities but other new opportunities as well. What life experience are you sculpting with a relationship you love to go home to? What other life experiences are created from being in love and loving? This all sounds so logical, but how often do you use your imagination to support what you do not wish for? Your imagination uses your emotions that are engaged in your present experiences, being the preview to what is next.

Your imagination is so powerful and I find that many do not even pay attention to what they are imagining. Your imagination is not just there to entertain you; it has real purpose and is a powerful tool for manifesting. Use your imagination as the machine that it is to create what you say you wish for.

You Are A Conscious Creator

"Logic will get you from A to B. Imagination will take you everywhere."
– Albert Einstein

Your Emotional Imagination is so magnificent; this is the one-stop shop for manifesting. I encourage you to honor your imagination as a sacred tool that brings your emotions to life. Through Power Wishing, you will learn how to enhance the use of your imagination as an advantage rather than a liability to all that you desire to create. Or better yet, you become a Conscious Creator and your imagination is your "Magic Wand." *As a Conscious Creator, you no longer create a life by default; you create experiences proactively.*

As you deepen your practice of Power Wishing, your imagination automatically becomes in sync with quickly creating using the awareness of your emotions. Imagine how it feels to walk around smiling and saying, "Ahh ... this is so good. I expected this. Yes, I saw this in my imagination and I played with how this moment would feel and here it is!"

Possibilities are a reality within your imagination. Logic is based on information that feels concrete and has boundaries, while your imagination is free of boundaries, space and time. Imagination is your playground to creation without the present reality dictating your outcome.

We use our imagination as a way to preview what we wish to create. Just like when we watch a movie and our emotions are being triggered, when we imagine, we are triggering our feelings and creating our "Ask." As we imagine our desires, we tend to feel good and say to ourselves, "I like this," "I want this," "I wish to enhance this."

As a Conscious Creator, it is your choice to put yourself in environments that are productive in supporting your Life by Design. Personally, I do not like to see scary or violent movies. I know that I get very affected by these graphic and suspenseful scenes, and I choose not to expose myself to these movies as they activate my imagination in a way that does not serve me.

I share this concept with my children and also suggest that they do not see these types of movies either. So, like kids do sometimes, they would tell me they are seeing a comedy and then go see a violent horror movie. When I would pick them up from the theater, their eyes would be wide open and they would be jumpy and paranoid. It was quite comical. They would eventually confess that they did not see a comedy and share how they did not feel so good afterwards. I joke with them about this and ask them to explain to me the thrill of feeling so scared and paranoid. How many times have you gone to the movies and watched someone being chased or hunted, then you walk out of the theater looking around you as if someone is chasing you or hunting you?

Expose your imagination to surroundings that support the creations you wish to enjoy as your life. Why would you waste your energy imagining what you do not wish for or expose yourself to visual scenes and emotional experiences that do not serve you? If you have a strong emotional charge towards something, your imagination will process this as real, and your body takes in what is being given to your cellular body as if this scene has really happened. This process creates a point of reference for attraction. Why would you create a point of reference to attract what you do not wish when this can be avoided?

There is so much value in being aware of where you place your emotional energy for creating your life. Are you aware if the thoughts in your head are mostly positive or negative, critical or encouraging towards what you wish as a possibility in your life? Where do you expend your energy? Where is your focus? Is it based in fear or love?

I enjoy keeping things playful when getting my message across, to create awareness. I had participants in one of my workshop place two cups in front of them and I said, "A penny for your thoughts." I asked them to place a penny each time they had a thought that does not serve them in one cup and then place a penny in the other cup when they had positive thoughts. This included thoughts towards themselves or towards another. Sometimes we are not consciously aware of our thought patterns; this gave them a point of reference outside of themselves. Now they could gauge where they were placing their energy. I'm not sure if everyone was honest about his or her pennies, though we had a good time discussing this. There were some who worried what their cups looked like and tried to control this. You can only imagine the energy they spent on worrying about this. Others compared their cups of pennies to those around them. They had a good laugh at how exhausting this was.

Many did share that they were surprised at how critical they were of themselves and how much energy they gave to what others were doing versus how they were feeling. It was a good example of how we may or may not be paying attention to our own actions, and instead focus on others or projected expectations.

Even as a Conscious Creator, there are still challenges and growth; the difference is you live a life without the chaos of feeling hopeless. You trust in your ability to create and feel the presence of your connection to Divine Love.

Playfully Create Your Life

Personally, I love playing in my imagination. I know the power of a few minutes of this kind of playful visioning and how much I can create with this practice. To me, this is always efficient life planning.

What if you imagined that everything – Source Energy, every feeling, every thought, your body, your mind and your surroundings – is a support system for you to have all you dream of? What if you truly believe this and that it is all at your command waiting for direction from you?

Imagine that as you reflect about everything in your world; the good, the bad, the ugly and the beautiful are here to support you. You are supported to have everything you wish for. The belief you choose based on your observation is what makes the difference. You are the one that makes the choices on how to utilize these resources.

With this knowledge, you can let loose in your imagination to create knowing that everything is on your side, and you have an abundant amount of resources. When you create this way, you release resistance towards whatever shows up, because it is all a support system for you towards the creation of your reality.

With this unrestricted way of playing in our imagination, we are taken to scenes and possibilities without the interference of our thoughts to organize or impose rules and boundaries. Our imagination, just like a drawing board, has the opportunity to create, erase and adjust whatever we wish to imagine. It truly is like directing a movie. Having said that, we also have the benefit in our imagination to witness our thoughts and shift them towards what we wish to experience without allowing the past, or what is in our present reality, to limit the possibilities we desire.

As you journey with these formulas, let's keep it simple. Life has enough of its own complications. There is no right or wrong, only your feelings make it so for you. I am sharing these concepts with you in a practical way. Play with these concepts and see how you feel. Have humor as you start to witness your life more as your "Movie" and make choices as the director. We can all probably admit we have created some pretty funny scenes in our life. Maybe at times when you witness your life "Movie," you can step aside from being so emotionally engaged and feel as if you are giving advice or observing someone else in order to receive the answers you are looking for.

Enjoy this opportunity to create. Play in your imagination. Play with how you feel. What would you like to feel? What if your life had the experience you would like to feel? When I look back and trace some of the wonderful things I manifested without effort, I reflect on how I did this. Usually it was because I did not take myself so seriously nor was I so intense with what I was wishing for. It was when I felt "that would be nice if that happened" or "if this would happen," and I played with the excitement and then I let it go. *Poof*! It appeared easily with joy.

When we play with how we feel and then look at scenes of possibilities with how we can feel, this gives us more possibilities to feel the reality of this. The *how and when* will become clearer as you continue to strengthen the anchor of the dominant feeling you've created to receive.

Release the need to have things in perfect order before you can believe what you wish for is possible. Let the perfection go for now. Stay playful with the feeling you wish to have and this will become the anchor to align everything else.

Just keep playing with how good it feels to have the possibility of your wish become a scene in your life. Take action towards this, and speak internally of it as the story you wish to have. Read books. See movies. Exist in environments that support your good feelings. Be your number one fan.

Take Down That Wall

Each of my children has done the course Outward Bound, an outdoors education program, for a few weeks in the summer. One of the reasons why I like this course is that it symbolizes life challenges and finding solutions through discovery of your Self.

After my son's return from Outward Bound, he shared how he had a good experience but at one point he was so tired of carrying his canoe that it felt like the day was never going to end. There were a few kids that were having a challenging time and he was not feeling like a happy camper. We laughed about some of his experiences and then we shared about how this is similar to life. He expressed how at one moment he wanted to leave and that was all he thought about. I shared that it is normal to feel like leaving a new, challenging or sometimes annoying experience. Spending a few weeks without your phone, computer or home comforts can be uncomfortable for anyone. It is also super frustrating not to feel in control of your day, especially with a bunch of strangers.

When I asked him how he got through it, he responded, "I just had to finish, I had to find a way." He acknowledged that at that moment it was a struggle but then he pushed through what he was feeling and thought about the awesome meal he was going to have at the airport before he came home. He said he went into such detail of how he was going to pig out and imagined what he wanted to eat before he flew home and this distracted him. He actually sent me a picture from the Maine airport of the biggest lobster I have ever seen.

We shared that it is the same with life. Sometimes we *hit a wall* and we want to move forward but we can get so frustrated and find all these reasons why we cannot, especially if there are others involved. Our fears can also place us in our comfort zone, which keeps us from where we wish to be.

Sometimes as parents we do not place our children in situations where their comfort zone can be challenged in a healthy way. How do we expect for them to know how to deal with challenges and go within to find solutions?

As my daughter shared when she returned from her trip when I picked her up at the airport, "I have more inside of me than what I expected." To me, that was the success of her experience. How do we expect our children to know what they are capable of when they are in their comfort zone and we may enable them to stay there? What about you? Do you make it a habit to push yourself past your comfort zone in a healthy way?

Ice Cream

This was also clear to me when my little sister Grace was 12 and we were hiking the Grand Canyon in Arizona. We went to the bottom of the rim, spent the night, and then the next morning, as we were halfway up the trail, she reached her limit. She sat down and said "No More! I am done!"

"OK…" I said, "What should we do?" She felt like she couldn't walk any further. I shared with her that we had no choice but to finish, and if we went back down now, we would be further away from where we started. We only had one direction to go, and that was up the canyon.

I shared that we could go little by little and take it slow, but we had to move forward. I would speak to her in ways so she could envision herself at the top. I also validated how amazing she was to be able to hike the Grand Canyon at 12. I reminded her that she was accomplishing her dream and that I was right besides her feeling so proud of her. I shared with her that this was just a moment in her experience, not the whole experience.

So we started to hike back up, playing games like counting 10 steps and then stopping, and then counting 20 steps. We were also easily distracting ourselves looking for little animals. We played. Then we would ask people who were hiking to the bottom, "How much longer to the top?" We asked everyone! We still laugh at this story over 20 years later because everyone had a different version of time. Some would say another hour, others two hours, and one person said, "You are almost there, only 20 more minutes."

What really motivated us was when we heard from someone that there was an ice cream shop right at the top of the Canyon. We have pictures of us eating that ice cream like nothing else matters. I still remember how delicious it tasted combined with the sweet feeling of accomplishment.

Sometimes we feel like we hit an emotional wall. We cannot feel the possibilities that lie on the other side. Using your Emotional Imagination, you are developing habits that will support you to imagine how to get to the other side.

A few guidelines in utilizing your Emotional Imagination when you feel like you have hit "the wall":

- Take small steps; any step moving forward is still moving forward.
- Distract yourself ... play games in your head, play music or simply go to another experience where you have felt good and enjoy the memory. Distract, distract, distract ... similar to how my son focused on a great meal or my sister looked for animals along her hike. Simple but productive.
- Do not take a moment of not feeling good and make it your whole experience. It is just a moment of not feeling good. NEXT!

- Feel your feelings and then allow yourself the space to release your intensity. This does not diminish what you are feeling, but it allows you to move forward towards another feeling that feels better towards what you wish to accomplish. The goal is to create movement and find solutions.

Your Life By Design

Imagination is the "Magic Wand" of our free choice, our free will to create possibilities of a magical life. The seeds for which your reality is created begins and ends in your imagination. It truly is a very sophisticated organizational system for manifesting.

You are the master architect utilizing this powerful system as your drawing board with Divine Love and you create your life by your design. It amazes me how sloppy people can be with their imagination. I can only conceive that it is due to a lack of awareness. Because if you are truly aware of the power of your imagination and trust that you are the creator of your world, you would not be careless.

Remember, as an Amazing Soul you are given all you desire to create your magical life. The awakening of your imagination is activated by your feelings, which grow, inspire, support and activate your creations.

I will repeat this information over and over again to give you different ways to acknowledge that you are the creator of your world. I repeat YOU are the creator of your world. There is more waiting to be aligned for you as you discover the Divinity within you. You bring to life your creation by imagining what you believe is possible for yourself. Nothing is in your way of being YOU, except yourself.

I named this body of work *Power Wishing* because I know how powerful our desires can be. I wished to make the process of manifesting simple and joyful.

Whenever we think of wishing, there is a magical component to this and I am here to remind you that the magical component is YOU. Through these formulas, you will take your wishes to a heightened sense of knowing of your Authentic Self. You will know that you create your Life by Design using your Emotional Imagination having synergy with your body, mind, Spirit and Soul along with your surroundings. Your wish is the command that all energies follow with joy and ease. It is your belief that makes this so.

Power Thoughts

Foundation of Power Wishing

- o   I am a "Master of my Emotions."

- o   When I shift my feelings, I shift my outcome.

- o   My dreams are as real as my ability to feel them being true.

- o   I have everything to gain by being my definition of my Self.

- o   I am a gift and my life is a gift that wishes to give to me.

- o   What I believe is possible about the world around me is what I can expect to receive.

- o   With every experience I have an opportunity to embody who I wish to be.

- o   I am a walking sacred prayer.

- o   Imagination is the "Magic Wand" of my free will.

- o   Imagination is my ability to play with creating the experiences of my life.

Direct Your "Movie"

Your imagination is forming your potential reality through energy. Much like playing with dough, you are molding the possibilities of your life experience through your feelings. The key here, and this is where the efficiency comes in, is that it is far more productive to play in your imagination with your feelings and the possible outcomes instead of living out these experiences in your daily life.

Why figure out what qualities you desire in a relationship by having several relationships that do not offer you these choices? You can narrow down your choices of these qualities by imagining your experiences with feelings. As I have shared, since I can remember I have been aware of how my imagination activates my life and I have utilized this to construct everything in my life. I know with total certainty that if I sit and play out my ideas, dreams, options and even fears in my imagination, that I am actively creating my life.

Envision your imagination like a drawing board where you can sketch, erase and make adjustments to your design. When you build a house, it makes practical sense to have a clear architectural plan and design the structure rather than tear parts down each time you change your mind to figure out the design you truly desire. By creating an emotional foundation using your imagination, you are using your energy efficiently.

We are creating in our Emotional Imagination®; the result of that creation is what appears in our physical reality. This being the case, imagine the importance of understanding that you have already created what you are witnessing.

Your Life As A Movie

The concern I had with students in my workshops was their lack of awareness of when and how they were creating. Because of this lack of awareness, many of them used their emotional energy in very unproductive ways. They had reactive behaviors towards their lives and created chaos that they felt they were not responsible for. I truly pondered how I could support others to know the power of their imagination and how to effectually use it while feeling free to be emotional in this space. As I reflected on this one day, I started to laugh, as the answer was right in front of me with the way I utilize my imagination.

When I have something I wish to manifest, I close my eyes and play it out like a movie. I entertain possibilities while being in this space: I write my script and then see how this would play out as a film. Here I play with my feelings. I have the freedom to be happy, be in drama, be joyful or be angry and then I make the decision of how I choose the final scene to play out. I then focus my attention there and play some more with those scenes.

When I play with witnessing my life as a movie, it is like a meditation where time stops and I am able to make choices by observing my options – as if I have the control in my own hands and I am able to change the channel, edit my past, play with my present situations or imagine my future in a way that serves me best in present time, letting go of present circumstances. After I play with my "Movie," I know with total certainty that I will witness this as a life experience.

All along, I have meditated in a way as if I was imagining my life as a "Movie." Everyone knows what it feels like to go to the movies and to feel emotionally connected as you witness the story in front of you. This concept was simple to use as an effective technique; it resonated effortlessly with so many people, and my students love manifesting this way.

"That's Your Movie"

In my courses and corporate leadership training, I always smile when participants take what they have learned of witnessing life like a "Movie" to the next level. I hear people playfully getting their point across by saying, "That is your 'Movie,' not mine." Or "I choose to not make them a character in my 'Movie.'"

This technique can be used in a productive way to explain feelings without being hurtful. It is also an easy way to train your Self to create what you wish to experience as your life.

There are a few things to remember as you play out your "Movie":

- Acknowledge your present feelings.
- Focus on how you wish to feel.

- Imagine as if you are watching a movie performance with your desired feelings.
- Anchor the feeling you choose with different scenes.
- Focus on solidifying the emotions you wish to feel, trusting that the details will work themselves out.
- If you do not have a lot of clarity about your feelings, then keep playing with different scenes until you discover your true feelings.

Your Stage Is Your Emotional Base

If you have feelings of resentment, you will build a stage of resentment, and then you will attract a bunch of resentful characters or other characters that drain your energy because you have aligned with their resentments. If you have a stage that has excitement and joy, then you create those in your life that are excited about life and joyful about what is expected.

The other thing to remember as you participate with the scenes and feelings in your "Movie" is that you cannot create scenes where you control others, regardless of your justification in doing so. You may not write a script on how someone is supposed to act towards you or how you want others to share with you. Writing a scene that controls another's behavior is big NO-NO. What you can do is write your script of scenes that are about your own behaviors. You can imagine how it feels to have a scenario play out with someone else, but only focus on how YOU feel – focus on how you respond to others and how you would like to shift or enhance any of those behaviors.

Many times we can have reactions to other people's behaviors. This Visualization Technology® is a productive way to play out scenes where you stay anchored in your core values, no matter how another treats you. Your personal values are non-negotiable, and this can be reinforced in your "Movie," supporting you to naturally respond with how you value your Self. You can also imagine how it feels to have kind, generous people in your life. Play with scenes of feeling comfortable and accepting your Self. As you feel this, imagine a scene where you are in a large group or in a meeting or in a situation with a relationship. When you play in your "Movie," you also activate your memory. We have so much intelligence, knowledge and resources within us that are stored in our cellular memory. Many times, we are not conscious of the emotional patterns that we are repeating based on old memory. We can access those memories that support us and shift those that no longer serve us.

At times you may have the habit of making others the expert of who you are before you go within to access your internal knowing, forgetting that you are your main resource.

I have seen great results of participants mastering Visualization Technology simply through the concept of seeing their life as a "Movie." They began to utilize this technique as a way to make choices internally rather than exhaust themselves emotionally. You will learn the skill of witnessing; you will play out scenes in a moment's notice to make choices that are responsive to what you wish to create instead of reacting impulsively.

If you have a fear or negative thoughts, which are also natural, you can play this out quickly. Play with scenes of your worst-case scenario and then move on to creating solutions with other more positive scenes. Why play out a fear over and over again in your life that you would not wish as your experience? *Fears stem from misguided perceptions.* With patience, you will resolve your fears by facing them internally with new scenes that begin to feel comfortable. You will find yourself strengthening your "Movie" throughout the day as your experiences naturally begin to play out scenes that are a match to the expectations of your desires.

Your Movie Happens

When you clearly begin to use this way of imagining, in time you will notice that it becomes a way of life. There is a system to utilizing your imagination. This is not fantasy or magic, although it may feel magical to witness what you have imagined as your "Movie" happen in your real life! This truly is a sophisticated system for developing and using your imagination to work for you as a tool to manifest your wishes.

Sometimes you may forget that you are always imagining in your daily life. Sometimes there is awareness of this consciously and sometimes there is not, but your connection to your imagination is activated regardless, as are your feelings. If your imagination is a tool that is working for you no matter what, let's work with it to actively serve you.

You use your imagination to see your route to work every day before you arrive, or you play out your "Movie" of going to work every day. You imagine what your outfit will look like as you get dressed for an event, you play out how you feel about what you are wearing, and how you feel at the event. When you take a test, you imagine yourself passing and you play out your "Movie" of being super joyful as you look at your partner and imagine what the future with him or her would feel like.

We imagine so many different scenarios all day long. I would love to have a movie camera inside some people's imaginations to film the movies they create of themselves that involve others. I am sure we have created some scenes with others and placed them in roles that they had no clue they were even cast in.

Now think about this for a moment: if we are already living what we have imagined, then imagine how beneficial it would be to fine-tune this Visualization Technology technique to create your life "Movie" consciously. When we have a lack of understanding or discipline with our imagination, we can be unaware that we are creating suffering, challenges and unhappiness.

Let's say you had a hurtful experience and reacted in a way that caused more hurt to your Self and others. Sometimes we play out these scenes over and over again and keep reinforcing what we do not wish for. In order to shift our experience to another one, allow the hurt to be acknowledged and do not suppress it. This gives energy movement from where you can make new choices. Feel these choices play out in scenes of a movie, and then attach them to possibilities you would like to experience. With this technique, you are self-sufficiently shifting your experience to a new one, and also shifting your cellular memory of the past to be updated.

Awareness of your imagination and how it activates in supporting your beliefs and outlook in life is very important. It is with your Emotional Imagination that is writing your life "Movie." You hold the ability to shift your beliefs and your perspective by the way you direct your imagination. Do not make this more complicated than it has to be. Keep it simple and take this as an opportunity to have ownership of your life.

No Commercials In My Movie

Philosophers and scientists have an ongoing debate about where our imagination comes from. Instead of analyzing this, I prefer to focus on and the results and mechanics that our imagination creates for us. Sometimes we can become consumed with analytical thinking and repetitive thoughts that are not in sync with our emotional desires. These are bad habits that were created; I refer to this as "brain candy" and this does not serve you.

If you get stuck in analytical debate in order to justify the how and why of something happening rather than finding solutions, your focus shifts away from achieving results. When we focus on creating conscious results in our life, the details will be given to us.

If you find that you are getting stuck in the details instead of feeling your expectation, maybe ask your Self if you really do want what you say you are wishing for. Be honest with your Self and take notice of the chaos. Oftentimes chaos would not be there or you would not allow it to get in your way if you had clarity about what you desired.

Life is supposed to be joyful. We are given so many opportunities and tools to be peaceful and excited about creating life, our life. Make your vision your authentic "Movie," and do not settle for commercials that do not support this.

The End Meets The Beginning

Part of the way I process information and create formulas is by focusing on the end result I wish to create and then I work backwards from there with the details. Many people process step by step in chronological order to get somewhere, even though they may not be sure where they are headed. It's OK not to know what something will look like as an end result, but we can know how we would like to *feel* about the end result of what we are creating.

In Power Wishing® the attention we place the most importance on is how you wish to feel about your end results. If I know how I wish to feel as my end result, then everything that I create will be focused and will lead to this.

For instance, if you were to rock climb, you have your safety rope anchored to the mountaintop and you climb up towards the anchor that holds your rope to guide you. Imagine the feeling you wish to feel towards an experience as the anchor. As you stay focused on that feeling, then all will guide you towards this feeling as the base that creates your result. You simply take steps and climb towards your goal. Your feelings are already anchored like the safety rope, which is leading the way.

Some people may feel a bit of resistance towards fully acquiring the skill of creating their "Movie" because they do not believe it is possible to have what they wish for based on their present experiences. Because they are so focused on their present situation, if they start to create a "Movie" of what they believe they would like but currently believe is not possible, they feel like a fraud to themselves. But, how do you think your present life was created? Your feelings are energy that you have molded into the reality you are now experiencing.

When you feel your Self as successful, when you walk, talk and act successful, you are! What is the difference between this and using the same energy to feel, walk, talk and act out your fears that have not even become a reality yet? *"Fake it till you make it."* This is not about being untruthful or fake; it is about cultivating the energy of your desire to manifest. Or as Muhammad Ali summed it up best:

"To be a great champion you must believe you are the best. If you're not, pretend you are."

We all know that one can only pretend for so long, but this gives you the opportunity to step into the experience and make it your own.

When my siblings and I were growing up, my father used to say, "Act like you belong and no one will question you." He would say this many times as he taught us to use our imagination. At times he would even have us play out experiences to show us that no one will question us if we have the conviction within ourselves of how we feel. I remember as an eight-year-old child I was in line at Disney World, and my father told me to walk into the park. He wanted me to meet my brother who was already inside while he was buying the tickets.

I started to feel fearful because I did not have a ticket and I did not want to get in trouble with the park authorities. I wanted to see Mickey Mouse so much and I feared I was going to be thrown out. My father, who has a determined mind and a military background, is not one to challenge. He looked at me and said, "Act like you belong and no one will question you. Think of dancing with Mickey in the parade." Within seconds I went from fear to dancing with Mickey and walked right in to meet my brother. My Vibrational Language was clear: the dominant emotion shifted from fear to my pure happiness of feeling myself dancing with Mickey in the parade. Nothing else mattered!

I have to laugh because 40 years later I found myself at a black-tie gala remembering this moment with my father at Disney World as a child. My friends were already inside with my ticket as the performance had started and I did not wish to interrupt them. Security was tight and though it seemed impossible to get in, I felt the excitement of sharing the performance along with my friends, and I simply smiled, walked right in and went to my seat.

This is a simplified example of Visualization Technology, but it offers a profound understanding of the component of YOU yourself believing; seeing and feeling in something first is vital in order for it to happen. We can shift anything within seconds, and as we all know, life can profoundly change in seconds.

Power Wishing

"Men do not attract that which they want, but that which they are."

This is a quote from the classic novel *As A Man Thinketh* by James Allan. This goes hand in hand with the saying, "As within, so without." Clean up your Emotional Self and that will reflect in your outer world.

I find that others will usually question you about what you question about your Self. The value of using the visualization technique of the "Movie" is that you work out all your emotions first within your Self, which naturally becomes the outside reflection you manifest.

Every Moment Is An Opportunity

Aligning your "Movie" in a positive way with your reality leads you to have emotional discipline that sets you up for success. You must take physical action towards what you desire. If you wish to find a job, you can play out in your "Movie" all day long about how you feel about your job but you have to take action towards creating this in the physical. I assure you that if you play in your "Movie" with your feelings towards an experience you wish for, opportunities will be presented to you. But you must also take action towards reaching these goals.

This is no different than knowing that if a person eats a whole chocolate cake with lots of frosting every night and does not exercise, they will gain weight even though they say they wish to lose ten pounds. If they do not stop eating cake, losing weight will not be their physical reality. So either they accept they will not lose the weight and enjoy the cake or they find discipline to stop eating cake. Play out in your "Movie" how it feels to have the discipline you wish to have. Find a matching feeling towards how you would like to feel, even if you know this feeling from another experience. Create scenes of you easily fulfilling these goals. When you feel resistance, work that out in your "Movie." Your imagination is your editing room.

Sometimes you can be playing out your "Movie" and if for some reason you cannot seem to get past an emotion you would like to shift, this is perfectly OK. You have already started the shift with the intention to feel differently. No need to push, just feel. It is a bit unrealistic to think that you can feel a positive feeling right away when you have an intense feeling that is pulling you in the other direction. Acknowledging how you feel allows the opportunity for another feeling to come in. Every moment is an opportunity for another moment to feel differently. Be patient and consistent towards what supports the feelings you wish to feel.

You Are Worthy Of Your Dreams

To be able to accomplish what we desire, we have to move out of our own way. We are worthy of our dreams, and the component of feeling self-worth is the underlying foundation to receive with ease. As we choose to release the habit of self-sabotaging our wishes with techniques such as the *Stage Your Day Technique*[6], we realize that there are many opportunities to create expansion in our self-awareness.

For example, I choose to go on different adventures in order to accept being comfortable with a healthy discomfort. I do not wish to miss out on a realized dream of mine because of fears or anxiety that do not serve me. One thing I can share is that one common thread I have with the experiences of my adventures is that the anxiety in the anticipation of an adventure is always worse than my actual experience.

For as long as I can remember, I always had this dream of going to India. No one close to me had the same desire to visit this beautiful country so each opportunity that came also went because I did not have a travel partner, but traveling there was on my "bucket list." Though I often thought of going to India, my feeling about when this would happen was calm. I would say to myself, "One day, I will go to India, it will happen."

Then, one day I received a visit from a cousin that I love so much and had not seen in several years. We met for dinner and she shared that she had just returned from a wonderful trip to India. My eyes opened six feet wide as I asked how it was and where she went. I went on and on.

In India, I wished to do Panchakarma, which is a therapeutic way of eliminating toxic elements from the body, and my cousin gave me the name of a place where I could go. We discussed going together in the spring but it was unlikely that our schedules would coincide. I remembered the name of the place she mentioned and looked it up online. There was not much information about it and actually there were two places with the same name in different parts of India.

When You Know You Know

I could feel that this was the right time to go: my schedule was open and

---

[6] *The Stage Your Day Technique* is a visualization meditation that I created which focuses on setting up your emotional base. Detailed explanation of this technique can be found in Chapter 9 – Stage Your Day.

my children would be well taken care of by their father. I made my flight reservations, applied for my visa and I was ready. This was my dream and I was finally going! After making all my arrangements, I just assumed that there would be space at the place I wished to stay. I contacted them and they said they were completely booked. I remember looking at the email saying to myself calmly, "I am going to India." I wrote them back and told them a little bit about myself and that I was going to India no matter what. I received a note back saying that, "It just so happened that they received one cancellation."

When I would share that I was going alone to India with other people, the comments were usually, "Do you know where you are going?" To be sincere, I was not really sure. I am usually geographically confused so I could not give them a straight answer. Then more questions came. "Have you researched enough? Are you crazy? Why are you are going alone? Is it safe to go alone to India? There are many diseases in India, you will get very sick." The best one I heard was ... "Why India?"

On top of that, to add to the humor of my process of getting to India, I was working in New York City at the time and I decided to process my travel visa there. I walked into the office and smiled at the man in the visa office and asked if my visa could be expedited quickly. He looked at me with a smirk on his face. Then with a big smile and an Indian accent, he said to me "Oh, so you're going to India like that woman in *Eat, Pray, Love*!" I had to laugh and then the whole office started to compare me to the book. I shared with them that I had wanted to go to India before the book was written. This was also a comment I heard often. I wanted to make a T-shirt that said, "I am going to India and, no, it is not because of the book *Eat, Pray, Love*." Well, this was the way the visa company remembered me. They were very helpful in getting my visa on time even though I decided to reserve this trip a little less than a month from when I expected to go.

Some questions that others asked me were valid and practical, so I researched the answers. I also received some wonderful advice from people who had journeyed to India. In my gut, in my feelings, in my whole being, I was so clear on going on this journey. I would listen to some of my loved one's concerns, but my gut kept feeling, "Yes! Yes! Go!" The departure date kept getting closer and closer.

You know how you can have the feeling that something could happen at the last minute and then all of a sudden *BAM*, the dream is over.

Even though I did not know what to expect with the details, I did know what I expected to feel about my trip. The feeling of this is what I continued to play in my imagination to strengthen my dream. I also stopped sharing with others that I felt would not be supportive because of their own personal issues.

I allowed 20 years of different opportunities to come and go, but now it was my time to go to India.

On My Way

Well, the day came when I boarded the plane and sat in my seat. I took a deep breath. I touched my seat to feel that I was really on my way. As I was flying, I had a mini anxiety attack. It hit me. I started to hear everyone's comments, plus I was leaving my teenaged children behind for a few weeks. Was I crazy to go to India by myself? What if I got sick and never recovered? I was hearing all the *worst-case scenarios* in my head.

My flight was delayed getting into London and I was hustling to make my connecting flight. I was listening to all the voices in my head. For a moment I started to envision the "Movie" that would follow each one of them as I allowed the panic to creep in while I was getting lost finding my next gate at the London airport. I was going to a foreign place that I did not know, was being picked up by people I did not know and staying in a place where I knew no one. To add to this, I was now panicking that I just might miss my flight. *Was this a sign not to continue?*

I stopped. I took a deep breath and basically gave myself a talking to. I witnessed my anxiety then I said to myself, "I am here and I have a choice; either I go or not, but I know I am almost there." Because I spent more time being consciously proactive in my imagination about positive feelings about my trip, my body quickly reaffirmed that knowing. I had a moment, acknowledged it and went back to the feelings I wished to create as my experiences.

Logically, I could not answer every concern, but my feelings gave me all the answers. I went back to my feelings and had some humor as I witnessed myself running again through the airport. I started to feel excited again. Finally, I arrived to the first security check with the airline and the lady said to me, "I apologize but there has been a change with your seating." In my head I started to look for the *worst-case scenario* and instead I quickly said to myself, "I am getting on that plane, everything is fine." So I looked at her calmly and said, "Do I have a seat?" "Yes," she confirmed. I said, "Great, that is all I need."

I now had 20 minutes to board and I still had to go through a security check, so I started running. I arrived at the plane with just a few minutes to spare; I had not paid attention to my seat assignment so I simply handed my boarding pass to the stewardess. I was directed very graciously to seat 1A. I was upgraded to full first class service from London to India! Even writing this I still get chills thinking of the amusement and the irony of that moment. I must say it was a very comfortable flight.

Have Proactive Scenes in Your Movie

My first trip to India and the subsequent trips that followed were as magical and adventurous as the beautiful country and its people. I felt at home with the new family and friends that I made there. I am so grateful I chose to listen to my gut feelings.

Though it was not a comfortable decision, or even a logical one, in my feelings there was logic and comfort. I used *Stage Your Day Technique* to strengthen my inner voice and listened to my Emotional GPS. Though at times I may not have all the clarity of what my feelings mean, I stay consistent with feeling my feelings, knowing that the answers will come. I have learned to have patience until I have more clarity. I do not change my feelings because something does not make sense at the time or ignore a desire I have because it does not seem possible. I stay focused on the feeling I have inside of me as my intelligence as this is where I prefer to make my decisions and shift my feelings when I have new information. My feelings make everything possible and how I expect these feelings to serve my dreams is what makes the possibilities real. Consistency with the feelings that serve my expectation is very important. When you create consistency, you reaffirm what you say you wish for; it is a way to claim your experience.

There are many unknowns in life that we may not always be prepared for. Though we can prepare ourselves emotionally for when these situations arise, we can deal with them in a proactive spontaneous way. *You make it a habit to be proactive in your life when you build on what is positive about your Self. When you look for the positive in your Self, you know how to look at the positive in a situation while being aware of the whole situation.*

Your positive emotional base carries you and supports you to vision in a way that expands your best qualities. It is easy to find what is wrong; to find what is positive benefits you from where others would falter.

When situations arise that may shock me, I wish to be able to respond with choices that sustain my life in the best way without being in my own way. Personally, I do everything I possibly can to be proactive in my life, as I feel it is easier to have a Life by Design than by crisis. Being proactive encourages you to have emotional habits that support you. Choose to focus on trusting your Self and the "Movie" you wish to have as your experience.

Yes, there are many unknowns still to come in my life ... there have been and continue to be many beautiful unknowns that I have treasured as gifts to my Soul and for these I am grateful. My prayer is that I am always open to these possibilities. I also encourage my children to have experiences that are out of their comfort zone. I support them in learning something different or traveling to somewhere unknown that is outside of what they are familiar with. We often venture together in this and I am so proud of them for exploring life in a positive way.

Where do you experience adventure? What are your dreams? If you could choose to have one dream come true, what would that dream be? Do you dream often? Do you believe they can come true? How do you imagine your dreams being true? What are you waiting for? Later is now.

Feelings Write Your "Movie"

Let's have fun in creating your life as you vision it. Just like when you watch a movie, you sit back and witness what you are watching. Now this will be your life preview. If you witness your experiences as a "Movie" being played out right in front of you, you will have the opportunity to respond to your life rather than react. Life becomes more and more like a candy store – all you have to do is choose.

As I have shared, our life is a "Movie" made up of our feelings and then our beliefs, thoughts and actions follow. We edit the script of our "Movie" by shifting our feelings. The shift of our feeling brings a different scene to our "Movie," which creates movement towards the outcome we desire. We have the choice to write our script and make our own "Movie." When we are not connected to our internal Emotional GPS, we can feel like we are watching a movie that is not ours.

Let's say for a moment that your script is written by your feelings. If you are used to allowing others to tell you how you feel, or resign yourself to not acknowledging your feelings, or respond emotionally based on others' reactions, then how can you write your own script? Then your "Movie" is written for you and blame, resentments and anger may also be written in your script. When I have observed this happening to others and they ask me how to get ownership of their script back, I share with them to use their imagination towards this. Sometimes people do not even know what it would feel like to have ownership of their life. They are unfamiliar with making decisions based on how they feel. They have trained themselves to feel emotion not as their definition, but as a reaction towards other people's feelings.

Many of us have had moments where we feel like we have lost ownership in certain areas of our lives, like a relationship, responsibilities, career, etc. The first step is to find what it could feel like to have ownership of your life choices and freedom to be your Self without feeling wrong or being what is expected of you. Play with the different scenes of feeling free to be your Self without negative consequences and explore going back to another time and place where you have felt this way. Give your Self full permission to dream. Once you can connect to a feeling that matches the experience you wish, this projects direction that acts like an anchor for your experience to move forward.

There can be experiences that we would like to change or resolve, but these experiences have already happened – these experiences are in the past. Release your focus on fixing a past situation or being fixated on any one experience. Feeling a little bit better is still feeling better.

Although we cannot change the past, we can shift the way we view the past. Playing with the experience as a "Movie" allows you to do this without judgment or emotions that do not serve you or another, as you are being a witness. In doing this you release attempting to change something that has already happened and instead resolve your feelings about it. Remember, the experience you wish to resolve was created from a feeling. Focus on the experience or the situation and connect to it emotionally in order to understand the emotional root of the cause that created this experience. When you have this knowing, you can shift the emotion so you do not repeat the same experience.

Focus On Resolving Your Feelings Rather Than The Situation

Once you have resolved your feelings about a certain situation, other circumstances in your life that are attached to that feeling will also be resolved because it is a domino effect. I feel it is far more efficient to manage your life this way instead of going from experience to experience to resolve each issue separately.

Shift the underlying feeling that is the root cause of your

challenges, and then you will shift all the experiences that are connected to this old belief that may not serve you any longer.

Invest time in knowing your feelings, as this is running your life experiences. You can organize your life quite nicely by knowing which feelings you wish to experience and which ones you do not. Those feelings that no longer represent you, well, it is time for them to go "bye-bye." Shifting these feelings will be easier and non-negotiable as you start to witness your Self have more of the life that represents you.

Writing your "Movie" is based on the feelings you would like to embody with the beliefs of who you are choosing to be in your script. This "Movie" transcends "What Is" presently and affects your beliefs, thoughts and actions, which set the tone of your Vibrational Language. You are attracting with clarity what you are expecting with synergy, as your Vibrational Language clearly dialogues this to transform "What Is" presently to "What If" as your reality.

You Get What You Feel

Many training techniques in visualizing and manifesting ask you to envision the end result with the end result being a tangible physical goal. Yes, I agree that this can be beneficial, but with Power Wishing Visualization Technology, the physical end result will naturally appear when you know how you wish to feel about what you expect.

As you explore your feelings, there will be pictures and scenes that come up in your "Movie"; trust that these are giving you clues or messages. These scenes have information, so as they come up, ask your Self what they mean or how they can benefit you. Hear the answers from an emotional space. Remember, no need to get caught up in the "brain candy" of how you will manifest the details … they will come.

We have spoken about manifesting based on your feelings being your end result. Now let's look at creating your end result as a physical goal with the physical details being your base and why I feel this way is more challenging. Let's say you wish to manifest a house, so you first focus on the details of the physical elements of your home. For example, you outline the results for the house by detailing that you want a white house on 23rd street for $500,000.

In this way of manifesting, you have limited your possibilities by controlling what you believe is possible, limiting the Universe to expand in co-creating with you. Because you have exercised your free will to choose by stating the details of what you want, even if co-creating can bring you enhanced opportunities, this will be challenging. Now what? Let's say that a better opportunity appears with a green house on 24th street. You may have doubts, or you may not even recognize this opportunity, because it is not a match to your specific wish. You have created a false sense of emotional security based on a plan that is physical. Because you have chosen your expectation based on solely a mental plan, you will try to process your opportunities as logic and most likely pass up, or not even recognize, something that is outside of your "plan," your expected outcome is from a physical perspective. Some would say that the Universe is supposed to help bring you the specific white house on 23rd street. Then again, the Universe expands our "Ask" and maybe this "Ask" was limiting.

Let's look at another approach; now imagine manifesting a home by having a healthy emotional base where you attract alignment for your vision of expectation. Emotions have fluidity and create expansiveness towards opportunities.

With the emotion-based formula of Power Wishing, you create a platform for so many expanded possibilities to be reality. Imagine a result based on the feelings of trust, confidence and awareness that the best opportunity will appear for you. You have certainty that you will know how to recognize and take positive action towards what you are expecting. Now we are talking.

When you focus on your feelings that are connected to what you are wishing for, then you are open for the Universe to co-create with you in an enhanced and expansive way. Trusting all the details will work out and are mirrors reflecting these emotions. You also strengthen the trust that good things will happen *for* you.

When I have supported clients in buying a new home, they are amazed at how the details get resolved when they make sure they have solidified their base of emotional expectation. They experience ease along with feeling like the Universe handled details they did not even foresee. They tell me about the wonderful and loyal realtor that they met, how the bank gave them a loan with no hassle and that the whole process happened in such a flow. Some even find homes so quickly they are in amazement. I have even had clients who find homes from people they know, and they share with me all sorts of "coincidences" that make the experience even sweeter. We laugh in my lectures about people having to make sure they have the belief that they can receive easily and quickly, as this is key. When you own how you feel emotionally, chaos no longer has a lead role in your "Movie." Solutions take over the lead.

Stay Focused On Your Feelings

Let's continue with this example of buying a house. The key to this is to stay focused on your feelings as the emotional entrance to what you wish to create.

A gentleman named Mark, who is an attorney, was attending my lectures. After a few months, we would laugh at how he would break down his feelings and overthinks things like a case study. This is the story he told me. He saw a house he loved and then felt the house was not a possibility for him because he could not afford it. Mark shared that what he had learned from my lectures was that he had a choice. He could either stay focused on visualizing the house and ignore the feeling that he cannot afford it or he can be aware that he loves this house and acknowledge that he feels that he cannot afford it *at this time* and choose to focus on his issues with money.

He said he had the "Mental Courtroom" appear in his thoughts. If he focused his wish in the first manner, he might manifest the house. But why manifest a house and create more debt that would add to his financial burden? Having a new home with more debt is not a great way to enjoy a new home. Then he added, "If I felt I could not afford the house, there are probably other areas where I feel the same way about my finances." He took what he learned from the Power Wishing lectures and cleaned up his beliefs about money, believing that other areas in his life would also get cleaned up automatically.

I often share that to me, it is far more efficient to clean up the limitations and chaos in your life through your beliefs than by working through each experience that is probably connected to that belief. Mark chose to focus on the feelings that he had towards money, which shifted naturally his beliefs. When he passed in front of the house, he said to himself that he couldn't afford it "at this time." He was wise enough to use phrases such as "at this time" knowing that with this language it is possible to create positive openings in his energy to manifest.

As Mark utilized Power Wishing as his support system, he said he did not feel that he is *working* on himself due to lacking something; he embraced Power Wishing as another way to process. Mark chose not to obsess over what he felt he was lacking, or what he was anxious about; instead, he had focused on clearing up his beliefs towards money. This created a hopeful feeling towards his financial future. He said, "When I took a moment to reflect, I realized that I had been so distracted with other things and the house was no longer a focus." His focus naturally had shifted towards a side business he had created with a hobby that was also bringing him income.

A few months later Mark decided to take a new route on his way home and he happened to pass by that house he was interested in once before. He noticed a house a few doors down that also had a for sale sign. With a sense of excitement and to his surprise, he took down the number to see the house. He said at that moment, "What's the worst that can happen? It will be fun to look at this house." He smiled when he noticed how different he felt driving down this street compared to last time. He shared with me that he was astonished that he no longer felt the same anxiety associated with the possibility of owning a new home.

He acknowledged he is not at the financial place he would like to be *yet*, but things have shifted. He is happier and occupied with more joyful activities, even making extra income with his hobby. He noticed that he is also spending less money. He had thought it was time to sell the house he lived in now because it felt like there were always new repairs, but he took notice that there had been no repairs in the last few months. He laughs with me when sharing that maybe the techniques he has been using from Power Wishing are working because his "Movie" is looking really good and is going the way he visualized it. He laughs again, sharing with me how much easier things are for him because he shifted the way he defines them.

In all sincerity, I understand that there can be moments when we feel it may be better to go back to an old pattern of beliefs. This is common. When Mark felt challenged by returning to his old habit of worrying about a lack of money or overspending towards unnecessary items that are not in line with his goal, he took a moment to step back and to witness his "Movie."

Getting off track can happen and this is normal and understandable. He centered himself by reaffirming how he would like his end result to feel. Using the Power Wishing technique, he also developed wishes to support his end result of feeling abundant in income and being debt free. He anchors this feeling when he feels off track.

Think of what you would like to shift or resolve and how many years you have worried about this. It has taken you years to create this pattern and sometimes there is a comfort in this. When we are changing our beliefs, it can feel uncomfortable for a moment. I like to see this feeling of discomfort as a way of our emotional body checking in to have us reaffirm if change is what we really wish to experience. The more you reaffirm your present belief when this comes up, the less you will be challenged by old habits that used to create emotional comfort for you. Your new pattern will begin to feel comfortable *sooner* rather than later.

Finding The Feelings You Wish To Feel In Your Script

Release concern if for some reason you are not able to feel your end result yet. You can resolve this by asking your Self how you would like to feel. Sometimes there is not yet a feeling attached to your desired experience because you have not experienced what this feels like, or you cannot remember because other feelings are dominating you. For example, lets say you are wishing for a loving relationship, I suggest that you ask your Self how you would like to feel, take that answer and in your Emotional Imagination let go and be in a daydream of wishing and then ask to have a memory where you felt loved or you loved. Just close your eyes, take a few deep breaths and ask your body to show you scenes of a time where you have felt this. It can be with a past partner, a family member, a friend, a mentor or even a pet. Trust that your imagination is guiding you by whatever experience you witness.

Release questioning what is shown to you and just trust. Know with total certainty that there is a reason for what you are seeing and/or feeling. Continue to play with whatever scenes come up and keep asking your Self how you would like to feel with trusting that you will be taken to other feelings and scenes. You will know when you have witnessed a scene that feels as a match to how you would like to feel.

When this happens, take a moment to anchor this as the knowing of what you wish to expect from your experience. Basically, you are saying to your Self and your body that, "*Yes,* this is what I expect to feel *now* in a relationship." Your imagination will strengthen the possibility you wish for by matching the same feeling with another experience, by acknowledging that you already know what this feels like from another memory. Your imagination processes this as an opportunity to expand a familiar emotion to strengthen what you are asking for now.

Know that you are the director of your "Movie"; therefore, if there is something you would like rewritten, you are empowered to edit the script you have created.

Stay up-to-date with your Self, assess your beliefs and shift the beliefs that no longer serve you. Check in with your beliefs towards what you are wishing to create. Take the new belief that you desire and simply connect that belief with the feeling of knowing what it feels like to live with this as your "Movie" called *Life* and write this into your script.

You Are The Director

You, and only you, write your script.
Only you can edit your script.
Only you know what "Movie" is right for you.

When you allow another to write your script, you lose your editing rights and you lose the flow of living as your authentic Self.
Write your script for YOU, for your dreams … if you choose to write your "Movie" as your Authentic Self, the characters you cast will match your life definition. Think about that for a minute … casting a "Movie" with characters that match who you truly are instead of casting a "Movie" with characters matching your false Shadow Self.

The outcome of your life "Movie" will be beautiful love stories of your Authentic Self in partnership with Source Energy … imagine the possibilities of these scenes.

What do you believe?
What is your belief system? This, and your imagination is what create the plot. Knowing what it feels like creates your "Movie."
And then you play … play in your imagination like you used to as a child. Whether it was imagining being a famous baseball player or a movie star or living in a certain place, playing in your imagination is not just for children – it is a brilliant way to succeed.

Witness the world as the entertainment you are plugged into.
Words can either create or limit.
You create one experience; you can create another.
Witness the world you have created.
Believe in your prayers.
Believe that your desires are heard.
Believe that there are those who want the best for you.
Believe in the good.
Believe in the beauty.
Believe in You.
Believe in Love.
The Light and forgiveness …
And the magic of all there is …
And all that is left to still explore.

Your Life On The Big Screen

Know that this is your "Movie"! You wrote it and you are the director. Sometimes we are not clear of what script we want to write. We get confused and caught in the chaos of other people's "Movie" and their script for us and we can feel stuck. It is OK that sometimes you lose track of your script. When these moments happen, close your eyes and just play with whatever comes to your imagination. Know that you can rewrite your script at any time; make edits instead of rehashing the reruns.

Ask to have clarity or patience to enjoy the moment in your life without having the grand plan.

Find guidance through your feelings and connecting with Divine Love. Know what feels good and create an outside world that supports these feelings. All is well; this is just an experience that was created by you, which means you can always create another one.

Get clear about what story you are writing for your Self. Write out your story and read it as if you were looking in on your life. Know the story that you tell. Own your story and believe in it before you share it with all those around you. It's not that you cannot share, but before you receive others' opinions and projections of how your "Movie" should be, get clear with your Self first.

Let go of speaking what you no longer wish for as your life experience. When you repeat the drama of telling a story that did not bring you joy or serve you best, you repeat the history and recall the cellular memory of this experience again. Leave the past in the past.

It is not what happens to us; it is what we do with it that makes a difference. In your Emotional Imagination, you can shift your perspective of your story. By shifting your perception of what you are observing, you create change for other possibilities. You can choose how you wish to feel about your world. This is your choice; you always have a choice.

Your imagination is how you write the script for your "Movie" of life. Your "Movie" becomes alive by the emotions that you choose to observe it with. You can choose how you create your script by choosing the emotions you wish to feel. Your emotions are the signal of what you are expecting to happen. Therefore, how you feel about what you expect is how your life will be.

As you play in your imagination, you are creating the script for the life you wish to experience as your reality. Enjoy yourself as you playfully explore how you feel and how you wish to feel. Play with different opportunities of what you would like to expect.

Know with total certainty you are the creator of your world. Be open to changing your mind. Be open that others will change their minds too. Be open that others will change their minds at different times.

Create consistency of those behaviors and habits that support you. Stay focused on the actions that support the script you are writing. Feel those "good" feelings to attract more of them as a match.

Be aware of all your surroundings and know you have created your stage for your "Movie" of life.

Know that on your stage you are creating the performance of your life, and YOU will be writing the reviews when you depart this life.

Power Thoughts

Direct Your Movie

- o   I am creating what I imagine.

- o   When I own my emotions, chaos does not have a lead role.

- o   I write the script, edit, cast and direct my "Movie."

- o   I own the rights to my "Movie."

- o   I have fun playing out my "Movie" as my life.

- o   My emotional discipline sets me up for success.

- o   My feelings guide me to more joyful scenes.

- o   It is not what happens to me, it is what I do with it that makes the difference.

- o   I know with total certainty that I am the creator of my world.

- o   I am worthy of my dreams.

The "Ask"

The Power Wishing® formula was partly created on understanding why sometimes when you ask for something, you receive it and others times you do not. Why does this happen and what is the difference? In this chapter you will receive insight on what effects your ability to manifest, and like a chemist, you will become aware of how to modify your outcome through adjusting your wishes and beliefs. Adjusting the emotional execution of your "Ask" is a key component of the formula as this will make the difference in how and what you receive.

Wishing is asking, and this is something you do all day long in so many different ways with your Emotional Imagination. Look around you: what you have manifested is based on the feelings of what you believe is possible and is what you expected to receive with this belief.

"Ask" is not just a verbal request; it is also when something you see attracts your attention emotionally. We create our "Ask" when we go to the movies and we feel engaged in a desire towards what we are watching. An "Ask" can be something as simple as when you see an advertisement and you wish you had what was being promoted or when you feel emotional about a TV show you are watching and are drawn to how the scene makes you feel. Even when you see someone in a relationship and feel you would like to have a similar bond or when you visualize a new car and you can feel yourself driving it. You are even asking when you watch the news and there is a connection to your fears hopes and desires. Our "Ask" is even activated through feelings, smell, sound, taste and physical sensation. All day we are getting intuitive hits and an emotional charge when we are connecting energetically. These are all moments when you are sending out an "Ask," and these moments all have emotions attached to them whether you are aware of this or not.

Millions Of Thoughts

One day I was giving a lecture about Power Wishing. I instructed the audience to begin this process by writing 6 to 12 wishes. During my presentation, my daughter, who was sitting up against the wall behind me on the floor, put her hand up with a question. It was quite a large audience and I was surprised to see my 12-year-old child waving her hand to ask a question. She really has a mind of her own and for a moment I thought to myself, "I have no idea what she is going to say." She clearly asked aloud, "Mom, why are we only allowed to write down 6 to 12 wishes instead of a million?" There was an awkward silence in the room as I thought for a moment about my response. I was impressed that she felt that 12 wishes were limiting and that a million wishes was the way to go. I shared that in a way, my daughter was actually on point. We are asking and wishing all the time, all day long. We ask for a lot more than 12 wishes per day, whether you are aware of this or not.

Actually, a number of years ago the National Science Foundation (NSF) estimated that your brain may produce as many as 12,000 to 50,000 thoughts per day depending on how deep of a thinker you are. Other estimates run as high as 60,000 per day! If you have 50,000 thoughts a day that means you have hit a million thoughts in 20 days.

Wow! Imagine if we conducted an analysis of your wishes to create a summary of all the emotions connected to your thoughts. Now add to that varied feelings of being overwhelmed, reactions that you have throughout the day and the projections of others. What do you think your "internal report" of expectations in regards to decision-making would look like? We could make the assumption that with so many thoughts and feelings there is probably chaotic energy and some mixed messaging going on internally. Imagine now, as the chemist that you are, that you clean up your Vibrational Language by being in touch with your feelings so that you communicate consciously with clarity to your Self, others and the Universe. Naturally, your day would go smoother if you give clear messages to your Self. It is very important to have awareness of whether you are giving mixed messaging to your Self and the Universe and if this is so, Power Wishing is an essential tool to clean up your message to be clear.

The "Ask" in Action

I experienced a beautiful story that is a true example of the beauty of our gift to be able to ask and receive what we expect. When I was 14 years old and in the ninth grade, I moved for a short while to Houston, Texas where my mom lived at the time. It felt quite different living in Houston compared to Miami, not only because of the weather and culture, but primarily because I lived in a two-bedroom apartment with my mother compared to living in a house with my father and six other siblings. In Houston, I attended an all-girls Catholic school, starting in the middle of my ninth grade year. In the early dawn I had to take a bus to school because we lived on the other side of town. I remember feeling uncomfortable because it was still dark outside when I waited at the bus stop and then I rode alone with the driver of the bus until he picked up others. I arrived to this new school and all the girls were mostly fair-skinned with blond hair, and I had more the Latina look with brown hair. I remember walking through the halls and feeling overwhelmed, not only by my own life as a 14-year-old but also because everyone already knew each other and I was not connected to any of them.

Most of the girls at school seemed perfectly dressed in their uniforms and they wore them heavily starched, looking clean and crisp. At the time, we could not afford nice clothes, and my worn shirt seemed different, so I felt out of place even more.

I was so relieved when I met a girl who was sweet and friendly. I remember looking in her eyes and knowing in my heart that she was genuine. We had an instant bond and we became the best of friends, but I only ended up attending this school for six months because I moved back to Miami that summer. I enjoyed my time with this very special friend and the best part about our friendship was the kindness that her family shared with me. They were Iranian and warmly invited me to their family gatherings. They enjoyed having me over for dinner and we laughed and spent a lot of time together.

When I left Houston, I lost contact with my friend, and I do not remember why. We were each other's confidante and support in a new school together. Thirty years went by and I thought of her often over the years with a gut feeling that one day I would see her again. I would remember her and had a specific memory of a bracelet that I left with her.

It was a very special bracelet that my Cuban grandmother gave me; it had been hers when she was a young girl and some of the charms belonged to her mother. She had given it to me when I was 13 and I had cherished this charm bracelet dearly. I would play with the dangling charms and I loved the sound they made when they clicked together. It was also special to my grandmother because it was one of the few possessions she had brought from Cuba and the gold from this bracelet was from her family's gold mine.

For some reason, I never asked my friend to return the bracelet after I left Houston. It had meant so much to me – I couldn't remember why I would leave behind something so important. Years went by and I would think about the bracelet constantly. I had no idea how or if I could get it back after 30 years. At one point, I thought to Google my former friend, but I am embarrassed to admit that I did not even remember her name. Although I had forgotten her name, I never forgot her kind soul and the warmth of her family.

My grandmother was a very special woman in my life; she truly filled a void. She was my grandmother but also a great companion. She took me places, enrolled me in classes, taught me how to sew and supported all my hobbies, besides instilling many values in me. Traveling was important to my grandparents; they would save their money and wait for a tour from an American Express promotion. They took me to Europe several times. Even though as a young girl I felt like everyone on the tour was at least 90 years old, I was nicely spoiled and they brought me to what seemed like every museum that existed. I always had a flair for clothes and I aspired to be the best dressed and not being able to afford designer clothing did not stop us. My grandmother would take me downtown and we would buy a pattern, some material and make the design ourselves. I had permission to always be creative when I was around her. To this day, I see something in the store and if it is very expensive, I look at my daughter and say, "We can make that!" I think of my grandmother often and I am grateful for her presence in my life, especially since I share a similar relationship with my daughter.

My grandmother modeled behavior of determination with focus to get things done without having her ego get in the way. "Can't" was not in her vocabulary; she would always find a way. She went from being part of one of the wealthiest families in Cuba to living in a foreign country and doing what she could to create a life for her family here in the United States. My grandmother was detailed about her thoughtfulness, and I learned a lot about kindness from her.

So back to my dear childhood friend who made such an impact on me in the six months that I lived in Houston. I gave her my beloved grandmother's charm bracelet and then I returned to Miami and we lost touch. After 30 years of not seeing my friend, my own daughter was now turning 14. It was the day before Christmas and as a gift to my siblings, I made them copies of a special picture of my grandmother with President Johnson. It had been two years since my grandmother left her physical body and on this day my father asked me if I would clean out her room of belongings. This left me feeling so connected to memories of her, and I especially thought about her special bracelet.

Making The "Ask"

As I sat around the dinner table at my father's house with my siblings explaining the visit my grandmother had with President Johnson and giving them a copy of the picture, this overwhelming feeling of regret came over me. I looked across the table and wished I could pass along this bracelet to my daughter, and I felt so disappointed that I did not have it for her. In that moment, as everyone was conversing back and forth, I acknowledged my feelings of disappointment to myself. As I remembered my grandmother and felt my feelings of love for her, I sincerely apologized to her for losing the bracelet. I asked for forgiveness from her and I forgave myself as a young girl. I felt it was important to take responsibility for losing it and I acknowledged this.

Then I clearly felt my desire to give this bracelet to my daughter. I felt my desire and my determination to do everything possible to find my bracelet again. I played out the scenes of looking everywhere to find my old friend from Houston. I imagined myself going to my old high school and looking her name up in the yearbook. I played out these scenes with such will and desire. As I did this, I felt that I still did not remember her name but I remembered her and how our friendship felt. As the doubts came up, I felt totally certain that a solution would be made clear. As I was playing out my scenes, I said in my prayer with all my heart that I wished for this bracelet to come to me. As I staged my day, I felt myself trusting my prayer with total certainty for no logical reason along with my genuine apology.

Even in the middle of my family talking and carrying on in conversation with one another, I was playing in my imagination and connecting with all my heart and soul to see myself recovering my bracelet. In this space of prayer, I gave my gratitude for Source Energy enhancing my expectation and resolving this with me. I made a commitment that I would do everything possible to recover it. Then I let it go, knowing that there would be a way and it would appear to me. I also included my grandmother in this prayer.

The conscious "Ask" that I made for my bracelet is what I describe as *Stage Your Day*. As you practice the *Stage Your Day Technique* consistently, you will find that you are able to *Reboot* at a moment's notice, any time, any place.

I let this prayer go and continued the evening with the knowledge that I was going to find my friend. What happened next was such a confirmation of "Ask and you shall receive," and "Ask and you shall receive what you expect." Power Wishing was created based on the way I have prayed and continued to witness how things materialized in my world. Those who use Power Wishing have certainty in understanding the unfolding of my prayer with the circumstances that you will read about. They know firsthand from using these powerful visualization techniques that when you create a clear emotional "Ask," believing what you expect to receive becomes truth in the physical world. At times, you will receive so quickly that you will at first be surprised. But as you will notice, using the Power Wishing techniques will become a lifestyle of consciousness.

I have included a copy of the email below to share the amazing result of my prayer that became a reality so quickly. Three days after my "Ask," I opened my email and received this:

From: Clera@_____
Sent: Sunday, December 27, 2009 12:56 PM
To: info@SimpleResults.net
Subject: Hello Old Friend
Hi! I am pretty sure I have found the right person. Are you "Missy" Carricarte who went to high school with me in Houston, Texas at Saint Agnes Academy? We were inseparable!
Clera

WOW! I remember sitting in front of the computer in shock and at the same time smiling at how there really is a perfect system to asking and receiving. No matter how many times I receive confirmation of my prayers, I always sit in awe of gratitude at how wonderful and empowering this is. I wrote back to Clera immediately and shared with her a long message of how happy I was to hear from her. I acknowledged how I thought of her often and what a dear friend she was to me. I also explained the story of the charm bracelet, how I thought of seeing it again often and how I had just prayed three days earlier to find her!

She responded with a long story of how she found me. She too had thought of the sentimental charm bracelet that she had from my grandmother. She had carried it with her from home to home throughout her life and always felt that it should be returned, as she knew how much this heirloom meant to me. Her story continued: her own daughter had asked for a charm bracelet for Christmas and because of that, she told her the story of me. She shared with her daughter that she had this bracelet that belonged to me and kept it in her safe at the bank. Her daughter asked why she did not find me yet? Her 10-year-old daughter then recommended that they Google me, and they found the website for my company Simple Results.

We reconnected through many long emails. In one of them I shared that something must have happened for me not to ask for my bracelet back because it was so important to me. With the good memory she has, she said, "You do not remember? We exchanged bracelets; I lent you the one my mother gave me when I left Iran and you lent me the one from your grandmother when she left Cuba. We exchanged heirlooms." When she reminded me of this, my heart sank. With all the changes in my life at that time, I lost her bracelet so I did not feel it was correct to ask for mine back. I felt terrible and she was so gracious about this, even though her mother passed the year before. The best I could do was recreating a bracelet similar to mine. I went to every jewelry store in the old Cuban area in Miami to find old charms to give to her daughter a bracelet.

The Magic Of The "Ask"

Clera lived in California and I lived in Miami, so she said she would send the bracelet to me and I laughed as I told her, "It has been over 30 years, and I can wait to see you in person." We made arrangements to see each other in Washington DC. It was such a joy to reconnect with my friend after so many years. This was a Divine blessing!

When we met in Washington, I was so happy to meet her daughter. She is witty, intuitive and such a joy. Clera and I spoke about our high school days and she remembered everything. It was a challenging time for Clera and me and we shared so many great memories together. I spoke to her about how I was going to go to the school and look her up in the yearbook. She laughed, reminding me that she too started school midyear because it was the year of the Iran hostage crisis and her mother had her leave the country to stay with her aunt in Houston. I would have not found her in the yearbook because we both arrived midyear after the pictures were taken. I shared my deep appreciation for her and her family, and she shared another memory with me. Because of the Iran situation, at the time many of the kids in school were not very accepting of her. That I accepted her immediately meant a lot to her. I was surprised that she was touched by the way I embraced her, as I did not pay attention to any of the prejudice. I felt just as awkward as she did and we clicked.

Imagine that Clera held onto my bracelet for all these years? What a beautiful testimonial to my prayer being answered after only three days – and I received the added gift of my dear friend's kindness and integrity, once again. My whole family was touched by this story and I share it often with others as another testament to the power of wishing, the power of hope and reaffirming that love and kindness is timeless.

Your prayers are heard and answered, and propelled by your beliefs. Ask and you shall receive" ... what you believe. I say this again and again because it is an important component of the formula. Pray, believe and expect what you believe. This story is so powerful in many ways, especially reaffirming the knowing that your dreams are heard because they matter and there is love that answers them. By using the tools of Power Wishing, you will formulate your feeling to consciously serve your expectation. In your asking, you are making a choice towards your life. You are choosing to enhance or shift or resolve or recreate an experience through your emotional awareness.

When I express conscious or deliberate focus, I define this as simply being aware of your present moment. The same way I made an "Ask" for my bracelet, even with people around me, I was present. I witnessed my daughter, which activated in me a desire to ask for my bracelet. In a few seconds I felt what I desired and where I had doubt. I cleaned up my doubt in my belief by asking for forgiveness to create a sense of worthiness to receive. Then I felt my end result of feeling the bracelet in my hand and feeling the joy of giving this to my daughter. I felt this as a real experience, not a forced feeling but *a natural knowing*. I also took responsibility to do everything I could with action in the physical to support the alignment of my prayer.

I believe with every bit of me that Source Energy gives what I ask for and I am responsible for asking and taking action for the way I wish to receive. This free will allows energetic support to clearly provide me with my expectation and expand my prayers in ways that serve my best outcome. In no way did I allow the details of how and when to interfere with my knowledge of this, and I made it energetically clear I was willing to participate by taking action. This was all done in a matter of a few minutes. To me, it is not the time you spend on a prayer, it is the belief of expectation you have when you create your "Ask," without emotions that cause conflict. A prayer that is quick, clear and to the point. If suddenly you had an emergency situation that you had to resolve quickly, do you think you would go into a long dissertation in your asking and have a mental conversation with your Self? No! You would pray very simply, emotionally direct and spontaneous with all your heart and Soul commanding your will to be done. The most efficient asking is through your heart and Soul, with the purest of desire.

Clear "Ask" = Clear Response

The different components of Power Wishing all guide you to take emotional responsibility for creating your life. This awareness of accountability towards your life allows you to know that you are competent to make adjustments that shift what you are experiencing.

It is as simple as feeling cold and getting up to adjust the thermostat. You are capable of adjusting your experience; you release the need of waiting for someone to change the thermostat for you. Why stay cold and be upset because someone else did not notice you were cold?

If you avoided being consciously aware of why you feel uncomfortable, you would not know what to adjust. You would stay feeling uncomfortable and feeling cold would eventually be the norm for you. However, taking a moment to ask how you are feeling, and being aware of this answer, means you realize and acknowledge that you are uncomfortable with being cold. Then the solution of adjusting the thermostat becomes clearer and you take action to resolve this. In doing so, you are also shifting a feeling of helplessness to empowerment. You own that you can create a life happening *for* you rather than by default.

Awakened Life

Sometimes we may know what to wish for and sometimes we may not have as much clarity. This is perfectly fine; you do not have to know everything before you do something. But you can start somewhere, and that somewhere is with your feelings. Start by paying attention to those intuitive hits, which I referred to earlier as your Emotional GPS.

If you are navigating your life on autopilot and are not checking in with your Emotional GPS, then the heart is no longer the vehicle for defining your feelings. Then one day you wake up and notice that you are way off from feeling the way you would like to feel about your life. You wonder how you got to this point of disconnection and you do not recognize areas in the life you are living. You also feel disconnected to your emotional body and this is when life becomes task-oriented and not Soul-driven.

Your life is not a to-do list. You are here to have a joyful life, not just survive it. We have all gone through phases where we resign to life as a compromise, feeling we are limited in our possibilities, and bypass our Soul's voice. This is understandable. But when you choose to live an awakened life, it is then that you will feel your entire being shine and you will create the abundance, joy and peace that you yearn for. You will know this is evident, as you will feel like a magnet that attracts more of what you love.

If you wish to manifest something in your life, be it health, a book, a career or a relationship, your feelings about what you wish to manifest are what will bring it to life; your expectation is what makes it a part of your life. You can support your "Ask" by being in environments that encourage what you desire. You can also see a movie or read a book to inspire your feelings.

Why manage a dream using a cycle of sabotaging thoughts, worrying about the details of how and when it will happen? I call this mental habit of processing "brain candy," and I believe that it wastes creative resourceful energy. It is like wishing to lose weight but then waiting until you have the perfect diet, or until you have to go to the grocery store to get new food, instead of working with what is in your control, now. There are things you can control now. There is no perfect plan; change is the only plan you can expect. Sometimes you just have to step into the experience without a *perfect* plan. Expect your life to unfold with details necessary for your plan with the feelings that you love and activate your desires with positive action and know all will be well. Step into the experience of your definition of your life as your plan.

When we play with possibilities in our Emotional Imagination®, we plant the seeds for them to come true. This goes for both positive and negative visions. If you go back and reflect on most of the experiences or things that have come easily to you, it was probably when you played with the notion in your imagination and did not take yourself so seriously. The feeling connected to what you wished for was clear and to the point, positive and without intense beliefs that did not serve you, or harsh words that reinforced negativity. It felt easy. You released controlling the outcome with a relaxed confidence without the do-or-die intensity. Basically, that feeling with a smile of ... *well it would be nice if this happens, but if it does not I am still good.*

Your Wish Granted

Knowing how to recognize your wish is something that you may overlook when you are waiting to receive. Remember, now you are a Conscious Creator co-creating with Source Energy and your opportunities are grander. Because you are being supported this way, things may not always be the way you think they should appear. I have a lot of humor about this because some people have this idea of the way they are *supposed* to receive their wish. When we let go of being *in the box* and allow the partnership with Divine Love to serve our wish in an expanded way, the possibilities are incredible. Just remember when you make your "Ask," ask with a huge smile and trust that you know how to recognize your wish coming true even if it comes in unexpected wonderful ways.

For example, say you are praying for a love relationship. In your mind you have a way you expect to receive this. You think love can only be found where you live, even though we all know love can be found anywhere. A great example of this is a client who was looking to manifest love in her hometown of Seattle. She wished for this loving relationship and *poof*, it showed up! But she lived in Seattle and her potential love mate was living in Boston, and because she assumed that she would find love in Seattle. She chose to ignore that this was an answer to her prayer of finding love, even though the relationship felt good and had the positive components she was asking for. After ignoring this opportunity for months, even though the man offered to travel to see her, she broke it off even though being with him felt great. A few months later, she found out that this new love interest was actually going to be transferred to Seattle. This story was fortunate, as they rekindled their relationship and are happily together now, but she almost shut the door to this opportunity completely. Everything and anything is possible!

Do not close the door to an opportunity just because at that moment it does not look like what you prayed for; pay attention to how you feel about it. "You never know" is a phrase in Power Wishing that is said with a huge smile, because what we do know is that by co-creating with Source Energy, we can expect grander and more wonderful manifestations than being on our own. Many times, it is beyond what we can imagine and we cannot always foresee the details being handled for us. This is why trust in knowing that all is working in your favor and being open gives life to your wishes.

Trust that your Emotional GPS lets you know about opportunities that are in your favor, even if it does not look that way in the moment. Trust that you will know. Trust that you are loved and your back is covered. Trust that your prayers are heard and answered. Trust your feelings and that you know how to take action with certainty. You can only get it "right" and goodness happens for you. Remember, Source Energy has your best interest in mind. It is all in your favor. Be more playful with the opportunities that come into your life and witness your wishes being granted in ways that are beyond your dreams.

Your Wish Is Your Command

Remember "As so above, so below" means that through your prayer you have used your Emotional Imagination to "Ask" for your desire and it has been anchored as a command in the "as above" as a feeling, an energy. You have clearly stated that your wish is to be birthed as your reality in your day-to-day and with this you have also activated spiritual support to freely assist you. In order to bring your Emotional Imagination to your day-to-day reality, the "so below," you must act with physical behaviors that are aligned to support your expectation.

To activate your "Ask," which is ready to be birthed in the physical reality, you merge the energy of your "Ask" with matching emotions, behaviors, habits, actions, words and thoughts that support how and what you expect to receive in the "so below." You are forming your energy of feelings and thoughts to have destiny here in your physical reality.

Based on your choice of actions, you will either strengthen or weaken the opportunity of the reality you wish to have. We have shared that the Universe processes as a computer and acts based on the programming it is given. A computer is not emotional; it is not changing the order unless you give it different programming. Actions that are not aligned with what you have asked for give another type of programming, which like a short circuit, can cause chaos and create delays.

When you are in a place of blaming versus observing, or defending your Self versus sharing your perspective, you are creating chaos for your "Ask." This also goes for betraying, gossiping, breaking commitments without communicating, being untruthful or speaking and re-living a past you do not wish for in your future. All of these choices draw on negative chaotic energy. It is that simple. You may even clog up the system or deplete the energy to a point where there may be a malfunction. This may show up as feeling super tired, having no energy, getting mad for no reason or feeling like your circuits are crossed. When this happens, there is not a *God* or life circumstance to blame. Remember, you programmed the Universe through your "Ask," by what you expected and the actions you took towards this.

Release being a victim to the "BBB Syndrome" (But ... But ... But ...) and get away from excuses. Excuses that are often made to rationalize the reasons why our dreams have been sabotaged. This syndrome affects millions of people every day. The cure may seem so obvious to some, but is often overlooked; it is simply to acknowledge what you have created. Release the conversations of blame and guilt and do something positive as your step forward. Own it and move toward being responsible for your next choices. Replace the "But" with a solution.

Have the discipline to stop making excuses in your life regarding what you know you should do for your Self but are not doing. This also goes for using others as excuses of why you cannot do what you should do for your Self. Release using your energy to beat yourself up and make yourself wrong. Take a moment to reflect what energy you are reinforcing and which energy you wish to choose. Each time you are holding another accountable, think about what you are asking for. Think about what you just said about that situation as if you are making a literal statement.

Another way I witness others doubt their opportunity to ask for what they wish for is through information overload. I humorously call this the "PBI Disorder," (Paralyzed By Information.) This "PBI Disorder" affects those who keep accumulating information from all kinds of sources but never really make a decision. They are paralyzed and to keep them in this state, they always need some more information to make the "right" decision. The issue is that they created information overload, which stops them from taking action in their life. How much information do you really need to make a decision that feels right? And again, who is the expert that you empower to advise you on what information you need to make the "right" decision about your life. You know yourself; life experience will give you information to know your Self better.

You can only get it "right" when you listen to your instincts and know that you are your best advisor.

Have awareness of how you would like to feel and move forward. Next! Keep it simple and be disciplined to move forward. No need to psychoanalyze yourself. Sometimes you just need to say, "Next!" The awareness of how you wish to feel is all that is necessary. What is the worst that can happen? You are capable to make another decision that feels better. Staying stuck is not an option, moving forward towards your dreams, as your truth is the only option. Then again, what do you believe?

If you find yourself going over and over and over something, then know that you are stuck in your drama and are not ready to move forward. If this is the case, own it and do not blame anyone or any circumstance for where you are. Find discernment on when just saying "Next" is appropriate and when it is necessary to examine the root cause of your experience to be able to move forward.

Yes, we are working with energy and the greatest energy of all is Love. Nevertheless, some things require pure discipline; make choices that serve what you wish in your reality. Certain types of choices use energy that go towards the positive current of your wish. Choose actions and behaviors that serve you and continue to strengthen the beliefs of your expectation.

Once I was giving an evening lecture and I was discussing the details about how to formulate your wishes as described in this book. A woman stood up and asked if I could go through her wishes; she wished to release drama in her life. We started creating the wishes and went through the system. As we were going through them, I could feel, based on the wishes she was creating, that there was reluctance. So I asked her, "Do you really wish to get rid of the drama in your life?" She said, "No. I like it." She laughed and we joined her.

I asked her, "So why would you go through all this for something you really do not wish for?" She shared that people tell her she should get rid of her drama, so she thought she had to, but after going through the wishing exercise, she was clear she did not want to get rid of her drama. Personally, I thought this was great because Power Wishing supports you to have discernment on what you believe *for you*.

Everything Is In Your Favor To Grant Your Wish

Sometimes our wishes are made clear to us through daydreaming. This is also a form of prayer and imagination where we are asking. Lose your Self in your Emotional Imagination and play with possibilities.

Let's take a moment to play with asking for your wishes:

Take a few deep breaths as you center your Self.
Feel your Self consciously connecting to Source Energy.

Then take another deep breath and imagine for a moment what it would feel like living with everything supporting you, where you are not limited – No fear towards anything you desire, you are free.

Feeling certain that everything is in your favor to grant your wish.
What would you wish for? Really, what dream would you claim?

Continue wishing for the life you dream of.
Now imagine your wish being true, right now.
Feel this as real.
Visualize it and see it like a "Movie."

Witness your feelings towards the "Movie" of your wishes being real.
Are you excited about this?
What is stopping this from being real now?
Do you feel confident about the possibility of your wish coming true? What is the worst thing that could happen if this wish came true?
What is the best outcome with this wish coming true?
What qualities of your Self will enhance with this wish being true?
What could you shift to support this wish being true?

Wish for the emotional support to make this happen.

Play with these questions and answer them to bring your dream as a life experience. Your dreams are there for a reason and that is to have them come true.

If you feel unsure of your wish coming true or feel fear is standing in the way of manifesting your wish, I recommend that you observe any feelings that may be blocking your wish, as you notice them ... resolve them by finding solutions.

If you cannot imagine or visualize your wish coming true easily, then ask yourself what you would like to support your desire. Then, create a wish for emotional support to shift those emotions that may not be serving the manifestation of that desire. You can also wish for better ways to respond to your challenges, and shift that energy to recognize them as blessings.

If you feel unsure, fearful or doubtful of your wish coming true –
Ask yourself:

Why do I feel frustration/doubt/fear with this wish?

What emotional support could encourage my wish to be able to manifest my desires with grace and ease?

How will this emotion/shift support me to recognize that I can manifest my wishes with grace and ease?

If you are not sure what to do, ask for clarity.
Keep the "Ask" simple and basic.
Set your Self up for success.

If you see yourself using energy and actions that are not in the positive flow towards what you wish, take a moment to realign yourself.
If this should happen, take a breath to relax, knowing that you are aware and acknowledge that you wish to show up differently.
Also know that you can immediately make a choice to do this.

As you begin to use my empowering intention-setting technique *Stage Your Day*, this will accelerate your wish into manifestation, by creating a positive emotional anchor towards your wish as a daily practice.

Celebrate Yourself

The great news is that every experience is an opportunity to embody more of who you wish to be and experience the possibilities you desire.

I wish to acknowledge how courageous it is for you to look at your world and take inventory of where and who you are. Acknowledge yourself for paying attention to your life, for consciously participating and showing up. This is unique and wonderful. This is to be celebrated and not to be taken for granted.

You are to be celebrated! Celebrate yourself! Your "Ah-ha moments" are giving you the answers to strengthen the base of all that you wish for. These moments allow you to anchor to feelings that will attract a life you desire. These moments are strong foundation-builders for your "Ask." Facing or acknowledging your life with conscious awareness is to be celebrated!

Do you celebrate your accomplishments? Do you know how to recognize your best qualities and how they add to the life of others and your Self? How do you acknowledge your Self and what you have created?

After you make your wishes, let go and allow the process to take place. Your responsibility now is to take actions that are aligned with what you have asked for to reinforce your expectation.

Enjoy exploring with all the possibilities that you dream of. If you believe, then it is real. Feel it and then you will see it. We are alive with our dreams and blessed with the opportunity of what we ask for.

Power Thoughts

The Ask

- My emotions anchor my expectation of my wishes.

- I build my life from what feels good.

- When I feel an emotion that has a charge, I pay attention to it.

- I am a magnet of my beliefs.

- I emotionally engage in my world positively.

- I express the power of gratitude in my life, which multiplies more of the good.

- I value my life as precious by valuing my choices.

- Ask and I will receive.

- Everything is in my favor to grant my wish.

- I know how to enjoy playing with all the possibilities I dream of and feel them be true.

The Magic Wand

We all love magical stories that take us to another place and time where everything is possible. Hopefully, after experiencing Power Wishing®, you will feel even more supported to view your life as magical, as you witness your daydreams appear as your life. Using daydreaming as a useful and effortless means to create, I like to use humor to activate my imagination, and this supports me when I cannot feel my answers come to me as quickly as I wish. For fun, in my imagination I would daydream as if I had a magic wand and with my magical wand I had the power to bring to life what I asked for. Asking for what we wish for is how we activate our *Magical Wand.*

Through the years that I have been teaching Power Wishing, I often have participants pretend they have a "Magic Wand" that creates anything they desire. Actually, I bring a magic wand to my courses and have participants come up to the stage and I will say with the voice of a playful magician, "With this *Magic Wand*, grant yourself 10 things you would love to have in your life right now. This *Magic Wand* belongs to you and is commanded for you to easily receive your wishes right away. All you have to do is quickly state 10 wishes now."

What do you think happens next? Usually there is a blank stare on the participant's face. I watch them go through the "mental filing cabinet" in their brain and there is a hesitation in stating these wishes. It amazes me how challenging most find it to name their desires. Now, if I asked them to name 10 things they do NOT want in their life, they have a running list and there is no hesitation! Why is that? Remember, this is your Vibrational Language® talking.

Imagine that your Vibrational Language is communicating like an advertisement on a billboard, requesting a match for what you are asking. If your billboard is clear with what you do NOT want in your life, it is advertising this – what you do not want is what you get. Advertise what you wish to attract. *Being aware of what you do not want is one thing, focusing and "looking" for it is another.*

Sometimes we are not fully aware of how we are asking and we can be disillusioned in feeling that life is giving us what we do not wish for, but in reality it is giving you what you did ask for ... as it always does.

I would like to share with you a story of a client that I worked closely with and I will use it to illustrate how she processed her thoughts and how this affected her "Ask." As you read this story about Lila, I understand if you feel frustrated at times. Her process can really go in circles, but then again I'm sure many of us can relate. If you are able to observe Lila, you can see how one may not be aware of how we are *really* asking. In her story you can observe when she modified her "Ask" and received a different outcome.

Lila's Story

Lila[7] has come to see me as a personal client. We have worked through some of her childhood challenges that she was holding on to by shifting her beliefs. But today she is sharing with me that she continues to have the same conversation with herself over and over again in her head and feels stuck. I ask her, "If I had a tape recorder that could record your thoughts, what would that recording sound like?" I share with her that maybe she would be surprised to hear how she really speaks to herself.

She was interested to hear herself aloud so she could truly understand what she was asking and believed was her true expectation. What was holding her back from moving forward in the area of her work? She continues and takes a moment to rant.

Here is Lila verbalizing her inner dialogue aloud to me:

I cannot take this anymore!
This winter is so cold! I am freezing! I have so few hours of sunshine a day.
This is making me crazy; I am going crazy with no sunshine.
I feel sad! I am indoors most of the time. I used to be an active outdoor person. I moved to this small apartment in Paris and I feel trapped here now. Why did I do this? I knew I would not like it here but I got this amazing job opportunity and it paid me the money I wanted.
I told myself that this would only be for a maximum of two years.

---

[7] Please note that throughout the book clients' names and some details have been changed to honor the identity of the individuals.

How is it that it is now five years? What happened to the time? I feel so trapped. I knew the first month I was here that there was no way I could do this. But I promised myself ...

I made a deal with myself, that it would last only two years! This way I would have enough money to move where I wanted. I kept telling myself it would get better and I tried to make it better. I always let myself down. But what could I do? They kept on giving me more raises. If they did not keep giving me more money, I would have left. But they keep giving me more money and they made it hard for me to leave.
What could I do? It really is not my fault. But now I feel so hopeless, I am stuck here. I am too old to get another job that pays me this amount of money. I have been getting sick a lot lately too. I need my insurance and if I worked at another place, maybe I won't be able to get insurance. How can I afford that?

Today, I saw an old picture of myself snorkeling in the ocean when I was on a vacation. WOW! It reminded me of how much I used to enjoy the water and the beach. I had totally forgotten those feelings and what it felt like to be outside in the sunshine and in the sea watching those beautiful sunsets. For a moment when I saw that picture I remembered how good it felt to be outside and feel the salt of the ocean. I even remembered (she starts to laugh) *that when I was little I believed I could be a professional swimmer.* (She is smiling and disappears into this feeling in her imagination and re-lives those moments, and then she stops.)

I have to live in reality! Feeling these happy times only makes me feel worse. I miss my friends. Judy keeps calling me but what can I say to her? My life sucks and I just keep telling her how great it is. I keep avoiding her because I just figured by now I would have left Paris and this job and would have been able to say my life was great. But I am still here. If I was to talk to her, she will know that I am not happy and then I will feel more miserable. It scares me to think about how good it would feel to go into the water because I feel so trapped. If I started to feel what that would feel like, it would only make me feel worse.

I am never going to be able to move out of this place. This winter I will probably slip into a depression and not get out! That happened to my Aunt Sally. And if that happened to me, then I can't work and who would ta care of me, I am alone.

Lila continues to tell the story that keeps her stuck in this drama. It is a story that she no longer wishes as her life, but one that has created a comfort. She lives a life of feeling *comfortably numb.*

As she continues with her story, she activates more of the same feelings she does not want to feel. What an irony. How many times do you think she has gone over this story and has seen this "Movie" in her head with all the emotions she is feeling? As she continues to repeat this story in her imagination, she is clearing giving mixed messages or signals. She is strengthening the very life that she says she does not want, by continuing to bring her past into her future.

How did you feel when reading her story? What tapes do you have going on in your head? Remember, these tapes are making your "Movie."

Discovering the Underlying Emotion

Using Lila's case study, let's decode her Vibrational Language. Maybe you will relate to some of these steps for yourself with a similar or different experience and it will support you to reflect on the way you process. Lila says that she continuously has this dialogue with herself. She has gone over the same conversation in her head many times. It is very common to have a certain story repeat in our mind, but here I want to examine how this story is self-created and how Lila can shift her story to create the results she desires. Lila is obviously frustrated, feeling upset and disappointed. We can all relate in some way to having these feelings towards a situation we feel stuck in.

My question to you is, "Do you stay in that upset or disappointed space in your imagination, going over and over the same story or do you move to a place of better feelings?" How long do you stay stuck in a situation you do not want, if you have one presently ... how long has it been? When you have resolved a situation that you feel stuck in, did you accomplish this by crisis or with being proactive?

Reflecting

LILA – *I cannot take this anymore! It is so cold! I am freezing! I have only two hours of sunshine a day. This is making me crazy; I am going crazy with no sunshine. I feel sad! I am indoors most of time. I used to be an active outdoor person. I moved to this small apartment in Paris and I feel trapped here now.*

Why did I do this? I knew I wouldn't like it here but I got this amazing job opportunity and it paid me the money I wanted.

REFLECT: When you hear yourself going over the same story again and again, ask yourself ... "Is this the story I want as a reflection of my life?" The story you repeat to yourself over and over is your life – your "Movie!" The good news is that she does know what it feels like to have an amazing job opportunity.

LILA – *I told myself that this would only be for a maximum of two years. How is it that it is now five years? What happened to the time? I feel so trapped. I knew the first month I was here that there was no way I could do this. But I promised myself ... I made a deal with myself that I would stay for only two years! This way I would have enough money to move where I wanted. I kept telling myself it would get better and I tried. I always let myself down.*

REFLECT:

She sold herself a story and then tried to keep finding ways to buy into her own story. She made a deal with herself that she would stick it out for two years. She compromised. When we compromise, it's like we are buying a big commercial time slot. Because she stayed over two years, she feels she has betrayed herself, by compromising her vision.

LILA – *But what could I do? They kept giving me more raises. If they did not keep giving me more money, I would have left. But they keep giving me more money and they made it hard for me to leave. What could I do? It is really not my fault.*

REFLECT:

Basically, she is not in a good place emotionally. She does not feel responsible for the circumstances that have kept her trapped and unhappy. She betrayed herself and takes comfort in blaming others. She blames it on the fact that they gave her more money to stay. She has chosen not to be accountable for her decisions. So where does she go from here? Because she has chosen to blame others, she is blinded from acknowledging her pain or circumstance from a place of taking responsibility or feeling empowered. Being accountable does not mean she has to make her Self wrong. She is also paralyzed emotionally with what I call the "BBB Syndrome" – the But ... But ... But ... Syndrome.

LILA – *But now I feel so hopeless, I am stuck here. I am too old to get another job that pays me this amount of money. I have been getting sick a lot lately too. I need my insurance and if I worked at another place, maybe I won't be able to get insurance. How can I afford that?*

REFLECT:

With these comments, she is building a case of reasons for her lack of action; in doing this she strengthens what she does not want with her *case of reason*. Because she is not willing to acknowledge and take responsibility for where she is, her commercial is really getting long and taxing on her Soul.

LILA – *Today, I saw an old picture of myself snorkeling in the ocean when I was on a vacation. WOW! It reminded me of how much I used to enjoy the water. I had forgotten those feelings and what it felt like to be outside in the sun and in the sea. For a moment when I saw that picture I remembered how good it felt to be outside and feel the salt of the ocean. I even remembered* (she starts to laugh) *that when I was little I believed I could be a professional swimmer.* (She is smiling and disappears into this feeling in her imagination and re-lives those moments, and then she stops.)

REFLECT:

The good news here is that the photo of herself woke her up to feelings, at least for a moment. This means those feelings are still accessible. No matter how small that inner voice is, it is still a voice that can still be heard. This is good news because this is where we begin. When she looks at this photo, she is asking to feel the same good feelings at this moment. She remembers how good it feels. Connecting with one second of feeling good is powerful, similar to the saying, "One man of strength is worth a thousand." This is her Soul speaking. Remember, your Soul knows and its job is to do everything possible to keep you awake to the life you wish for.

LILA – *I have to live in reality! Feeling these happy times only makes me feel worse. I miss my friends. Judy keeps calling me but what can I say to her? My life sucks and I just keeping telling her how great it is. I keep avoiding her because I just figured by now I would have left Paris and this job and have been able to say my life was great. But I am still here. If I talked to her she would know that I am not happy and then I will feel even more miserable.*

REFLECT:

She has now alienated her friends and other people who love her. She lives for a story that is not true. Soon she will be saying no one loves her and she is alone, even though in reality she has taken actions to push others away.

LILA – *It scares me to think about how good it would feel to go into the water because I feel so trapped. If I started to feel what that would feel like, it would only make me feel worse. I am never going to be able to move out of this place. This winter I will probably slip into a depression and not get out! That happened to my Aunt Sally. And if that happened to me, then I can't work.*

REFLECT:

She now uses her Aunt Sally's behavior as a model for her future and to strengthen her case. OK, can we see how Lila's story can keep going? It can just spiral down to a place where she continues this drama and keeps strengthening the story of what she does not want in her life.

Strengthen Your Story With Feeling Good

As we have discussed, some people feel if they remind themselves of what they do not want and go over stories that hurt them that this will prevent those stories from happening again. Or they deny themselves to feel good so they do not get hopeful and then disappointed. Some believe that this is better than what they assume will happen if they take action towards their Soul's voice. This isn't so! Technically, you only reawaken memory and strengthen a stronger point of attraction towards what you say you do not wish for.

How many times do you think Lila has gone over this story in her head and with her feelings? In her imagination she feels the intense emotion of feeling trapped, hopeless, too old, and worried about getting sick and being alone. What reality do you really think can come from this? She may not realize it, but she is asking for more of what she does not want. Her "Ask" is in the story she keeps telling herself and she continues to strengthen the emotional buy-in to her story. Besides having commercials in your life, you have huge billboards advertising a story you say you do not wish for.

Lila wants a different life experience and if someone would ask her if she wants to relocate with a better job opportunity, she would say "Yes!" In that moment, she would let you know how badly she wants to live in Miami. She can say she wants to move all she wants, but the underlying and more powerful raw emotion of the story she is telling herself is, "I am trapped and it is hopeless, things keep getting worse." She may say she wants to move, but feeling stuck and the excuses she has created to justify why she is stuck will continue to be the base of what she will attract especially if she continues to justify her case against her Self.

How can Lila receive a great job opportunity, a move, a new life in beautiful Miami full of sunshine? Is this possible? Of course it is! The good news is this is totally possible. She has already created a similar experience elsewhere; now it is just time to create another one. What has to happen here? How can she change these intense emotions?

First, she has to start with a "good" feeling that she already has. No matter how small the voice of that feeling is, this is a start. Keep it simple, one good feeling can lead to another and another. Building on what is positive and aligned with your Authentic Self has more force and strength than the illusions of fear.

How does she find those good feelings when the other not-so-good feelings are so loud at the moment? Remember when she looked at that picture of the ocean and she connected with that feeling of being there? She had a moment of feeling "good." Even though she continues to cancel out this feeling with her "BBB Syndrome," this is a start. In the manifesting process, what can sometimes happens at this time is that the feelings that keep us stuck seem so overwhelming that we do not believe the little glimpse of a feeling of how we wish to feel could really make a difference. This is false.

If you desire to shift a situation that seems overwhelming to you, look for what feels good. It does not have to pertain to that situation. It can be anything: pictures, items, places, or music reminding you of feeling good. This will remind you that this is your focus.

There is more good news! Even though Lila is mostly focused on her "BBB Syndrome" as the substance of how she is asking and how she will receive, she is aware that she feels really bad. Although she is not totally acknowledging where she is and not taking full responsibility because she feels trapped, she is aware of her unhappiness rather than being numb towards this knowing.

She also feels that she cannot fully acknowledge her feelings until she has a solution, but a positive solution will not come to her through the way she is focusing. So many times people feel they cannot feel better until what they want appears; this is completely counterproductive. How can you ask for what you wish expecting the opposite as a result? If you are waiting to be happy until you have what you want, or believing if things were different then you could be happy, it is like going down a bottomless pit in an endless pursuit.

No matter where you are, you can start somewhere. Baby steps lead to miles, base hits lead to more homeruns than just homeruns alone. Lila can start with some good emotions that she is aware of; she can use them as her anchor to receive what she desires. Even starting to imagine the sun on her face is a good place to start. Her goal is to build from emotions that support the possibility for her to be in the space where the "What If" of being in Miami and the "What If" of a good job opportunity can be more of a possibility of her reality.

Presently it is not possible for her to have a lot of good feelings towards what she desires. No worries. For Lila to let go even for a moment and change her feelings when she has little hope is very challenging especially when defeating emotions are so charged. What she can do is deviate her attention to other things that are not related that will make her feel good. Finding other ingredients of happiness and joy to add to her emotions will offset the intensity of her feelings she lacks. Mathematics of energy is on your side when you build from what feels good, this equates with far more power than all those feelings that are not so good.

Imagine it like this. One can have lots of "bad" relationships over the years and then that one new good relationship makes all those bad ones feel like a distant past. You even hear people comment on how those other relationships brought them to where they are now. Anything good can happen in a second where the past hurts become a distant memory.

If Lila could get out of her own way and shift her focus from "What Is" as circumstances, by playing with the feeling of what she would like to feel a little more every day, she will replace her present circumstances. And really, what would she have to lose by being in the space of "What If?" More disappointment? She is already disappointed. Being more depressed? She is already there. We have everything to gain by playing in our imagination with the feelings we would like to experience. To feel a sense that it is possible to feel good is a good start; this is also called hope.

Her goal is to build from emotions that support the possibility she is wishing for. "What If" I could be in Miami, how would that feel? "What If" I could feel the sunshine on my face? "What If" I got a good job opportunity there? "What If" for a moment in time, I could feel this without struggle, as if the Universe is supporting me and I trust this?

She may go in and out of this good feeling in her imagination, but she can bring herself back to connecting to experiences that she already knows feel good.

In Lila's story, if we read in between the lines, she has also told the story of what she wishes for. Maybe the voice was not as strong, but the storyline is there to build from. She knows what it feels like to have a good opportunity, what it feels like to have the sunshine on her face, to swim in the ocean. She already has a base of experiences to align how she would like to feel now and can create from this as a base for the expectation she truly desires. Now if she starts to build on these feelings and images, what would start to happen? The other experiences where she can feel good, peaceful and enjoyment with excitement will carry over to complement what she is asking for in expected and unexpected positive ways. These then lead to other similar daydreams.

I will continue to narrate Lila's story. Some days she feels better than others and feels that maybe there is a possibility. She is not sure how it will happen but that becomes less and less important. She now keeps a picture of the ocean on her desk and looks at it several times a day. This reawakens this knowing in her cellular body memory. Before she used to feel hopeless at the thought of this, but now she disappears into the warm sun in her imagination, which feels much better. Her energy reaffirms this and strengthens her core with this knowing of feeling good.

A few days later when she was in the office, she saw a co-worker who was so excited as she told Lila that she is being transferred to Miami. "Can you believe that?" her colleague said!

A Moment Of Choice

Lila connected with her co-worker's excitement and held that feeling and it felt good. She even asked her if there were other opportunities and the co-worker said, "No, it appears that this was an unusual offer." Then the "BBB Syndrome" kicked in and began to attack her hopes and feelings. Then she got upset that this did not happen for her. I mean she has been in cold Paris longer than her co-worker, this was supposed to be her dream. But then Lila surprised herself. She gave herself a moment to be in her drama and to be upset, and then she chose to let the voice of the "BBB Syndrome" go. She was exhausted of feeling those feelings. She stepped back and witnessed where she was headed with that "BBB" voice and she just stopped herself from going down that road. Lila took a breath and asked herself: *"If I could choose, how would I like to feel?"*

Lila stayed consistent in supporting feelings that made her feel good. She used the Power Wishing tools of *Stage Your Day*, which supported her awareness of her *emotional intention*; even though she was a bit disappointed, she regained control of her "Movie." She released how the outcome was going to happen and stayed focused on how she wanted to feel about the outcomes she was waiting for. She was just tired of her complaining and surrendered. Maybe her surrender was not from a place of empowerment, but it is still productive because she stopped fixating on her issues and this opened a space to allow something different.

She decided if it is what it is, then she will make the best of it. She even started to go to the gym and walk outside more often. She thought, "At least I can feel better about myself and be outdoors more, even if it is not Miami."

A few months later, another rumor starts, that there may be another opening available in Miami. Lila was hopeful and went to her manager to inquire. They said there were currently no openings. She told her management that she would be interested in moving to Miami if there was an opening. To her surprise, her manager had no idea she was willing to move. Her manager even went as far as saying, "You will be the first person I will let know if there is an opportunity." Lila was surprised at this. She thought her manager already knew of her desire to move. As she pondered, she realized she never told anyone of her desire to go to Miami. In this moment she also acknowledged that she thought her manager was starting to have something against her because she gave the Miami opportunity to someone else. How many times do you assume others know what you are asking for and then judge them based on this?

She was a bit disappointed that there did not seem to be openings, but kept on her routine of going to the gym and even joined a book club and met new friends outside the office.

She was feeling much better about herself in her present circumstances; she even lost some weight that she had been carrying for the last year and bought some new clothes. She stayed consistent with feelings and actions that served her wellbeing and had the attitude that *whatever happens will happen* and in the meantime she was going to enjoy this beautiful city.

Even the weather was getting better. Maybe her attitude was not always very happy, but she was making solid improvement and finding the good.

A few months later, her manager came to speak to Lila. She said, "Lila, I apologize for giving you such short notice, but would you be able to move to Miami within a week? The management understands this might be challenging with the short notice and we would give you an up-front bonus to move quickly." Her manager also added that she hopes she will take this opportunity as it offers her a promotion in an area that Lila mentioned she desired when she moved to Paris, but was not available at the time. And of course this is not the end of her story, only another beginning.

Be The Story Of Your Dreams In Action

As in Lila's story, we can be unaware of how we continue to tell a story that we do not want as our life experience.

"If you are not in the process of becoming the person you want to be, you are automatically engaged in becoming the person you don't want to be." – Dale Carnegie

Yes, when you connect with your dreams you awaken them and you awaken the person you wish to be. They may even awaken in an unexpected moment that reminds you of a dream you forgot. To wake up does not have to take years; it can be in a moment's notice like so many stories after 9/11 or with a chance meeting of someone. *Do not overlook your awakening because of the way it happens; pay attention that it did happen and hold onto it, strengthen it.* Do not allow your logical mind to take you away from being awake to your dream being true. Yes, there may be change but change can mean positive consequences.

What is your belief about being able to have what you wish for? Do you need to imagine the worst-case scenario before you can feel comfortable and then playing out different worries and possible negative outcomes, because your expectation. Maybe this is a habit to make sure you have covered everything, but in the meantime you are also picking up past memories to support the worst-case scenario you are imagining. When you go over different scenarios with the same dominant feeling of fear or worst-case scenario, it strengthens this possible outcome. This Universal Computer receives this as a command to serve your "Ask" or prayer, and to have your wish granted.

If the most dominant vibration with your wish is the worst-case scenario (because remember, you needed to make sure you really, really went through every worst-case possibility), so you receive what you expect. "Ask and you shall receive." *Poof*! Prayer answered. Worst-case scenario is in your reality!

When we receive what we didn't want, we often cannot understand why what we think we really wished for is not happening. Then we want to understand what happened?

Keep it simple: ask yourself what expectation was your focus when you made your "Ask?" Focus on the possibility you wished for in your imagination, play out your worst-case scenario to resolve them, not for them to own you.

An opportunity that is new, innovative to be birthed was shot down because of how you were focusing, not because of the idea.

Your Dominant Consistent Feeling Wins

The strongest point of references of your "Ask" is what attracts, meaning your most dominant consistent feeling as it relates to your thoughts. Of course, you may have other desires that are more positive for you, but those get outvoted if the list of what you do NOT want is more dominant.

If we seem to not be getting what we want, we translate that to lacking something within ourselves – we must be at fault.
There can also be the belief that something must be wrong with you and so you focus on what needs to be fixed in you or where you feel you are lacking. You believe that only then you can succeed.

We are often taught to pick ourselves apart and focus on what we feel we lack, even though there are so many positive qualities to focus on. Sometimes we look for what is wrong in ourselves before someone else can find it. We place a lot of energy in working towards all that we are missing or feel we do not have yet.

Our culture often trains us to enhance our physical appearance, alter our emotions and point out where our lives need "fixing." Self-help books have good intentions but often tend to break you down and give you lists of things to do to improve your life because you lack something, not because you wish to enhance your life. While some may be motivated to succeed this way, I wholeheartedly believe that if your emotional foundation is built from a place of lack, this can exhaust you on so many levels.

The feeling that you're not enough and need to find what to fix to feel better is a never-ending cycle that can give you the feeling of never "keeping up." Any transformations you make based on this energy will be temporary. You start to reinforce the training that you need to "keep up," you are "not enough" and "need to fix" your Self, as a way to motivate but this all stems from a place of lack. The idea of needing to "fix" or that you are "flawed" for who you are is disempowering, and this is a type of energy that blinds you to what there is to love about your Self, and your surroundings. Imagine the difference of attempting to accomplish your desires with the feeling of lack in you versus from a foundation where you feel empowered? Whichever way you choose, your dominant vibration becomes your dominant feeling that attracts. Find what you love about your Self and your surroundings and have this be your dominant feeling that attracts for you.

Pay Attention To You

So I ask you ...

Where do you spend your emotional energy? This is the place from which you are asking and creating what you are expecting to receive.

When you are happy or have received a wish granted, what emotional energy do you receive this with?

Where does your energy go when you are dealing with a situation that bothers you? How do you continue to direct your focus towards that situation when you think about it?

Do you wake up feeling more excited about your days than not?

If you give time to creating or updating your life vision, designing it from the perspective of how you wish to be emotionally engaged with the world in and around you, would your world look the same as it is now?

Is your outside world a reflection of your inner dreams?
How would you like to feel in your world? What are doing about this?

Are you ready to receive the possibilities available to you with ease?
Do you believe this is easily possible?

Different Approach = Different Outcome

Activate what you DO want by releasing the habit of constantly making a list of all the things you want to "fix" and complaining daily of that which you do not want.

Stop the self-sabotaging habit of breaking your Self and others down. JUST STOP IT! Have the discipline to stop doing things that are not what you wish for.

Believe you have a choice. Create awareness and remind your Self of what you love about your Self. Honor the whole you.

Yes! You can desire to improve yourself or your life, but think of it as an enhancement. Release the habit of feeling like you need to "fix" your Self and others. When we feel insecure about our own list of things we would like to "fix," we often can create a habit of making this list for our loved ones. We break down our accomplishments and those of others instead of rejoicing in them.

Exploring your emotional life is not, in my view, the same as "searching." You are not lost! You are exploring effective ways to manifest and communicate the Amazing Soul that you are as you define your reality. You are whole and complete, and connecting with others in this way gives the best opportunity for the best outcome of your relationships and harmony with others.

Power Thoughts

Magic Wand

- o Asking for what I wish for is my "Magical Wand."

- o My past hurts are a distant memory.

- o I can choose how I wish to feel.

- o I accomplish my desires from an empowered foundation.

- o Different approach = different outcome

- o I am conscious of where I spend my emotional energy.

- o I am whole and complete.

- o I connect with my best Emotional Self for the best outcome of my relationships.

- o I create a magical life where all is possible.

- o I receive the possibilities that are available to me easily.

Language Your Life

Words Are Your Sacred Language

Language Your Life® focuses on how your language guides your skill of manifesting. This important part of the Power Wishing® method is comprised of understanding the principles of writing out your wishes and acknowledging the power of your words. Your language, both verbal and written, keeps the direction of your vision towards the way you expect to receive in the physical world. Language Your Life is a component of Power Wishing where you compose your "Ask" using specific language combinations. You use writing as a tool to claim your wish, hope, desire and prayer into physical reality.

In Power Wishing, there is tremendous respect towards the meaning and emotional weight of your words. We honor words as potent and instrumental tools in aligning your experience with your intention. Our language is sacred and holds the power to activate our reality. You will learn to articulate and claim your desire with emotion-based language that represents wholeness and respect towards yourself and others.

Words carry emotional messaging and as you begin to consciously use Language Your Life, you will have a heightened awareness of how your communication affects what you attract. Use your words wisely as they can either be a weapon or a tool towards your Self or others.

Words Are Your Literal Command

From here forward, think of everything you say and do as a literal command to manifest. Meaning, every joke and conversation to yourself and others is taken as it is said, as if it was written on a piece of paper and submitted as a request and responded to in the same literal way. Sometimes we say things we do not mean and think that this is okay. We act as if words and feelings have little value. Use the gift of your words to say what you truly mean and to honor your life and others.

The Japanese scientist Dr. Masaru Emoto conducted one of my favorite experiments. He performed a series of tests observing the physical effect of the vibration of words, prayers, music and environment on the crystalline structure of water. He has proved that if water is exposed to a word, it will respond to that word. Water exposed to words such as *war* or *hate* deteriorated quickly, whereas those exposed to words such as *love* and *thank you* did not deteriorate. He also showed how loving words purified water that had been polluted. Words are a vibration; there are many scientific studies that confirm the effect our words have on our DNA, your physical body. This research backs what I know with certainty based on the results that I witness in my work and in my own life.

Reflect for a moment when someone says something that hurts your feelings and how it affects you physically. Your stomach may hurt or you may get a headache. For me, it is refreshing to know that if others need proof, then this concept can be shown with evidence as a tangible fact. Then again, your feelings should be proof enough. Also, if thoughts and words that come from us have an effect on water crystals, and we are about 60% water, think of what kind of effect they have upon us, as well as the people and events that come into our lives. It also goes to show that prayer of high consciousness positively affects the matter outside of us.

It is important for us to choose the words we use carefully. Release the notion that "words are just words." As our society progresses, it is interesting to see how the use of language has changed. I feel that there is less and less respect for the way words are used and valued.

Reflect for a moment on how you use your words. Do you feel your words as they are spoken? Are you conscious that they are bringing to you what is actually being said? Words bring opportunity. Are you aware of what you say to others? Are your words healing? Do you value the opportunity you have with your words?

Language holds a frequency just as music does. Both words and music can affect the rhythm of your life. From the Universe's perspective, which takes your words literally, it makes no sense why one would say something that one does not mean. Logically speaking, it makes no sense to be hurtful to others or our Selves. We already know that positive and negative thinking have a major impact on surrounding environments, besides the impact on ourselves. Furthermore, why would you speak in a way that is hurtful to yourself?

Awaken To Your Blessings

"Everything is energy and that's all there is to it. Match the frequency of the reality you want and you cannot help but get that reality. It can be no other way. This is not philosophy. This is physics." – Albert Einstein

If you think everything that surrounds you, along with your words, thoughts, and actions, and is here to support and love you, how would you approach your life? Would this affect your choices? How would you use this support? If you totally dropped the notion that you are not supported, or energy is not in flow with you, and shifted to knowing fully that how you make choices is how everything responds with you, how would your choices be different? Would you language your life differently?

How you perceive what is surrounding you is your choice. Know that all is in perfect order as blessings for you; it is your choice to awaken them. Can you visualize your Self with your arms open wide, receiving gifts of love and abundance like rain falling, and having so many wishes being granted and given to you? Would this shift the way you live your life? You empower these opportunities with the energy you give it.

Everything you feel, think and do is a language that is creating your life. Taking ownership for what and how you are languaging your life is what encourages the outcome you desire. When your Vibrational Language® expresses the ownership of your choices, the need to feel disempowered or victimized is released. Owning your choices creates a life that is happening *for* you and you live knowing that your physical reality is created by you.

When you use your words, you are claiming your hope as an actualized reality in the physical world. Your words reinforce your Vibrational Language, communicating how you expect to receive what you have asked for. In your Emotional Imagination®, you have designed your "Ask." Now, as you will phrase this "Ask" as your Power Wish, your words are the action that claims this as the physical experience you expect to have. The expectation of what YOU, dear Amazing Soul, must first and foremost believe you deserve. The belief of what you expect determines what you will receive. This is why it is important to take time to mold your dreams with your Emotional Imagination, write it and take action to have your dreams and beliefs match the way you wish to receive.

The Prayer Of A Conversation

Paula, a client of mine, told me about a conversation her friend Sarah shared with her. At lunch, Sarah was discussing how she would love to live in California. She and Paula discussed the possibility of living there with ideas they were excited to experience. Paula said they went on and on happily chatting away about the weather, the food, etc. She said it felt great, as she knew with this conversation they were creating their "Ask." They were naturally visualizing the feeling, the taste of the food, the job opportunities, etc. Paula knew that with this conversation, she was sending out a prayer and it felt special to have this conversation that felt like a prayer with another. Imagine for play that this conversation actually is a prayer, which is being sent off to the Universe to be matched. The prayer is fully charged with good expectations. Perfect!

Paula shared that she just sat and smiled, feeling this possibility, and she let it go. Paula then started to shift her conversation to the wonderful phone call she received from her cousin. She was staying in the good groove of wonderful feelings as she shifted to another area of her life. She rest assured that she has anchored her prayer with confidence that all will come her way. She trusted this state of allowing.

Sarah took a shift emotionally and started to say that even though she would like to move, she heard that it is so expensive there and people are not what they seem. She went on and on about why this would not be a good idea. Paula just looked at her and made a choice not to engage emotionally or verbally with Sarah's doubts. She instead chose to be supportive by just listening and when Sarah asked her what she thought, Paula then told her that maybe she is not ready for the move and that this is okay. She was willing to talk things out with Sarah and use the conversation for her to create clarity, but Sarah was not interested.

Paula reminded Sarah of when she arrived in New York City 10 years ago. Prior to that, she would daydream constantly about living in the big city and then one day, "out of the blue," she was on a plane and met the woman she now works for. She moved from Michigan to New York within a month and it felt simple. Paula smiled at this memory as she was now excited about the possibility of moving to sunny California and could feel the warm sunshine on her face. She just knew it would happen, and felt this excitement. Paula shared with me that as soon as she felt this certainty, regardless of where Sarah was at, surprisingly her thoughts went to remembering a dear friend who lives in California who told her to visit and said she could stay with her. Paula could not believe she had forgotten this until now, and so she decided she was going to call her to make plans to visit. She smiled to herself, as ideas are now coming to her to align the expectation of her wish. She was feeling thankful, knowing that all is in perfect order.

Paula's focus was not towards the details of how it will happen because she trusts they will be shown to her and she will know how to take action that is in alignment with them. Paula shared her appreciation towards the fact that she had not always felt she could command her destiny by her emotional emphasis on what to expect. In sharing her conversation with me, she also realized that she had no judgment towards her friend and that was refreshing.

Your Dream Is Calling

I understand that sometimes we are not able to fully capture the feeling of trusting what we wish to manifest. Work out your doubts in your "Movie" and then use your words to reinforce what you wish for. In these times especially, you can use your words to support your Self. If you wish for something, ask for it, feel it, dream it and own it. Why wait? Do not place your life on hold. It is way too precious.

A very successful businessman was seeing me for a personal session and he shared with me that he had a dream to write a book. This desire was burning in his soul and he could not escape this feeling. I asked him, "What is stopping you?" He shared that it is his fear of what others will think about him, especially his children. With a smile I shared with him that they were already thinking what they wished of him regardless of whether he wrote this book or not.

He had a twinkle in his eye when he shared his feeling about why he enjoys writing. He said, "I feel so vulnerable and emotionally naked and in a strange way writing gives me liberty to be myself." He continued, "I feel I have lived my life restricted in who I am. I am not complaining about being successful, I have been blessed, but I have also had to play a role." Nevertheless, he felt the greater his achievements were, the more he felt like a prisoner to the responsibilities in his world. He did not wish to change his life; he just desired to embody more of his true Self and passion to experience more of what he enjoys. He felt that life is short, and he just had the experiences of his dear friend passing at the age of 51.

Then I shared with him to think for a moment about what would feel worse for him: what he perceived others thought of him or how he would feel if he did not write his book? He said, "Not writing my book would probably pain me for the rest of my life." Then I added, "Then you have your answer." I also added that after listening to him, that not meaning to he might be a bit angry and resentful towards those he thought would judge him. I said, "The funny thing is that you are spending all that energy reasoning why you are not writing when you have not even given those that love you a chance to like what you write. What if they like it?" Then I asked him, "Check in with your Self and make sure you are not using other people as your excuse not to write your book." He responded sincerely saying, "I am used to being successful at everything I do and writing a book is way out of my comfort zone." We shared some more and as he was leaving we both laughed at the simplicity of this and how we can make something more challenging than it really is when we have fears. Well, actually fears that have not even happened. Sometimes we create so much emotional anxiety from the mental torture we place ourselves through, that our fears can paralyze us.

So often we use the energy to create what we desire by assuming what could happen without even asking for what we truly wish for. *When you are in a state of fear, you are still asking for what you expect.* Save your Self the mental anguish and just ask for what you desire from your Self and others. Sometimes you are not clear of how to language what you are asking for or you are not even clear about what you want. This is when you can either use your Emotional Imagination to find clarity on your feelings or have a conversation with someone who is a supportive listener so you can hear your Self out loud.

No Matter What, Use Words That Honor Who You Are

This is an important point I like to make in the coursework of Language Your Life. Using words to demoralize a person's whole being is a huge dishonor. There is not a good enough reason to be driven to communicate this way or to get someone's attention in this way. I have heard people say that they believe if they are mean, then it gets the other person to pay attention or listen. Yes, it may, but it will also result in hurt and resentment. To break down a person with cruel words or to use trusted information as a weapon, even if you feel that what you have to say is valid, will only be experienced as painful. This is not necessary.

When you demoralize a person, they cannot hear what you have to say; they are closed off because they feel hurt about what was said. This causes them to feel bad and spend energy defending themselves. It creates an emotional mess. Then, instead of dealing with the original issue of why you felt hurt, these demoralizing words become used as a platform to create more hurt.

It is said that it can take many years to build a relationship and only a few hurtful words to destroy it. I sincerely believe this. This can be avoided, especially with children who repeat the movie of these hurtful words for years and years as they grow up believing they are true. Maybe in the heat of the moment an adult said something very belittling to the child. The adult could place that into perspective, but for the child it came from someone they loved and respected, so they took it as a truth about who they are. Be very careful not to speak hurtful words to children. Their egos tend to be vulnerable; such rebukes can result in them feeling worthless, which was not the intention or end result you wished for. Of course, the same goes for adults. As adults we are all still vulnerable, especially with those we love. Speak with love, purpose and passion, using gentle words with yourself and others. When expressing your Authentic Truth, be the voice of honest expression.

Self-Love

We have discussed your words in relation to others and towards what you wish for. I also have shared that I believe with total certainty that words, like everything that surrounds us, have vibration and affect your DNA, which reflects in your manifestations. This includes health, wealth, relationships, everything. Many times we do not pay attention to the way we speak to ourselves; this is detrimental to our whole being.

I had a client who was losing her eyesight quickly and the doctors could not figure out why this was happening. A former client referred her to me, because she felt that through healing sessions with me her friend would be able to get to the root of what was happening based on beliefs she might be carrying that were now affecting her physically. My new client began to share with me about how she did not understand why this was happening to her. She was very confused and frustrated. She was also a bit defensive when we explored how she might hold beliefs that could be causing her to lose her eyesight. She explained to me that she was here because she had exhausted all other avenues and was desperate. I listened to her as she talked, and I was compassionate with her.

As she continued her conversation with me, she let go of her guard and spoke more freely. I wrote down notes of what she was saying. She started to tell me about her life and how she used to enjoy herself a lot more. Since this issue started with her eyesight, she had become so focused on fixing this that she was beginning to feel obsessed with it and did not even want to see friends.

She had been a schoolteacher and she stated that she hated to see how children were mistreated. She felt they were not able to express themselves freely. This is why she stopped teaching; she could not bear to see parents not acknowledge their children's feelings and a school system that she felt was breaking them down. She started to cry and said that she did not understand why people could be so cruel and mean. She had a hard time watching the news and hated to see what was happening in the world. She sarcastically said she did not have to worry about watching the news anymore since her sight was so bad. She kept saying that it was so hard for her to see people hurting each other. She talked about this for about 15 minutes as I continued to write down notes.

After she shared, she felt she got a lot of her feelings out and I appreciated that she was truly present with me. When she stopped expressing herself, she took a moment to just cry. I shared that I was not sure why bad things happened to good people, and agreed that it did seem unfair. I told her that I thought she had a very compassionate heart and this was why it pained her to witness hurt in the world.

I shared with her that I understood how challenging it was to see the world this way, since she was such a loving, nurturing woman. She then shared a childhood memory that she had forgotten about a cruel thing she had witnessed as a child. She continued, saying that the most painful part was when she attempted to share with her mother she felt her mother ignored her.

We discussed this for some time as it naturally tied into the way she felt others treated her as an adult and her sensitivity with children being treated similarly. After we talked about a few experiences that truly pained her to witness, I said to her, "Did you know that in the last 15 minutes you said the words 'I hate to see' 17 times?" The woman was shocked. She used the words "I hate to see" before so many things. "I hate to see the way the world is going." "I hate to see how they are treating children in schools." Again and again she said these words.

She was so surprised because she felt she was a positive person. I explained that she is a positive person but perhaps she was just tired of feeling she was up against the world. This made her feel defeated and then she felt angry. But this was her way to "protect" herself from what she was witnessing. She also shared with me other disempowering beliefs such as "I always give in too easy. I should say 'No' more often." I shared that these were some beliefs she could work on shifting and that I thought these beliefs were an accumulation of her feeling overwhelmed at her situation and created her anger.

Ah-ha Moment

I was feeling quite positive of the new awareness she was sharing, which was allowing her to begin shifting her beliefs quickly. She was now open to acknowledging the way she had been expressing herself at this moment in time. She was also totally surprised by her language and what she had been saying to her Self. She was even more surprised that she was not aware of this.

She expressed that she was a woman of prayer and she had been praying so hard. I was gentle in my explanation to her and suggested that she step back for a moment and, without blame or shame or feeling bad towards her Self, imagine that her prayers were being taken literally. What would they be asking for? She had that "Ah-ha moment" of what she had been clearly putting out into the Universe and what she was saying. Basically, it was hard for her to see the pain she was witnessing and she did not want to see this pain anymore.

Let's say that all this was her "Ask" of free will and there is Loving Energy that does not judge what you are asking and only wishes to give to you. In doing this, let's say that the Universe says, "She is making the 'Ask' that she cannot bear to see how mean people are because it is too painful." And so the Universe responds to her request of "I cannot bear to see." Then as she continued to reaffirm this every day with stronger feelings, words and thoughts, the Universe said, "We have a request for more, 'I cannot bear to see.' Give more of 'I cannot see.'" Now imagine that your body is a part of this whole opportunity that loves you and gives you what you have asked for. How would the body respond to this? She answered, "By not having to see; and giving me poor sight."

She understood that in no way was she consciously creating these behaviors to harm her Self; it was a defense mechanism. On another level she felt relief, because she now understood that there was a system to energy, and feels a sense of empowerment to shift her circumstances. She had felt angry with God and now felt inspired to pray, knowing that God was on her side and that she could utilize this knowledge.

We did quite a bit of work. My focus was not the healing of her eyes, as that was the effect of her beliefs. To focus on her eyes as the cause, she might recreate something else with the same beliefs that have affected her eyesight. We worked on her beliefs and her feeling powerless and not able to feel she could be hopeful in a world that seemed hopeless, which left her feeling victimized. We went to the cause of these beliefs with the experiences that created them. This was literally an eye-opening experience for her. She continues to be aware of her beliefs and knows how to shift her language to serve her Authentic Self and desires, and now, years later, her vision has improved significantly.

Your Words Are Your Choice

Many years ago I heard a yogi master say that when you use words to gossip or hurt another, you connect with that part of them. You connect to that negative part of the other and you bring that energy back to yourself.

Now, why would you want to strengthen a connection to someone's insecurity, jealousy or fear, or what you say you dislike? You know the saying, "If you do not have anything nice to say, don't say anything at all." I liked this saying because I feel there are many ways to say something.

You cannot be responsible for the way other people think or what they say. You can be responsible for the energy you give to what others think and say.

Your Words Voice You

When in doubt, choose words that build, enhance and expand the sacredness of you and another. Personally, I am very sensitive to sarcasm. Because I believe people mean what they say, I take words literally. I do not buy on any level that something said sarcastically was meant to be just a joke. I feel it is a cowardly way of saying something negative that wants to be said. It is often a way for an insecure person who does not know how to communicate to hurt others. Sarcasm hurts.

Sometimes we cannot shift our feelings towards someone or get happy when we feel so angry. Saying nice things to someone who has just hurt us may not be possible, but what is possible is to remember that your words are voicing you.

Words Are Our Gift To Attract, Our Gift Of Free Will In Action

If in the moment we cannot feel better, we have our words to help us; how we speak to ourselves can hurt or heal us. We use negative words to hurt others and often to speak poorly of ourselves. We lie with our words and then justify our lies. We text hurtful words and then delete them as if they never existed, but they live on with the one we hurt.

We all know the power of our words, so why do we still make decisions to use them in ways that hurt? I believe that they hurt not only others but our Selves.

If you were to make a choice to live from the truth of who you are, the voice of your Soul's perspective, what kind of conversation would you carry on with others? How do you speak to yourself? Would you allow or would you like another to speak to you the way you speak to yourself? How do you wish to feel about the way you voice to yourself or others?

Reflect for a moment on how you communicate when you are disappointed or angry. Reflect when you have been kind with your words when you have felt this way and the outcome that came from this.

Why waste your words on negativity when they have the power to elevate, enhance, encourage, express and create goodness? Words are our gift to attract, our gift of free will in action. Another way we use words is when we compare ourselves to others and then create self-doubt or jealousy. Or, when we judge another by assuming, when we all know that we cannot really know the real story of any person. You are in control of the way you choose to use your words.

Your Story, Your Words

How are you telling the story of your past? Is it someone else's observation of your past telling your story? Are your words repeating the past you do not wish for into your future?

It is OK to talk about your past, but in a way that brings the parts of your past that serve you now. What parts of your past do you wish to be awakening in your future?

Verbalize the story you wish to live by using words that foretell a future that you desire. How you verbalize your observation of your past says what you expect of your future. Imagine that the words you speak go into the atmosphere and the air circulates like magnets to connect a match.

Now with this imagined in your mind, knowing your words connect to bring about your reality, reflect on whether you are using words that create the reality you desire. Your words write your "Movie." Many people would be debt-free or release being in unhappy relationships if they would stop talking about how many bills they have or all the things they do not like about their relationship. Communicating through complaining does not result in resolution; it only causes the "Ask" to return more of what you are complaining about!

Use your words to bring into your future your past in ways it served you or use them to bring into your reality what you wish for. Use words that redefine your challenges as adventure and opportunity.

It's Your Choice ... Your Choice Of Words

Sometimes I have days where I feel like complaining and using words that are not so positive. On days like these, I give myself permission to have a "bad" day, with some clear boundaries. We all have those days. My teacher Frank used to say, "If you are going to have a fit and get upset, make sure you have a really good temper tantrum, give it all you got and then be done with it." Give your Self permission to be disappointed, upset, angry and plain old mad. The objective is not to stay there too long.

Do your best to be conscious of your words and do not connect with those that may trigger you. Even on "bad" days, do your best not to say words that you will regret. Attempt to find another way to share your feelings without breaking down the person. Stick to the issue or speak at another time when your emotions are not so charged.

"If a child tells a lie, tell him he has told lie, but don't call him a liar. If you define him as a liar, you break down his confidence in his own character." – Jean Richer

When you speak of another, understand this is also a prayer for your Self. *What you pray for another you pray for your Self, what you speak of another you speak of your Self.* Take the opportunity to share beautiful words with another because you are aware of their presence and the value they are to your life. Share good feelings, share beautiful words. Please do not assume that people know how you feel, especially the ones closest to you. Many times our family and closest friends are the last to hear us say beautiful things to them.

There is a dear friend of mine who recently passed away. I am quite good with expressing myself, but I must say, that in desiring to write to her family I have found it challenging to finish my note. What does give me peace is that when I saw her a few months before she was bedridden I felt this urge to talk to her in depth.

I looked at her and told her how much I appreciated her and shared with her all these kind things that I felt for her. I shared sincere words of gratitude for her with so much love and admiration. I remember leaving the conversation feeling grateful that I had listened to myself and shared for no other reason than because I felt it in my heart. There was no special reason to do this, as I did not know she was ill at the time, and neither did she. I am so thankful that I shared when she was present and that I did not miss out on a moment to share my gratitude for her.

Your Words Are A Reflection Of You, Your Beliefs, Your Soul

Your words are a high sacred language. If you knew that your words are sending a prayer for yourself, would that change your choice of words? If language can create an environment for love to live in, are your words used as an opportunity to enhance this?

Words are an action that creates direct intention of more action; the body and the mind respond to your words. The energy of words is converted into your relationships and life experiences. As you speak with love as the base of your words, this aligns the expectations of your dreams with love.

Your words have the potential to accelerate, neutralize or enhance the dominant emotion of attraction. See your word as law. Your word is your belief. Understand that if you give your word, you are giving a promise and have created an energetic obligation to fulfill the promise you chose to make. Many times one can use words to prove a point to be "right." At times like this, release the need to be "right" with your words and replace being "right" with sharing your perspective with harmony to honor others.

Your Word Is A Vow To Your Self

As I have shared, there were times I only had a prayer and with this prayer the only thing I felt at the time was that I had my word. I sincerely believed that this was powerful and would start the flow of what I wished to receive, especially since I was having a challenging time. I have understood the power of my word as a valuable component to who I am.

When I was younger and living on my own, I felt insecure about the fact that I did not finish college. I did not have much money and I felt socially awkward, but I knew that my greatest value and security was in my character traits. Valuing my Self for the trust and honor I show others and valuing others in my life are a result of an education from life experiences.

There was a point in this stage of my life where I did not have enough money to pay my rent and I did not want to lose my apartment. Even though it was not in a good part of town, it was what I could afford at the time. I had to decide if I should tell my landlord that I could not pay the rent when it was due or tell her in advance. I decided to call the landlord before the rent was due because I already knew the truth and felt it was not proper to withhold this information. I was responsible for what I was supposed to do and I had to be willing to face the outcome. If she said we could not work it out and I had to leave, then so be it. Even though I feared that this could be an outcome, I believe that being straightforward with someone and not misleading them will always create better options than the alternative. Plus, in reality she was not the cause of my financial issues, so why should she take on responsibility towards this? Being this responsible at about 19 years old was not so easy, but I knew enough to let go of the worst-case scenario "Movie" in my head. I believed that whatever was to happen, I would be worse off if I was not up front.

Before I called her, I acknowledged to my Self that I had always paid on time and felt my intention to pay and be fully up-to-date. So with that feeling, I spoke to her about my situation. I relayed to her that I was not sure what I could pay, but I would pay something weekly. I assured her that I would not leave her in debt and she could trust my word. To my surprise, the landlord agreed and we made a payment arrangement. I felt grateful and responsible to make good on her trust.

I can remember being parked in the driveway of that apartment sitting in my car in the heat of summer with no working air conditioner and a broken car window that did not roll all the way up.

I smile now because I realize the humor of how at some points in your life it can feel like that moment would be forever – and now it seems so long ago. Of course, I paid all of the rent that I owed and eventually worked my way up to move to another apartment.

Your Word Is As Good As The Action You Put Behind It

If you asked me the name of this person, I could not tell you, but after 30 years I can still remember how good it felt to be trusted when I felt that I did not have much to offer a landlord who barely knew me.

Many people who see me in my lectures and in my community have no idea of the challenges I have had in my life. How could they? They see a successful woman and business leader living a very nice life in many ways, and they might assume that I have always had it easy. But I have endured so much in my lifetime, like many have, and I have grown through my challenges. Like all of us, when we look back maybe we would have made different choices with the wisdom we have now, but at the time we did not have the insight we have today. We all did the best we could at the time. The point is to move forward with who you are and what you know now with the person you are today.

Choose To Define Challenges Differently

These formulas that I share here with you have transformed and continue to shift my life. This book is written as a reflection, like a mini case story of my life with techniques that are proven to work. Over the years they have been perfected through experiencing them in my life and seeing the results of others who use them as well. As I move forward in my life, it is not a reflection of a past that I do not wish to recreate. I am continuously growing and enhancing possibilities, creating momentum with my possibilities realized as my life experiences. This does not take away challenges I may have; I just choose to define them differently.

I can remember being really upset one day as I sat in my car in front of that apartment I was struggling to afford. At the time, I was in sales and I could not understand why people were not buying from me like I thought they should. I had a good product and, in my mind, I thought I was presenting a great pitch and felt they were really missing out.

Frustrated, I sat parked in the driveway in tears, blaming others and feeling powerless. Having an understanding and knowing of energetic work and feeling stuck made me feel even more frustrated. These were humbling moments.

That day I took time to reflect what I was doing that was creating the lack of movement towards what I wanted in my life. I saw my tape recorder in my car that I would use when ideas would come to me while I was driving. Most of the time we are told to rehearse our sales presentation in the mirror, but I felt that I needed to hear myself. So that day I taped my presentation as if I was in front of someone. Then I waited three days until I listened to it so that I was removed from that moment and could witness the recording outside of myself.

Well, after three days I heard myself and I was shocked at the difference of how I thought I was presenting myself and what I heard. I realized right then and there that if I had a chance of being successful in sales, I needed to at least start with cleaning up how I verbalized my thoughts and feelings. At the time, I felt other things were out of my control, but I did know I could control how I spoke. Sometimes we can feel so overwhelmed that we are not sure of how to shift internally, but we can start with how we communicate. So I spent time paying attention to my words, verbalizing what I wished to aspire, every day being aware to have my words in sync with what I wish to strengthen as my belief.

How many times have you thought you said something to another and really it was said so many times in your head, but you never really said it to the other person? Have you had a conversation with someone when you were really worked up and what you think you said or the way you think you said it was not necessarily the way it happened?

I find that at times this is a habit that is true for a lot of CEOs and executives I advise in my leadership courses. I have them tape-record themselves, as an exercise. Many times what they thought they were communicating compared to the way they expressed it out loud was not a match. After their awareness of this, along with using Power Wishing tools and techniques, they started to listen to themselves and others differently.

Language To Avoid In Power Wishing

In Power Wishing, participants quickly realize that the spoken word carries emotional accountability. There is deeper meaning and more value in a word than we may initially think when we just say it. Words create your story, shape your "Movie" and connect you in supporting the world you wish to create with being a positive influence with others.

Words to avoid –
ALWAYS – NEVER – TRY – DON'T – NOT – I GUESS – I AM SORRY— BUT

Words That Block The Flow Of Receiving

Using "always" or "never," especially in a righteous manner, blocks you from being open to new information or receiving another possibility that could change your mind for the better. It also limits your expansion in a relationship and in conversation. Many times you may have thought you would "never" do something or "always" do it the same, but then things can change. Even if at a certain moment you feel you would "never" or "always" do something, when sharing with another, these words can cut off a healthy exchange of ideas. Reflect for a moment on the times you have said, "I will never" or that you would not accept this or that or ever do this or that. What about when you have judged another and said you would never do as they have done? And then things changed, you changed and you ended up doing what you *never* thought you would do.

The word "try" does not clearly compute as a direct command to the Universal Computer. How can the Universe "try" to support you? It either does or does not. How can our minds process "try?" What action is your mind supposed to support with the word "try?" Try to pick up a pencil, try to get in your car, try to fall in love, try to get a job ... it translates to "I'm not sure I want to" or "I do not know what to do so I guess I will try," or "I am not ready to do this, I have hesitation," or simply, "I am not willing" or "I do not want conflict right now so I will *try.*"

So imagine what action you are "trying" to tell the brain to perform. What action is the brain supposed to take with the word "try?" If the word "try" did not exist, what would you say instead? Maybe you mean to say "attempting" or "making an effort to do something." With these words there is movement. Use this as an opportunity to be clear in voicing a situation or a feeling. I highly suggest taking the word "try" and "can't" out of your vocabulary unless you wish to stay stagnant in a situation. Use your choice of words, to move *towards* something versus blocking it, or choose to communicate clearly to claim the emotions that will support what you wish for.

Be aware of how you use the phrase "I guess." Many times this can be used in a disempowering way. Sometimes, we use the word "guess" hoping not to offend someone else with our opinion or because we fear rejection for being wrong.

If you are asked something and you feel you know your response, well then share. You were asked to share what you know. What if something good will come of this? Give others an opportunity; you may be pleasantly surprised. If you do not know, you can say, "I do not know at this time." Clarity with our words supports healthy relationships. Let's play with the notion that the truth is always known, that if you are not verbalizing sincere truth, it is felt through your vibrational energy anyway. So without using the phrase "I guess," how would you consciously answer questions you were asked?

As you Language Your Life clearly, you will choose words that will eliminate chaos. You will be clear in your message with yourself and others. This is a beautiful way to be truthful, as well as to honor another.

To me, using the phrase "I apologize" versus "I am sorry" feels very different. I am conscious of when I use the phrase "I am sorry" versus "I apologize," because it is valuable for me to pay attention to how I am taking responsibility. I feel that when I apologize to someone, I own my behavior differently than when I say, "I am sorry." When "sorry" is used, it can often feel like it can be a way to brush the other person off. I have often heard the phrase "I am sorry, OK ..." which to me has the tone of "Now get over it!" or "Let's not spend too much time on this, I said I was sorry." It is like shooing the person away not to make a bigger deal out of something, and I feel it avoids responsibility.

Saying you're sorry to keep the peace, even though you believe you were not incorrect, can be used to avoid more drama, but it is not authentic communication. Sorry can also be used to communicate in a way that does not have the other person feel inferior towards your strengths. When you apologize to someone, I feel you are making a statement or a request to discuss the situation in an emotionally healthy way. Acknowledging something for which you sincerely feel regret, remorse or even sadness plays an important part in the healing you may hope to experience with another. With an apology, you own that your behavior has hurt another. You wish to be accountable for your part in this "Movie" and to find a resolution if possible.

Your Words Have Light

For a moment, feel that you have Light around you and this Light is your Vibrational Language. Your words give energy to this Light. When you speak authentically with honor towards another, your commitment to this integrity creates a synergy that only accelerates the manifestations that surround you.

Understand that if you give your word, you are giving a promise and have created an energetic obligation to fulfill the promise you chose to make.

Many times one can use words to prove a point to be "right." At times like this, release the need to be "right" with your words and replace being "right" with sharing your perspective with harmony to honor others. As you clean up your language and reflect on how you use your words, understand how important it is for you to be honorable with your word. How can you create an honorable life if you do not even honor the simplicity of your word? It is OK to say, "No" or "I am not sure at this moment" or "Can I get back to you?" or you can change an agreement. If you are not ready to do what you say, then do not say it. If you commit to doing something, do this because you mean it, not because you just said it to manipulate another into doing something for you. Saying you are going to do something and then not doing it creates chaos energetically. That energy could be used to circulate abundance and accomplish a goal but instead, it is like pushing back a prayer we said we wished to receive.

There are many unexpected situations that can come up where we could create chaos and may not respond appropriately at the time or when things seem out of our control. So why create chaos with what is in our control, with what we agreed to do? Be conscious to clarify your words and your agreements because we do have control of our words. Your word is a vow to your Self.

Everyone wants to be loved and visible. When you keep your commitments, you are languaging to others that they matter and are visible. You can choose to speak with another with love or hurt, your choice. We have all made choices with words that were not very kind. No matter how conscious we are, this can happen. The best thing to do when you are aware of this is to acknowledge it to the other person and clean it up with words that replace hurtful ones – your choice, your words, your Light.

Words Confirm Your Perspective

Having verbal discipline also supports you to be the authority of your mind. If you do not mean something, then do not say it. Imagine that your words give you Light and blessings. Every time you abuse this privilege, you take away Light and blessings from your Self. There is no other person or God controlling your words so take responsibility for your power to create; this is within your control.

When you take ownership of your word as law, you improve your ability to materialize things you want in your life. Be careful what you ask for and how you validate this by what you continue to say.

Since we know that your word is law, then refrain from thinking or speaking in terms of things being hard, evil, ugly or difficult. In Language Your Life, we totally avoid words like "impossible," "worry," "trouble," "problem" and "hate."

Problems are situations that are challenges to overcome.
Impossible is a belief of what you think you can expect.
Worry is a feeling that delays your dreams.
Hate blocks the opportunity to love.

Your words confirm what you desire; this also confirms your perspective. I remember that I took my children with me to bereavement counseling right after their father left this physical world. My son had not ever had the experience of counseling before this but he was open. The psychologist asked him a list of questions and then said to him, "I would like to know the way you think." He then asked my son, "When you see a half glass of water, do you see the glass as half full or half empty?" My son immediately answered and said, "It depends how thirsty I am." That was a classic moment. I felt like telling the psychologist that our sessions with him were complete. My son had measured the fullness of the glass based on his feelings of expectations. He was in control of what he expected because he knows how to observe the possibility.

Words Of Love

Do not lose an opportunity to tell someone you love him or her. Not because it could be too late one day ... but because life is too precious to let another day go by without saying it. Many times we leave our loved ones for last, thinking they will always be there later. Like the shoemaker whose family has no shoes.

Take care of who is closest to you first before you spend energy caring for others, as the ones closest to us sometimes need our care the most. Later is now.

Communication is a treasured gift that gives us the most amazing opportunity to verbalize kindness and love to those closest to us, even strangers. Have a proactive life of communicating positively and sharing love. Why? Because you can respond to your life with words that praise and feel good.

Speak as if you are speaking in prayer, a sacred language where words create the environment for love to live.

Power Thoughts

Language Your Life

- o   I know the sacred power of my words to activate my reality.

- o   I communicate with emotional accountability.

- o   Using words is my free will in action and my gift to attract.

- o   The words I use are a part of answering my expectations of my life.

- o   My words have love at the base of their expression.

- o   I honor my Self and others with how I use my words.

- o   I live proactively sharing love because I can and it feels good.

- o   I use gentle words with my Self and others.

- o   I am responsible for the energy I give to what other people think and say.

- o   I use my words to let others know I love and value them.

Exploring What To Ask

This chapter is designed to bring you clarity of the emotional understanding of your Self. Through the reflective questions in this chapter, you will take a look at different areas in your life and reflect if there is an area that you would like to be different or would like to enhance. You will also reflect on what emotional foundation you would like to strengthen for the expectation to receive the life you dream of.

An important part of Power Wishing is to recognize the feelings with which you are making your "Ask" and to be aware of a positive or hindering trigger driving your expectation. In this chapter I offer you the opportunity to explore different angles of a feeling in order to identify what underlying belief is connected with your expectation. You will explore questions that will help you discover any unacknowledged feelings or triggers that may be affecting the realization of your life dreams. With this awareness you will clearly create conscious written wishes to solidify an emotional foundation that claims your expectation. You will also begin to do this consciously as a lifestyle.

Take a moment to feel what is your greatest wish, what it would be like to receive this wish being granted. What emotional support would you ask to easily have this granted? Your emotions are the anchor directing your expectation to fulfill your dream. Like a wind that easily pushes a sail, allow your emotions to gently bring your wish as your life experience. Move the emotions that are not in alignment with how you wish to receive out of your way. Just like you would make a pros and cons list towards a situation, create this with your emotions.

Keep what supports you strong and let go of what blocks your abundance. Stop settling for your dreams not being realized. Life is your opportunity to be alive with your dreams. Yours! You cannot expect another to feel the same passion or desire as you do about your dreams and the importance you place on them. If you are waiting for others or society to agree with you before you live for your dream, you might as well sit back and get ready to watch lots of commercials in your "Movie." These commercials will be advertising other people's beliefs and will distract you from your "Movie." The opportunities and experiences that are in your life must be an added value to what you wish as your life. If not, cut out the commercials and get to the "Movie" of your Life.

Many of the wishes you may design from these exercises may seem so simple at first. But sometimes, what is obvious is overlooked and what can be resolved in a simple manner is made unnecessarily complicated. Do not undermine the power of simplicity to easily resolve any situation – keep it simple. Our goal is to realize joy, laughter, fun and love for your Self and others every day and Power Wishing® is a vehicle for this. Once you have a deeper understanding of what you would like to ask for, you will learn how to write a Power Wish to reaffirm what you are asking for. This is also a powerful way to express your authentic truth. Writing your wishes and seeing the confirmation of what you desire on paper gives you a sense of organization and supports you in releasing the intensity of having all of these feelings and aspirations.

Affirmations On Another Level

Let me take a moment to clarify the difference between affirmations and Power Wishing. Power Wishing is a systematic formula of awareness that empowers you to utilize your emotions as a vehicle to finely tune your outcomes. You are able to use your emotional base as a steering wheel. When you know how you feel consciously, you decide which direction you wish to steer. You are driving the expectation of your journey.

An affirmation is a wonderful way to make a positive statement or declaration of the truth you wish to experience as your reality, a positive step in giving you clarity to knowing what you wish to choose. However, I will share with you that if you are working to convince your Self that your affirmation is possible without being emotionally connected, you may manifest it, but not necessarily with the emotional foundation that serves you the best in receiving it.

When I think of an affirmation, it feels like a car that is not completely touching the road. You are in a great vehicle, which is a positive thought, but not on the road ready to ride. By this I mean a grounding of your emotions to anchor your ride to the expectation of your journey. Now imagine that your affirmation is grounded by the direction of your Emotional GPS. Having your affirmation manifest with the support of a positive emotional foundation as the anchor to receive takes the language of the affirmation to an authentic reality where you claim a healthy expectation. There is a very different outcome when an emotional connection supports you to truly be connected consciously with emotions that anchor your affirmation. The ride on your journey is smoother, on course and authentic. Hear yourself ask for what you aspire and feel your emotional connection with what you are asking for.

Remember Power Wishing is emotionally based wishing, so you ask for the emotions that will strengthen your foundation to receive. What I find to be an issue for some of my clients and students is when there are emotions that they did not think played a role with their wishes.

Sometimes, I will ask you how something *serves you* and you may wonder how drama, or sadness or anger could serve you. For a moment believe that everything you have created, everything you do on some level is done because you felt it would do something positive, maybe protect you or give you love or motivate you to be better.

When you are aware of a behavior or emotion that no longer serves you, you can shift the behavior or emotion without losing the result. You can continue to bring the result into your life without the behaviors that no longer serve you. When you ask yourself, "How did this behavior or habit serve me? If I know that it has served me, why did I create it and how did I believe it would serve me in a positive way?" With this understanding you can appreciate your belief and keep the positive result while releasing the need for drama, anger or sadness to create the same result with a behavior that is no longer positive. You are able to only keep what does serve you.

So for example, if you wish to release procrastination and are having a challenging time doing this, I would ask you, "How does procrastination serve you?" You may say, "That is crazy, it stresses me out." But if you think about it as a behavior that does something for you, then maybe you would say, "It motivates me to get organized and focused quickly." Then you would ask your Self, "How do I feel when I am organized and focused?" You may comment that you feel positive or secure. When you have this awareness, then you can wish for a positive way to feel those emotions in other areas, letting go of procrastination as a vehicle to get there.

Observe that everything has a positive aspect, and that you created it because you believed on some level it would serve you. Knowing this simply without judgment or mental chatter releases the behavior that is no longer positive and shifts it to another behavior that is.

Let's explore some feelings and some beliefs in a playful manner. Witness your Self answer these questions.

Do your best not to take your Self so seriously. Please remember to keep it simple.

Explore the questions that resonate with you, and know you can go back to this list when you need to, as certain questions will resonate with you at different times in your life.

As I have shared, we all have created some pretty funny scenes in our "Movie." The good news is you can rewrite them, edit them or have new ones ... so let's emphasize that you have awareness and knowing as you answer these questions.

Take a moment before you read them to center you Self to hear the answers from your heart and let your logical mind take a rest.

Let's Explore Your Emotional Habits:

Do you feel you struggle within your Self to express your true feelings?
In what area(s) do you feel you struggle or feel challenged with in sharing your feelings?
Does struggle motivate you?
Do you struggle for what you wish for and this gives you the feeling that you deserve it because you have worked for it?
Do you believe that you deserve opportunities that come easily?
If an opportunity came quickly, would you trust it or would you feel there must be a catch and you look for how you may be tricked or fooled?
Do you believe that things can come easy to you?
How do you express this belief?
How do you feel when you receive things easily?
Do you feel in order to receive you have to give first?
Do you believe that if you receive, then you are in debt to the other?
Are you a giver and not a receiver because in that way you feel you do not owe anybody anything? How does this serve you?
Do you believe that change is risky or positive?
How do you feel when you wish to make a change that you believe in and are challenged by a loved one? Does that shift your perspective in a positive way?
Do you take a risk for something you wish for?
How does it feel to take a risk when others oppose you? Who nurtures your beliefs?
When your wish is almost manifested, do you embrace it and receive freely or with drama?
Where do you have drama in your life? How does drama serve you in this area?

How do you feel when you easily move in the direction of where you say you would like to be?

What feeling stops you from having the life you say you wish for? How does this serve you?

How does it make you feel to stay comfortable knowing what to expect even if the expectation is not what you desire? How does it serve you to stay in your comfort zone, even if it means not taking opportunities you have dreamed of?

How does not knowing what to expect feel?

How does it feel to succeed at something you have been striving for?

If you feel like you will not succeed at what you wish for, how does this make you feel? What do you do with this feeling?

When do you become self-critical of your Self? How does this serve you?

What does feeling successful do for you? What do you do with these feelings?

Do you feel insecure or doubtful with those who challenge you? If so, how does this serve you?

Do you give your power over to others who challenge you and allow them to be the expert of you?

How does this statement feel to you? – I feel I am living a life that has been chosen for me by what I believe is expected of me from others.

How does this statement feel to you? – I am living a life I have chosen.

Why would you allow your Self to be in surroundings where you begin to mentally reduce your Self or shut down?

How does hanging onto toxic relationships that do not support who you are serve you?

How does a relationship that uplifts your Soul feel?

What does a relationship that reminds you of what you love about your Self feel like?

How do you support your Self to be authentic?

Do you truly believe that you know how to live a happy, healthy productive life? How does this appear in your reality?

Do you feel at any level that owning your happiness would hurt others?

When do you feel the most peaceful? What emotions give you peace?

Do you wake up in the morning wishing things looked different? How does this serve you?

How does it feel to wake up in the morning embracing what you have created with excitement and purpose?

What passions do you experience in your life?

Do you feel peaceful when you are at home?

Your Life Is Non-Negotiable

Let's say that your Authentic Self took a moment to step outside of you and observed your life as you are living now. What do you feel would be the viewpoint of your Soul if you were witnessing from a non-physical place, where there is no judgment or consequences?

Take a moment and reflect about your life as an observer:

What would you observe?
Is your personality a voice that is in sync with your Soul's desires?
What would you enhance in your life, NOW?
What do you appreciate about your Self?
What decisions would you make, NOW?
What would you shift in your life, NOW?
How do you become more secure within?
Well, let me ask you ... how did you become insecure?
Have you become fearful to make decisions?
What is the desire in your Soul that you really, really want?
How are you going to bring this desire as your life experience?

Sometimes we are not able to rectify why things are the way they are or why you did this or that. Let go of why and move forward. Do not start psychoanalyzing your Self. NEXT!

Take the pause button off your "Movie." Let go of why and just move on to how you wish to feel NOW. Make the decisions to support this and take the action to make it your life.

The easiest way to shift a fear into strength or insecurity into security is to embody your best qualities regardless of the circumstances around you.

Be the best of your Self and do things that remind you of this. Make this a habit. And if your surroundings are not supporting you to feel your best Self, well then shift your surroundings or you will become your surroundings.

You choose your surroundings and you are influenced by your surroundings, so invigorate your Self with places and people that support the life you wish to live.

The Time Is NOW

The time is NOW. Do not wait for a crisis to motivate you to where you know you wish to be, or with decisions you feel burning in your Soul that you desire to take. Make decisions and be motivated in times of joy to build with joy and abundance. Pray in times of joy, give thanks to create more joy and multiply what you are thankful for. When you praise and bless, you magnify these blessings for your Self and others. Enhance what you love and make wishes for plenty more love in every area.

The desire to live happy, peaceful and honoring the strong desire of your heart and soul is not wrong; it is honoring the blessing of your life. The desire you feel is there for a reason.

My Core Values Are Valuable

Support your Self with the core values that define the incredible Amazing Soul that you are. Value your knowing. Name them. Own them! Name five core values that you love about your Self. These values are non-negotiable, regardless of what happens around you. This will also bring you back to center of being anchored in who you truly are. The same way your blood type does not change, regardless of the circumstances you are experiencing, your core values remain the same.

Do not negotiate your personal core values under any circumstances. Infuse these values into your "Movie." They are your supporting role in every scene. What you love about your Self is non-negotiable.

Those that love you and support you would not wish for you to negotiate them. *Allow and trust that the world will come to you based on the identity you own for your Self.* Know with every bit of your being, you are loved and there is great love for you. Have total certainty that Source Energy loves you and that you are seen and loved for all that you are. This includes your choices and experiences.

Ask! Ask for clarity, ask to know how to enhance all that you love about your Self and your life, ask for guidance and feel loving respect for your life of wishes granted.

Know That You Know

Trusting your feelings and intuition is key to all areas of your life. Instinctively knowing what feels right for you and trusting this, as your base *is* your life security. If you do not trust your Self, then the unknown will feel overwhelming and fearful. What if those experiences that feel overwhelming or fearful are opportunities given to you to master trusting your Self and bring you one step closer to your dreams?

Example of wishes to strengthen your expectations:

I know that my prayers are heard.
I believe my prayers are answered in the best possible way.
I am supported with love for my prayers to be answered in a way that is greater than my expectations.
I honor my Self as sacred and I feel honored by God.
I trust my own personal belief of Source Energy/God/Creator/Universal Energy/Love.
I deserve a good life. I do not deserve to be punished for my choices of honoring my Self.
I am living my life based on choices of honoring my Self.
The emotions I will enhance to expand my life are _____.
I expect _____ to happen in my life from now on.
I know that all that surrounds me is working in my favor.

Your Greatest Expectation Answered

If any of your answers are not a match for the expectation you wish for, no worries. You will create wishes to counter this with positive emotions. If you wish to feel stronger towards a belief that supports you, you will make wishes to enhance this. Remember it's your "Movie."

Through this process of questions and reflection, create clarity of what you expect in the life you are designing. Maybe some of this self-exploring will lead to other thoughts and questions or answers that give you clarity. Trust that everything that you feel is in perfect order to bring you closer to your greatest expectations.

The Reflection Of Your Prayer

Because of old habits, we may tend to pray for "help" when we feel we are lacking. Now imagine for a moment that your prayer carries emotional energy that is literally being transmitted in and out.

Now play with the notion that Universal Energy is like a big mirror. You send a prayer that has the energy of lack and then you receive a reflection back based on lack. The dominant feeling that you are praying with is reflected back to you as the foundation in which you will receive.

If at times you have doubts for what you expect with your prayers, this is understandable. Then make a conscious "Ask" to receive what will resolve your doubts within you emotionally. In the heat of our emotions, without realizing it, we can send out our prayer with excitement and then take it back with doubt or fear. Or we feel alone and separate from this Loving Energy to hold our prayer to answer it. This causes an energetic reaction of having the gas pedal on the floor, only to slam on the brakes and place the car in reverse.

What I am sharing with you is that shifting the emotion from which you ask will shift the way you receive because the emotion shifts the expectation. In times of need, ask to connect to a better feeling and ask for more of this to embody you, as opposed to asking out of desperation.

If you pray like a beggar, you receive like a beggar. Your manifestations will reflect this feeling back to you; you will not feel fully deserving of what you are receiving.

If you pray from a place of lack, you will receive struggle in your answer. There certainly are times in life where we can truly be in need of something, feel as though we lack something or genuinely be in desperation. This is a part of life! Sometimes we can be in such a strong place of emotional need that just the idea of feeling good can even be challenging.

This is all understandable. I am not suggesting you deny this being true for you or pretend all is well; I am simply sharing for you to ask for a better feeling to shift the feeling that does not serve you or in this case, ask to have the feeling of desperation released from you.

Wishes Can Only Involve Yourself

You cannot wish for another person. Any wish to influence the behavior or actions of another is a big "no-no" in Power Wishing. This is an important aspect to Power Wishing, as you are the director of your "Movie." You cannot direct other people's "Movie," even if you feel like you are the starring role in their life. Give them love, wish them more love and the rest will follow. Respect other people's journey. Stay out of other people's business and focus on your own. Do not wish for things to be different for them, wish for them to know the best of themselves and that they are loved. Wish them peace and wellbeing.

As we have shared, you can wish to change your attitude towards others. For example, you can ask to easily and patiently communicate with family members or a friend. You can wish for guidance or resolution within your Self towards another. You can create a wish that releases your negative feeling towards someone. You can ask to have understanding or forgiveness towards your loved ones. You can wish for yourself to feel different towards another but it is the other person's choice and decision to be who they are. Allow them to be themselves and stay focused on you.

At one time or another we may have been better at identifying what is lacking in our relationships rather than focusing on the blessings. Relationships go through different phases and sometimes we feel we are real experts on what the other is lacking. The next time you become an expert on someone else's lacks, whether this is a reality or not, take this ideal opportunity to check in with your Self first to confirm if you feel you are lacking any of those qualities within your Self.

Quite often we place so much focus on the other person as the reason that we do not have what we feel we should, either personally or in sharing our life with them. Stop making other people responsible for your choices. Release this from your energy. I am not validating their behavior; I am reminding you that you have choices on how you respond, not only to them but also to your life. Sometimes you are blessed to build closer relationships, and sometimes they dissipate or you have to walk away. I truly believe that when you honor yourself and others by being authentically sincere with your heart, many things happen to support the wellbeing of all. At times we may not be clear on what that looks like, but if we trust that honoring another will bring wellbeing, then whatever may come will be welcomed and a blessing for all.

Here are some thoughts to ponder and examples of wishes to honor your relationships:

Core beliefs that will support you in relation to others:

I know how to trust my choices in my relationships.
I know how to trust my emotions.
I know when to communicate with others in a non-defensive way.
I know how to communicate with others in a non-defensive way.
I know how to allow others to have their feelings without taking them personally or making the other wrong.
I know how to allow others to be themselves without being offended.
I know how to witness others without judgments.
I know how to listen to who they are without projecting my beliefs onto them.
I know how to strengthen my core belief that I am good enough for someone to truly love me for who I am.
I know what it feels like to be embraced for who I am authentically.
I know how to feel lovable, even when I feel I have disappointed my Self or another.
I know what it feels like to be in a loving relationship.
I know how to reinforce a foundation that supports the possibility of healthy relationships I desire.
I release drama in the relationships that surround me.
I know that I can see the truth of my relationship without feeling helpless.
I release blame towards others and my life circumstances.
I release the belief that relationships disappoint me.
I release the expectation of loved ones disappointing me.
I know that I have discernment about what my true feelings are and what feelings belong to another.
I know that I am able to create the relationship I believe is possible.
I trust that whatever happens in my relationships is for the best good.
I trust in my relationship with God/Source Energy to support me for resolution with painful situations.
I know how to express my core value as my identity in my relationships.

These are just a few examples of Power Wishes for relationships. If there is a particular relationship you would like to focus on then I suggest that you make the wish specific to them by using their name.

Expect What You Pray For

Here is an example of a client of mine named Margaret who came to work through relationship issues she was having with her husband. She complained about her relationship daily. She attracted a man that over time she felt did not respect her, who also triggered her to feel unlovable. She wished for a relationship with someone who would reinforce all she loved about herself, but instead had a partner who was very critical of her. She was frustrated and got upset because she was exhausted of praying. She also said affirmations for what she desired but it felt like things were actually getting worse. She was unhappy with a man who was not what she asked for. Or was he?

When Margaret began asking herself real questions about their relationship, being able to witness it without shame, blame or making herself wrong, she was able to observe things with a different perspective. She stepped back and did not focus on who was right or wrong, good or bad, saint or villain – she just observed. In observing her relationship as if she was looking at a case study without emotional projections, she could create an opportunity to have another possibility. She could move out of the pattern of blame towards her husband to know where she was accountable to take responsibility for her role in the relationship. Leaving his issues separate and focusing on her Self, she began to witness where she could make shifts.

She received clarity that her beliefs about her Self and what she believed about her relationship affected how she was receiving the answers to her prayer. Because of her self-critical beliefs, it would have been very challenging to have the healthy relationship she truly desired as she was praying from a place of being critical and resentful towards her situation. She began to focus on her Self and created wishes to enhance her positive qualities, along with releasing her own critical behaviors.

What she wished to receive in another she reaffirmed within. She also wrote wishes about releasing blame towards her partner. Her attention transferred towards her Self and away from her relationship. She knew that she wanted to feel whole and heal her Self before making a choice about what was truly going on in her present relationship. This also began to affect her in a positive way in other areas; she felt valuable and lovable as she prayed and expected to receive what she wished for.

Remember, keep it simple ... in Power Wishing we go back to the sophistication of basics as a powerful foundation to rebuild or strengthen your emotional structure.

Here is an example of some wishes that supported her:

I easily release the need to be critical of my Self.
I easily release the need to be critical of others.
I easily release the need to have critical people in my life.
I know how to easily have a relationship with others without being a critic.
I easily accept compliments.
I know how to compliment others.
I know what it feels like to easily love who I am.
I know what it feels like to easily be loved.
I easily know what it feels like to be loveable.
I know how to love another by focusing on the positive aspects of them.
I easily release the habit of blaming _____ for my discontent.
I know how to release complaining about _____ and replace that with finding positive attributes about _____.
I easily accept responsibility for my choice of _____.
I simply release holding others accountable for my choices.
I easily know how to release complaining about my relationship.
I easily release complaining about my past.
I know what it feels like to easily recognize where I am presently loved.
I know how to easily accept the love that surrounds me.
I know how to forgive my Self and others without shame.
I easily know how to pray, feeling hopeful that my prayers are answered.
I easily know how to pray, asking for supporting love in my life.
I know how to easily recognize my prayers being answered.
I know how to trust the action I take towards my answered prayers with enthusiasm.

What You Ask For May Already Exist

After her base of core beliefs felt solid and she witnessed them appear in her reality, she then started to make other wishes, manifesting the relationship she now knew was possible. In the case of Margaret, she chose to shift away from the relationship she had at the time, but many times what you are asking for in your relationship may already exist; it just requires a shift in *your* perspective to see it. When you shift, you are able to recognize things differently. When we shift the way we are observing the relationship, it has an opportunity to appear differently and then we can make a conscious decision for our choices.

I have often heard people compare their different relationships, and when asked to do this I have to ask myself how one can gauge a relationship against another for being better or worse? As I reflect on my different relationships and ask myself if I can gauge them, I feel that it is not possible. Every relationship brings different gifts and each is experienced at different stages in your life.

We all desire love and one of the ways this is experienced is through our relationships. Relationships, among many things, are doors that awaken aspects of us that can only be awakened through relating with others. At times we can take on beliefs about who we are because of the way we feel in a relationship. These beliefs may be true or may be a projection of another's beliefs onto you. I know if a relationship is positive for me based on how I feel about myself in relating with that person.

Ponder for a moment the times that you have created a relationship at a time when you felt secure and certain of who you are. The relationship was created as a by-product. It was an added value; it was not your sole value. You will find that in knowing your Self, you release the pursuit of chasing happiness and success because you know that by being your Authentic Self, you can create this anytime. I believe that relationships and desires are all positive excuses for us to discover more of ourselves. When we are in a relationship, this usually takes us to knowing ourselves differently.

Ask And Receive Your Answer

Ask, ask, ask. Ask your Self questions, and know your Self emotionally. Take moments to ask questions so that you may have the opportunity to be proactive towards answers showing up as your life. Your life experiences are steps that take you closer to your dreams being realized.

Asking For Love From Others

Now take a moment to reflect and feel which beliefs listed below resonate with you. Which do you relate to in reference to the way you ask from others? Pay attention to the questions that give you an emotional "gut feeling," so you may gain perspective of the beliefs you hold. This is your journey. Yours! Take your time to step back and witness and to allow yourself to sincerely explore your answers. Write out your answers so you can use this material to convert as your wishes.

Explore how you feel asking others to share in your desires:

Do you feel comfortable asking for what you want from others?

When it comes to asking others, have you ever regretted not asking for something?

Do you feel someone else (a boss, spouse, friend, salesperson, etc.) is in "control" of your result?

Do you change asking for what you wish for because you feel another person may be uncomfortable with what you are asking for?

Do you assume that the ones closest to you should know what you want and you should not have to ask for what you want from them?

If you have to ask for something that you feel should be a given because of the type of relationship you have with this person, do you stay quiet or do you communicate?

We often think that the ones closest to us can read our minds and know what we desire. Reflect for a moment on your patterns of communication and how you ask for what you would like to receive.

Do you wait to make sure that you have all your bases covered before you ask, meaning you probably never ask because you are waiting for the "perfect" moment or time?

What exactly is the "perfect time" anyway?

Do you clearly ask for what you desire from another and give them the opportunity to show up for you?

Do you blame others when you do not get what you want and hold them accountable for your choices?

When you clearly shared your wish with another, did you assume they felt a certain way or did you listen clearly to their response?

Do those you ask from truly have the capacity to give to you the way you desire?

Do you silently ask for a lot of things in your head, but because you may be anxious of how others will react, you do not ask directly?

Do you create behaviors so others will clue into what you need?

Do you believe it is demeaning to ask for certain things that feel to you like they should be a given, such as help at home, a raise or a promotion?

Do you become bitter or resentful because you did not get what you were asking for?

Do you believe it is impolite to ask for what you want if there are other people around?

Do you believe that asking for what you want is selfish?

Do you withhold asking because you feel you will be perceived as self-centered?

Do you feel your needs or desires are perceived as inferior or less important than the needs of others?

Do you feel others have bigger needs than you and you should not ask?

Have you had hurtful experiences when you have asked for what you wanted in the past?

Have you experienced an unpleasant history of receiving bad reactions from others when you ask for what you desire? Has this led you to not ask again?

Are you honest with the reasons why you are asking?

Do you fear that asking for what you wish for may alienate or infuriate others so it is safer not to ask?

Would you prefer not asking rather than risk being humiliated?

Do you feel you will be judged or rejected for asking? When do you feel this way?

Do you believe that you have so much and so it is not right to ask for more?

Do you believe that if you ask for too much it means you do not appreciate what you have?

Do you believe that you do not deserve to ask for something if your life has so many blessings?

Do you believe that asking is a way to let others in your life know that they are present and you trust them?

Did you know that there might be many people that would love to give to you if you let them know what you wish for?

Did you know that when you do not ask, some people might feel this as rejection?

Did you know that feeling gratitude for your blessings is asking for more of what you love and that you deserve more of what you appreciate?

Love Is Not To Be Sacrificed

Do you make time to reflect within your Self to have clarity on your decisions or do you find your Self seeking outside influences to reflect *for* you? Sometimes I hear people share that they take time to reflect and that outside influences do not dictate them. Then I hear them share the reasons why they have not made an important decision and yes ... this had to do with some influence outside of their Self.

The reasons are because outside influences convinced them in some way that they are powerless. Or they feel they have to sacrifice themselves for their children or parents or for other reasons. I am sure if those they feel they are sacrificing themselves for knew this, they would feel terrible and guilty that someone they love felt they had to sacrifice themselves. Do you feel you have made sacrifices? How does the feeling that you have made a sacrifice for the ones you love serve you? If this is so, what do you expect from them because of your *sacrifice*?

Let go of feeling you have to sacrifice on any level. Replace this with a choice.

Your True Wishes Are Known To You

Ask questions that really dig to getting real answers and allow your Self to receive real truth in your answers. At least know your truth for your Self. If an answer does not come right away, know that it will. Everything will come together. Having trust and patience with your Self, knowing that you are loved and supported in ways that may not be apparent in the moment, is a wish to strengthen. Sometimes we are not aware of how long we have avoided hearing our own answers. In order to fully know what your core belief is with what you desire, you must sincerely be honest with yourself.

You can only get it *right* with honoring your Self with truth. Truth defined by you as your emotional knowing. We can shift and have moments where we have different awareness. Your genuine emotional journey allows you to make choices that are in alignment with the present possibilities available to you and know how to activate them as wishes granted.

There is no judgment, there is no lack, there are the definitions we place based on our perceptions.

Connect lovingly towards how you feel, ask yourself questions and feel the answers knowing you will have the solutions. Also, know that connecting lovingly towards your Self resonates in your surroundings. The beautiful gift of embodying the real YOU is the alchemy that balances out your life in a soulful way.

Money Comes Easily To You

Yes, we all live a day-to-day life that may make us feel unable to dream of a different reality. For a moment, take a step back to witness your life with knowing that you can shift your reality. First let's witness the way you may be focusing your prayers. Say that you are in financial hardship and the natural reaction to this is you pray for more money because your bills are piling up.

Obviously, if you felt you had a choice, you would wish to receive more money without struggle, not by working longer hours or spending more time on the road. What if you could receive more income without the struggle? I am sure you are saying to yourself, "Of course I would love to have more financial security without struggle." My question to you is, "Do you believe this is possible to receive without struggle and challenge?"

If you do not believe this is a possibility for you, here are some examples for your wishes:

I know how to trust that money can easily flow to me.
I know how to receive more financial income without struggle.
I know how to work efficiently with my time.

If you already believe that more financial income is possible without struggle, then your Power Wish could be:

I recognize other opportunities for increased income with ease.
I know how to trust myself to recognize financial opportunities.
I easily with confidence take action towards opportunities present to me.
I am a magnet that easily attracts more income with my talent.
I know how to increase my income with what I am presently doing.

Money, Money, Money

Let's continue on the subject of money. When you feel stressed about your bills and you need *relief* from this pressure, you may feel that wishing for more money will bring you this *relief*, and this is obvious.

The awareness I would like for you to have is that relief can be created through more money or other opportunities. Because money is the only way you are expecting to receive more relief, you may not be open to recognizing relief is actually coming to you in other ways or there is opportunity for relief in other areas. Yes, you are praying for more money, but perhaps the strongest dominant feeling is receiving relief and money is one option. Therefore, relief may come in others ways where money may not give you the relief you expect and possibly feeling relief in other areas will support you to be relaxed with creating more money. With Power Wishing, we go for the big picture, not just the pieces of one area.

So let's play with this for a moment. What if you wished for relief in unexpected ways? This way you are open to other possibilities besides money. Create a wish for knowing what it can feel like to receive relief from different possibilities, that you trust this, you recognize this and you believe that you deserve this. This way you would feel more relaxed and have more positive beliefs about creating money, and therefore money will come more easily because you are relaxed.

Ask your Self, "If I felt relief in this area of money, what would be different in my life today?" Play with those opportunities in your "Movie." Create scenes in your "Movie" of the feeling of having relief now, with plenty of abundance in different areas of your life, including more money.

Again, the feeling that matches what you wish for will create the foundation for your expectation. There is an Energy of Love that loves you without conditions that desires to enhance what you have asked for based on your expectation. You are not alone in your desires; you have Source Energy boosting up your prayer.

Let us consider the way one may be asking when there is a feeling there is something lacking in life. We have established that you do not want to continue to attract more lack, but perhaps, unintentionally, this is the message you are sending out.

When you feel you do not have what you wish, it is possible that attached to your prayer are feelings of being unworthy to receive, or feelings of being a victim, or other beliefs that may dominate the frequency of how you receive. Your prayer is: "I am lacking … help!", "I am lacking money because I feel unworthy" or "I am not talented enough to receive the money I wish for easily!"

So the Universal Computer gives you back the answer to your request with the message of "money received with struggle to prove yourself."

Situations are emotional; emotion is what has brought you to your "Ask." Ask with the emotion of how you wish to feel supported through your experience.

So if you feel you lack talent to receive the money you wish for, then ask to recognize the value of your talents. Ask to know how to honor what your talent is. Ask to find opportunities to expand your talent. Ask how to shift your focus from what you lack to what you wish to enhance.

Your Emotions Are A Magnet

Many times people focus on creating wishes in each section of their life: a relationship, money, a car or a job. They believe that these manifestations will bring them some kind of satisfaction.

In creating wishes based on things, people may begin to act and feel like a different person in each different scenario in their life depending on what they think is expected from them to create each thing they say they want. They may present one side of themselves in their job, another in their relationship, and another with their family because the focus is about getting what they want. This can become an exhausting chase, trying to figure out how you must be to create a match to your wish.

Through Power Wishing, you instead create an emotional foundation that is the magnet that attracts all that you desire to feel. Life becomes emotionally stable and your Authentic Voice is strengthened and represented in all areas of your life, equally as the authentic you. Release the habit of creating emotionally messy patterns by giving other people, circumstances and things power to make you happy or give you peace.

Your life choices become really clear when you are emotionally healthy and when you find what you are looking for within your Self. You do not have to be perfect in your emotions in order to achieve. Just follow your Emotional GPS and strengthen what you wish to build internally. Then all that you accumulate is an added value to who you are and you release the fear of losing anything. The outside world adds to your life but cannot take away from you what is yours internally.

"Don't aim at success – the more you aim at it and make it a target, the more you are going to miss it. For success, like happiness, cannot be pursued; it must be a result … as an unintended side-effect of one's personal dedication to a course greater than oneself." – Viktor Frankl

When you are able to view your life as a discovery of YOU instead of accumulating an identity outside of yourself, then life is like a treasure hunt rather than a road of faults. Focusing in this manner, the treasures that seemed hidden are now alive within you, which only creates a reflection of this outside of you. Then you are more aware of what you love about YOU and you find more love within your Self. You attract more love. You feel happy and then every light is green and every parking spot is yours.

Dreams Are Possible, When We Are Ready

At one of my workshops, a woman named Lysette stood up and announced that she would like to change careers. She had a good corporate job but really desired to work for herself as a massage therapist. She stated that one of her biggest concerns was that she feared she could not create the clientele to financially support herself. Interactively with the group, we formulated Power Wishes that would support her emotional base to have security in her decision to change careers. During the seminar, four or five people raised their hands to say that they would be her first clients. She looked around at the people and started to cry and everyone was surprised. Why would she cry if she just received what she said was her biggest concern that she wished to resolve? I witness this often and understand that people rarely know how to receive what they have been asking for. She had never asked for clients out loud and when she received this so easily, in that moment she recognized her fear of taking on this new change and not knowing how to receive so easily. In continuing to explore her underlying belief, she realized that she did not deserve to be able to do what she would enjoy for work. She believed that she did not feel it was possible to do what she enjoys and still make an income. To her surprise, the strongest belief that came up for her was that her mother would not be proud of her choice of this new career and would be disappointed in her.

I suggested that before she goes into detail with wishes about the business plan of her new career, she strengthen the emotional foundation within herself. This way the business would have an opportunity to succeed with an emotional base of self-worth and acceptance of her choices. It seemed as though she held a belief that massage therapy was not as professional or respected as her executive position. She admitted that she was sabotaging herself with beliefs, even though she greatly desired to shift careers.

She was concerned about her mother as she is close with her and did not wish to feel she would disappoint her. She decided to be proactive towards those feelings in the hopes that her mother and she could even be closer. As I shared earlier, you cannot wish for another to feel a certain way as we can only shift ourselves. But Lysette understood that the best opportunity she had for her relationship was to reinforce within her what she perceived her mother felt she lacked. Where she believed her mother would be disappointed in her, Lysette reflected on areas where she might be disappointed in her Self and addressed her beliefs in these areas.

153

Based on her feelings, the following wishes would serve her transition:

I trust in myself.
I trust in my decision.
I have confidence in my ability.
I feel worthy; I have self-worth.
I release the struggle of having to work so hard.
I release the fear of working for myself.
I know that I have the capability to be financially independent on my own.
I release the belief that I must receive financial abundance through struggle.
I can be compensated financially to support myself with work that I enjoy.
I know how to accept my choices.
I release fear of judgment from those I love.
I allow others to be disappointed without feeling I have to change my choices.
I know how to acknowledge my Self with my courage to follow my dream.
I accept others' perceptions of my decision without feeling I have to change my choice.

Reflect for a moment about your beliefs on receiving:

Do you feel that you desire something, but then feel insecure or unworthy about receiving it? Do you have to overcompensate in order to receive?
Do you have a habit of sabotaging your opportunities? Awareness is a key factor.
Is there something you truly desire or a change in your life you would like to make? How would you feel if this could really materialize?

Poof! Your Magic Wand Grants Your Wishes

What if your "Magic Wand" gave you something you truly desire, right now? No questions asked about why you want this and all you have to do is receive your wish.

Are you ready to have this now? How would that feel? What is the greatest fear you have about this occurring? Name it. What do you fear about having what you truly desire?

If you did not fear in having it, you would have created it. Fears are perceptions of what we believe could happen. It ultimately is the deciding belief that affects your possibilities. Make wishes to release your fears towards the possibility so you may receive and reinforce positive emotions that support the possibility you wish for.

I can assure you that if the issue of not knowing how to receive is coming up for you, as it did for Lysette, it is also showing up in other areas of your life. As for Lysette, the focus was on her business, which gave her insight into the underlying emotions that connected to her receiving. As Lysette shared more in the workshop, she was able to connect to her experiences of receiving in other areas of her life. With this understanding, she simultaneously cleaned up other areas in her life that had to do with the same issue.

Health – Wealth – Prosperity: Our Birthright

I believe that it is a natural part of our existence to be healthy and wealthy in all we desire. We live in a physical world. Being wealthy and having things is not the issue; it is the power we give these things that can lead us to feel a certain way. It is the reasons why we created the need for these things that makes the difference. If money is one's identity of success, then there will always be the fear of not being successful if you do not have money or an intense fear of losing it. If one feels successful internally, then money and other things are not what define them.

Emotion-based wishing is powerful because you can create far more of what you desire from feeling worthy than attempting to create more financial abundance by focusing on how you are not. Feeling worthy as a base will create more than just financial worth. It is the magnet that attracts more wealth and abundance to you.

When you are enhancing the best of you, focus on being a better person because of your dedication to your Self, not because you lack something. Enhancing your best Self manifests your dream.

Focusing on enhancing and expanding who you are and living true to this gives you all you are asking for. Life accomplishments are not about what you accumulate, but about the pursuit of all these experiences, which are taking you to a discovery of you.

Love Sustains All

Remember that no matter what you create or what you wish for, the most valuable element, what sustains all, is love. Create your wishes through love, sharing and gratitude for your blessings, while being present and authentic.

Power Thoughts

Exploring What To Ask

o   I strengthen the claim of my expectation by writing my wishes.

o   I trust that all is well and I expect to receive all that is well.

o   I know the power of simplicity.

o   I am driving the expectation of my journey.

o   I have dreams that are to be lived; this is why I have them.

o   The dreams that hold dear to my Soul are non-negotiable.

o   The time is NOW.

o   My life is a discovery of my Divine Self.

o   I am a magnet that attracts more wealth and abundance to my life.

o   Love sustains all.

Writing Your Power Wishes – Guidelines

In the Guidelines of Power Wishing® we will explore the details of writing your wishes. You will understand the process as it relates to different areas of your life and will begin structuring your wishes specifically. This section is designed like a workbook to ponder and explore within. Refer to what you need; skip over what does not apply; and go back to it when you fine-tune your wishes. Write your wishes playfully, have fun and allow your imagination to envision all that you truly desire, with the expectation to receive this. In writing out your wishes, take yourself literally as you ask for what you desire. As you read your request, see what is really being asked for exactly word for word, as if it's an order taken by a waitress or a command programmed into a computer. When reading your written wishes this gives you perspective to create clarity.

Create A Ritual

Wishes can be written at any time. Nevertheless, I feel that creating a ritual with writing your wishes can bring conscious awareness and give importance to this process. This is your life and you are claiming your choice of how you wish to experience it. Give importance to what can support the way you love, feel, think and wish to live. Ritual may have different definitions for different people, though universally it means *formal procedure, service, ceremony, habit, practice or routine*.

Nature is a wonderful guide for us; it has its own cycles of energy that can support the flow of your wishes. In ancient cultures, and even today, we can measure and take advantage of the movement of the celestial system to assist us with everything from planting seasons to decision-making. Changes of nature are influenced by the lunar cycle; the new moon is known as a time of giving direction to new beginnings. It is a good time to "plant" your intentions and make your wishes. In astrology, each lunar phase has a specific purpose or theme. For example, a certain month may have an astrological sign that may have traits that are also a focus for you, so utilize this energy to accelerate your manifestation.

You could also write your wishes on the same day every month. I suggest that you only write your wishes once a month to allow some space in time to witness the growth of how you are manifesting. Allowing time to pass also gives you the ability to recognize and reflect on what is appearing in your reality based on your expectations. As you reflect on your wishes monthly, you will observe a pattern of how you receive. Then each month you can make adjustments to receive the way you expect.

Use a Handwritten Journal

I suggest that you handwrite your wishes. You may type them in your computer first but then transfer them to a handwritten journal. Handwriting is an action of grounding and claiming your wishes to be a physical reality; this is an extra step that reflects a deeper persistence with your intention, the same way there is a more profound response when you send your personal sentiments with a handwritten note rather than via email.

When you begin to intentionally state to yourself what patterns you would like to shift or enhance and what you truly desire on a monthly basis, you create a rhythm where you are fine-tuning your Vibrational Language® to be in synergy connecting you to everything you wish for.

When you start to write your wishes, there may be a long list of so many things you desire. Believe me, you will get to them all and create more along the way. As a suggestion, begin your focus on one main desire and create wishes to emotionally support this main desire. Your written wish should be short, sweet and to the point. Write down a minimum of 6 and no more than 12 wishes per month. In the beginning, keep focused on the emotions of a main desire, and then as that desire gets resolved, you may like to add a few more towards other areas. Remember that the manifestation of your desire depends on your belief towards it, so focus on how you expect to receive. Keep your wishes precise and simple. Keep one focus at a time. Play with dreaming and wishing, knowing they can come true.

Positive Emotional Patterns

Through Power Wishing you have consciously asked for change, so expect that things around you will begin to shift. Imagine if you have a line of stacked dominos and you pull one because it is your favorite number; the other dominos in the line have to change as a result of this shift. This is true with your experiences, people, events and your own attitudes that will change as a response to the shifts you have asked for in your life. Welcome these new changes. Some may seem positive and others not. Be patient and release judgment towards what appears negative. Things are not always what they seem. View the changes around you as evidence that your life is changing as a result of what you have asked for.

Yes, Power Wishing is about witnessing your wishes come true, but to me it is bigger than this. It is about understanding your emotional patterns. Keeping a Power Wishing journal will help you notice patterns in your life. Acknowledge and validate the themes that reoccur, witness them and make new choices. Embrace those wishes that come true as you are strengthening the construction of your life with positive emotional patterns, which is the greatest wish of all.

Guidelines for Writing Your Power Wish:

- Use positive language that supports your desires.
- Use clear and concise language to describe your "Ask."
- Use clear and concise language of how you expect to receive.
- Address underlying emotional blocks to create an emotional release or shift.
- Keep it simple, one desire at a time.
- Enhance positive qualities and strengths to support your expectation.
- Use present tense format as if the wish is already realized.
- Use the words and phrases from Language Your Life® to describe how you wish to receive: "with joy and ease," "harmoniously," "quickly," etc.
- Avoid asking from a place of need, struggle or lack; know you are worthy to receive.
- You may include the phrase "for my best good" in your wishes as a way to honor co-creation to enhance variations of your wish that would serve you best.
- Sometimes we may expect to receive a certain way; "Ask" to be able to recognize your wish being granted.
- If you are not sure how to handle a situation or know what to wish for, you can wish for guidance and also make a separate wish to recognize this guidance.
- You cannot wish for others to do things or be a certain way.

Review and Reflect

You can review your wishes whenever you want, but do not read them every day or obsess over them. Allow them to breathe. My suggestion is to reflect on them once a month and grow in trusting your process. Let them go once your intentions have been purely set. Continue to grow with who you are. Trust this, trust your Self and trust that you are loved more than you can imagine and are never alone. Enjoy life from this perspective.

Some wishes become realized soon after you write them. Others may take more time, and you can continue to adjust them monthly until they come true for you. If some wishes seem to be taking longer, then examine the underlying emotions that may be hindering this wish from manifesting or make adjustments to the wording of your wish. If you bundle up too many expectations in your wish, you could lose the potency and direction of your "Ask." As you evolve, so do your wishes and you will adjust them accordingly.

Your Words Are Magnets

When you write your wishes, use words that work to attract what you desire and avoid words that block receiving. For example, the word "need" implies that your wish comes from a place of lacking something. When you say, "I need more money," it feels as if you are asking to receive something that you are deficient of. Asking from a base of lack can only set the stage to receive more lack and challenge as a match.

The phrase "I attract money into my life easily" or "Money comes more easily to me" is setting the stage to ask from a place of feeling worthy where you are enhancing your current situation. You are asking from a base of already knowing how it feels to have money and wishing for plenty more. Therefore, you will receive the match to this. This is a specific and immediate implication that you are ready to receive without struggle. Again, be aware that your emotional beliefs are in line with what you are wishing for.

Replace the words "need" with *Desire, Wish, Command.* Feel your words as a magnet attracting for you.

Another example of a word to avoid is "lose." The word "lose" is a common word associated with weight, but the real meaning of "lose" connotes that you would like to find what you lost again! Language Your Life recommends that you replace the word "lose" with "shed."

Using a word that is not the most effective can feel like driving a car with one foot on the gas pedal and one on the brake. The car may still move forward but it is also slowing down and may even jolt back. It is a contradictory effect that cancels itself out. This is basically what we do when we ask for something but have a belief system that prevents us from receiving what we are asking for.

The goal in creating a powerful and effective "Ask" with your wishing is that you have a clear and concise belief of how you expect to receive your request. It should feel like you have your foot on the gas pedal and you are driving straight forward with ease with your GPS fully charged with an emotional foundation that is on target.

One of the best ways to review the language you are using to write your wishes is to first read them literally – very literally, as in without any emotional connection. Review them this way to assess your language. Later you will read them to feel if they ring true for you.

It is also very common that when people ask to be able to pay off their debts, they ask for more money because they need to pay their bills. I would also suggest that you create another wish to be "debt-free." Also, if you are feeling pain, ask to be "pain-free." Use words that bring to you what you wish and, if ever in doubt, use the phrase "free of," as this clears you from the weight of what is holding you back.

Say these words out loud to yourself and sense which words feel better to you and which ones have more resistance or less resistance:

Pay Off Debt vs. Debt-Free
Approval vs. Self-Worth
Comparison vs. Honoring Individuality
Chaos vs. Balance
Defending vs. Communicating
Need vs. Desire
Doubt vs. Confidence
Fear-Based vs. Empowered
Shame vs. Acceptance
Surviving vs. Living
Could vs. Can
Problem vs. Challenge
Worry vs. Concerns

Each word can refer to the same thing, but upon comparison, there is one version that holds a more encouraging energy to support you. These words have a supportive tone that can be used to master your Vibrational Language to accelerate what you expect.

Positive Word List

When creating your written Power Wish, you can use the following words as suggestions to illustrate positive vibration:

- Awareness, Abundant, Acceptance, Adept, Awaken, Alertness
- Blessed, Being, Beauty, Balance, Belonging
- Creative, Clarity, Caring, Compassion, Conscious, Connection, Centered, Courage, Choice
- Discernment, Divinity
- Essence, Enthusiastic, Enlightenment, Evolve, Ease, Embrace, Expanding, Empower
- Faith, Flow, Forgiveness, Focus
- Grace, Graceful, Gratitude, Giving, Guidance, Greatness, Growth, Generosity, Grounded
- Happy, Harmony, Harmonious, Heart, Heart-Centered
- Inspired, Inspiration, Intent, Intuitive, Integrity
- Joy
- Kind, Kindness
- Love, Light
- Mindful, Manifestation
- Nurturing
- Open, Oneness
- Peace, Power, Peaceful, Positive, Play
- Radiant, Release, Receptivity
- Strong, Serene, Self-Love, Supportive, Strength, Success
- Tranquil, Truth, Transform, Trust
- Universal, Understanding
- Vision, Vulnerability
- Will, Wisdom, Wholeness, Worthy, Wise

More Word Suggestions

When you write your wish, remember you are giving an exact clear order claiming what you expect. Write exactly what you wish for and how you wish to receive it; this is your Magic Wand. Sometimes this may mean releasing emotions that are in the way of your expectation.

Here are additional word suggestions to construct your Power Wishes:

- Easily
- Releasing … fear, struggle, doubt, rejection
- Without struggle
- Discernment
- Resolving
- Gracefully
- Enjoyment
- Deserving
- With ease
- I know what it feels like to …
- I trust that …
- I recognize …
- I acknowledge …
- I know how to …

Shift Your Wish from Lack to Empowerment

Sometimes we cannot feel empowered towards a loss, or what we feel we are lacking. This feeling can also occur when we wish to do something for someone we love but feel helpless. Create a wish of how you would like to feel, even if you do not feel this yet. In doing this you are creating the anchor of what you would like by fine-tuning your language and this will gently offset the intensity of feeling lack or helplessness and support you to receive differently.

An example of asking from a place of lack:

I know how to feel inner- strength (or understanding) in dealing with my loss.

Examples of enhanced wishing:

I easily recognize the strength I possess within.
I am easily shown where I am strong without creating experiences to prove this.
I ask to be shown the opportunities to strengthen my healing process.
I ask for peace.
I know what it feels like to be peaceful.

An example of asking from a place of lack when worried about another:
Please don't let my mother get worse.

Examples of enhanced wishing:

I easily release my feeling of helplessness towards my mom.
I strengthen my trust in the love that surrounds my mom to support her with her will.
I send my mom love, may she feel my love.
May the love I feel for my mom strengthen her, if this is her will.
I send Absolute Love and healing Light to my mother. May she use this love for her healing, if this is her will.

As you say a prayer for another knowing that you have the best of intention for them, in Power Wishing we are very respectful and honor others and their choices. Make sure you place "if it is their will" so it is *their* choice to receive your prayer as an enhancement to *their* life wishes.

An example of asking from a place of lack:
Please help me with my job.

Examples of enhanced wishing:

Show me the opportunities for a career that is a match to my desires.
I easily recognize opportunity for the career of my desires.
I know how to get out of my own way to ask for what I believe is possible in my job.
I easily appreciate the value I contribute to my job.
I know how to appreciate the opportunities I have now.
I know my appreciation leads me to other opportunities.
I effectively communicate my wishes.

Exploring Power Wishes

Below are *different* samples, separated into categories, of how to format your wish as you write them. Be playful and go for your greatest potential as you design your emotional foundation to support your dreams. Feel free to personalize the construction of your wish with your own phrases.

ACTIVATING YOUR POTENTIAL

"I easily recognize decisions that are in alignment with my potential."
"I easily find myself taking action with my decisions that are in alignment with my potential."
"I know what it feels like to be patient with myself while achieving my goals with inspiration and ease."
"I easily find myself embracing the habit of self-discipline, feeling energized as I follow this."
"With ease, I know what it feels like to recognize my accomplishments with appreciation of myself."

SUCCESS

"I easily find myself initiating action to support my success with enthusiasm towards _____."
"With ease, I completely release the self-sabotaging habit of creating worry that inhibits my success (or you can be specific.)"
"I know what it feels like to easily replace my worry with trust in my abilities to succeed."
"I easily find myself having clarity of how to attain my goal of _____."
"I easily find myself taking action toward the clarity receive of how to attain my goal of _____."
"The habit of accepting chaos as a way of motivation is easily lifted from me completely without feeling unproductive."
"I easily know what it feels like to replace chaos with joy and experience this as a normal way of life."
"I easily trust what I value in myself, especially in the area of _____."
"I know what it feels like to make decisions based on how I value myself as a secure foundation for my success."
"I easily take action with trusting the decisions I make, especially in the are of _____."

COMMUNICATION

"My inner thoughts serve my wishes to be fulfilled with ease."
"I easily find myself communicating my wish in a non-defensive way."
"I easily find myself being consistent with communication that is in alignment with my wishes."
"I easily find myself feeling safe to trust who I am as I express my thoughts and feelings to others."
"I easily approach decisions with awareness of my communication which honors the clarity I have to succeed."
"With ease, I find myself listening to others while honoring my boundaries."
"I easily find myself responding to challenges in a way that honors my heart and Soul with calmness."
"I easily find myself communicating my challenges with solution oriented language."
"I easily release my fears of being myself when I communicate with others."
"I know how to easily trust that I can effectively communicate with _____."

CREATIVITY

"I easily find myself expressing my creativity in ways that feel good to me."
"I easily express my creativity in front of others enhancing my visibility in a positive way."
"I easily find myself allowing my childlike nature to guide me into new ways of having fun, with spontaneous joy."
"I easily find myself taking time to be playful with being creative in my imagination."
"I easily find myself using my creative imagination to find solutions to my concerns."
"My imagination is easily inspired to envision new and beautiful experiences with joy."
"With ease, I know what it feels like to use my imagination to support me to envision my goals as reality."
"My imagination is a consistent tool that I easily create positive possibilities with."

JOY

"I easily recognize the experience of having joy in my life."
"I easily choose joyful experiences rather than unnecessary drama."
"I easily acknowledge the joy in my life."
"I feel a joyful ease with experiencing my Authentic Self in my daily life."
"I easily know what it feels like to attract happiness in my life."
"I easily find joy replacing my sorrow with _____ ."
"I am easily able to stay joyful in all my surroundings without being influenced by the negativity of _____ ."
"I joyfully find myself pursuing those activities that increase happiness in my life."
"I gracefully and easily find myself experiencing life in a way that brings me meaningful joy."
"With joy and ease, I know what it feels like to be in a healthy and loving relationship."

SELF-LOVE & SELF-WORTH

"I easily recognize my self-worth."
"I easily know what it feels like to be worthy."
"I easily acknowledge my value."
"With ease, I know what it feels like to recognize my emotions without doubting my feelings."
"I easily release the need to identify myself with my insecurities and replace this with appreciating myself."
"I easily know what it feels like to peacefully accept myself for who I am."
"I easily find time to nurture myself."
"I easily accept being nurtured by others."
"I easily release feeling guilty for taking care of myself."
"I easily know what it feels like to enjoy doing things that make me happy without feeling stress."
"I easily release critical and unworthy Self talk."
"I easily reinforce my best emotional Self by taking moments in the day to center myself."
"I easily release all self-defeating behaviors and replace them with self-love."
"I easily know what it feels like to love my Self."

FRIENDSHIPS & FAMILY

"I easily find myself seeing the good in others when I gracefully connect with them."
"I easily find myself genuinely feeling relaxed and interested in developing new friendships."
"I easily release the tendency to control _____ in our relationship."
"The tendency to project my insecurity of _____ onto others is totally lifted from me with ease."
"I easily find myself desiring to be present when spending time with my family."
"I easily know what it feels like to feel peaceful and happy to go home to spend time with my family."
"I easily release my critical approach with _____ and replace this with acceptance of their decision."

RELATIONSHIPS

"I easily know how to ask for what I wish for in a relationship without doubting that it can happen for me."
"I easily find myself effectively communicating in a positive way my feelings in my relationship with _____."
"I know what it feels like to have clear discernment towards choosing potential loving partners."
"I easily find my actions supporting the loving connection between _____ and me."
"I easily attract a male/female partner who shares my understanding of what love means."
"I know how to have healthy boundaries that support the best of me in my relationship with _____."

FINANCIAL WEALTH & STABILITY

"I easily release all doubt of supporting myself financially."
"I trust in the financial plan I have created to support my financial wellbeing easily."
"I easily know what it feels like to have wealth."
"I know how to create wealth without struggle."
"I easily have fun making money."
"I know what it feels like to be debt-free."

"I easily know how to successfully stay within my budget."
"I easily find myself taking responsibility for my finances and feeling empowered with my decisions."
"I know what it feels like to release worry about my finances."
"I easily know what it feels like to replace worry about my finances with enhanced positive energy for my financial abundance."
"The habit of overusing my credit cards is completely lifted from me with ease and accomplishment."
"I easily replace the habit of overusing my credit cards with being creative utilizing what I have now."
"I easily feel confident in knowing how to mange my wealth as it continues to increase."
"I know how to easily feel financially independent with fearing my future while being debt-free.

SHIFTING HABITS

"I easily know how to keep consistent behaviors that support me by being conscious of my actions and reflecting on them throughout the day."
"I easily find myself using moments of confusion as a constructive way to have clarity and to remove the chaos in my life."
"The habit of procrastination is easily lifted from me."
"I easily know how to live my life with my values regardless of the opinions of others."
"I easily know how to live my life with my values while respecting the opinions of others."
"I easily know what it feels like to have patience as I witness my life unfolding."
"I easily trust that life is unfolding in ways that serve my best interests and I have patience with this."

Stage Your Day Technique

Through years of practicing and teaching visualization techniques and various forms of meditation, I am often asked by my students and clients, "How do you meditate?" I get asked this question over and over again and many people share their concerns about whether they are practicing meditation correctly or not. They wonder if they need to do it a certain way or have a certain set-up to practice.

Meditation is a reflection for the Soul to be heard and given a voice. My belief is that there are many ways in which we can meditate in our life. Any moment when you are present in your being can be a meditation. When you take a moment to focus, you are consciously connecting on a vibrational level. You are a walking sacred prayer and your life is a reflection of your prayers answered. Meditation supports you to be present in the reflection of this.

Focused Intention

By taking a moment to have focused feelings towards an experience, you strengthen your emotional foundation as a meditation. Imagine for a moment that you are building a house. The most important focus in building your home is making sure the foundation is solid. Once completed and holding all your personal belongings inside, you rest assured expecting that your house stands safe and secure because of the solid foundation you focused on building.

Like building a home, you lay a solid foundation of feelings: wellbeing, worthiness, trust and a sense of deserving with ease knowing what it feels like to love and be loved. Imagine more of your life being built from this emotional foundation.

The building of our emotional structure supports everything in our lives but is sometimes overlooked. Sometimes, we build a life on a foundation of emotions that do not serve our happiness or we find ourselves attached to the habit of building from a foundation of struggle or using a foundation we did not lay for ourselves.

Meditation allows you to take a moment to create awareness of your emotional foundation to choose what strengthens your foundation and what does not. Then we can choose to enhance what works for us or shift what does not through the energy of meditation or prayer. Using meditation as a tool for focused intention, you create a solid healthy emotional structure for yourself that will support whatever experiences you have in your life.

Meditation is not about connecting or re-connecting to God or supporting Love that surrounds you, for I believe we are always connected. It is more an *observation* of this connection as a partnership and an anchoring to a conscious awareness and appreciation of this. *It is about feeling the knowing of Source Energy as a co-creator with you.* It is also about strengthening your trust that you are fully supported by this partnership and all that surrounds you with so much love.

Meditation is any time where you consciously go to a place in your imagination and acknowledge your feelings, where you take a moment to play with all the possibilities of what you desire. This can also be in the present moment, where you feel time stop as you consciously connect with your Self. In this space, possibilities are felt in a way that feels real and where you have genuine acknowledgment that there is so much love that surrounds you. In this space you are asking for what you expect to receive.

Reflection For The Soul

I share my *Stage Your Day Technique,* as well as other meditations such as the *Reboot* and the *Movie Technique,* as a valuable way to meditate and anchor your intentions for creating your world. Meditation exists in different forms. There are many great teachers, books, videos and information for both formal and informal meditation. My style is to keep things simple and support people to practice a meditation that personally resonates with them and gives them the results they wish. To me, when you take a moment to consciously connect and reflect, to be with yourself this is also a meditation. There is no wrong way of doing this. You can only get it right when you are caring for your Self in a positive way. I have done many different forms of meditation at different times of my life. Sometimes I would sit and meditate for lengths of time, while other times dance was my form of meditation. As my life changes, so does my form of meditation. Whether you follow a formal way to meditate or if you wish to daydream or dance, these are all wonderful practices.

Whatever works for you is the best meditation. How one meditates is personal, as is one's definition of God, which is to be respected. What works for someone may not work for another. Once I had a client who lived a busy life and had several thousand employees. He would say to me that he needed to meditate but felt he could not sit and quiet his mind for 20 minutes and this was causing him such anxiety. I looked at him with humor and he said, "But isn't that the right way to meditate? I am supposed to sit for 20 minutes or longer and not allow thoughts to go through my head." I shared with him that this may work for some people, but for him and so many others with so much going on in their head, this may not be the best meditation practice to start with.

Many of us may have anxiety at just the thought of attempting to have no thoughts. He saw the humor in his situation: how could he have so many thoughts, so many exciting projects, so much going on in his mind, and then expect himself to have no thought. The reality was that his worries, thoughts and feelings were all going a thousand miles an hour. So, for him to sit and clear his thoughts, and have a silent mind in a deep meditative state was perhaps not the best option for him to begin as a meditative practice. He would be ignoring his thoughts, pushing them away rather than transforming or transcending them. He enjoyed running, so I suggested that he run and get that "runner's high." This is a form of meditation as well. I used to run quite a bit and I found that this, along with other forms of exercise, is a powerful way to create and connect where there is a silence to hear and see clearly. In that state of *runner's high*, I felt present without resistance to allowing prayer and anchoring my expectation.

At the moment, my favorite meditative space is the beach. During my walks on the beach before I go to bed, I hear the waves and it calms me. I have less wandering thoughts because the thoughts that do show up in my mind support the choices that sustain me. The sound of the waves and the smell of the salt air take me to a feeling of being present with such gratitude. I feel myself wrapped in prayer with such love from Spirit and all aspects of my life. As my mind floats in rhythm with the waves, my imagination drifts to feelings of peace.

Sometimes I see pictures, past memories that are enjoyable and feelings that add value to my vision. I have had many different experiences with life, love, loss, and illness. I have grown and with this growth, I have released questioning what is a "right" or "wrong." Personally, I do not attempt to control my mind or my feelings, I prefer to be in a state of allowing and witness like a Movie.

I connect with how I feel, and if something does not feel good for me, then I focus on going to a place with my experiences that can feel peaceful. This supported me to become liberated of the habit of viewing my experiences in a judgmental way and I feel my mind relax in a peaceful state with no real thoughts.

The practice of your meditation should not feel as though it is more work. It should feel inviting, relaxing, nurturing and comforting. Meditation is a way to enhance a solid foundation of self-love. It creates a space where you feel good about connecting with your Authentic Self and the "Love Energy" that surrounds you.

Yes, meditation is valuable for sure, but your practice is personal, so do what works for you. It can be formal or casual, individual or in a group – a dance, a run, a walk, a swim or simply sitting and breathing.

My Emotional Gifts

Our life is the creation of our emotions attached to the pictures we create in our imagination. Your emotions are your gift … your birthright. By recognizing this awareness of your emotions as a gift, you allow your emotions to perform as an inner navigation system to fulfill all that you desire. Now imagine that our Vibrational Language® carries our expectations that were set by our emotions. For a moment, pretend that your Vibrational Language is like a perfume that enters the room before you are even seen. When you place a perfume on your body, you have an intention of the way you would like to be perceived with this smell. Your intention is like an aroma that precedes you, attracting to you what you expect.

Your Vibrational Language is what is communicating everything about you. If you take a moment to set the direction with your intention, then your day unfolds smoothly and flows in alignment. You release questioning whether an experience is good or bad; you simply observe it as a component of your expectation and align your emotions accordingly.

Stage Your Day Technique

Stage Your Day Technique is a practice that supports you to set your intention before you start your day. We all have busy lives with so many thoughts that are racing through our head along with huge "to do" lists and it can sometimes feel like we are chasing our day. Many times we are not present and it feels like our day ended before it even got started.

Besides feeling chaotic, this can also lead us to follow the direction of the energy of others rather than attracting the energy to support us.

I realize how vital and effective it is to take a moment to focus on how I wish to feel before my day even gets started. I created the *Stage Your Day Technique* because it makes such a difference to the way I respond to an experience versus reacting to it. My energy is organized with more clarity and not easily influenced by other people's energy surrounding me that may be chaotic.

By imagining my day before it happens and playing with the emotions I wish to feel that day, I am setting my emotional stage. Basically, I am commanding with my Vibrational Language that no matter what happens today, I expect for it to play out on my stage of calmness, excitement or confidence … whatever I wish to feel for the emotional foundation of my day.

When you play out scenes in your "Movie," you are looking at options and making choices. With *Stage Your Day*, you are setting your day with the emotional foundation to support your "Movie." You create your stage with intentions that serve and empower you. You run through your day positively, refusing to give any power to any thing, person, place, condition or circumstance. You practice this knowing and set this intention to your emotional stage. With this practice you are announcing energetically that what is to appear in your day must fit these criteria. In *Stage Your Day* you are also grounding your intention with the love of Source Energy, consciously partnering and acknowledging this love that expands your desires. In this meditation you are projecting what you expect. The more you practice this proactively, the more you will be aware that what you project is what you expect.

Your Day Is Your Intention

Stage Your Day is practiced before you start your day; before you even step out of your bed. This is an ideal time to set the intention for your day. It can even support you to release any negative feelings or energy that you may carry with you from the night before. Let's say you went to bed with thoughts or concerns that you would not like to transfer over into your new day. If you do not take a moment to clear your thoughts, they would just blend into your day. What about if you had an amazing dream that felt so good? Taking a moment to ponder on it and integrate it towards your day can be very beneficial.

Of course, you can do *Stage Your Day* at any time or you can use the *Reboot Technique*, a quick mid-day method to quickly strengthen your emotional stage of your day. This powerful and effective technique can be used quickly at any moment to reinforce your intention towards what you expect. The *Reboot Technique* also supports you to realign with your intentions with what you wish for if you get off course or "off your stage."

When I began to explain *Stage Your Day* in my courses and classes, I first asked how people start their day. We would have a lot of laughs as people explained their morning. Usually they are woken up by a loud alarm that they place on snooze several times, and then they race out of bed to get themselves together quickly. They are basically on automatic with their routine. I ask them, "What are some of the thoughts you have before you get out of bed?" Most respond that they are undesirable thoughts about having to go to work *again* or they are anxious thoughts about their "To Do" list. What they are expecting was not always so great because they usually have to wake up to do something they feel they are not choosing.

Jonathan was a student of mine and he shared a story that I heard often from many of my clients. He gets up in the morning with the loud alarm clock and feels like he immediately picks up all the problems in his life where he left off before going to sleep. This reinforces a continuation of what he says he does not want. Then he has breakfast and engages in conversation with his wife about family matters when he can feel the tension of his relationship, which is lacking romance. Then he is rushing his kids out the door. He feels nothing in his life runs smoothly. He leaves the house and during his first moments to himself, before he gets to work, he hears the news blaring in the cab. He buys the paper and reads it on his way to work so he can feel informed of national and world politics, crime and whatever else is of crisis in today's world. So imagine for a moment how the stage of his day has been set. He has started his day with chaos and frustration and this is the foundation from which he builds his day. This can be avoided by taking a few minutes to himself while he is still in bed. By playing out his day and commanding his expectation, the day could be totally different. Sounds so simple and it is. Because Jonathan was taking one of my courses, we had a few weeks to share together.

I asked him if he would be open to implementing *Stage Your Day* before he started his day. He was all for it as he shared that he was feeling exhausted and was so tired of his routine of feeling like he is "putting out fires" all the time. Jonathan worked in the financial industry and he naturally followed a routine in his daily life and enjoyed order.

He was committed to implementing *Stage Your Day* to his daily practice. After a short time using this method, he shared his results with the class. He said, "At first, I did not know where to start. I was so wired to rush out of bed that I had to be aware of staying in bed for a few minutes more." He shared that staying in bed longer and not rushing out on automatic pilot was challenging but it made a big difference with how he felt. He noticed he was calmer, more patient and kinder in his communication with his wife and children.

After a few days of doing the technique, he started the practice formally and he immediately took notice that he wanted to shift the way he felt about going to work. He was feeling stressed even before he got to the office but could not understand why because he really loved what he was doing. As he played with creating a stage where he felt calm and excited before he went to work, he realized that the way he conducts his morning had so much to do with how he was feeling.

In the few minutes of setting his intention and then asking himself what he could do to give himself support, he saw it very clearly while staging his day. So he made some changes to his morning routine. He laughed as he shared his story because the things he shifted were so simple and obvious.

Before he got out of bed he set his stage with calmness and excitement and anchored to this feeling. After he would rise, he stayed in a morning routine of taking time for himself with a shower and getting ready to support him to feel centered. He then greeted his family saying "Good Morning" to everyone and asked him or her how they slept. This was different approach for him and his family appreciated his attention. He also helped his children to organize themselves better for the next day before bed so they did not feel so rushed in the morning. He did the same for himself. His family was surprised at his morning cheer. Without effort, the conversations in the morning naturally shifted to being more pleasant rather than chaotic with issues. He made it a point to positively engage with his family each morning before he went off to work.

In transit, he made a few other changes. He chose to smile while he was walking and when he entered the cab he turned off the news and later used the 45 minutes on the train to read something that he enjoyed that was non-related to work. By the time he got to his office, he was calm and felt creative, which led to being enthusiastic and feeling excited.

He began using the *Stage Your Day Technique* for his morning because he felt this was the most challenging time for him and he was aware that he needed to get out of the bad habits of his morning routine.

Before he began using *Stage Your Day*, everything seemed so overwhelming and as if he needed to make a big change in order for his life to shift. He shared with the group that this practice allowed him to step back and witness his life more clearly. It was most surprising to him that the simple things he shifted made a huge difference. This new routine now seemed like commonsense to him and he felt in sync to start his day off joyfully and with ease. When he was rushing on automatic pilot, he did not even notice how stressed he felt and how his unproductive habits were setting him up to have unnecessary chaos and challenges.

A month after the course, he wrote me to share that he was beginning to use *Stage Your Day* to play out his whole day. He now understood that he could resolve even large challenges with the awareness of simply shifting habits and staging the way he wished to feel.

Proactively Stage What You Expect

While using the *Stage Your Day Technique*, you can witness the possibilities of your day as scenes with the emotional foundation you are choosing for your stage. Play out the flow of your day, witnessing your Self having this emotion throughout your day.

Start to witness your Self going through your day and even imagine the interactions you assume you are going to have. Choose to edit parts where you prefer not to react, delete actions that do not serve you and reinforce what does. *You can create, resolve and shift any emotional experience you desire through the energy of playing with your feelings.*

In this space, work out whatever perceived fear you may have for the day knowing that you have created the reality you are experiencing now and so you can also create another one. Play with your emotions internally. This is much easier than playing out experiences in your real life that can be hurtful or repeating emotional patterns of the past that do not serve you. Knowing how you wish to feel towards an experience sets up an emotional point of reference in your energy, which creates a system of "like attracts like."

The gift of *Stage Your Day* is that in this space of being proactive you are free from your past; you are not your past and limiting beliefs. You are what you wish to create. You are free to *be* in a time and space where your present circumstances do not dictate and you can create based on your pure emotional desire of what you wish to be your reality.

Although we are grateful for our logical mind, it can also block us from believing our dreams are possible. By loosening the control of our logical mind as the guard gate to protect us, we can see past our patterning and beyond our fears and perceived limitations. Allow your heart to create what love generates.

Your World Is Your Stage

As you reinforce your inner emotional system with feelings that feel good, you release patterns that no longer serve you. Naturally, the emotions you designed for the "stage" of your day become a magnet for your experiences. You are announcing your stage instead of leaving it to chance. You are creating a stage for like matches to step into your world instead of chasing them. Those that are not a match to you leave your stage and you no longer feel the need to spend the energy to engage with them from a place of lack or fixing. Joy and self-love have replaced this.

By feeling good and experiencing a life that feels good to you, the need for drama, chaos and unhealthy people is released with ease, as this is no longer a magnet for the reality you have designed. Your stage is set so that those that are not a match for you no longer surround you and you bless them on their way. Your stage is one of wellbeing for all.

When you play with the possibilities you wish to create, just stay focused on how you wish to feel. Releasing your feelings of worry on how things will happen allows space for the feelings you desire to take the lead role on your stage to organize the details.

Once you feel a possibility as a real experience through your emotions, your cellular body accepts this as if it has already happened as a reality. This reinforces your point of attraction for these experiences to manifest and downloads your DNA to activate and respond accordingly.

The *Stage Your Day Technique* supports you to be able to witness your emotions without the interference or limitations of your personality. This is a beautiful opportunity to honor your life using the energy of your full potential without fear, judgments, projections from others or hesitations. It is a pure energy of absolute safe love for you.

In this energy, feeling lovable and loved, you reaffirm the deep knowing of the Absolute Love of All That Is as your partner in enhancing all the possibilities you desire as your reality. When I share of Source Energy of All That Is, I am referring to an Energy that is always with us. An Energy that we are always connected with unconditionally. Some may call this Energy the Universe, God, G-D, Yahweh, Jesus, Allah, Buddha, Christ

Consciousness and others. As I have shared, how you wish to define this Energy for yourself is personal and I fully honor and respect your belief.

When you pray, "Ask," wish or daydream about your life experiences, know that you are not asking for a favor or being evaluated on whether you should or should not have what you are asking for. Know with total certainty that you are worthy and deserving of all that you are asking for. Feel and trust that the Universe wishes to give you all that you ask for and it does. You receive what you are asking for, so having an awareness of how you are asking creates the knowing of how you will receive. Let go of any notion that there is an energy force that wishes to deny you. Through what you believe is the possibility of your reality, you consciously activate this Love within and all around you.

The *Stage Your Day Technique* is a powerful tool to practice emotions that feel good. By taking a moment each morning to support yourself in staging your day, you clearly give your emotional blueprint to the Universe and command the life you choose to design and begin to witness it as your reality.

When you *Stage Your Day*, you also give love to all those that surround you. Envision a blanket of love and kindness to the world. Praise others, bless your life and give love to all that is your experience.

Use this moment to give thanks for your life, your health and thank your body for working for you without having to ask. Feel your heart full of excitement and love for everything. Feel thankful that you can create your life and give wellbeing to others. Bless your opportunities. This is a moment where you consciously love. Wrap the ones you love with beautiful golden Light and tell them you love them, you love them, you love them. This is all one needs to do remind the ones you love that they are loved and this awakens more love within them.

Your Feelings Serve You

Everything in life is started with a feeling. Feelings are energy and to deny our feelings can create all kinds of blocks that do not serve us. This can create chaos, confusion or even illness. Your feelings are to be embraced as the "Magic Wand" to create, shift and enhance your life as the magical experience it is intended to be.

When you *Stage Your Day*, you are setting yourself up to respond to experiences based on your emotional vision and you are bringing life's creations to you. How do you wish to feel? What do you wish to feel? Activate what feels good to you!

Knowing your Authentic Self is a journey; there is no final script; there is a continuous story that you are writing.

"As above, so below"

> *As above = Your imagination as a prayer / Source Energy as your partner supporting your prayer through the Universal Computer*
> *As below = The physical form of your prayer anchored as your day-to-day life experience*

Stage Your Day Morning Practice:

In the morning, before you get out of bed, take a few deep breaths.
Go to that place between waking and sleeping and bring back the feeling of a time and place where you were very relaxed and peaceful.

Then take another few deep breaths.

Stay in that space and if there is still "busyness" in your mind, simply transfer those feelings to your heart knowing they will be converted into peace. Do not worry about the details of those feelings.
Place your focus on your heart, because everything we wish to create in our reality, we wish to create with the energy of our heart as our emotional foundation. It is through our heart that we wish to receive; where we wish to make decisions and where we wish to have love as the base of all things.

Then, with those feelings in your heart, feel a golden cord going from your heart anchoring to the center of Earth. Imagine this cord pulling beautiful, loving, grounding energy from the Earth up through the soles of your feet to the center of your body.

Be conscious of your breath as you continue to breathe in and out, feeling a calmness knowing all is well ...

Feel energy moving through every part of your cellular being, throughout your body, towards the top of your head ... you can feel this as a color filling your body or simply a feeling.

Now feel this energy go out through the center of your head.
As you do this, imagine an image of yourself as if you are inside a golden cocoon soaring towards the magnificent rays of the sun.

In this space, feel your Self moving up towards the warmth of the sun surrounding you. You have comfort knowing all is well and you are fully supported with love for all you wish for. In this space of feeling the warmth of pure love connected to all of you, your physical and non-physical, take a moment to give gratitude for another opportunity to have your possibilities realized as you consciously feel the presence of supporting Love.

Begin to daydream and feel your Self activate the experience of the day you are about to start. Ask yourself, "How would I like to feel today?" Focus on the feeling you would like all your experiences to be initiated from.

Remember that you know what it feels like to experience the feeling you wish, whether it is joy, calm, love or confidence. Place whichever feeling you would like to feel as if you are anchoring them to a stage. These feelings are the stage where your experiences will come from.

Ask yourself how you wish to feel towards people and situations today?
Remember, you cannot control how you want other people to feel. You can only manage your own emotions and process. What you activate in others is a reflection of parts of yourself or the opportunity to make a choice to support what you believe is possible for yourself.

Now again, run through your day including people and situations in your imagination with the feeling you wish to have as your stage for your day.

If there are any areas where you feel some resistance, stay there for a moment and play with resolving this. If you still feel overwhelmed, anxious or frustrated ... this is OK ... no worries ... remember, this feeling will pass or be transformed to how you wish to feel. Sometimes this can feel very easy and sometimes it is more challenging.

Do your best in being patient with yourself, and ask for clarity or support.

Ask for an experience that is similar to the way you wish to feel to reinforce your knowing. Know it is easier and more effective if you can change something while daydreaming, as this will shift that feeling and experience in your day-to-day reality. Stay as playful as possible.

Then move your consciousness to where you feel a flow of the feelings you enjoy, focusing on where you feel inspired, loved and can express your best Self. Be aware of staying focused on what is productive in your life.

Next, with a sense of playful joy, take these feelings of how you wish to feel throughout your day and place them into raindrops. Feel these raindrops wash over and through your body, moving into every bit of your cellular being. Know you are anchoring this feeling within you and it has integrated with your Vibrational Language, creating a point of reference for the physical world to respond. This is your own personal fragrance.

Now take a few deep breathes, and feel your Self again bathing in the golden sun rays as if this is love is reinforcing how loved you are. Take another breath and imagine you are in your golden cocoon looking down at an image of your physical body feeling solid and whole with your possibilities.

Witness your Self break through your cocoon and merge with your physical body through the top of the center of your head, reinforcing all the knowing of how you are loved with all your possibilities granted. So be it! You have claimed this to be so. Open your eyes and begin your wonderful day.

At any time throughout the day, whenever you get a feeling that you would like to shift, you can take a deep breath and give your Self a wonderful rain shower of the feelings you have chosen to reinforce your emotional stage.

This is living consciously, being proactive and commanding the foundation of the life you live … your stage.

Allow these positive emotions to wash over you and connect to the feeling you wish to merge within every part of your cellular being, strengthening the anchoring of this to your day.

You Own Your Stage

As you continue to practice *Stage Your Day*, you will notice that you will be witnessing your world with more clarity and observing how everything is connected. You may feel less of a need to interact all the time as your Vibrational Language will release the feeling of being needy or insecure as your attraction and instead become a language of feeling stable and certain. If for a moment you go to an emotional space that does not serve you, no worries, you will not be there for long, as you will gently use the technique to go back to your emotional wellbeing.

Through the practice of this Visualization Technology®, you will notice that your interaction in your day-to-day comes from a natural flow of your best Self. Your days will be more enjoyable with ease. Any challenges you will face will be with a knowing that all is well and you can shift your experience. These challenges will become less frequent and seen more as situations to resolve. You will have challenges and hurts, this is life ... the difference is that they will not consume you or define you like before and will not last as long. There will be healthy awareness of processing. You will continue to anchor with the feelings that support your stage of creating your life of emotional choice with ease.

Soon you will observe that your morning *daydreams* become your reality. Enjoy an easy way to create your day with this practice. If you can feel it and believe it, so be it! You have loving support around you to make this so; your dreams as your reality is your birthright. By creating a clear vision of the life that you choose to live, you will manifest your wishes. When you take ownership, the world around you will respond.

Stage Your Day Technique – Quick Reference Guide:

First thing in the morning, connect with your feelings ...
Anchor your heart with a golden cord to the earth and feel your Self rise to the warmth of the rays of the sun and allow this feeling of warmth to remind you that you are greatly loved.
In this space, ask your Self how you are feeling and simply listen.
How is your body feeling? Scan your body as you ask.
How do you wish to feel?
Daydream.
Ask your Self to find a moment when you have felt the way you wish to feel right now.

Play with this feeling as a dream, anchoring this as your stage.
Witness this and know this is a real possibility.
Embody this feeling within you and observe your Self experiencing the day
you are about to begin.
Simply smile and give thanks for your day of possibilities.
Infuse your day with love and share love with those that surround you.
You claim this now, so be it!

Sleep: Rest Your Body and Mind

As you have consciously started your day, complete the cycle of claiming your life by staging your night. Sleep is a wonderful way to rest and renew your body, and it is important to rest your body and relax your mind. I also believe when we sleep, we are rejuvenating our Soul. Your body may be resting but your Soul is awake and attentive and continues to support all you desire while you sleep.

What if you have a "support team" in the unseen – angels, guides and ancestors – all there willing to assist you? They are simply waiting to be asked by you, as they respect your free will. What if your sleep time became a magical journey where you felt taken care of and nurtured and woke up feeling rejuvenated? Let's say that you have the opportunity for all of this in your sleep.

Assume that your brain does not know how to relax because it's constantly on call every moment, every day, every year of your life. Without giving it a sense of direction when you go to sleep, it is free to find thoughts and experiences that may or may not be pleasant for you. Sometimes we forget the last thought that we chose to have before closing our eyes. What was the last thing you experienced in a book, or on a computer or on TV or in a conversation before drifting off to sleep? Let's say that the brain feels that its job is to continue to support that last feeling or dominant thought while you sleep. The brain finds reinforcement to your last thoughts or concerns. The brain is such a hard worker, so it goes searching your library of information and experiences all night. Usually the information your brain finds may result in dreams of more worry and unrest, causing you to wake up feeling tired. Again, what did you subject your Self to before going to sleep? The mind stays awake with its potential and capacity to bring you information. Lead your brain to look in the direction to reinforce your wishes, not your fears.

Direct Your Dreams

What if before you went to sleep you chose to believe that those in the unseen are there to support you in a positive way? What if you asked for support believing you will receive it through a dream or inspiration?

I suggest using your sleep for many valuable opportunities. Turn the TV off before bed. Take a shower or a bath and disconnect from your day. Spend some quiet time beneath your sheets visioning an intention for your sleep, like a nighttime journey.

Ask the Loving Energy that surrounds you to show you messages in the form of dreams or inspiration that will reveal their meaning to you and provide you with guidance to gently release anything that no longer serves you. Replace it with what serves your heart and Soul now in every area of your life.

Personally, before I go to sleep I reflect on my day, either by myself or by saying prayers with my children. We name our family members and other loved ones as we wrap them in white Light, reinforcing that we love them and ask for them to have the blessings they desire. We send love to the world. We ask for forgiveness for those we may have hurt and towards our Selves for any hurt we may have caused to others or for missed opportunities. We bless our life, and ask that we be guided or supported. Then we say at least three things that we are grateful for that happened that day. Finally, we pray that we know how to show up with love and kindness in our hearts always. It is a gift to be able to fall asleep with a feeling of peace, knowing that your day is resolved, and this will set the foundation for a restful sleep and allow you to wake up feeling refreshed and renewed.

There Is Great Love For You

Meditation is a powerful, joyful opportunity to shift your life experiences by simply taking a moment to go to a space within yourself and feel your emotions regarding an experience or towards what you wish for. In a meditative space, you have the opportunity to move past your perceived limitations and away from the chaos of life and move in the direction of your "Ask." Basically, you are able to shift away from the present "What Is" to the possibility of "What If."

Meditation, prayer or focused thoughts are all similar practices for me because in all of these practices one is in a state of being versus doing. Meditation is a proactive way of setting intentions for your life.

Awareness of emotions creates direction in your life and whenever you take a moment to focus on your breath with awareness, to appreciate your life and the good that surrounds you, you multiply what you define. This is also about having quietness to "hear" or feel the Energy of Love and for that Energy to give to us. This is a *sacred time to remember that you are never alone and there is great love for you.*

Morning Practice

Visualize the start of your day through the Stage Your Day Technique.
Affirm your sense of purpose.
Ask.
Witness it done.
Expect it.
Take action.

Evening Practice

Prepare for a peaceful, restful sleep.
Complete your day by setting the intention to release it on an emotional level, whether by awareness or forgiveness.
Reflect on a few things that you are grateful for.
Create an "Ask" with God/Creator/Holy Spirit/Universe/Spirit Guides to support you in a peaceful and restful sleep.

Fine-Tuning Your Expectations

As with all the information I present to you, I encourage you to enjoy finding your own unique flow with these systems. I invite you to have awareness of what resonates with you, and then perfect this as your own practice. Because this not an instruction manual, but rather, principles that guide you and enhance your life skills, soon you will have a lifestyle that supports your best Emotional Self.

I have named this work Power Wishing® to encourage fun and lightness as we design our lives. Now that you have reviewed about writing your wishes, I am going to share how you can continue to drive the energy flow of your "Ask" of what you expect in your physical experience to clearly anchor this structure.

I view manifesting as an exciting opportunity, and there are disciplines that can fine-tune your expectations. Having disciplines is not about control or restriction but about being empowered in the physical world to support your Self. Life can be heavy enough, so the more organized, relaxed, and trusting we are with our emotions the more a peaceful life and magical experiences become the norm.

It Is All Inside You

I am a person who expresses my emotions; they are the antennas with which I interpret my world. I have always been this way and, on many occasions, I have been told that I am too sensitive. In a world where people often prefer to avoid being emotional or understand themselves emotionally, I had to acquire the skill of balancing my sensitivity.

Having said that, I also like to get to the bottom line of most things quickly, and I have learned to have my emotions also support this in a healthy way. Power Wishing is designed to get to the bottom line of having what you long for, cutting through the "red tape" of chaos and drama to have a life of realized hopes.

Let's imagine for a moment that you have all these wonderful seeds of Divinity inside of you that hold the vision and the know-how of the life that you desire. These seeds are waiting to be awakened within you to be the reflection of your physical life. You already have Divine life within you; there is nothing you have to find or invent, and the seeds are there for you to awaken. This is what I am referring to when I share about encountering your Divinity, your greatness; it is already within you, waiting for your discovery. Your emotions awaken these seeds to grow. Through your feelings, you are making your "Ask," asking for what you believe is possible to activate and then your free will invites the creation of Source Energy, which, like the Sun, nourishes what you expect.

Once you awaken the seeds of your Divinity, your true Self, these seeds of have programming to support you. *Just like plants have a process that is programed for growth, if you stay open to the Light of who you are and stay away from darkness, your dreams will naturally grow and continue to attract what will nourish them.*

The key is to be aware of what you believe is possible. You are engaging emotionally as you activate your possibilities with your belief of expectation. Therefore, if how you feel about what you are asking for is not aligned with how you wish to receive, basically if you do not believe it can happen, then take a step back and clean up your emotions towards your expectation.

Make choices towards supporting how you expect to receive and stay away from the weeds of doubts that will strangle your growth. Trust the Creator that co-creates with you for all you ask for; use this knowing to trust within your Self that you will make the necessary choices.

I find that when people are not manifesting the results they wish, it is because they are holding contradictory emotional beliefs. It could be that they are feeling one way emotionally and in their physical experience, with their logical thinking, they are denying what they are feeling. This translates into living a divided life where they have a reality they say they do not wish for. I created this emotion-based wishing formula to assist the whole of you, so that your body, mind, Soul and spiritual Self are harmoniously united.

I believe that accomplishing your goals is not the most challenging part, identifying what you desire and making a conscious decision to activate that in your physical life is. Once you identify what you desire the rest is mechanics, a system where your awareness allows you to make adjustments to easily choose your reality. As with growing a plant, you give it time to grow, fertilize as needed, prevent weeds, and make sure it receives sunshine and nourishment. Exercise this system of mechanics to grow your emotional seeds; trust what you cannot see and expect them to blossom.

The Activation Of Your Divinity

To create your reality of choice, you can fuel the development of the seeds of your Divinity with what we will define as the growth stages of your "Ask": *Awareness, Acknowledging, Witnessing, Aligning, Allowing and Surrendering.*

> *Awareness* of desiring a flower is the start of its growth, but a flower has no chance to exist before a seed is planted. Your Divinity has no chance to be awakened unless you give awareness to who you truly are and ask to have this self-awareness exist.

> *Acknowledging* the seed in the ground as you plant it gives the flower the opportunity to bloom. Once you anchor your Divinity by owning your choices, every possibility you desire can grow.

> *Witness* the growth of your possibilities – with beliefs that are positive, with surroundings that nourish your beliefs positively and with emotions that are sunshine to cultivate your desire. As with growing a flower, it may take some time before you see the flower bloom in its completion. Every once in a while, you see glimpses of the flower coming up from the Earth, but it is a process. First there is a leaf, then a stem, and then a bud unveiling itself into a flower. Have disciplines to continue to check on this growth from a place of excitement, trusting that Love is co-creating the expansion of your expectation with you.

> *Align* what you expect with physical actions and disciplines to reinforce the belief of the dream you hold dear to your heart. Align your decisions to take action, to nourish and enrich the blooming of your expectation.

> *Allow* what *you know you know* to be the truths you believe even before your physical reality manifests this to you. In the process of allowing, you are not trusting in the unseen blindly. You are engaging, as you have planted your seeds with your feelings. Your feelings are powerful and valuing them is an expression of self-love and appreciation for your life. Trust the Love that surrounds you that wishes for you to have your life in full bloom. Love creates everything; self-love is a mighty power to construct anything you choose to happen. Have convictions with the seeds you are planting; nourish them with confidence. Strengthen your seeds by taking actions with integrity that support the growth of the direction of your life. Take care of yourself; honor what you are growing in your life.

> *Surrendering* is keeping the faith alive. If you planted a seed and have cared for it properly, the best way you know how, then why would

you keep pushing it into the ground to make sure you planted it correctly? Why smother the growth of your expectations with insecurities of doubt or weeds of negative influences? This would only hinder the growth you have asked for with uncertainty. When you plant a seed, you water it, nourish it, trust the earth's way and then allow it to grow. Surrender with certainty and move to another part of your life that brings you joy to reinforce your trust.

Awareness

Life is constantly in motion. The Earth is always moving, as is your life. Emotions are meant to be in motion; this is a natural way of being. Being present with your awareness will organize your internal Self to release creating life experiences you would not consciously choose. Not consciously choosing creates a life that is on automatic, with habitual feelings driving your reality. The opportunity with your awareness is to inventory those automatic survival habits and refocus them to serve you in the direction of where you aspire to be.

As you continue to awaken the awareness of your Self, you will shift your life as different experiences come into play. There will be times you will not know what to do with the awareness that you are experiencing. When this happens, be patient and even if you may feel like being silent in your awareness, trust that the knowing within you will guide you. In those moments, when you feel there is no guidance yet, always choose love and kindness towards your Self and others. Let go of feeling pressured to do something that does not feel authentic to you and especially avoid behaviors that do not honor your best Emotional Self. The beauty of awareness is that it generates a doorway into your world, inviting you to discover and manifest possibilities through the discovery of your Divinity.

Acknowledging

Awareness creates the consciousness of what you are observing. *Acknowledging* what you are observing gives form to your present reality. When you acknowledge where you are now – the good, the bad, the ugly and the beautiful – you are in the present moment. You are stating that you are in the driver's seat of your life, not a passenger. You can choose whether you place the brake, drive forward or stay idle. This also prevents your decisions being driven by someone else.

You become present in your life. It does not matter what your present circumstances are; what matters is that you acknowledge them and this gives a foundation to have the opportunity to shift your present reality into what you wish for now.

Acknowledging what you believe you can expect from your present reality makes the difference of what choices you will make.

Sometimes people fear that if they truly face what is happening by being present, it may be too painful and so they believe denial will protect them from the pain. Or, people feel that if they acknowledge something they have been avoiding, that means they have to make a conscious decision now.

Understand you are making decisions through your emotional state, and if you acknowledge truth for your Self, you can drive the energy of how this will continue to manifest instead of the lack of acknowledgment of how you really feel keeping you stuck. To pretend that things will get better when one continues to feel worse about a situation is only keeping in an unhealthy cycle.

Acknowledgment is not forcing your Self to feel a certain way; it is acknowledging the truth for your Self so you can have the possibility to experience the way you wish.

Another reason for lack of acknowledgment is because one may have a challenging time accepting that some things are not forever, life brings changes, even though one wishes them to be so. This can be difficult to accept.

Acknowledging is also acceptance of what is. In this knowing, let go of resistance. Just let go of resisting what you are witnessing and accept it as is. Accepting things as they are can be liberating, even if logically this does not seem so.

When you acknowledge things are what they are and still do not know what to do, it is often best to just let it be for the moment. As you let it go for the moment, use the Power Wishing formulas to ask for guidance, clarity and positive truth. Enhance your trust in the Love that surrounds you and within your Self, knowing the situation will be resolved. Allow your Self to make choices that support you.

Sometimes lack of acknowledgment is because one may have a hard time accepting a past decision and not be able to face the situation clearly. Admit to your Self whatever pain or disappointment you experienced, so you can be free from it owning you. It is useless energy saying something is the way it is, when it is not *for you*.

Acknowledge how you feel now and how you would like to feel. Acknowledge what you would like to see differently in your life and know that this acknowledgment is a first step to change.

Acknowledging awareness is a language in itself and people define what is in the scope of their awareness based on the dialect of their beliefs, life experience and what they believe they can expect from life. I ask that you be sensitive to each person's varied perception of how they define what they are aware of or not. What may be clear for you may not be for another. As you do this powerful work for your Self, allow others to have their awareness based on their own personal timing and beliefs. You can share your awareness while having discernment between what is sharing and what is projecting onto others.

Acknowledge that you are empowered and can make choices; therefore, you release resisting because you can handle whatever comes your way. Acknowledge and accept the truth of who you are. This is natural to the Soul and creates a rhythm of life that is beyond magical.

Witnessing

Witnessing allows you to make choices that are empowering. Can you remember a time when you have witnessed something and were grateful you could observe it rather than react, a time when you were able to step back and give your Self a moment to make a conscious choice? When you practice witnessing, you train your energy to focus with a response in alignment with what serves the possibility you desire.

No one person, situation or force has the power over your choices. The more you practice witnessing, the more you will naturally make choices in the moment without having to step back. Witnessing allows you to create habits that are responsive rather than reactive based on your past or fears. This is especially beneficial when you are shifting a major area in your life.

You have probably spent years with the same programming and life is moving so fast around you that the energy flow that you created may not support what you wish to be possible now. Many times what may occur as a *bad* experience may have been created from *bad* habits, and when we witness, we can catch a *bad* habit and create habits and disciplines to support the experiences we desire. Continue to work within and witness. When you have anchored the feeling of your belief of positive expectation, nothing can stop you except the creation of failure in your imagination.

By witnessing, you are able to get out of your own way to allow yourself to observe your connection to the experience, just like you are watching a movie. Witnessing allows you to catch your Self from setting your Self up to fail and to re-position your Self for success. You will also notice blessings that have always been there and abundance that is waiting for you. Imagine you are watching a movie about YOU, the Amazing Soul that you are. You are witnessing different experiences. Watching this, you are present and non-reactive, though you are engaged with the experience in front of you. As the witness, you feel opportunities differently. It is as if you step back for a moment, giving your Self space to have discernment for your choices and to be a fan of the choices you are proud of. Witnessing allows you to observe your life while being present.

This ability to witness allows you the opportunity to respond with energy that is in sync with All That Is and all you expect. Witnessing is living in the now, where your wellbeing is balanced and your perspective is fresh, without the emotional baggage of the past. This takes patience and the desire to let go of patterns, control, judgments and projections. Witnessing allows you to take an empowered role in your life by making emotional choices that respond for you, creating a life that is happening *FOR* you.

Your Presence Holds Love For Another

In witnessing others, you may observe situations that are unsettling to you. Be conscious to be in a place of non-judgmental witnessing so you can present to respond, and have discernment with the present situation rather than projecting on to another because of your discomfort.

Know that through your witnessing you are still engaging in love for others by being responsible for your actions and honoring them for who they are. Your presence holds a Vibrational Language® that is so powerful and is an accumulation of more than just words. The same way a hug can say so much more than words can. When your presence holds love for the other, this reminds them to hold love for themselves. Never ever underestimate the power of love, especially your love.

Aligning

We live in a physical reality. If you wish to manifest your prayers of awareness and what you have acknowledged as the life experience you wish for, then you must take actions that are in alignment with your prayer. As you witness your life, you will know when to take actions to bring your wish granted. Through your "Ask" and witnessing you will be presented with these opportunities, but it is YOU that must take action.

Allowing

We now come to the part where you allow and let go. You allow for what you have anchored as your expectation to be claimed, to breathe and grow. I remember in the early days of my spiritual studies when I first heard the word *allowing* and I was not sure what that meant. Especially to the A-type personality that I was, I had questions. How do you just allow? Allow what? How does this work? I felt programmed in thinking that I always had to *do* something in order for something to happen. What I realized was that I already did the work and continued to take action through my Emotional Imagination®. Just like allowing a seed to grow, your "Ask" needs some space to allow growth. Many times one can be impatient and not allow time for everything to align to manifest.

In one workshop, I explained this concept with a visual example and with humor. I took some soil and placed a seed in the soil. I then said, "When we plant a seed, we water it, fertilize it and let it go so nature takes care of the rest." Then I said, "Imagine that your 'Ask' is the seed and you planted it with your intentions but instead of allowing what you have asked for to manifest with what you believe is possible, you constantly touch the seed, look at the seed, ask the seed 'Why have you not grown yet?' You step on the seed and you poke at the seed, smothering its growth process because you feel like you have to constantly *do* something. You start to complain that the seed has not grown yet, so you start to water it even more and then you drown it. When you find out the seed has gone rotten because it was overwatered, you forget you were the one who gave it so much water and blame the Universe for not giving you what you asked for." We all had a laugh at this funny example that shared my point.

Allowing is an action, in the sense that you are engaged in trusting what you have planted. You reaffirm this trust by doing other things that bring you joy. I will say over and over again, let go of what appears to be in the moment as your reality; your present reality does not have to dictate your expectation. Hold onto the emotional expectation you wish to receive and allow this to grow.

The most challenging part of being an Amazing Soul, is to allow your Self to stay faithful and true to your Self in moments where you feel your reality is not a reflection of honoring your wishes. In these moments when you feel doubt and have darkness in your hope, stay true. Imagine these moments like a roller-coaster ride and just hold on with what you wish to be possible and allow the ride, because like a roller coaster, the doubt will end. In these times, do your best to allow your Self to witness what is around you and know that by holding onto what you believe is possible all will be as you wish.

Create discipline to allow things *to be* in moments of challenge; this takes patience, as our natural reaction is to control what we do not like. When you are transitioning your experience to another, do not allow the chaos to be a storm, instead feel it like a wind that is passing. Allow what you are witnessing to pass, because not what you wish to create, do not let an experience you do not wish for have control over you. Conquer them by allowing them to pass like a gust of wind taking away what no longer serves you.

At times when we have an expectation and witness that there does not seem to be a flow with others around us towards what we wish for, we can become disheartened. Allow others to be in their "Movie" and you stay in yours. What I am sharing is different than tolerating others. If you are tolerating with resistance and not in the space of allowing, a sense of resentment will be your expectation. If this happens, be aware of your feelings, acknowledge them and see if you can release your resistance to holding them responsible for what you wish for. Let go of what no longer serves you. This includes experiences as well as others.

As for your Self, when you release the resistance towards showing up for your Self and your dreams, you allow others to explore their dreams differently. Having a release of resistance within and feeling a flow of harmony even if it does not seem logical, is freeing. What is logic anyway, when it does not feel connected to who you are?

Surrendering

Surrendering fully trusts the process of allowing. Letting go and surrendering means you are engaged with yourself and your skill of moving to the rhythmic dance of receiving because you are trusting that all is working in synergy with your belief that all is as it should be towards your dreams.

Through surrendering you have this feeling inside your Self that you have done all you can up to now and consciously you are choosing to let things be and trust the outcome will be for your best.

Your surrender is allowing the space for the Universe to show up for you. You are also acknowledging that in this space of co-creation something else may show up for you that is beyond what you can imagine. What will show up for you will be aligned with your feelings, it just may be better than what you imagined.

When I used to hear the saying, "Let go and let God," it sounded disempowering to me. It felt like I was handing over my heart's desire to some *God* that was going to decide if I could have it or not. My young rebellious Self was not going to allow this *God* to make this decision for me. After I shifted my relationship with Source Energy, I totally feel empowered with "Let go and let God." God does deliver what you believe. This Source Energy is not moody, it does not dictate, it enhances creation of what you believe is possible and delivers this fully ... the same way I believe that love magnifies the good in our world.

I believe there is such respect for us from God. I feel God knows and we have been given everything that is necessary within ourselves to create all we desire. I personally believe God loves us without conditions; therefore, with this type of love, we are given everything to use with our free will. To me, if this was not so, then it would be a conditional *God* that is contradicting the message of unconditional love. Having been given free will, it is a testament that there is respect towards our choices. God will step in to co-create when there is a prayer. In asking, you have exercised your free will, therefore inviting Source Energy to co-create with you. It is as if there is always a knocking at the door, but in order to receive who is knocking you must first open the door. If you trust in Source Energy to deliver to you, then release doubt the moment your "Ask" does not seem to be what you expected. Surrender and do your part to show up with being accountable for your choices and allow this Love to carry you to your wish realized.

It is so liberating when you trust and surrender to the order of things that you witness. I feel very blessed that I trust experiences in my life as an order to bring me what I have asked for. Sometimes I am aware that I may be disappointed and feel like I am on a roller coaster and I acknowledge this even at times when I feel challenged with my beliefs. Then I reaffirm my trust that everything is in perfect order by strengthening my beliefs. We can be disappointed, but again this does not have to dictate the end result of what we wish for.

Why do some see what they do not wish for as a *sign* from God? Sometimes, we take the slightest defeat as a *sign*. Or we doubt that God is with us or we are being denied because things at the moment do not look the way we expected. *Please remember, small or large obstacles do not equal defeat; they are defined as life experiences.* Surrender in knowing that all is working in your favor, even if at the moment you do not understand. This is why it is called faith and so in these moments strengthen faith in your Self and your beliefs.

A Huge Thank You

I think we can all look back and be grateful that some experiences we believed at the time were major disappointments have moved out of our lives. Can you remember your first love that you wanted to marry or the house you wished to buy or the job you did not get or other examples? Do you now look back with such gratitude that you moved onto a different experience? It is a blessing when there was a greater intelligence that had our back; what we were disappointed about then would have been a bigger disappointment if it had stayed in our life. This greater intelligence held on to the knowing of what we were truly asking for, even if in the moment we forgot. You are not in this alone. Remember there is great love for you always.

Timothy

As I write this, one there is one case study that comes to mind is a client named Timothy. He came to a workshop of mine in late 2011. He seemed interested in the work and wanted to come in for a personal session. He then returned in early 2012 for another workshop with his wife. Only recently in 2013 did he see me for personal sessions. His recent testimonial expressed how his process of working with me truly required an open mind.

A major part of my work is to create awareness that things we perceive as the issue are not necessarily so.

Timothy came to me with a phobia of flying and heights that he wanted to overcome. It was limiting his business opportunities and he also wished to go on a vacation with his wife. I listened as he expressed that he wanted to focus on conquering his fear of flying. After a brief conversation, he immediately understood that the phobia was the effect of a greater cause and what he perceived as the cause was not actually the cause.

When you let go of the story you have been telling your Self of why things are the way they are, only then can you be open to another possibility of your story. Having said that, I realize this takes courage and requires a release from judgment. Timothy was able to move away from the story he always told himself and realized that it was much more layered than he thought. Now we could get to work.

In his own words … "A big part of our behavioral pattern is deeply embedded in us, and shaped by all of our experiences – both the good and bad. It is very difficult to have the self-awareness needed to not only evaluate the problem, but also have the correct solution. This is where Anne Louise comes in. She has an amazing gift to be able to dig deep and quickly identify where the issues really stem from, and then be able to 'reverse the behavioral pattern' in a way that leaves you in awe. Your job is to just be honest with her (by the way, she'll know if you're not!) and let the process work. Don't fight it, don't wrestle it, and don't question it too much. I assure you that the answers will reveal themselves in due time. Just enjoy the ride!"

He admitted to often projecting his negative feelings towards people he really loved, as if they were part of the problem. He shared that he often wondered about the "What Ifs" in a "grass is greener on the other side" way. He wanted more of this, or a little bit of that, thinking that it would make him happier.

He spent months self-reflecting and seeking answers for himself and tried to define *why* he felt he desired to seek guidance through this work to begin with. He contacted our office several times to inquire about the process, but he wasn't quite ready. He felt he wanted to enhance his career, his relationship and his life but mainly work on his fear of flying. It had gotten in the way of so many opportunities through the years and he was ready to conquer it once and for all. He admits, "I went to Anne Louise for these reasons and these reasons ONLY. However, I sensed something much more profound was going to happen, and deep down inside I was ready for it."

Upon beginning his session, Timothy recalls that from the moment he entered my office, he knew that our session would go much deeper than he initially expected. He was actually relieved by this. We spent the first 15 minutes discussing why he was here and he discussed wanting to reach his potential. Then, based on my intuitive reading of his energetic memory, we started a discussion about his father who had passed away when he was 47 and Timothy was 22. At first he said, "This has nothing to do with my father." Then he surrendered to this moment of sharing completely, with a rush of relief. For almost all of his childhood, his father had abused him. He was abused physically, verbally, emotionally and spiritually. His father was a bully and oftentimes did it in front of others. Timothy admitted that when his father passed away, that the first thing he felt was relief. "He was not around to destroy my life anymore," he admitted. "I also have several siblings; I didn't have to witness him abusing them or his second wife either."

Timothy is a wonderful person who strived to be the best he could be, for himself, for his wife, for the community. I could tell his intentions to create a good life for himself and to be respected in our community were genuine. He had never really confronted his feelings about his abusive childhood and thought that this was just his story, but it was not a crutch in life. He felt that he had forgiven his father and that it was what it was.

After our discussion, he felt safe to feel his emotions towards his father versus using his thoughts as his feeling of the relationship. There was also an unconscious fear that if he allowed him Self to feel, he would be overwhelmed by his feelings. I find this is a very common reason why people choose not to connect with a painful experience and this is understandable. Though I assure you if done properly, one feels relief because it is no longer running you, as you will see in the case of Timothy.

He was ready to surpass these tragic memories and move past them. Being numb to an experience, though, can have its effects. When you do not acknowledge the pain of a trauma, it takes an energetic toll on your Soul. This does not mean you need to re-live the trauma, but in order to move forward, acknowledgment of your feelings is what creates healing and resolution.

During this personal session, Timothy and I explored beliefs that he held and worked on healing his DNA, or cellular memory. We shifted the focus from his mind to that of his feelings. He connected with his Soul and asked himself who he was ... not as a logical question with a check-off list, but from a Soul perspective. More importantly, he felt that it was important to figure out who he was *not*, in order to make room for him Self.

After our session of clearing and shifting beliefs, he shared the following in his testimonial:

My Soul is not afraid of flying, despite what my mind tells me.
I am nothing like my father.
I had not, on any level, forgiven my father.
I had not, on any level, forgiven myself for anything related to my father.

Everything will be OK.
I was emotionally immature and lacked "emotional poise."
I had no emotional boundaries.
A lot of the things in my life were emotionally about me, so I emotionally engaged in things that were meaningless. A lot of my reactions to things were as if I was in crisis mode; everything was an emotional overreaction. Everything will be OK.

Usually when we awaken our feelings, our body also goes through a transition. His body had been holding the space for his feelings about the relationship with his father for so long. We often forget the stress our body feels when we repress emotions, guard our feelings or hold onto a story.

Many times after I share this work with clients, they will have tears of release at odd moments. I remind them not to worry about defining their tears; just allow and be grateful you're releasing the memory without having to re-live the trauma. We may have fear of facing a situation because we feel we may fall apart and that facing it may be worse. I believe the anxiety of what we believe we are going to face is usually far worse than facing our pain.

Timothy, a vibrant entrepreneur always on the go, also shared that when he went home, he felt numb for about three to four days and spent a good amount of time just crying and shedding tears kept inside for so long. He felt naked and that actually felt good. He believes the first session lifted the fog and created more clarity in his life. He felt harmony, which aligned his mind, body and Soul. He began to witness and was able to observe his life as a "Movie" when needed.

Dig Deep

During the second session, as Timothy said, "We really dug deep." The goal here was to reconnect with certain experiences in an attempt to ultimately be at peace with them. We got into a meditative state and I was able to get him to retrieve the first memory of the trauma. He connected with the emotions and circumstances that his "three-year-old Self" was experiencing at that time.

While it may have been uncomfortable to re-live these experiences, Timothy later shared that it was easily one of the most profound experiences of his life. The shifting began in a big way because of his acknowledgment. Real healing began quickly.

As a three-year-old kid looking for dad's love, what Timothy got was seriously damaging abuse. He grew up needing to create an emotional defense mechanism to protect him Self. He had bullied children when he was younger and was somewhat of a bully as an adult. Though Timothy is a wonderful man with positive qualities, he realized he did not really trust people; he was guarded, judgmental and argumentative. Even worse, he felt inadequate, unworthy of anything special, and unloved. Ultimately, he felt like he must have done something wrong to deserve the abuse and carried this to his adult life. Of course we all know logically that there isn't anything a child could do to deserve to be abused, but our emotions do not play to logic.

This is so common with those who have been abused. This is also why I am cautious with the phrase "like attracts like." Because when someone has been abused it does not mean they are an abuser. One component of my work is that people are able to share aspects of themselves that they would like to shift without feeling shame. In this vulnerable yet safe space, they feel emotionally safe to share without feeling judged.

During the third session together, something really profound happened. As we discussed abuse, his own experiences did not come to mind, but instead he put himself in his dad's shoes. You see his dad continued the abuse that was done by his father. By repeating the behavior he observed, Timothy's dad was simply seeking the love and affection he never really got from his father. This in no way validated his dad's behavior, but allowed this full circle witnessing of his story of his painfully abusive childhood, which released Timothy from the burden he buried himself under for so long. He instantly felt a great deal of compassion towards his dad. Instead of thinking, "How could he do this to me?" He now thought that he must have felt awful, trapped, confused, etc., to have behaved the way that he did. This was not about him wishing to save his dad or feeling sorry for him; it was about compassion that led towards genuine forgiveness.

Then he had an emotional breakthrough. He shared, "I started to think, if I feel compassion towards him, then I definitely should feel some compassion towards myself! I really know now that this abuse was completely unprovoked by me. His abuse of me was not my fault. Period."

We worked on forgiveness and then I suggested that he practice the *Forgiveness Prayer* to release his pain.

For the first time ever, he genuinely forgave his father, and himself, for everything that occurred. He actually came to a place in his heart where he could feel love for his father. I remember when he shared with me that he genuinely felt love for his dad and even told him he loved him with his thoughts. He also added that for the first time he was able to remember the good memories of his childhood. This is one of the reasons I do the work I do and feel such passion for sharing ways where love can expand.

What came out of this forgiveness was nothing short of profound. For 30-plus years, Timothy had made decisions (mostly unconscious) based off of his "old" mindset, the mindset of an abused person. Once he forgave himself and his father, he immediately stopped identifying with the experience on a deep emotional level. "I know it happened to me – I am not in denial – but I am not emotionally, physically or spiritually tied to that experience anymore. I am free from the chains that held me for so long," he shared.

Since his sessions, Timothy has checked in with our office but is amazed that he didn't feel the need to come back in for another session for now. He was so pleased with the results that he shared a wonderful testimonial with us and even gave us the following bullet points explaining how he felt his life had shifted since participating in this belief work:

- My defense mechanisms that served no purpose are gone.
- My anxiety has greatly diminished.
- I am no longer afraid of heights, tight spaces or flying.
- My desire to be a bit of a "control freak" is gone. This allowed me to trust people much more and this has helped my business and relationships.
- I observe much more than I speak now. It is amazing to witness my life this way.
- My business is doing better because I now feel like I deserve GREAT, BIG things. Not surprisingly, I actually started to chase them.
- My relationship with my wife has improved drastically. The energy in our home is so much more relaxed and she can express herself without fear of me being verbally overbearing.
- I stopped talking to many of my friends and acquaintances. Simply put, I chose these friends when I had the old mindset, and I needed to move on and create an environment that was going to help me accomplish my new goals.
- I am significantly more open-minded.

He continued to share, "I rarely get upset anymore ... at all. This might sound strange, but not having your temper there to 'guide you' takes some getting used to. Ninety percent of things that pissed me off before don't even get my heart rate up anymore. Heck, I barely notice that they even occurred."

He continued to say, "There was a very aggressive impromptu 'cleansing' process occurring. Everything from my diet, to my clothing, to the music I listened to, to the shows I watched changed. It was pretty strange when you go to watch 'your favorite movie of all time' and can barely sit through the first 20 minutes of it because you don't enjoy it anymore. I truly feel like a different person sometimes without this emotional baggage that I carried around for so long, and quite simply, this enhanced version of me just requires a different stimulation ... A more positive vibration."

May I add to this that Timothy flew from Miami to California to take his wife on an amazing summer vacation, and he took several flights for business as well!

The Harmony Of Acceptance

In making choices with your new awareness, there may come judgment from others or your Self. You may judge your Self for past decisions or judge others. This serves no purpose and only blocks the opportunity to receive the gift of awareness from your decisions.

When judgment is released towards your Self, and replaced with acceptance you will actually begin to witness with awareness the "Movie" of others without judgment. You will simply make a choice if you wish to add this scene to your "Movie" or not, without making your Self or others wrong. This also creates scenes of harmony in your "Movie."

Some People Will Agree With You And Some Will Not, This Is Life!

Sometimes you may feel that if you hold out waiting for others to agree with you, or for the "right timing," things will work out. The reality is that there is no "right timing." You are just hoping that others will agree with you to avoid any perceived pain when really it is just your decision.

If you wait to do things in other people's timing, your wish may never happen or you may unwillingly do things at a timing that is for someone else.

Then the YOU that wishes to experience a life of choices will shut down inside. It will be as if you are alive but have died (are dull) inside.

I would rather feel challenging emotions that guide me in the direction of my dreams than challenge myself with avoiding my feelings. When challenging emotions occurs, connect with your Emotional GPS and start an inner dialogue with yourself. Give your emotions a voice; reflect and create the space to hear *your* voice of reason, and then take action. Just do it.

When we depend on the "Mental Courtroom" of logic to decide our *case,* we tend to create more chaos, confusion and, in a way, we sentence ourselves to an emotional prison; or even worse, being an "emotional hostage" to others.

If you wish for a new experience, spend time feeling the emotions that you would like to feel in connection to this new experience. Do not worry how you will get there or what will prevent you from getting there or anything else. For a moment in time, feel excited about the possibility that you wish for! Dream, play, daydream ... have fun with this. Soon, the new feeling you wish to have with the desired experience will have all the support to create the logical way to live this experience.

It may sounds obvious, but I often remind others that logic is not an emotion, and this helps to create perspective. Your logic was created through your past emotions and beliefs and is influenced by the perspective of others. At times, this can be a positive influence with what you wish for; nevertheless, make sure your logic is up to date with what you are wishing to create.

Keep noticing the feelings you enjoy feeling and those that you would prefer moved out of your way. It is natural to seek validation and find proof to accept your feelings. We are a society that gauges and makes statistics about so many things, but what if you were able to know how to validate yourself from within with ease? When you release the need for validation, the outside world starts to respond to you without much challenge. You also release the habit of needing to challenge yourself.

Whether the outside world validates you or not will be the least of your concerns because the feelings of self-validation, happiness and peace are so strong within. The outside world will be more of a resource for the reality you wish to choose. When you have healthy emotional boundaries, you will strengthen your discernment on how you allow the projections of others to affect you. With your discernment, you will easily separate the projections of others from your own and recognize those that are yours that you wish to own.

After all, how can anyone else truly validate your feelings? They are yours and only you have all the facts and history to be the expert of YOU. Validating yourself from a genuine place of your Soul allows you to speak and listen to yourself clearly as you make an emotional decision.

Healthy Emotions Are My Lifestyle

As you deepen your practice of Power Wishing you will strengthen your inner voice and gain discernment of your authentic beliefs. You will listen to yourself without guilt or feeling bad about taking actions that support your beliefs. And somehow there is a knowing that this supports others you love as well. *Now, healthy emotional decisions are a lifestyle, whereas before you defined them as emotional risks.*

You will have a stronger sense of Self. You may still ask for other people's perspective, but this will be a choice. They are an added support system to strengthen the definition of yourself as you continue to define your life.

The beautiful part of supporting others during a challenging experience is that you can stimulate them to find their own voice by holding space for them. When someone shares their feelings with you, they have an opportunity to hear themselves from a different perspective.

Ever think out loud to a friend and then all of a sudden the answer comes to you? Allowing others in your life as this type of support with healthy boundaries gives you an opportunity to reflect on a decision from a positive place, and be consistent with choices that are in alignment with you. You have the opportunity to own your feelings without blame or judgment towards your Self or others. You are able to move away from the excuses of not showing up and operate in a space free of drama or crisis. Guess what else happens? You attract calm and ease; imagine this replacing judgment as more of your life experience.

As you embark on this journey, you will own your feelings without the need for validation from others or the need to have permission for your choices. This is liberating for you and for others, as you release them from being responsible for your choices. You may even notice you will communicate differently in your relationships. This process creates an honoring of you and this mirrors towards honoring others.

As you read my work and the information I share with you, I gently remind you to be mindful that others may not feel or think like you and their beliefs are their choices, not yours. Then again, you might be pleasantly surprised at those you get to know differently and maybe create another type of bond. This is also a valuable practice for you, as you would appreciate the same sensitivity and respect as well. You would appreciate to be honored for your timing with your awareness as you may make changes in the beliefs you have held for years.

My work is about awakening your awareness and giving it form to be productive in your life; it is not about a right or wrong way of being or doing. It is simply about bringing awareness to the emotions that create clarity about the world within you and around you.

The definition of the world you create is personal and should be respected by you. May you joyfully own your feelings passionately with self-love, knowing that you are deeply loved.

Power Thoughts

Fine-Tuning Your Expectations

- o Goodness is happening all around me and I recognize this.

- o I accept the truth of who I am and this creates a rhythm of life that is beyond magical.

- o I have the ability to witness my world and respond in sync with my expectations.

- o My belief of what I can expect makes the difference.

- o I surrender to trusting my abilities.

- o I trust my emotions and this is reflected in my actions.

- o I know all my personal details and history and therefore I am the expert of me.

- o My feelings are not right or wrong; they are simply my feelings and I honor this.

- o I experience self-love as a mighty power to construct anything I choose to happen.

- o Healthy emotional decisions are the base of my lifestyle; I no longer define them as emotional risks.

Your Voice Is Your Truth

There is a voice inside of us, and it speaks to us. Your inner voice reminds you of who you are and what you love about your Self. Keeping your Self aware of your voice gives you discernment when there are times you doubt your Self because outside voices sound louder. Allowing your voice to be heard can reassure yourself of the truth that belongs to you, the truth of who you truly are.

Many times people disregard their voice. Time passes and their inner voice that once spoke of pure love and acceptance for the discovery of you becomes quieter. They begin hearing other people's definition of who they are as their voice. And because life can move at such a fast pace, unconsciously they have allowed others to replace their own voice. One day, they wake up and they want their voice back!

Life can be challenging at times. Knowing your truth even in the midst of chaos is so valuable; you can remind your Self of what you love about who you are and what you believe is possible. It is valuable to stay conscious of listening to your Self – you have a lot of great things to say. Your voice has purpose, it has intelligence, and it is YOU. Meditation is also a positive way to strengthen the clarity of your voice.

The Voice Of Our Dreams Is Non-Negotiable

Our life is an accumulation of experiences. We all have moments of searching, experimenting, finding, succeeding, failing, speaking our truth and losing our truth. By "truth," I am referring to your beliefs and how they ring true for you.

The Greek philosopher Heraclitus of Ephesus said, "The only constant in life is change." He also said, "Good character is not formed in a week or a month. It is created little by little, day by day. Protracted and patient effort is needed to develop good character." We are changing, life is changing; therefore, things in your life do not stay the same. If you allow your Self to live with the character of your truth, then you can flow with whatever change comes. There is rhythm in living authentically; the fear of the unknown is quieted with the voice of certainty of who you are.

How could fear direct the main stage of your life's performance, when voice of your authentic Self is clearly running the show?

We can all probably agree that we have changed parts of our truth at some point in our lives. Hopefully, as we have more life experiences, we become clearer about how we define ourselves; we have discernment towards our values and our dreams that are non-negotiable.

We have "Ah-ha moments" that reveal our truth; we know when there is a truth to live by. Release questioning your Self about something you know is your truth; make it a habit to go straight to living it. Life can be really messy when a group of people says they love each other and are not in their truth. When you step into the experience of being in your truth as your life, you will be pleasantly surprised at how much easier it is to live this way.

It Is Always A Good Time To Live Your Truth

Create peace with your Self if your truth today may be different than what you believed yesterday. Create peace with your Self even if your truth today may be different than what you wish for tomorrow. The evolution of feelings is a natural progression of life; your beliefs shift because life continues to evolve. Be at peace with who you are. No matter what other voices try to define you, define your Self with your own voice. Everyone benefits from this.

It is funny how people can be judged if they choose to change their beliefs or perspective. I see this like clothing: when you were a child you wore certain clothes and, as you grew, those clothes did not fit anymore. With clothing you simply would go through your closet, take inventory of what fit you or not, and then replace it or maybe adjust the clothing. But you did not try to wear a pair of pants at 30 years old that was yours when you were 10 years old. We should review our beliefs the same way, inventory them and see what beliefs are still appropriate.

Thank goodness that people are able to change their beliefs and shift their perspective. This has created positive change, developed technology, expanded knowledge and love. How many times throughout history have we witnessed someone make a choice based on their belief, and at the time people thought it was crazy although today it is celebrated? Others' perspectives cannot gauge our truth; they too are changing and evolving. *You evolve based on the expansion of your imagination, what you believe is possible and your willingness to change your mind by making changes to your own beliefs.*

Your Actions Are A Match To Who You Say You Are

Once when I was driving back from a lacrosse game with my son, to my surprise, we had one of those memorable "out of the blue" conversations. At the time he was an eighth grader playing on the varsity team. His life experience was different than those of high school students so he had some questions. He started to share conversations he had heard about marijuana and then asked me what I thought about alcohol as well. I shared with my son that I can say the same thing about drugs, alcohol, sex, cheating in school, lying, etc. Your actions are a match to who you say you are, your character.

The question is, "Are your choices in line with what you respect and love about yourself?" It was such a powerful conversation about character values and making choices based on your belief system of who you are. I reminded him that only he could gauge his values through his actions.

Then we continued this conversation, sharing about friendships and school. I shared with him a hypothetical example and asked him if he has a habit of stealing. He laughed and said, "No mom, of course not." Then I asked, "Why?" He replied, "Because I don't." Then I continued, "Is it because stealing is not a part of your character?" He answered, "Obviously, it is not." So I continued and said, "If a friend steals something from you, does that give you the right to steal from him?" He replied, "No." I said, "Why?" He replied, "Because I do not steal." "Exactly!" I said. "It is not who you are! No matter what someone else does to you, you do not change your behavior and you do not shift who you are. Don't be moody with your character. Either you are or you are not a person who steals, no matter what." I also explained to him that sometimes we can falter and may react to a situation without our best character traits, as we are emotional beings and not robots. Another part of character and bouncing back is taking whatever accountability is necessary to move forward.

The conversation was really good, so good that it inspired the tagline of my company Simple Results, *"Character is not a mood; it is the foundation of who you are."* We often want to find validation or permission to support our feelings, especially if it is considered a risk. We want to give our emotions a voice of reason to make it easier to process what we are feeling and to therefore express ourselves to others without feeling doubt or fear of rejection. Hoping to receive validation or create proof for your feelings is a natural desire. While support and unsolicited advice from others can be helpful at times, if you are not clear with why you are making your choice and how you feel, it is important to check in with yourself. Have some clarity about your feelings before you hear other people's perspectives, so you can have discernment with how you are processing this information for your Self.

Allow others to be an asset to you and to enhance your perspective so you do not miss out on making a valuable decision for yourself. Set others up in your life to support you, not to fail you. Then again, what beliefs do you carry about believing that there are healthy environments to support and love you? I feel that if my surroundings stimulate me in a positive way, I can accelerate my growth by merging with the influence of this positive collective consciousness that surrounds me. The same is true when it is not so positive.

How can anyone else really validate your feelings when feelings are a personal experience? Who could be more of an expert on your own experiences than you? Who understands your desires more than you? And if you may not understand them completely, they are still your feelings that are connected to you. When others share their advice and opinions with you, they are basing it on their own beliefs and experiences. Again, all can be well and good. Having discernment on what is well and good for you is what has value.

Look For The Good

You get what you are looking for. Look for the good and good will follow! Own the beauty and good qualities of your life by making choices that reflect what you are looking for and the likes of this will be found.

However, if you find yourself in a mental cloud of confusion on a matter, it is best not to discuss it with others right away. Do the emotional digging on your own to eliminate the risk of being inadvertently drawn to opinions that support your fears as a misaligned belief.

One Truth = One Life

In the private space of your imagination, check in with your Self to feel if there is a truth that is burning in your heart that requires to be lived differently than the way you are living.

If you live a dual experience in your life or feel conflicted, alter this to a choice of living transparently. Sometimes when we are conflicted, we wait to see what will happen. To me, this is basically waiting for chaos to happen. Usually the false truth that is fed by your fears is what ends up dominating your life experience by default. Imagine for a moment your Vibrational Language® communicating for you, the dialogue that is attracting your life experiences.

If you are living according to your false self, then you are attracting based on the false truth of who you say you are and what you say you want. This creates an emotional mess and is very draining to your whole being.

Having one truth inside your heart and another playing out in the experience of your life does not support a healthy emotional foundation or relationships and creates mixed messaging that disturbs your abundance. It also doesn't support a healthy body; it is stressful on your body to live separate from your Self. Living differently than your Authentic Self is not being truthful, especially to you.

Distorting the truth is also not being truthful. When we are untruthful, we are only appeasing ourselves because of what we cannot face. In reality, it serves no one.

"We tell lies when we are afraid … Afraid of what we don't know, afraid of what others will think, afraid of what will be found out about us. But every time we tell a lie, the thing that we fear grows stronger." – Tad Williams

The Truth Sets You Free

I believe that the truth does set you free, along with others that you may be holding prisoner with your falsehood. When you are living outside your truth, you are sharing a false sense of who you are. There are many reasons why people justify living in this way. One could be because they do not wish to hurt the ones they love, but in essence this is exactly what they are doing.

"Some people will not tolerate such emotional honesty in communication. They would rather defend their dishonesty on the grounds that it might hurt others. Therefore, having rationalized their phoniness into nobility, they settle for superficial relationships." – Unknown Author

If the truth always comes out, then allow truth as the genuine expression of your life. Let your truth be what represents you. Why attract into your life from a base that is not you? And if untruths surround you, there will be a peace within your Self knowing without the need to defend your Self.

"Honesty is a gift we can give to others. It is also a source of power and an engine of simplicity. Knowing that we will attempt to tell the truth, whatever the circumstances leaves us with little to prepare for. Knowing that we told the truth in the past leaves us with nothing to keep track of. We can simply be ourselves." – Sam Harris, from his book *Lying*

I remember when I discovered that my friend's daughter would lie to her mother about details of her personal life and kind of silly things. I asked her why she lied, and she said, "Because the truth would hurt my mother's feelings." We discussed how she felt for a while, then I shared with her that from my viewpoint the reason why she was lying would hurt her mother more. She has led her mother to believe that her daughter is a different person than who she truly is. She was not giving her mother an opportunity to have an authentic relationship with her; in reality, she did not know how her mother would respond. I assumed her mother's feeling would be hurt more at the notion that her daughter did not trust her.

A relationship like this is not relating; it is more like surviving each other. I shared that if her mother did not accept her or her truth, then she did what was proper in respecting her mother with sharing truth. Choosing to build her relationship with her mother with respect and honor is her responsibility and what is expected from her character. This goes for any relationship; with the foundation of untruth, you are setting up the relationship to fail.

On the other hand, when you give your loved ones an opportunity to know you as your genuine Self, you are setting the stage where there is opportunity for an authentic bond – where there is capacity for mutual understanding and acceptance, setting up the relationship to succeed.

You Are Responsible For You

Once, I had a client named Rose who was feeling hurt and upset that her marriage ended. I listened carefully to her as she shared her feelings for some time. As she continued, she lost track of what she was saying and shared herself in a more vulnerable and raw way. She was surprised when I repeated back to her that she mentioned several times that over the years she and her husband both focused on separate interests; they both worked hard and basically lived separate lives. She said that she felt she could not really be herself in her marriage and that her husband did not really know her. She kept many feelings and experiences to herself and felt they were more like roommates than a married couple.

After she was done expressing herself, she cried and had different emotions reflecting on her years of marriage. She sat in amazement that 15 years had gone by and they did not know one another and this made her feel a bit lost in a world she thought she knew. She felt frustrated that she felt he did not see her for who she really was and disappointed she was not her Self. So I said, "Perhaps your husband really did not divorce YOU, he divorced your false Self." Her face lit up as this resonated with her deeply. He did not know her and she was not herself around him. She presented to him who she thought she was supposed to be in the relationship. She was frustrated in the marriage because she felt limited to be who he wanted her to be. Rose still had all her feelings towards the marriage, but realizing that she was not really her Self gave her a feeling that she was not necessarily a failure and that she had a chance for happiness if she would be genuine about who she is.

Nevertheless, she acknowledged that she stopped paying attention to who she was and who he was because her focus was on her belief that you are to stay married no matter what, so survival took the main stage. Her belief to hold onto a marriage contract was stronger than giving the marriage a chance by being who she really was inside. Perhaps if she had shown up as her truth, things would have been different. We worked on releasing her resentment towards her husband and on her feelings of blaming him. This was not about blame but more about her taking responsibility for her feelings and moving forward.

Many times when we are not our true Self with another, we blame them for this and build resentment. If you think about it, how can you blame another for taking away your voice? I understand that situations can be challenging and we may change for another or make compromises based on their promises, but we were the ones who made the choice. As adults we can make choices; in reality, that is what we are doing when we choose to be authentic or not.

Rose and her husband had children together so the separation felt difficult for them. I do not think anyone marries in the hopes of getting divorced. The children were confused about what was really happening. They were being told one thing and then the behaviors of their parents showed another. Their reality felt chaotic, because they were confused about what to believe and trust. They felt the blame that their mother and father felt towards each other and did not know how to process this as they wished to love both parents. This especially affected one of their children to feel insecure about trusting her Self and this was reflecting in her behaviors.

Divorces, breakups and family disruptions can be very painful. But mixed messaging can be more damaging. The truth may be hurtful and not something anyone wants to hear, but sharing what is really happening can avoid unnecessary damage to the relationships.

I share with my children that if they know there is something they need to be truthful about and if we communicate it right away, we have an opportunity to deal with the consequences in a noble way. Confronting the truth sooner rather than later allows the issue to be dealt with instead of adding more feelings of hurt and betrayal. We all have done things that we need to own up to, and taking responsibility for them can seem like the world is going to end, but we all know that is not so. Keeping inside what we wish to share or clear up can be worse, do what you feel you should do to resolve the truth to free up the energy for healing.

If others feel hurt by you sharing what is truthful to you, this is a different type of hurt. You are acknowledging your truth and willing to take responsibility. The other person does not have to agree or may be disappointed, and you may have to work on healing with each other. But at least there is a base of truth to work with. This is healthier than building a relationship on lies disguised as truth. *Building from truth – meaning each person's perspective of their truth, each owning their feelings – allows for the possibility of healing.*

Share your truth gently and take responsibility for your feelings without expecting others to be responsible for you or expecting them to change for you. There is no need to be harsh with your truth or project it onto others, as this can cause unnecessary pain. I remember hearing a saying that went something like, *"Truth with a knife is not truth, it is just hurtful."* That has stuck with me because people should be aware of why they are sharing their truth or telling someone their truth – what is the reason, to hurt or heal.

Authenticity Attracts Light

There is no Light when we build from a foundation of falsehood. You honor another by being your Authentic Self. We are an example of what we believe, especially to children. Children especially should be able to trust that those they hold dear to their hearts are transparent with what they say and how they live. We ask so much from children to live a life of values; the ones closest to them must be the example of this.

If I could leave you with one message to fully embody and trust, it is that the power of being your Self creates a blessed life.

Acknowledging who you are by being authentic, you bring more blessings into your life, and you are a blessing to others when sharing this way. Your authentic presence creates a clean energetic connection; others feel emotionally safe with you, as a person that they can authentically connect with. Trust that your Authentic Self brings positive energy to your relationships and creates healing, prosperity and synergy that is positive for all. Do not pay attention to the way things may appear; pay attention to being authentic in your life and trust that all will be well because of this. Do not waiver on this and create the stage for others to do the same.

Expand Your Soul's Playground

There is a saying that I use ... *"Unite with Light-minded Souls."* By this, I mean surround yourself with people who share a love that supports you with an environment you believe in. Where do you feel loved and invited to share your true Self with others? Make a mental list. Where are those places and who are those people? If a place or person does not make the list, there does not need to be any drama, no long ceremony of blame. Sometimes things are what they are. Next!

And if there are situations that you feel you are not able to change at this moment, no worries. Having clarity of what you would like to do is already creating movement in that direction.

My dear friends are truly supportive of my sensitivity and with who I am. It is important to us that we feel comfortable just being; we do not feel this pressure to perform for one another. No need to feel that we have to be *on*, be a certain way or do certain things to keep in each other's good graces.

I often mention in my seminars that I find it interesting how sometimes friends are not necessarily truthful with each other because they feel it is a way of being polite. Why should anyone have to lie or make up that you or your child is sick in order to not have to show up somewhere? To me, it is untruthful to show up with a smile if you wish you weren't there, for whatever reason, big or small. Of course, I am not suggesting anyone be impolite. If you choose to be a guest in someone's home or accept an invitation, receive this graciously by adding value to the other with your sincerity. Others may have their reason why they may decline an invitation from me. I wish to thank them for being sincere and not choosing to do something that is uncomfortable for them out of an obligation and then eventually creating discomfort for all of us.

Personally, I go to places that I truly wish to go to. I feel it is a disservice to the host to show up to an event or a dinner party with the energy of not wanting to be there. If we know the power of our energy to manifest and words that support this, why would you lie and use something you do not wish to manifest as an excuse? For example, my child is sick, a death in the family, an accident – these things you do not desire. At the time, telling the truth may seem overwhelming, but the alternative is worse.

We all have a vibrational energy that is a language that tells the truth of what we are feeling. This is why at times you hear what someone is saying but your gut feeling tells you they mean something else. In reality, their Vibrational Language is what you are hearing clearly, even though at the moment you may not be able to process that gut feeling.

When your intentions are clear and you are present, you give positive Light to others.

Enhance your surroundings by using your presence and energy as a positive influence. If you are not able to do this for whatever reason, stay home. Honor yourself and another by being sincere and energetically clean.

The Truth Of A Lie

Take a moment to reflect on this very common habit of justifying lies that so many of us have become accustomed to. What would be the worst thing to happen if you told the truth? What if in telling the truth something full of life happens that clears the air? What if the truth carries a force that is clean and that will not attract drama, as lies do? When I speak of "truth," I speak of truth that is gentle and kind, not hurtful or spiteful. What if the truth truly sets you free?

"A truth told with bad intent beats all the lies you can invent."
– William Blake

Expect From Another What You Give

It is simple; if you desire truth from others, embody truth. We cannot wish from another what we are not willing to be. What you expect from another, be this yourself. Be the example of what you expect from others in your life.

Accept the truths you wish to live by and play with them in your imagination so you practice being comfortable with them as your experience. See yourself living with what you expect to receive by being your Self. Be conscious of your awareness towards how you feel, believe that the consequence for being your Self is positive.

Release others from being a certain way in order for you to be your Self and have the life you say you wish. Demonstrate to others who you are and how you wish to be treated. Think of it this way: how can you expect others to treat you as you wish if you are not showing them what you expect by being your Self? This is conflicting on so many levels. You are setting them up to fail. Set up those in your life to succeed in having a healthy relationship with you by being your Self. You will be pleasantly surprised with others as they embrace your Authentic Self. You have everything to gain by this and so do they. You will also find that you are more accepting of others as they are.

Through this process, it is possible that a relationship may shift in your life. If the relationship ends, then bless them on their way. Appreciate the presence they have in your life and honor them. Pray for another the same prayer you would wish for yourself. Treat them with dignity and trust the process of evolution for all. As you bless relationships to take the course that serves you both best, you make room to receive a match for what you wish for, and free them for the same.

Be True To Thy Self

This reminds me of another client, Celia, who had been married for 12 years and then decided to divorce. She and her husband remained respectful and amiable during the divorce. They did not have children in the marriage, even though my client would have liked to. Her ex-husband had disclosed to her that he would not marry her unless she agreed to a life without children. She had married him for love, although a bit reluctantly under this condition, and accepted this fate even though she had a strong underlying desire for children. For several years they knew that they were not as happy as they expected but kept the marriage going. They were able to do this by focusing on being very successful professionals and traveling often (separately) for their work.

Finally, instead of continuing to be in denial, they both came to the decision to be in their truth about their marriage. By this time, the marriage was quite predictable and basically ran like a business.

Once they came to their decision that it was over, it was over. For many on the outside, it seemed so surprisingly quick and without drama as they both seemed fine. Their family and friends did not even invite conversation, it just was what it was; their marriage was over and they both moved on.

Later my client came to see me again and felt that maybe she had a chance to have children. Being in her mid-40s, she felt that maybe it was too late, but she still imagined it for herself. She kept playing with the idea in her imagination and now that the divorce was final, she was excited by the vision that maybe some day she could be a mom. After so many years of putting this vision on the sidelines (even though it was never forgotten), she became present with enjoying the feeling that this could be a possibility. On the other hand, her ex-husband was now in his early 50s and was oddly also regretting that he did not have children. He played with the idea of what it would feel like if he had children, imagining how different his life would have been.

Let's fast-forward to what happened a year after their divorce. Celia meets a man with three children and is gracefully welcomed into the family to share with his children. Even though she was happy, she still has this burning desire to have her own child. She cannot deny her wish, so she shares this with her boyfriend after five months of dating. She is now pregnant with twins.

Her ex-husband falls deeply in love with a new woman who has two young children of her own and the children accept him with genuine joy. He feels like he knows how to be a father to these children and enjoys his new family so much.

A Magical Life

Their love stories continue to unfold and show us that anything is possible. Definitions of truths and life change. Beliefs shift. Relationships end and new ones begin.

By the way, even though this couple divorced, they are presently happy for each other, as they feel fortunate they chose to be in the truth of their relationship, which I believe led them to their present happiness. There is no sense of regret; it almost seems as if their marriage was in the far distant past with the experience of new love.

Sometimes in the moment of present circumstances, things do not look possible. This is why whatever you wish for; do not base it on what seems possible in your present reality.

It is amazing what can happen when people stay on the course of their definition of truth and stepping into this as their life, they also find others that define life the similar. Stay up to date in a positive way with your truth in your relationships. Not everyone has to agree, but it is important to ask questions and answer in a way that is truthful.

I am so passionate about empowering others to believe in being themselves. Living in your truth really has so many beautiful benefits and miracles. I have witnessed this time and time again. When you are choosing to be genuine, you trust moments differently. You trust with a knowing that these moments are scenes in the "Movie" you designed for your Self, feeling a strong connection to your Self and Divine Love.

Being open to the different opportunities that are presented to you, and trusting that this will create possibilities that you can manifest easily in your life, is a good belief to have. I believe that when we consistently feel struggle or the exhausting effort to make a relationship work, it is because we are going against a flow that is naturally aligned with who we are.

Live with your inner Self and your outer personality as one. Do not discourage new possibilities for living as your true Self because you have been comfortable with a personality that was not a full representation of you or was a misrepresentation of who you truly are. It really does not matter why you have not lived fully in your truth, what matters is the decision to live this way now.

There is less effort in being you. Life seems magical but in essence it is a response to you being you. This is what truly creates miracles ... all else follows.

Be The Example Of What You Believe Is Possible

Remain attuned to your beliefs that serve your whole being and have total certainty that this will serve the ones you love as this is basic Universal Law. Again, do not concern yourself with others' reactions, as this is for them to work out. Concern yourself with being virtuous and truthful as you honor others, as this is the greatest security to preserve your wellbeing and the integrity towards others.

No matter how wonderful your life has been up to now, no matter what you have experienced as the best moments in your life, know with total certainty that you will have plenty more positive experiences as you expand and awaken to living with authenticity.

Imagine yourself living with your definition of what is virtuous for you, feel what you can expect from this feeling relaxed with the freedom of being you.

As you continue to be an example of what you believe is possible, this will be reflected in your reality. Your life is a reflection of your desires and expectations. You cannot create what you do not believe you cannot have, nor can Source Energy create this for you. As you create what you believe is possible, Source Energy honors your creation. Also, please know that whatever you define as a mistake from your past is insignificant compared to what possibilities you have now.

"The Light is more than some abstract, unknowable energy force. Light is Truth. If Light is truth, then darkness must be lies. Each and every lie we tell to others and ourselves casts the shadow of separation upon us. Every time even the most minor deception is revealed and the truth is made known we are re-united with the Light. So, let there be Light. Those are the words by which you can create your own magnificent world."
– Renee Bledsoe

You Create One Experience; Therefore You Can Create Another

All of life is in constant motion; you cannot stop the evolution of life around you. Therefore, nothing stays the same from one moment to the next. If you try to remain the same or hold onto old beliefs that no longer serve you, the motion you create is struggle. It is that simple.

If there is motion anyway, then allow the motion move forward, not backwards towards your past. You would not get to your destination by looking in your rear view mirror. Choose to look forward to the destination of your dreams by being more of an expansion of your true Self. The time is now to fully honor the gift of your life by honoring your Self and those you love by being you. Everything is possible ... everything is possible with love, especially self-love.

Your Voice Is Your Voice And No Other Voice Compares

When you listen to your Self, the voice inside is powerful and knows you. Listen to your voice as a song that you love to play over and over again. You are alive and the world is full of possibilities. Feeling good about the way you feel, life is presented as a dance to this song. Your Emotional Imagination® is colorful and full of dreams being true.

You are crystal, crystal clear with your voice as you step into the outside world. You notice that though you feel crystal clear, not everyone feels the same way you do. This can be uncomfortable at times. Nevertheless, you allow them to have their "Movie" and you have yours.

Sometimes, the doubts of the people closest to you can have you to second-guess your Voice. You love them so and out of this love do not wish to disappoint them. When this happens, you may feel you should be more of a reflection of who they say you should be, even though it does not bring you peace. Then the voice inside you that loves them feels that maybe it is better to silence your voice as to not lose a loved one.

Others may hold the belief that living for your dream is not being responsible. You can feel the voices of those who love you challenging what you wish to expand in your belief and love towards your Self. You step back and witness this "Movie" and know that everyone is different, so you may attempt to explain your Self but it seems to not make a difference to some people that you love. Because again, they have their "Movie" and you have yours. You start feeling the forces of social pressure step in to challenge what you believe is possible. You gently hold strong to being you, feeling this as a good thing.

You would not make others wrong for not agreeing. You may encourage others to be themselves. It may even feel like you start to experience a negative consequence for being different. But as you reflect, you actually have noticed more harmony and calmness in your life by being the expression of your voice and are confused how this could be wrong. You still stay strong knowing how to stay in your "Movie." Then that one day comes when you arrive at a crossroads and must make a decision.

At times you felt so sure but surprisingly you get an attack of the "BBB Syndrome." This could happen to any of us at any time when we begin to rationalize our situation and feel we should rethink being ourselves. "But ... but ... but ..." You start questioning your Self. You feel hurt for the way you were questioned or belittled by others for what you feel. You are now aware that there is risk to owning what you believe. You ask your Self, "What is my greatest risk for being my voice?"

And then in an instant ... BAM! Instead of this questioning leading you to your own "Movie," you end up in your "Mental Courtroom," inside your head with beliefs presenting their case and stating their arguments. You are trying to discern whose voice you are hearing – your parents, loved ones, society, manager, co-workers? These other voices are influencing YOUR voice.

Is it challenging to hear your own voice when there are other voices in your head? Are your emotions and logic also wishing to make their case? We all have these kinds of conversations going on in our head from time to time; emotions versus our logic or society challenging who we believe we are. Because of this, you start to ask the opinions of others, thinking this will help you have clarity. You choose to ask questions in the hopes of receiving supportive answers from the ones you are hoping to convince. But this does not always produce the best answers.

At times you really wish to hear your Authentic Voice again, the voice that kept you company but in this moment other voices in your head are louder and your voice fades. You feel as if you are starting to surrender to the voice of others. You recognize how long you have done this in certain areas in your life.

Then the case in your "Mental Courtroom" starts to strengthen, fueled by the opinions of others, of those you are hoping to convince. You start thinking and fears come up, then you feel guilty of being foolish or crazy with a belief that you hold dear to your heart, a belief of your Self and possibilities of dreams that made you feel so good. Now you are tired.

You feel defeated and then you think, "How can I argue with 'the expert witnesses,' the ones that know so much, the ones that are older than I, the ones that have lived with me for so long, have had more experience or preach the word of God or loved ones that say they love me?" You give over your power as if these people are truly the authorities on the subject of YOU. They say they are being critical because they love you and they want the best for you. You do not agree, but your fears now also take the place of your voice.

You are exhausted. That once strong voice of yours becomes silent. Not realizing it, you become numb and create a life to reacting to others' definition of who you are.

Then you feel foolish whenever your voice wants to be heard. You are silent in your Soul's calling and believe you will receive a consequence of rejection if you start that *talk* again. Now you have trained your Self to stay silent, or convinced your Self that there will be a stronger negative consequence if you keep listening to your Authentic Voice.

When the belief you held close to your heart starts to voice itself, you remember that the jury can and will go back into your "Mental Courtroom" and it may be worse. Fear becomes the main witness in your belief system. Your actions are now mainly motivated by fear, so you do whatever to avoid consequences for being your Self, which translates into not having a life of your own.

Renew Your Voice; Wake Up Your Soul

At one time or another, we have all gone against ourselves. It is time to release voices that do not feel harmonious and loving in your head. The time is now to listen to your Self. If not now, when?

When you feel that you are going against your Self, close your eyes and go to a favorite memory of when you felt calm or happy. You can comfort your Self and bring your Self to your center. Play with this like a movie, and you will feel better.

As you deepen your practice of Power Wishing®, you will begin listening to your Self differently. Your "fix-it" voice, your chaotic emotional energy and the habit of slipping into the "BBB Syndrome" will have less of a presence in your day-to-day life. You transform the voice of the dreams in your head to reflect your attitudes and focus. With respect and honor towards your Self, you hear the actions you can take to enhance the positive aspects about your Self that you believe in.

Listening to your true voice also moves unnecessary influences out of your way and makes room for those that add value to your life. Those who wish to control you are not expressing love; they are controlling and selfish. This is not love; it is selfish manipulation.

See yourself as a chemist, mixing and blending emotions and beliefs to create your possible outcome. Now experiment with this formula and watch it become your life.

Release challenging to trust your inner voice and you will be pleasantly surprised at how easily your days flow. If you look at this in a practical sense, you will see this as a formula of using your energy productively and efficiently. Your wishes will be granted in a productive and efficient way.

You will also benefit from clear discernment of how you are influenced by others. Guess what else happens using your energy in this productive way? You will accomplish more in the same amount of time without feeling exhausted. It is so exhausting to fight within your Self and amongst others to be heard or seen for who you know you are. Next! Allow your energy to work for you, which keeps your Emotional GPS fully charged and on target for your wishes granted.

You do not gain from unnecessary pain. Keep it simple and joyful, as there is everything to gain from this.

What You "See" Is What You Are Feeling

We become our dreams based on how we believe they can be true. Power Wishing is not a system that is robotic. It is a Visualization Technology® that brings awareness with formulas for you to build on as a part of your day-to-day life.

Power Wishing supports you to play energetically with different ways of dealing with certain situations; to review your beliefs to wake up to the best of you; and to own your life choices while allowing others to own theirs. In this energetic play, you transform the energy of your choice into a reality in your life.

It is a normal survival skill to do the same thing over and over and over again and create a pattern that you feel obliged to defend, even over your Authentic Self.

Ask your Self questions to go deeper into finding answers and become more familiar with the fullness of your Authentic Self. The voice of your questions and answers guides you to breaking patterns that are outdated for you – patterns that you created to *survive* your life and not *live* it.

If we do not question ourselves from a place of empowering ourselves to be aware and awake, then, without realizing it, we fall asleep to the wake-up call of our true self and confuse our habits for false awareness.

Sometimes you may not know how to support the dreams of your loved ones because you would have to go outside the box of what you expect from them. You would sincerely have to be there for them without an agenda or a love that controls.

Do not expect from others what you are not capable of giving.

We all choose different ways to support ourselves financially, physically, spiritually and emotionally. Where do you go to be supported for who you wish to be as an expression of your life experience?

Knowing yourself takes time, consideration, patience, experience and, most valuable, love. Knowing others also requires an open mind and heart to allow the other to simply be.

Who others are is not a reflection of you; it is a reflection of who they are. They are accountable for the world they are creating, as are you.

Are You Choosing?

Choose to be your Self. Even if you feel you cannot make different choices right now in your present circumstances, at least be aware of the choices you would like to make. Be aware of what choices you believe are in your control and choose them; do what you can now. Later is NOW.

Hopefully, sooner rather than later you will be so uncomfortable with not being your Self that you take action with your choices now. The choices and opportunities are always there; it is you who makes the choice to take them. Ask your Self, "What is the best thing that can happen if I listen to myself?" There is such greatness on every level waiting to match your greatness. What are you waiting for? Later is NOW.

The Reboot Technique

The *Reboot Technique* is another tool that you can choose that will support you to break patterns, in a moment's notice. In my seminars, I noted that my clients needed something they could do quickly in the heat of the moment – to strengthen themselves before a business meeting or when they feel really excited and wish to stay in that state rather than go into a pattern that does not support their joy. So I created the *Reboot Technique* as a fun and effective method to center your intentions to manifest quickly.

The Powerful Amazing Soul

Now for a moment let's play with knowing that you are so powerful and you can make things appear in your world. YOU ... this Amazing Soul!

The super powers you have been gifted with are your feelings and beliefs that activate the creation of your world.

Long ago, as an Amazing Soul, you were given knowledge and training on how to respect and use this great power you have been given. Your deep understanding of how to use your Emotional Imagination to activate your feelings and beliefs in your outside world is inside you. Basically, you are your own superhero!

As your own superhero with strong character values, you have accepted the responsibility of this power to create your world. You know that only YOU have the power to make things happen for your Self. You can love others, but they also have the power to create their own world and they are responsible for managing their own "superhero powers."

In accepting this great gift and having this power, you agreed to the following terms in your contract:

- You can no longer blame anyone. This includes but is not limited to loved ones, parents, society or circumstance.
- You must take full responsibility for what has been created as your physical world.
- You are responsible for the Vibrational Language you give off to others and society.
- Life circumstances or your past do not dictate your future, and you accept that you have control of this.
- You take accountability for your life being based on your choice of what you believe about your Self and what you believe you can expect from this world.
- You can create your life as a reflection of a dream or a nightmare; your choice.
- You are experiencing your Self as a human being, exploring your spiritual Self as an Emotional Self in the physical.

As an Amazing Soul who has super powers here on Earth, it was shared with you that there was the possibility that you might create unwanted desires from time to time. This is expected as you have vulnerabilities and are expanding. You are also exploring love; love for your Self and with others.

Just in case this may happen, you received the *Reboot Technique* as a back-up plan as a way to recreate and strengthen the knowing of the voice of your best Emotional Self. This is a gift that you can use whenever you wish to bring yourself back to knowing the Amazing Soul that you are.

You are aware that unwanted experiences are a possibility. When this happens you "Reboot," because you know that experience is an opportunity to know the contrast of what you do not wish for. You use this experience as awareness to strengthen your emotional anchor and move forward with greater intensity.

Reboot, Refresh, Recharge. This is a must to keep your super powers active to their fullest capacity. Know you can "Reboot" anytime, anywhere and the results are lightening quick!

The Reboot Technique:

Close your eyes and take a few breaths.
Know just by awareness of your breathing that you are consciously connecting to your Self and Source Energy.

Right in between those breathes ... Go into the unwanted desire ...
Feel this or a situation that is not a reflection of who you believe you are at this moment.

Acknowledge the scene and let the "Movie" of this play out for a moment.
Feel the way you feel about your Self in this scene.
Knowing how you feel at this moment, ask your Self how would you like to feel instead?
Feel this feeling the best you can ...

Ask for a memory that has a similar feeling ... play with this feeling of what it can feel like.

Knowing that you can make a different choice, watch your Self play out any scene in your imagination with your new feeling of choice.

Ask for any memory that reminds you of what you love about you. Use this memory to connect you more with knowing that how you wish to feel NOW is a real possibility.
Playing with the feelings that you love will activate more of this ...

Grab onto this feeling in your imagination NOW as if you literally take your hands and grab it. With your hands take that feeling you wish for now, and see the scene of the unwanted desire and cover the scene with this new feeling.

Feel the same situation with the feelings that are possible now. Take this feeling and rewrite your present scene to what you know you can expect. Breathe ... Next!

Own the feeling you are choosing, you have the power to own this feeling. All other feelings that you do not wish to own as your own are vanished. You are a superhero, and YOU make a difference in this world by your presence.

Your Character = You

"Be more concerned with your character than your reputation, because your character is what you really are, while your reputation is merely what others think you are." – John Wooden

There are many changes in life: countries get destroyed and there is war where humans devastate and are left devastated; weather patterns that are uncertain; people who do the unthinkable.

There are many uncertainties. But what you can be certain of is YOU: your character, your values, the way you treat your Self and another. Your love is the reflection of your world.

Character Is Not A Mood; It Is A Choice.

It's your choice!
Why be someone's version of you?
Choose to be your true and best Self.
When in doubt, choose your Authentic Voice!
When in joy, give more joy.
Believe love heals all.
Your Soul Will Win!

Imagine This

Imagine a world where everyone practiced the utmost honesty with himself or herself, where no one would cause each other pain. Where we all lived without regret, we hold ourselves responsible and honored each other's choices. The world being free of self-importance, self-righteousness with no deceit, regrets, blame or excuses. Imagine yourself creating this world because these are your virtues and because of your presence, others choose to enhance their world also.

Power Thoughts

Your Voice Is Your Truth

- o   I am the example of what I believe is possible.

- o   I manifest plenty more positive experiences as I live with authenticity.

- o   I created one experience; therefore, I can create another.

- o   My voice is my voice and no other voice compares.

- o   Life circumstances or my past do not dictate my future.

- o   Reboot, Refresh, Recharge.

- o   I am accountable for my life based on my choices.

- o   Greatness on every level is ready to match my greatness.

- o   The time is now to fully honor the gift of my life by honoring my Self.

- o   Everything is possible ... everything is possible with love.

You Get What You Expect

I have a passion for hearing people's stories. I am genuinely curious and intrigued to listen to what others believe and what they have created as a result of this. It fascinates me to witness their beliefs and see what they have manifested and how this is reflected in their world. It is all based on their belief of expectations. People have lived their stories attached to their beliefs for so long, they are usually not even aware of the beliefs that are running their lives.

When was the last time you reflected on your beliefs? Your feelings, words and images that you play over and over again in your mind reinforce your belief system, which creates your life. Understanding and acknowledging your beliefs is vital, because your beliefs are running your life. *You get what you expect.* Do you know who you are according to your beliefs? Where do your beliefs come from? Are your beliefs really your own?

Mirroring Positive Qualities

There have been times where I knew I needed to shift beliefs about myself, but my surroundings at the time were not supporting the beliefs I wished to carry. So I would immerse myself in books and movies in order to absorb the attributes of the person I wished to mirror and to embody those positive qualities I wished to enhance in my Self.

It is also powerful when you hang around others in surroundings that you admire. I find myself being around people who I believe are smarter than I or who have an interest that I admire; they stimulate possibilities within myself.

My grandmother was from Cuba and she lived a very privileged life until she left her home country to immigrate to the United States. Like members of many other Cuban families, she was sure at the time she left that she would go back to Cuba and her life in the States would be temporary. I remember that as a young girl I spent a tremendous amount of time with my grandmother. She had a great influence on me in regards to the person I am today. Besides knowing several languages and having studied in the best schools, she was a very determined person. She had me learn new things, and taught me with patience. Since the age of eight, I accompanied my grandparents on trips to Europe, where we would travel to museums to study art and music. She wanted to give me the experience of understanding the world from a broader perspective.

She was an entrepreneur, her family was entrepreneurial, and if there was one thing that I learned from her, it was that she had very clear beliefs. She owned her belief systems and lived by them; "no" did not exist in her vocabulary. She may have challenged me on my belief systems or our beliefs may have been different, but I felt there was mutual respect between us. At times she would get frustrated with me and say, "When you get something in your head, you do not let it go!" She was right and some things have not changed.

Like my grandmother, we could get lost in our hobbies. She could always entertain herself, and I do not ever remember her being bored. She would tell me that I was always inventing something new, but she would be right next to me making sure I had what I needed for my invention. Neither of us needed much outside entertainment. My grandmother was an artist, and I was creating or spending time exploring. I feel that I am an artist with my words, my work and my life as a creation, and I appreciate the encouragement my grandmother gave me.

At the same time, she was a businesswoman, a highly educated, experienced woman who did what was necessary to support her family, whether it was selling valuable assets, investing in a business or in a piece of land. After leaving Cuba, she also did babysitting for three dollars an hour at strangers' homes. I would go with her, as I was curious about how other people of *means* lived. She would read books in different languages as she continuously educated herself; this was a good example for me.

After leaving Cuba, my grandfather, an MIT graduate, sorted mail at the post office to be able to support their family. Amongst my grandparents, there was an attitude of resolving and figuring out a solution. They did not ever take on a "poor-me" mentality. I do remember my grandmother speaking of her past, but one story in particular she repeated to me several times, which I feel has a great impact on the way I share with others.

As You Believe, So It Is

My grandmother had five sons and one daughter. At the time of the Vietnam War, four of her sons were in the military at the same time. I cannot even imagine what that must have been like, especially after leaving your home country to make a new life for yourself. She felt she owed a lot to this country, as did her sons.

At one point, she disagreed with President Johnson and thought to tell him so; this was not a surprise if you knew my grandmother. As a woman from Cuba with no political connections or background in this country, she decided to write her senators and submit a letter to President Johnson. I have a newspaper clipping with the headline "Johnson says, 'I need to speak to this woman, she has something I need to hear.'"

Basically, President Johnson received her letter and personally called her. Then my grandmother and grandfather were invited to make an official visit to the White House.

In my office, I have a picture that I treasure: it is a close-up of just my grandmother and the President walking together up a set of stairs, seemingly having an intimate conversation. She would point to that picture and share this story that I will always remember.

She said that she shared with President Johnson that he should always fight communism because she, along with many others, had made the ultimate sacrifice. She had four sons in the military and now she only had three living sons because one died in action.

She would share with me that though President Johnson was compassionate, they did not agree on some issues. Over my years with her, she would repeat over and over again this part of the conversation. He said to her, "Mrs. Carricarte, we may not always agree, but we can reason with each other." This is what she would say to me when we would think differently. In all sincerity, this knowledge is a precious and beautiful gift that my grandmother left me.

She expressed to me that people should reason with each other rather than pushing each other to believe what the other believes or deciding who is right or wrong. This does not mean that people always agreed, but this style of communication can bring out positive results.

I can attest that this was not always the style of communication my grandmother took on, as she was strong towards her beliefs, but I felt that we reasoned with each other and this allowed me to appreciate our differences, along with others.

Imagine. How did she get to the White House? No contacts, little money – there is no logic to this. I share this as an example to remind you that the convictions of your beliefs are how things get resolved. Of course, you must take actions when opportunities present themselves, but the desire and strong belief that it will happen is the ticket.

As you believe, so you conceive.
As you believe, so you aspire.
As you believe, so you perceive.

Your Perspective Creates

There are many individuals who choose not to allow other people's perspectives to dominate their lives, even despite criticism. They follow their beliefs, despite the risk of losing everything to gain what they believe. Sometimes I hear people say, "I will have to lose everything in order to live what I believe."

In my perspective, living what you believe is gaining everything. What are you really losing if you are not living according to what you believe? What you are really losing is your perception of loss, and let's be clear – you are imagining a loss that has not even happened.

I have listed some people who overcame their present reality, in which it did not seem possible to succeed by other people's perceptions. Nevertheless, they followed their beliefs and trusted being led by the burning desire in their Soul, their beliefs. The valuable quality that these people had in common was that they were able stay expansive in their own minds, thinking of new possibilities regardless of what the outside world was telling them.

I Have A Dream

"Don't ever let someone tell you, you can't do something. Not even me. You got a dream, you got to protect it. People can't do something themselves, they want to tell you can't do it. You want something, go get it. Period." – Chris Gardener, from The Pursuit of Happyness

Michael Jordan, one of the greatest basketball players in the world, did not make the basketball team in his first year of high school. He said, "I have missed more than 9,000 shots in my career. I have lost almost 300 games. On 26 occasions I have been entrusted to take the game winning shot, and I missed. I have failed over and over and over again in my life. And that is why I succeed."

J.K Rowling, the author of *Harry Potter*, spoke to the graduating class of Harvard in June 2008. She said, "You might never fail on the scale I did, but it is impossible to live without failing at something, unless you live so cautiously that you might as well not have lived at all – in which case, you fail by default." She should know. The author didn't magically become richer than the Queen of England overnight. Penniless, recently divorced and raising a child on her own, she wrote the first Harry Potter book on an old manual typewriter. Twelve publishers rejected the manuscript. A year later she was given the green light from Bloomsbury, who agreed to publish the book but insisted she get a day job because there was no money in children's books. What if? What if she stopped at the first rejection? Or stopped at the fifth, sixth, seventh, eighth or ninth rejection?

Harland David Sanders, the famous "Colonel" and founder of KFC, started his dream at 65 years old! He was mad that his social security checks were only $105. Instead of complaining, he did something about it. He thought restaurant owners would love his fried chicken recipe, so he drove around the country knocking on doors, sleeping in his car, wearing his white suit and selling his special fried chicken. He received a "No" over 1,000 times before he received the "Yes" that turned his recipe into a business.

Walt Disney, the man who gave us Disney World and Mickey Mouse, had his first animation company go bankrupt. Legend has it he was turned down 302 times before he got financing to create Disney World. A newspaper editor fired Walt Disney because he "lacked imagination and had no good ideas." Several more of his businesses failed before the premiere of his movie *Snow White*. Today, his legacy includes a multi-billion dollar business and has affected countless childhoods that wouldn't be the same without his imaginative ideas.

Mark Cuban, the billionaire owner of the NBA's Dallas Mavericks, got rich when he sold his company to Yahoo for $5.9 billion in stock. He admitted he was terrible at his early jobs. His parents wanted him to have a normal job. So he tried carpentry but hated it. He was a short order cook but a terrible one and waited tables but couldn't open a bottle of wine. He says of his failures "I've learned that it doesn't matter how many times you failed. You only have to be right once. I tried to sell powdered milk. I was an idiot a lot of the time, and I learned from them all."

Theodor Seuss Geisel is the real name of the author Dr. Seuss, who gave us *Cat in the Hat* and *Green Eggs and Ham*. These classic imaginative books are read to children everywhere, in numerous languages. At first, many didn't think he would succeed. Twenty-seven different publishers rejected Dr. Seuss's first book *To Think That I Saw It on Mulberry Street.*

John Grisham, the American author, was first a lawyer. He loved to write and his first book *A Time to Kill* took three years to write. The book was rejected 28 times until it was accepted for a 5,000-copy print. He's sold over 250 million total copies of his books.

Steven Spielberg applied and was denied two times to the prestigious University of Southern California film school. Instead, he went to Cal State University in Long Beach. He went on to direct some of the biggest movie blockbusters in history. Now he's worth $2.7 billion and in 1994 he got an honorary degree from the film school that rejected him.

Stephen King's first book *Carrie* was rejected 30 times and he then threw it in the trash. His wife retrieved it out of the trash and encouraged him to resubmit it. The rest is history. He has sold more than 350 million copies of his books.

Stephenie Meyer, the author of the *Twilight* series, said the inspiration for the book came from a dream. She finished it in three months but never intended to publish it until a friend suggested she should. She wrote 15 letters to literary agencies. Five didn't reply. Nine rejected her. One gave her a chance. Then eight publishers auctioned for the right to publish *Twilight*. She got a three-book deal worth $750,000. In 2010, *Forbes* reported she earned $40 million.

Tim Ferriss, the man behind the *4-Hour Workweek,* changed how many people view work and life. Twenty-six publishers rejected him before one gave him his chance. His book has been on the bestseller's list for years, sold all over the world, and last year he published *The 4-Hour Body*, which went to #1 on the New York Times bestsellers list.

Many record labels initially rejected the Beatles. In a famous rejection letter, the label said, "guitar groups are on the way out" and "the Beatles have no future in show business." After that, the Beatles signed with EMI, and became one of the greatest and most legendary bands in history.

Winston Churchill failed the sixth grade. He was defeated in every public office election he ran for before he became the British prime minister at the age of 62.

Thomas Edison's teachers told him he was "too stupid to learn anything." Edison also famously invented 1,000 light bulbs before creating one that worked.

R.H. Macy had a history of failing businesses, including a dud Macy's in NYC. But Macy kept up the hard work and ended up with the biggest department store in the world.

Executives rejected Charlie Chaplin's act because they thought it was too obscure for people to understand. But then they took a chance on Chaplin, who went on to become America's first bona fide movie star.

Marilyn Monroe's first contract with Columbia Pictures expired because they told her she wasn't pretty or talented enough to be an actress. Monroe kept plugging away and is one of the most iconic actresses and sex symbols of all time.

Soichiro Honda was passed over for an engineering job at Toyota and left unemployed. But then he began making motorcycles, started his own business and became the billionaire brand Honda.

Vera Wang failed to make the U.S. Olympic figure-skating team. Then she became an editor at *Vogue* and was passed over for the editor-in-chief position. She began designing wedding gowns at 40 and today is the premier designer in the business, with a multi-billion dollar industry.

Albert Einstein didn't speak until age four and didn't read until age seven. His teachers labeled him "slow" and "mentally handicapped." But Einstein just had a different way of thinking. He later won the Nobel Prize in physics.

The first time Jerry Seinfeld went onstage, he was booed away by the jeering crowd. Eventually, he became a famous comic with one of the most-loved sitcoms ever.

In Fred Astaire's first screen test, the judges wrote: "Can't act. Can't sing. Slightly bald. Can dance a little." Astaire went on to be the most famous dancer of all time and won the hearts of the public.

After Sidney Poitier's first audition, the casting director instructed him to just stop wasting everyone's time and "go be a dishwasher or something." He went on to win an Academy Award and is admired by actors everywhere.

Oprah Winfrey was fired from her television-reporting job because they told her she wasn't fit to be on screen, but Winfrey persevered and became the undisputed queen of television talk shows and a leading businesswoman, philanthropist and billionaire.

Lucille Ball spent many years on the B-list and her agent told her to pursue a new career. She almost quit acting right before she got her big break on *I Love Lucy*. Now she is an American acting legend.

Henry Ford's first auto company went out of business. He abandoned a second because of a fight and a third went downhill because of declining sales. Believing in his vision, he went on to become one of the greatest American entrepreneurs ever.

Outside Influences Are Added Value

Choose your outside influences not as a distraction but as added value to strengthen the belief of the YOU that you love! What you capture as truth reinforces your beliefs about what you believe you can expect. It's that simple.

A number of people that I mentioned turned great failures into great successes. What I appreciate about their stories is how they chose to define "failure."

One does not need failure to succeed, but if something has happened in your life that you have defined as a "failure," have you allowed this to define you?

"I am thankful for all of those who said NO to me. It's because of them I'm doing it myself." – Albert Einstein

If I were to go deeper into many of these individuals' stories, I would bet that they all have many common threads:

They believed in their expectation.
They were passionate about what they created.
They did not have some intense business strategic plan, it all started with a feeling with which they created their beliefs
They had a strong core about what they believed.
They knew what was non-negotiable in what they accepted as "truth."
They remained persistent.
They no longer lived in the expectations of others.
They accepted themselves and their vision.
They did not compare the reality they wished to have to others or discount their reality because others had a different one.
They did not choose to stay holding onto someone else's belief about them that did not serve them, even if that belief got them started.
Their success started as a passion or hobby.
They owned their vision.
They chose to define success and failure by their own definitions.

How many of these common threads do you have? These people believed in themselves and held onto their own vision and beliefs regardless of what the outside world was reflecting to them.

Surround Sound

Ray Dolby was an American engineer and inventor who created the Dolby sound system that you hear throughout movie theatres, as well as the original cassette player. If you glance at most stereo systems, VCRs or movie listings, chances are you'll see Dolby's last name or the opposing double "D" trademark. The brand has been stamped on an estimated 750 million electronic products since Ray Dolby began his company in London in 1965. He died recently and his story encapsulated a lot of what I have been sharing that I thought to recount a part of his story that inspires me.

Tom Dolby, his son who is a filmmaker and novelist, said: "Though he was an engineer at heart, my father's achievements in technology grew out of a love of music and the arts. He brought his appreciation of the artistic process to all of his work in film and audio recording."

To me, this is what it is all about: do what you love and you will have all that you desire. Heartfelt passion is a powerful asset for a peaceful well-lived life with happiness. Do not undermine the power of your beliefs, passions, goodness and your values. Your feelings towards what you love, being the genuine authentic you, is the base of creation at its best. Mr. Dolby invented a technology that is used all over the world and it was his passion that he paid attention to, not the invention. His inventions were the byproduct of his love for music and the arts.

This is a quote by Mr. Dolby himself that sums up what I am sharing: "To be an inventor, you have to be willing to live with a sense of uncertainty, to work in the darkness and grope toward an answer, to put up with the anxiety about whether there is an answer."

He also shared, "I had to spend a lot of time traveling and giving endless demonstrations to skeptical engineers all over the world who had been taught that noise reduction was impossible and that only charlatans came along once in a while with the promise of noise reduction." Basically, because of a "proven" scientific belief, no one was interested in listening. Did he allow other people's beliefs to stop his? Obviously not. He invented this not only because of his love of art and music but because he was focused on finding solutions.

Here is an excerpt from an interview about Mr. Dolby's interest and passion for flying:

Interviewer – "If you were that elated at age 14, why did you wait until age 57 to learn to fly?"

Dolby – "I took about eight hours of lessons during college, but I realized that it was an expensive proposition, and I didn't have any money. I also didn't have the time it would take to learn, so I put it on the back burner. I just didn't realize how long it would stay there."

Interviewer – **"**How did you go about making it happen?"

Dolby – "One day I started buying flying magazines. I think that's when my wife Dagmar knew the handwriting was on the wall. She and my two kids – who were still small then — told me how dangerous it was, but I prevailed and convinced them that it wasn't, and finally everyone came around and grew to like the idea."

Trust Time Is On Your Side

I share with others to trust in the timing of things. Clients come to say, "And why now," or "That was supposed to happen then." But, what I have learned is that experiences will come at a time when you truly feel it is a possibility. If your dreams are not coming true today, it does not mean this is impossible. If situations in our lives are not in alignment with what we wish to do, continue imagining your desire and feel it as a possibility.

Sometimes there is a timing for different things in life. Now is the time for me to publish my book even though this has been a lifelong dream. At some point I just resigned to trusting time is on my side. The timing will come and trust that when the time comes it will be *perfect timing.* In the meantime keep a visual of your dream. Surround yourself with images, environments and experiences that are in line with your dream. Just like when I finally took my trip to India after 20 years of yearning for this experience, everything worked in such a perfect way and quickly. I can assure you I could not have planned it so well. As you see, Mr. Dolby had taken some lessons, and then let the idea go. When he started reading magazines about flying, he brought the idea back into his vibration, and then it happened. He learned to fly!

I have seen countless people experience the joy of manifesting their dreams. So many times it begins with a feeling, a visual. With your belief, you dictate the outcome and it will be in perfect time.

Inspire By Reminding Others Of Their Best Self

Of these amazing people mentioned, so many were inspired by others. I am sure many of their mentors were teachers. I would like to take a moment and honor the experience of my teachers who were just being themselves, but to me they were mentors who made a difference.

There was one teacher in particular who changed my life and is a big part of knowing the experience of what I teach. My history teacher's name was Mr. O'Brien and, even as I begin to write this, my eyes water. I was a student who could have been lost in the system, but this story reminds us how one person can have an impact, especially a teacher. I was a student he could have ignored and not given time to. I was polite, but as I shared with my own children, I would often not attend school; I was bored with my classes, especially in a public school with a few thousand students.

One day, this rosy-cheeked man in his mid-sixties, who often wore a white shirt that was a bit tight for his belly, came to my desk to speak to me. He basically said, "You are a nice girl and I am sure you are quite smart, but you are not in my class very often. Why?" I am not sure exactly what I said but I do remember clearly what he said. "Let's make an agreement. If I let you study anything you want for a semester that is connected to history, would you come to class every day?" I said, "Yes, of course!" He said, "OK, what would you like to study?" I said, "Socrates. I love Socrates." Imagine this coming from a tenth grader who did not enjoy going to class.

This brilliant, simple teacher gave me material to study and asked me to write papers on Socrates. I was in class every day. I would not let down a teacher who believed in me and allowed me to be my own person, especially because he ignited my love of learning. Mr. O'Brien, with his innocent smile, had me dive into Socrates' history and Plato's *Republic* in the tenth grade. This had a profound effect on me.

By allowing me to connect with learning that inspired me, Mr. O'Brien embodied the example of "learn what you love." It became easy to show up every day for *me*. By "seeing" me, and communicating with me, we both had an uplifting, powerful experience … one that changed my life forever. Mr. O'Brien taught me that doing what you love is being responsible. It is what activates us to explore more. His concern in what interested me and taking the time to mentor me reminded me that I mattered, and I pass this on in my teaching style.

Love What You Do And Good Will Follow

"Others may question your credentials, your papers, your degrees. Others may look for all kinds of ways to diminish your worth. But what is inside you no one can take from you or tarnish. This is your worth, who you really

are, your degree that can go with you wherever you go, but that which you bring with you the moment you come into a room, that can't be manipulated or shaken. Without that sense of self, no amount of paper, no pedigree, and no credentials can make you legit. No matter what, you have to feel legit inside first." – Chris Gardner

Education Comes In Many Ways

One day I announced to my father that I was no longer going to continue in college. My father looked at me and asked my plans, and also asked how was I going to make a living? I told him I was not sure but I was leaving college and then I would find a way to support myself. There was that moment of silence as I can remember waiting for what he was going to say, as it was important to me. I have often shared with my father that this was one of his great parenting moments. He said to me, "College is good for many things besides education. You make contacts that will be your friends for the rest of your life." Then he said, "I will support your decision under one condition – that you never stop educating your Self. There are many ways to receive an education. Educate your Self towards what you are passionate about and you will always create an income." He continued in our conversation explaining that if I stayed focused on what I loved, I would prosper in many ways. I appreciated this advice and support, and I took him seriously and continued my education in other ways.

I was blessed that both my father and my mother did not see my desire to be educated in the non-traditional ways as a failure. Today, my children love to be educated in both traditional and non-traditional ways. As I write this, my daughter is leaving to study at an art university in London and my son has his eye set on a recognized business university.

My parents encouraged me to find my passion, and build on that as my strength and base. I had a passion, as did others that I quoted, a fire inside our Souls whose voice was listened to. We must fuel that voice by reinforcing it with experiences that honor that who we are, regardless of what appears in the moment in the outside world. *As we shift our inner world from within ourselves, the outside world will reflect accordingly.* Remember nothing has power over us apart from the power we give it.

Know Thy Beliefs

As you dive deeper into the Power Wishing® formula, you will become more aware of what beliefs you hold. I will ask you to check in with your Self periodically and ask yourself, "Whose belief am I?" "Is this my belief or someone else's?" You will uncover what beliefs supported certain experiences of yours and what feelings are at the root of those beliefs.

These are questions to reflect on as you assess the beliefs that you hold and observe if you chose them for your Self or if you inherited them from others. This assessment allows you to break down your beliefs to understand the cause of the experience you create. Then you can systematically integrate emotions as a formula to support what you expect.

When you attempt to connect your experiences, past or future, with the attached beliefs you carry, you get to the root of your beliefs and emotional patterns. With this awareness you will be consciously aware of what you believe about the world around you and what you believe is possible.

So I ask you, "Whose belief are you?" We all have our stories, our history, our circumstances and this shapes what we believe. Now add to that the opinions of your mother, father, family, friends, and society, and you can see how our beliefs are shaped greatly by many influences.

The pressures of life and challenging circumstances can create doubt in your belief system and one day you may wake up and realize you are living your life according to other people's beliefs.

I have a compassionate understanding of why people can be confused about their own feelings and beliefs; I understand that we believe we do this out of love, responsibility or a sense of care for others, even if we have abandoned ourselves. Or maybe you are not strengthening your own beliefs because you are on automatic pilot with beliefs that you did not choose consciously. No need to make a big deal out of this; simply clarify between the beliefs that you wish to choose as the reflection of yourself and release the rest. Does this sound easier said than done? It can be this simple because this process of Power Wishing connects your emotions to your beliefs instead of using your mind and logic as your emotional gauge.

Fears = False Evidence Appearing Real

Sometimes we make decisions based on different fears. One of these fears may be rejection from the ones we love. Having this feeling is very natural. We often learn about rejection at an early age, and we quickly discover the pain of this. We carefully weigh the risk of taking the chance of being rejected and sometimes believe that we can avoid this pain if we do not make certain choices. But then we just create different pain – the pain of abandonment, the abandoning of our Self, and worse, the abandonment of our dreams.

Fears are False Evidence Appearing Real. How do you know if your fear is real? Yes, there are certain fears based on the reality you are experiencing now. There are also fears that we create simply because we may not have the answers and we are scared of the uncertainty. We may not know what to do in a situation or we fear ridicule or failure. Sometimes we even create fear towards positive feelings such as feeling loved and being successful. Your fears clearly state what you expect to receive. The question to ask yourself is how does this fear serve you? It has to serve you one way or another or you would not have created it.

Why is it that similar circumstances create different outcomes depending on the person? Is it the way they have chosen to give energy to their fears? *We choose whether fear owns us or we own the accountability of surpassing the fear.* Sometimes the way people get over their fears is by getting tired of experiencing the way their fears define them, which is not who they wish to experience as themselves.

No one can reject anything about you unless you reject it about yourself. Strengthen your emotional intelligence. Build your emotional muscle. Your feelings are not going anywhere. Use them as the force of energy they are, and give them a place that feels good to you. Stop being sloppy with your feelings and the way you imagine the possibilities of your life. You have a choice; you can have a *proactive* life or a *reactive* life.

Your Authenticity Is Non-Negotiable

Something happens when you choose to be your Self from a place that is authentic and gentle: a deep wisdom appears. It is as if the chaos and unnecessary energy have gotten the *memo* that you are going to honor YOU. Knowing how to hear and recognize the best of you on this personal journey allows guidance from a solid place within you where your authenticity becomes your strength and is non-negotiable. You start to hear your fears with discernment and you simply release them as unnecessary energy or address them.

You define taking care of your Self as being responsible versus being selfish. The chase of getting what you desire in your life as if you are a beggar shifts to a life that magically provides for you. Your character, values, and your Emotional Self become a vessel for your wishes granted with very little resistance.

Power Thoughts

You Get What You Expect

- My beliefs are running my life; I get what I expect.

- I know how to hear and recognize the best of me and I listen.

- No one can reject anything about me unless I reject it about my Self.

- Fears are **F**alse **E**vidence **A**ppearing **R**eal.

- Nothing has power over me apart from the power I give it.

- Doing what I love is being responsible.

- I inspire others by reminding them of their best Self.

- With my belief, I dictate my outcome.

- Living with what I believe, I have everything to gain.

- Education comes in many ways.

Collective Consciousness

Because we are living in a time where we have created the two-second Twitter update on our lives, it is challenging for many of us to know how to nurture our relationships and gauge our emotional experiences.

The media influence and patterned cultural beliefs are so strong that we have lost a lot of our natural intuition. We also live in a society where our children are brought up with information constantly being thrown at them. Information and imagery are all around us. This has created emotional confusion in a culture where people are out of touch emotionally with why they react the way they do and with being accountable for the results of their reality.

As we explore collective consciousness, it is not about making the media or our society wrong or right; it is about you being aware of the influences around you so that you dictate these influences and, if you choose to merge with them, then this is a conscious decision.

My kids will probably say that sometimes when I see an advertisement, I take it too literally. My first inclination is to believe what I see. Here is a humorous case in point. I was in fifth grade and about 11 years old. For class, we each had to choose an advertisement and talk about it. I chose a new deodorant at the time called Tickle. I saw all the Tickle commercials and I loved them – young girls were laughing when they put on the deodorant because it tickled them. I wanted this deodorant so much! I was very convinced that when I would try Tickle, I would laugh, be tickled and happy. I still smile at how persuaded I was by this advertisement. You can probably guess the rest of the story. I tried Tickle and nothing happened. I tried it again and still nothing. I was not laughing and it did not tickle me.

Should I have felt wrong for not feeling tickled like I saw in the commercials? Should I have gone out and conducted a survey to see how many people laughed or not with Tickle to justify my feelings? I share this example to be humorous about the fact that emotions are heavily influenced by the media and by our surrounding societal influences; therefore, if we feel different, we question ourselves in a way that is not always positive.

What if your emotions seem different than the way they are supposed to be according to others? Recognizing your emotions gives you discernment to gauge your feelings for your Self, for the experiences you wish to choose that are aligned with you – without the drama. Better yet, value the way you feel without the need to always have to justify your emotions. Wow, what a concept!

The Monkey, Banana And Water Spray Experiment

A scientific experiment that I like to share is The Monkey, Banana and Water Spray Experiment[8]. This experiment involved five monkeys (ten altogether, including replacements), a cage, a banana, a ladder and an ice-cold water hose.

The Experiment – Part 1

Five monkeys were locked in a cage, a banana was hung from the ceiling and a ladder was placed right underneath it. As predicted, one of the monkeys immediately raced towards the ladder to grab the banana. However, as soon as he started to climb the ladder, a researcher sprayed the monkey with ice-cold water.

But, here's the kicker; in addition, the researcher also sprayed the other four monkeys. When a second monkey tried to climb the ladder, the researcher again sprayed the monkey with ice-cold water, as well as the other four monkeys, who were simply watching.

This was repeated again and again until the monkeys learned their lesson: climbing equals scary, cold water for EVERYONE, so no one should climb the ladder to get the banana.

The Experiment – Part 2

Once the five monkeys knew the drill, the researcher replaced one of the monkeys with a new, inexperienced one. As predicted, the new monkey

---

[8] Sources -Stephenson, G. R. (1967). "Cultural acquisition of a specific learned response among rhesus monkeys." In: Starek, D., Schneider, R., and Kuhn, H. J. (eds.), *Progress in Primatology*, Stuttgart: Fischer, pp. 279–288.
Mentioned in: Galef, B. G., Jr. (1976). "Social Transmission of Acquired Behavior: A Discussion of Tradition and Social Learning in Vertebrates." In: Rosenblatt, J.S., Hinde, R.A., Shaw, E. and Beer, C. (eds.), *Advances in the study of behavior*, Vol. 6, New York: Academic Press, pp. 87–88.

spotted the banana and went for the ladder. But the other four monkeys, knowing the drill, jumped on the new monkey and beat him up. Now the new guy thus learned not to go up the ladder for the banana! Without even knowing why and without ever being sprayed with water, the new monkey learned this behavior and believed that he could not go up the ladder or get the banana. These actions get repeated three more times with a new monkey each time and ASTONISHINGLY each new monkey, none of whom had ever received the cold water spray himself or knew anything about it, would be initiated into the group by getting beat up and hence learning "the rule."

When the researcher replaced a third monkey, the same thing happened; likewise for the fourth until, eventually, all the monkeys had been replaced and none of the original ones, who had been sprayed by water, were left in the cage. This is a classic example of "Mob Mentality" where bystanders and outsiders uninvolved with the fight join in "just because."

The Experiment – Part 3

Again, a new monkey was introduced into the cage. It ran towards the ladder only to get beaten up by the others. The monkey turned with a curious face, seemingly asking, "Why do you beat me up when I try to get the banana?" The other four monkeys stopped and looked at each other puzzled (none of them had been sprayed and so they really had no clue why the new guy couldn't get the banana), but it didn't matter. It was too late; the rules had been set. And so, although they didn't know WHY, they beat up the monkey just because "that's the way we do things around here."

The bottom line in sharing the Monkey Experiment is that we can simply remind ourselves to ask *why* things are the way they are! There may be very good reasons why or why not. Decide for yourself and own why you do what you do.

Know And Honor Your Beliefs

Do not live your life just because it has always been done a certain way. Question why you do what you do, have awareness of what is running you. Your feelings, thoughts and memories repeat throughout your cellular body and create the foundation of who you believe you are.
It is important to understand your beliefs, because they determine what you expect to happen.

Are you living your life experience or someone else's? An easy way to tell is if your life matches your dreams and if you feel happy and joyful the majority of the time. When I share happy and joyful, this is a feeling that is natural, not a forced feeling that feels unnatural. Are your dreams a direct manifestation of your beliefs? Are you living the life you dream of? If you are not aware of your own feelings, beliefs and strengths, then influences can become your beliefs.

Know your own beliefs and have certainty that you are your own expert in your own life. Be aware of your surroundings and the media. Simply check in to see if the information that you are exposed to adds value to your life. *Separate what is expected of you with who you actually are.* We are programmed to think we have to do something or be something. What if you could be your Self without worrying about being your Self? Imagine that!

I will ask you again, "If you were to live from the truth of who you are from your Soul perspective, what would this look like?" An even better question, "What would your life look like if you were living from beliefs that are authentically yours?"

The intention is for you to create a synergy so the outside world responds with your inner world of desires. When was the last time you reflected and sat down to imagine and write the story of the life you wish to have and how you believe this is possible? How aligned is the story you would write with the story of your present life? Whatever your answer is, continue aligning your dreams with the story of your life.

A government cannot dictate your wellbeing, nor can your boss, a family member, a relationship, religion, the bad economy, etc. Many people have succeeded under harsh circumstances and social economic times – so can you. Our society is made up of a lot of beliefs. The strongest beliefs of our culture do not necessarily come from the "right" or "best" ideas but from the strongest marketer of the idea. Just look around at the political ad campaigns, the product advertisements and the headlines of our newspapers. The power of persuasion is everywhere.

The media is not only delivering information; it is a campaign to shape the way we think. This is its purpose. They are manipulating the public through powerful tools of persuasion and marketing. The media is a vehicle for us to witness an array of realities, realities that are the perspectives and opinions of others. It is your choice which one you wish to choose and to make it yours.

I share this to explore the influences that surround you in your life. Your life does not lie in the hands of others or the circumstances of the world. Yes, they may have an effect on it and this effect can be good or bad, but in the end it is your choice. Use your surroundings to clarify choices you make for your Self versus allowing your surroundings to define you.

Allegory of the Cave

Many times, we empower our surroundings and others' perceptions to dictate our choices. We do not question what we see and stop asking ourselves what we believe. We become robotic. Remember, awareness is the tool of staying awake to your Self and the world around you.

One of my favorite lectures that I give is on the comparison of the *Allegory of the Cave* and the movie *The Matrix*; there is so much rich information about human behavior in these stories.

The *Allegory of the Cave* is a powerful story about how we make illusions real, where shadows were believed as the truth. Even though what the prisoners in the story were witnessing was not the real thing and never had been, because they acknowledged the illusion for so long, they lost their ability to accept another reality. This happens with many people: they are trapped in the illusion of life without questioning. In *The Matrix*, people are basically freeing others from a prison created in their own minds.

In the *Allegory of the Cave*, the prisoners are essentially mistaken about what reality is. Because the prisoners are unable to turn their heads and instead solely focus on staring at the shadows that are in front of them, they can only identify this as their own reality. From reading the story, we know that it is a puppeteer creating the shadows that they believe is reality. Because they know nothing else but the shadows they see, much like one who only "knows what they know", they accept this as truth with no questions asked. The prisoners stay focused on the illusion of the shadows, even though they say they wish to be free. They are not creative with their imagination or questioning, so they stay focused on what they can grasp with their mind, as this is all they know and creation stops there. They define what they can expect based on the limitation of what was in front of them and went no further in their own process of creating possibilities.

One of the prisoners escapes and leaves the cave. He is shocked at the world he discovers outside the cave and at first does not believe it is real. He becomes aware that his perceived reality was a misperception. He expands to understand the goodness of his new world and his truth.

He sees the Sun is the source of life and goes on eager to explore this new world. With his excitement, he goes back to the other prisoners to let them know what he has discovered.

In the scope of this story, it is pretty impressive that this prisoner was able to bypass his beliefs of the illusion and move out of his comfort into excitement and he just expected the other prisoners to feel the same. This was a logical thought, since they could have freedom. This prisoner would rather suffer any fate than return to his previous life and understanding (or lack thereof) as a prisoner.

The escaped prisoner returns to the cave excited to inform the others of the world outside of the cave, the Light. The other prisoners laugh at him, and mock him for going out of the cave. They do not believe him and threaten to kill him if he tries to set them free. The others cannot understand something they have yet to experience. This happens with collective consciousness: one may resign to the majority and the majority may not always be the freedom or joy you wish or believe possible.

The Light Of Your Beliefs

"The unexamined life is not worth living." – Socrates

Many people, like the prisoners, do not want to break free from their perceived reality, even though they may complain of their present circumstances. In *Allegory of the Cave*, Plato casts the cave in a very negative light: the prisoners are chained, the images are dark and distorted, and the voices are misconstrued echoes.

In life, you can stay in your cave of illusion, with your false Self and beliefs that do not serve you. Or you can transcend this imprisonment of Self through feelings, beliefs and prayer, reorienting your whole life as an upward journey from darkness into Light. In this story Plato would say that knowledge is the *Light* to your freedom. I would share that your emotions and the knowledge of knowing your Self emotionally, exploring your life as an emotional journey creating knowledge from this, is the *Light* to your freedom of Self.

"The life you've led is not, in fact, the totality of what is possible for you. And if you can release yourself from the bonds you don't even see, you would then be able to see the world as it truly is." – Partridge

Love Your Self Through The Choices Of Your Environments

When we are exposed to toxic environments and people, it can be challenging to find the good in these atmospheres or to believe that good is possible and that we can trust ourselves. It is valuable to have discernment to know when the environment is influencing a behavior or your Self. My grandmother used to say two sayings in Spanish that I grew up with, "Tell me who you hang around with and I will tell you who you are," and, "Your surroundings either become like you or you become like your surroundings."

I have made different choices as we all have about the consciousness of our surroundings; I choose to believe that if an environment is not supportive to the consciousness I wish to enhance, I remove myself. Of course, I do everything possible to align those surrounding with my being, but if I know that this is not possible, I would prefer to use that energy in a more productive way. I feel that attempting to merge with surroundings that are not in sync with who I am will be a loss — loss because even if I wish to stay, I will be emotionally exhausted and by default the environment will have the influence.

Basically, toxic people and toxic environments only lead to a toxic mind, which influences a toxic heart. This only leads one to feel powerless. You cannot change others and if you wish to have any influence in your surroundings, you must be a high example of what you expect. I understand at times, there are situations that happen and you feel you cannot leave an environment.

When it is possible, do everything you can to experience other good in your life — spend time in other areas where you are free from toxicity to bring balance. Hopefully, either the toxicity will leave your environment or you will exit the toxicity. You do have to make choices to support your Self; do not expect things to just *happen* without action. At times we can experience wanting to make a decision that does not seem "logical" based on collective consciousness or beliefs, and also religion. But there are times we feel so strongly that we wish to break free from what is holding our Soul hostage.

Create disciplines that encourage your core beliefs about your Self. Use *Stage Your Day,* play with your "Movie" to create an opening for another possibility through your Emotional Imagination® and when opportunities present themselves, know they are an answer to what you asked for and use your imagination to be in anchored in self-love to move forward.

The Wonderful People That Await You

You can always stay open to other beliefs and understandings. Nevertheless, do not take on a belief that is not your own. Connect and check in with your Self and own what you believe with actions that are an example of this.

There are so many wonderful, incredible, good people in this world, many that are as like-minded as you. Allow these wonderful opportunities to be a part of your life; do not block them with toxicity. Toxicity does not deserve such a place in your life.

Keep your process simple, even if the circumstances seem complicated. Do not settle for what no longer serves you, do not justify why you continue in an environment that does not serve you or at least be honest with your Self about why you make your choices. There is one person you always go to bed with and that is your Self — at least be clear with your Self. I find that it is better to be alone than in bad company or company that does not serve my being. How many times have you been in company and felt lonely? I assure you if you choose your Self over toxic company and do not compromise your energy, you may be alone but you will not feel lonely or depleted, and sooner than later more wonderful people will be a part of your world.

Support yourself with environments that mirror the Vibrational Language® you desire to feel for your Self. Choose environments that support you and who you believe you are. You are here to have joyful experiences and share joy; to be loved and love with acceptance. Have the discipline to experience your life as your choice.

You are enough and there are many people who would love the opportunity to love you and be loved by you. Witness your inner voice as your cheerleader to have all that you desire, to guide you to choices that lovingly support you.

Changing Your Mind

Making choices, even if you have to change your mind, is taking responsibility. It shows you are being accountable for your decisions and not holding others responsible for your choices. Allowing your Self to awaken to choosing your beliefs through self-awareness is courageous. In essence, it is more than being courageous: it is releasing fear of believing beliefs that may be illusions and not really the truth of your life. Maybe they were not even your true beliefs to begin with.

I once had a teacher who made it really clear to his students that it is perfectly OK to change your mind. This understanding is so simple, and yet, so profound. Then why is this so challenging at times? It only makes sense that a part of our evolution is that we change our minds; we are always having new experiences as we are growing and changing. Sometimes our egos get in the way by sticking to a belief because we are adamant or righteous about it and *always* said we would *never* change it.

From time to time, it is important to assess your beliefs and check in to see if these beliefs you hold serve your life purpose. People change their minds all the time and they also change their beliefs. Imagine if you agree with someone and it is not your mindset, what happens when they change their mind? You sold out! Maybe they changed their mind to what you had originally thought ... Ouch!

The energy of your beliefs attracts your life and attracts others with similar beliefs. Many times we incorporate the belief systems of others. Here you will reflect on which beliefs are truly your own and which you would like to shift.

As you shift your beliefs, many changes in your environment take place because you attract differently. The *attraction* has shifted because your beliefs have changed, and therefore, you can expect a different reality. Making choices in your personal beliefs is a respectful way of experiencing your life and connecting to others. How many times have you judged another or had a strong opinion about something? Then, you have a life experience and your perception or judgment about that person or situation changes? Oops!

We know logically that not everyone will hold the same beliefs we do. Why then, when we feel challenged with a decision, do we doubt our own beliefs? Whatever you choose, own it, and be open to changing your mind if necessary. It is clear to me that being your Self is the only way to go. Molding your Self based on someone else's belief, when it is not your truth, makes no sense. *Being solid in your Self and your values creates a secure foundation that you can depend on.*

You Find What You Are Looking For

Years ago, I went to a small conference in Washington D.C. regarding challenges of the inner cities. This was an important conference to bring awareness to patterns, education and solutions. The first lady at the time was present and she personally visited each place that we discussed.

The goal was to find solutions that we all could use based on our personal experiences along with the information that was presented. In some of the presentations, many statistics were given to provide credibility for the information presented.

After visiting the inner city, the patterns within families became clearer to me. There were beliefs that families held onto for generations that kept them in a cycle of challenges. The beliefs inner-city residents carried about themselves made the difference between those who "got out" and those who continued the cycle. One pattern that was clear to all was the lack of positive male role models. I left there with the awareness that statistics may have had truth but that statistics can be limited by where they are gathered and who gathered them. It gave me the clarity that, in different ways, we also go about looking for "statistics" from others to support the belief we wish to hold or strengthen. Where are you going for your information and statistics to prove your point or justify your decision? Where do you go for reinforcement on what you believe?

Collective consciousness carries strong beliefs about many things. For example, when I was researching different beliefs in reference to illness and medicine, it was surprising to find some of the beliefs we held as a society. Many of those beliefs have changed over the years. Of course, there is a great amount of valuable information out there based on research, experience and testing; I am only sharing this to remind you to be aware of how you are connecting to the information or statistics. Challenge statistics that are not what you believe by not choosing to believe them for your Self. Buy into your beliefs, your knowing.

It is still challenging for me to believe that not long ago – in my own lifetime – African Americans were so discriminated against. To think that as recent as the mid-twentieth century black people were not able to sit next to white people or use the same water fountain or bathroom, and worse. And that there is still such discrimination that still exists seems surreal in a modern time. Segregation and discrimination had to become great political issues, along with people who gave their lives, in order for society to wake up and change its perception towards a different collective consciousness.

I still remember my daughter coming home and announcing how she admired Ms. Rosa Parks. She was a simple woman who took a stance clearly aligned with her beliefs of human dignity, again reminding us that it is what you believe in that makes you who you are. It also reminds us that one or a few people can shift collective consciousness by their beliefs.

Some Interesting Facts:

In the early Egyptian and Mesopotamian cultures, it was believed by several philosophers believed that the world was not round but flat.

Many feared the number 13 and it is considered an unlucky number in many cultures. In 1911 the word Triskaidekaphobia was created to explain this phobia. The superstition has become such a widespread belief that today 80% of buildings in the USA do not have a 13th floor. Approximately 1 billion dollars are lost each year in the travel industry because so many people refuse to travel on Friday the 13th. In other cultures, 13 is considered a lucky number.

Until 1945, no one came close to running a mile under 4.13 minutes. It was believed for a long time that no human could break the 4-minute mile. Then in 1954 Roger Bannister beat the record of running a 4-minute mile with a 3.59.4 finish. Now that everyone believed it was possible, it only took 2 months before another person beat his time.

I found so many of these interesting facts that reminded me that as our consciousness changes so do our beliefs and then so do the *facts*.

Belief In One's Soul Dictates Statistics

Many times collective consciousness dictates the outcome of someone based on their circumstances. What statistics does not calculate is the belief in one's Soul of what is possible and the desire to attain this. I often share with others about a student called Johnny. His story exemplifies how we can have a vision for others and hold a safe, supportive space for them even if collective consciousness has already dictated their outcome. We can also do this without interfering in their process to manifest for themselves.

I met Johnny about 15 years ago at the inner-city school I ran in one of the toughest neighborhoods in Miami. Johnny was a wonderful, vibrant eleven-year-old Cuban-born student. He had a great smile, even though his eyes did not always shine. It was obvious he had experienced hurt. We spoke often about his favorite subject, baseball. The times we spoke about baseball were when his eyes would light up; most of the times they were dim and not present. He loved baseball. He was always shocked that I knew so much about the sport. I would share with him that at his age I played softball as a lefty first-baseman and pitcher. Plus, I was a switch-handed hitter who made the all-star team every year. We would laugh, as he looked me up and down and commented that he never would have guessed I knew anything about the sport, let alone played it. Even though things were rough in his neighborhood and his life was challenging, he still had this feeling that he could be a great baseball player. I totally encouraged his dream because I could see that he could taste what it felt like to be a baseball player, and he lived his dream in his heart again and again. He started showing me a few baseball cards he had collected, strengthening his belief in his dream.

The foundation of him wanting to be a baseball player was based on how good he felt about himself when he played this sport. When Johnny was playing ball, especially every time he hit the ball, he was excited about his life. At that moment in time, he forgot about his problems and was hopeful about his future. I loved his passion. He would look for me in the halls so we could talk and this also made me feel good.

I spent time with Johnny imagining his baseball career, and we talked about how it would feel. We played with the "What Ifs." "What if you went on this team? What do you like about this team? What if you played this position? How would that feel?" We got so fired up imagining him being a baseball star and witnessing his success! Then I told him to read and watch everything he could about baseball. He got immersed in his passion, and I also witnessed him begin to override other doubts he had in school about himself. Even though nothing in his reality changed at home, I felt our conversations were good for him as I witnessed that he was changing his view of himself and life's possibilities.

Not long after sharing with Johnny, I ran into someone who was a coach and was equally passionate about baseball. He agreed to volunteer to work with Johnny. Now, not only did Johnny have a coach, but also he had an amazing male mentor who could mirror his dream with him. This was so exciting for all of us.

Because Johnny was having this feel-good feeling as he became more immersed in his dream of baseball, he was attracted to doing things for himself that made him feel better. His grades improved, he hung out with positive friends and he continued to activate more of that *feeling good* in other areas of his life.

In my time supporting the school's progress, attendance was up, funding was coming in and the school's organization and morale were improving. This was a good story in our city.

Mid-year, a group of psychologists came to the school to see about this feel-good story of our rising school. To my surprise, they began to analyze my work there along with my credentials choosing to not focus on the results that were happening. They were disappointed in the fact that I chose not to know the past history of the students. I knew that most of these kids had experienced challenges and some had trauma, but I was not concerned with learning all these details. Honestly, I felt like the weight of their pain could hold me back from moving the school forward.

Even though these new successful results of the school spoke for themselves, some thought that by supporting the students to believe in their dreams that I was setting them up to fail. According to their professional opinion, this "was not possible under their circumstances."

One lady chose to use Johnny as an example of how I was setting him up to fail. She began to tell me the story of his past. One day when Johnny had come home, there was a terrible fight in his house. Sadly, at age nine, Johnny had watched as his mother was shot dead right in front of him. This was terrible and my heart was so sad. I understood why he had lost the gleam in his eyes, though I also realized that he seemed sad less and less now.

We all understand that watching a horrid event like this could change Johnny's beliefs about himself and affect what he thought he could accomplish in the world he lives in. With that tragic event, everything seemed dismal and Johnny's hopes went dark. In that instant, he changed his belief about the future of his life, which is understandable given such a tragic event like this.

The reason I did not want to learn the personal background of Johnny and other amazing students was because I believed that if my feelings were tainted with sympathy and sorrow for their challenging pasts, I would not be able to hold space for them in the way they deserved. Every time I looked at a beautiful child like Johnny, and I would think of his past, perhaps my sensitivity would weigh down my ability to see the potential of his bright future.

What would happen if every time I saw Johnny and listened to him, all I would see was the vision of his mother being murdered before his very eyes? How would I, in the short time of being there to support him and the other students, successfully be able to encourage his dreams of the future if all I could see was his past?

I was concerned that my feelings would be too caught up in his tragedy that I would merge with the consciousness of others and begin to believe that these kids have little chance with their dreams. My mission there was to inspire these children to dream, allow them the opportunity to dream as big as they could. I felt my responsibility was not to learn about their past but to hold the space for them to strengthen the possibility of dreams in themselves.

If I or someone else comes with their own fears and worries about him, directly or indirectly along with his vulnerability, he may take on those projections of other people's fears and add these to his own. He also may not be able to tell that they were not his own fears, but those of other people. He may also make his decisions based on their recommendations that he should not hope so big.

So, if Johnny is expressing his dreams to me and I have energetic beams that I am emitting to him that have the message of "Life is a struggle" or "Poor Johnny, he has had such a hard life," I will be activating and connecting with that part in Johnny. I will be enhancing the part that does not serve him. Johnny will feel my pity towards him, along with my anxiety about life being a struggle, even though my words are different than my energy.

When Johnny shares his dream, I am to connect to his hope with my feeling of hope; this activates Johnny to feel even more hopeful. But, if I am telling Johnny to be hopeful and my energy is that he can never make it because of his life experience, well then "poor Johnny." In reality I would be buying into the collective consciousness of what others expect that he could accomplish.

I Will Heal – In My Time

Of course, I am not suggesting that we live in denial of tragedy or challenges. Whether it is a stranger we read about in the paper or a loved one, we can have empathy for their challenges and still hold space for their dreams. I am sharing Johnny's story to create awareness of how one can project on to another based on their emotions or beliefs about what they believe the other can expect for themselves. Be aware that when you may feel sorry or pity for others, this may not be the best support.

When we have pity, we connect with a feeling that does not lift the other with hope in themselves or their situation. We can be compassionate, gentle, listen to them and have empathy, which is different than having pity or feeling sorry for them.

How does Johnny, or any of us, take a painful experience that has created such a strong belief in our existence, and shift back to supporting our dreams? How can we avoid a painful experience from blocking us from having our wish be manifested or our dreams come true?

I am not saying that it is easy to shift the beliefs created from this type of traumatic event, but it is possible and it is a choice that you must make about how you are going to move forward.

It is valuable to feel our pain, grief and sadness in order to be able to transform it. Choices will be made in processing that pain whether you choose them consciously or not. One way or another, these feelings carry an energy that will form a direction. You can fall into a numbness or become resentful and angry, or you can deal with it by feeling what needs to be felt and then choosing from there on how you can move to another better feeling.

What often happens after a trauma is that we get used to an emotional habit that does not serve us to protect ourselves emotionally. It's as if pain or sadness is a food that you do not really like, but you continue to eat it because it is there on your plate. You become comfortable with it, and you forget what it feels like to have other food that tastes better to you. You are not open to experiencing what if feels like to try new food and to taste different things; you have too much fear it could make you not feel good, or in this analogy, have more hurt feelings. You stay comfortable in the same experience of eating the same food. Then, when someone offers you a new food to try, you don't try it because it feels easier to keep on eating what you are familiar with whether you like it or not. Before you know you it, you forgot what other foods taste like and do not venture to any new restaurants.

This can also happen with your feelings. You can get stuck in a feeling. You can feel like you are drowning in a feeling. This is all very real, and in no way do I mean to undermine the tragedy of a horrible experience that happened. Many of us have experienced traumatic events: abuse, illness, the loss of loved ones or other challenges.

Moving past pain is based on personal timing for everyone. This does not often happen overnight, so be patient and kind with your Self. Sometimes I hear others say, "I should be over this by now," and my response is, "Says who?" I share this because sometimes we tend to compare pain, create a scale to measure whose pain may be worse or compare the timing of our healing with another.

Your pain should never be denied because of how someone else feels about your pain or because of a comparison to another. Allow yourself the space to feel your feelings and heal in your own time.

In our society, we often know how to connect best with others because of similar painful experiences, from multiple support groups for those in pain to conversations over coffee that are about comparing painful relationships.

Take notice of the conversations you share with others or the start of these types of conversations with strangers. Now, this does not mean that you cannot share your feelings of pain with others. Have awareness when you share your hurt feelings. Is it with the intention to build a case of blame towards someone or something, or find resolution, which carries a different energy of the possibility for healing? Sometimes our focus that is in the direction of what does not serve us is simply bad habits and comfort zones, nothing more.

Being Stuck In A Moment Is Not Being Stuck In Your Life

Listening to your emotions is a choice. Life experiences can be painful; nevertheless, you can choose to live a life without hate, resentment and unnecessary energy that does not serve you. You can build courage to face your fears. Facing your emotions can be the most challenging part, even more challenging than the results of your pain.

We all can get stuck in an experience. We can carry the weight of our challenges and then create a life of more of those experiences that we do not desire. Choose experiences that support you instead of deplete you. You create the opportunity to have a joyful life even amidst the pain and chaos. Model others who have created what you wish to create in times of challenge. Imagine your possibilities with the best of you with what you wish to create in this reality and release worry about how it will happen. Instead, focus on knowing how it will feel when it does happen.

All Feelings Have A Purpose

"The love that you withhold is the pain you carry." – Ralph Waldo Emerson

If you feel something, there is a reason for this. Your feelings are your internal guide, your GPS of where you are headed. Painful feelings and physical pain are cues saying that you need to hear something.

Pain is an invitation for you to check in with your Self and provides an opportunity to make new choices, move forward, have a new understanding and accept changes that are occurring. It is the Soul's voice creating awareness.

Facing our emotions heightens our awareness to shift our pain, but we have to face our pain first. This is a process, and in the process we may unveil more pain connected to other aspects of our lives.

As I have experienced, something happens as you are transforming the pain; life does bring unexpected sweetness when we face our Authentic Self.

Pain may be an avenue to awaken and accomplish your purpose, but please know that pain is not the only way. If you find that you have more clarity after painful experiences or this motivates you to make decisions, then please make wishes to release this being your motivator.

My Imagination Actively Supports My Healing

Our imagination is always active, even when we feel our pain. Our imagination, in some form, is creating pictures for us that support our feelings. Our feelings are real, no matter what the reason. What we must have discernment with is if we carry our painful feelings of the past and make them true in the present when it is not the same experience. We can use our imagination to play out our pain and strengthen this hurt, or we can use the scenes that we are creating to move forward with healing energy.

About two years ago, I experienced three significant losses in my life within six months and this was very challenging. I will share with you that there were times that I was not interested in shifting the emotion I was feeling. The pain was so deep that finding joy in my day was challenging.

One of those losses was that of the father of my two beautiful children, who passed away tragically in front of their eyes. Then, I lost two others that were dear to me. Amidst all this loss, I mourned having a partner in parenting my children, and now I was witnessing the deep cries of my children's pain. It felt unbearable. I used these tools that I share with you to support me to shift my own feelings. I used my imagination to play out my pain, my hurt, my anger, forgiveness, healing, and I eventually created a new vision.

People with the goodness of their heart would say to us that "time would heal the feeling of loss." Whether it is my personal loss or that which I have witnessed with clients, I have to admit that I am not so sure that time will always heal that deep pain. I feel that time supports you to learn how to live with it. I used my imagination to choose how I wish to live with my experiences that caused me pain; in that space I could feel different options for this. I was able to shift my awareness towards other positive aspects of my life and lead my children towards a positive light. We each gave each other permission to honor our feelings, knowing with trust and love that we could transform them in our own time and we have.

Empower Others By Honoring Their Feelings

It can be most challenging to witness someone you love go through a painful emotion, especially your children and close loved ones. Without meaning to, we may wish to convince others to feel better or dismiss another person's feelings by rationalizing their pain. We often hear, "It's not that bad" or "Don't feel like that." This may be a reaction to feeling helpless to heal our loved one's painful moments.

For me, coming from a big family I felt I always had to do something if someone I love is in pain. I felt I had to help them or fix the situation. My children have been great in teaching me to handle this in a different way. They will say to me, "Mom, I am not asking you to do anything. I am just sharing with you how I feel." This is where I have learned to ask them if they need anything from me. "Can I do anything for you?" is a powerful way to support others. Remember, if the answer is "No," it means no. If their answer is no, then their answer is no. No means no. Listen to what others say. If they said it, take it as they meant it. Release the voice in your head that says, "No, what they really meant was" or "I know what they need." If they said "No," they mean no! Let them know that you respect how they feel and are there for them when they need you. Sometimes it can be healing for the other person to feel respected for their wishes. How do you listen to "No?" Do you honor this or do you spend time trying to convince them differently?

Empower others to honor how they feel, as you appreciate the same. Share that you are there for them if they need your support and witness them by holding a loving space for their emotions in the physical space and in your imagination.

Please keep in mind why you would be offering advice to someone if you have not been asked. If it is your intention to show compassion and understanding towards someone who is feeling pain, I suggest listening to them without sharing your opinion unless they ask for it. Acknowledging someone's feelings by listening is healing. You would be surprised at those who have not been heard or acknowledged for the way they feel. When I would conduct my teacher trainings to those in the field of emotional healing, one of the most valuable tools I would teach is how to hold space. I was respectful that they were experts in their field but would often remind them of the importance of practicing this technique with their clients.

There is much value for the person in pain to be heard and acknowledged, so they can connect with their inner Self to discover their own answers. This is where self-created healing can occur.

In other situations, sometimes people offer advice because they want the other person to be different. We may wish for the other to change so that we feel better about ourselves when we are around them. Have awareness when listening to others to release the habit of finding what is wrong or pointing out faults; there are enough critics in the world. Take opportunities to give positive reinforcement.

Witness your Self listening to others as if they do mean what they say or they would not have said it; stop giving your interpretation to what they have said. Listen to what people are asking for; help them be accountable. Give the message that there are positive consequences to communicating clearly what you wish. With this, you are creating a safe emotional relationship. If they do not mean what they say, then it is not your job to interpret what they mean. By not being their interpreter, you are supporting them to be clear communicators, and feel worthy to ask for what they believe they need.

Although you have the best of intentions, your desire to solve their pain may make them feel that they are inadequate to resolve their challenges themselves. Allow others to hear themselves so they can use their own intuition, skills and strength to navigate their way through a challenge. This can be common with parents and their children and also with significant others.

There is a time when we are ready to accept support, and usually when the timing is "right," we ask. In my experience, the most powerful method of supporting others is to hold space for them and allow their feelings to be expressed just as they are. Give them the space to share their thoughts without any response from you unless they ask for your advice or feedback. This takes discipline, but if you can move out of your own way and simply witness, you may just witness them get to the other side of their pain towards a place of peace. What if your presence gave them a feeling of love and being safe emotionally where they were able to talk it out and find their own resolution? When this happens, the relationship goes to another level and reaches a depth of honor and respect. I find that many people underestimate the power of their presence for healing.

I would suggest in situations when you feel you wish to support another and feel helpless to do so that you visualize giving them love, seeing them happy, peaceful with themselves and the situation. You cannot control another person's actions or thoughts, but you can pray for them. Utilizing your imagination to send others love is a wonderful practice; it will also give you peace because you are actively doing something positive to support them. At times when I felt a sense of helplessness towards witnessing those I love, this visualization has brought me great peace. Simply visualize the person in your imagination as if they are in front of you and share with them the love you feel for them without telling them how to be or what to do. Simply remind them that they are loved. We never know when someone is ready to receive the best of themselves, especially when they are having a challenging time. Visualize your love filling them and allow that to be enough.

Love is seeing in the other and holding that vision for them when they forget to see this in themselves.

When others feel loved, they are supported to make choices that support themselves with self-love. Never underestimate the power of love in your prayers to others as a form of communication of energetic healing.

Mirror The Good Experiences Of Others

I believe that we can listen to one another in a supportive way, but I think that it is challenging to find someone who can truly move out of his or her own way to be present to hear your story without projecting theirs onto you. Remember to have discernment about when to share your story and when you make choices that are based on the opinions of others. Because, if it happened to them in a certain way, it means it may or may not happen to you the same way. The good news of sharing with those who add value to your world is, if you like the experience they had, then you can use that as support and mirroring for the outcome you wish to have.

My Reality Is Realistic

Everyone has his or her own reality. Depending on the person, there are also beliefs about how they define what is realistic or not. I am sure you heard people say, "Come on, be realistic!" I have been told this quite often. Usually there is humor or sarcasm when this comment is given. I respond, "Be realistic according to whom? Whose definition of realistic am I supposed to define my reality with?" Or I simply answer, "I am being realistic. I am realistic with what I expect from my reality." I am totally comfortable that my expectation of reality may be different than others.

Your Perception Is Your Reality

What is reality? How do you define reality? Based on your definition or based on another's definition of reality? Your definition of your reality is based on how you observe your life.

Whose reality are you living? What does being realistic mean to you? How are you defining "Be realistic?" Do you base your reality on someone else's observation? Imagine how exhausting it is to not be in your own reality. You truly hold the ability to create your wellbeing and life experience based on your beliefs of who you are.

Look for the good. This is what will be activated within you and will connect you with all that surrounds you.

I have shared with my children that a thousand people may not agree with you and you may be the only one who believes a certain way. The certainty you have of your belief is worth more than a million others agreeing with you, when it is not your belief. One certain belief can make a difference; but more importantly, it is so important to honor your Self.

I let them know that it's OK that they may feel like the only one who believes in something. I remind them that I believe in them, and home is where they are loved, accepted and cherished for who they are and that they are free to share their beliefs of reality here.

Power Thoughts

Collective Consciousness

- I live from the truth of my Soul perspective.

- I am what I believe.

- I truly hold the ability to create my wellbeing.

- I am my greatest resource.

- I ask others from a place of gathering information, not to seek validation or approval.

- My Emotional Imagination presents me opportunities.

- I stay open to other beliefs and understandings as I have discernment of my beliefs.

- I have the discipline to experience my life as my choice.

- It makes sense to me that a part of my evolution is that I change my mind.

- It is clear to me that being my Self is the only way to go.

Your Perspective = Your Reality

When using your Emotional Imagination®, your vision for manifesting has no boundaries. If you use your Emotional GPS, your feelings can take you to places and experiences in the unknown that your logic simply cannot explain or quantify.

"Always go with your passions. Never ask yourself if it's realistic or not."
– Deepak Chopra

Logic looks for the secure return on your decision. Your logic will look to secure your decision, but as you strengthen your trust in your Emotional GPS, your feelings will create the security that is necessary to follow your gut instinct and make a positive decision for yourself.

When your emotions are able to act as a filter that gives information to your brain, then your brain is able to process updated information clearly, quickly and in sync with how you are presently feeling or wish to feel. With this synergy, your logic plays a supportive role by adding information to your emotions.

When you depend solely on logic to create your life, you are limited by old information. Imagine if the weatherman on the news opens up his report and says, "Well, today is August 12th and like the last August 12th, the weather forecast is rain." You look out the window as you hear this and say, "Yes it is August 12th, but it is sunny." You share this with the weatherman and he says, "Well sooner or later … it will be raining, it was like that last year." Some people are just stuck in the past no matter what the present looks like. Even when the future looks different, some people are just waiting for the past to repeat itself.

When you imagine and allow your dreams to feel true, you shift your emotional patterns and you update your belief systems as a message to your brain. It is like blaming the computer for not giving new information, when the programmer was the one who did not give new programming. When you play with possibility in your imagination, you use your feelings to create a "Movie" of what your life would look like "if," then you reinforce this image with your surroundings, actions, etc.

This way your brain can "look" to change its mind and receive fresh new emotional information to be able to experience different weather – even if your surroundings look the same. Support your logic to be up-to-date by using your past without making it wrong and to build from the positive aspects giving the brain permission to do the same.

My Brain Looks For What I Expect

We can all relate to being pulled in different directions over a decision in our life. The awareness I wish to bring is in understanding where your decision is being made from? Is it emotional or logical?

Is your logic helping you live a life defined by what others expect of you or keeping you in the past? Check in with your Self to see if your logic is supporting you in a way that will organize a plan to manifest your desire. Teach the brain to look for what you are expecting, as a resource for the result you expect.

Let's look at how we can receive two different outcomes to the same question. If we were to listen to a conversation of a brain looking for love, what would it sound like? You have an idea of what love means to you. Does it come from logic or emotions? Do wish to receive love from the perspective of the way the brain would see love as practical, making sure you checked off what a relationship is supposed to look like? Does your idea stem from your emotions of trusting how you feel and then allowing love to take form?

Let's say you have not found love. You ask the question "Why?" and you receive an answer from the brain's perspective.

A conversation about this with your brain:
You:
How come I have not found love?

Brain:
I really do not go out enough. I do not meet people because all my friends are married and I do not know anybody who is single anymore.
I am working all the time and when I get out of work I am tired.
I am alone and I cannot take a chance of losing my job.

The brain answers the question like it is answering a questionnaire. It may sound logical, but it has you accepting circumstances you wish were different without having the emotional awareness to shift them.

Practicality can be good, but not for everything. What if you ask yourself the same question from an emotional perspective? How would the brain look differently to support you to find answers that would affect your outcome differently? When we are able to understand the emotional cause, we can create a different effect.

The question would go something like this:

You: (think to yourself)
How come I have not found love?

Then you ask yourself:
What does love feel like? Do I know how I wish to feel about love? What would that feel like? When have I experienced love like this? Let me play with how I wish to feel about the possibilities I would like to experience from love.

My Logic Complements My Emotional Expectation

When we summon up a feeling, we direct the brain to find a memory of this feeling or one that is similar to reinforce our case. The memory reinforces the feeling, which allows us to build by directing it emotionally. The brain responds differently to a quest for emotion than it does to a logical question.

The goal is to connect you with your emotional support system, along with having your logic be a complement your emotional expectation.

You can shift how you seek to find answers. For example:

"How come I have not found love?"
Alternative: Ask yourself – How do I wish to feel about love?

When you think about love and you find that you are analyzing it with your thoughts, take a moment to go to your Emotional Imagination instead.

Like a movie, create scenes that feel good about being in love. Play with emotions of love in your imagination. From here you can create the opportunity for the brain to find other ways to support you because you have shifted your possibilities with different expectations.

"Well, I really do not go out enough to find a relationship."
Alternative: Ask yourself – What kind of experience would inspire me to go out?
"I really do not meet people."
Alternative: Ask yourself – What do I enjoy doing that will create opportunities to meet new people as well?

"All my friends are married."
Alternative: Ask yourself – How can I take time to be in my passion, as this will inspire me and strengthen what I value about myself to attract new potential mates into my life? (Remember, the more you value yourself, the more you attract those who will value you.) **Be interesting to your Self.**

"I am working all the time."
Alternative*:* Ask yourself – Why do I "feel" I need to work all the time?

"I am tired."
Alternative: Ask yourself – Why do I feel tired? Or Am I tired because I am not enjoying my work and working as an escape? Or where do I feel I am draining my energy? Or how would I feel to take care of my body to support the vibrant energy I wish to feel?

"I am not interesting to men/women."
Alternative: Ask yourself – What are the attributes about myself I like and how can I enhance these?

As we have shared previously, language is important: how you language to your Self can create a different response, which creates a different outcome. The simple shift in language in the way you explored about love created the brain to support you with options.

When your brain has an updated resourceful library of beliefs, it is a powerhouse to accelerate your manifesting. If you do not stay up-to-date emotionally, your brain library can only give you information from the past. When this happens, you may react to a new situation based on a past experience or you may simply stay stuck in your past and pass up a dream ready to be true.

Live your dreams; this is why they are there.

When you use the Visualization Technology® of your imagination to create new beliefs and to update old beliefs, your brain reinforces the different outcome you expect. This is a system, not some magical formula. Again, this is why it is important to reflect about your life and stay up-to-date on your dreams and aspirations. Have an updated inventory in your library of beliefs; understand how they serve you where you are now and this will translate into your future.

Activating Your Perspective – Look for the Good

In my own life, I have been able to share these powerful tools with many, and I have used them to navigate my own journey as well. My work is a way of life, and I have shared this information with my children since they were very young. As a parent, I have supported them to be, feel, think and trust themselves. I choose to communicate with them not only to express my love, but also to stimulate them to find their own voice and create their own lives.

As you will read in this story, witnessing a loved one in disharmony can be challenging. Here you will see my own challenge in holding space for my son so that he could discover how to resolve a situation based on how he chose his perceptions.

When I shared with my son that I was going to place this story in my book, we laughed. It seems so long ago, but, at the same time, it was a moment that was a big shift for him. He learned that based on how he chooses to observe a situation he has the power to create the results he desires. After this experience it was clear to him that he was in charge of making his "Movie," even though at the time all the other characters seemed so big and he felt so powerless.

I am going to take you through his thought process, as well as mine, so you can see how emotions and Vibrational Language® can shift an outcome – even if the process is challenging.

My Sweet Boy

One day my son came home from school and was very upset. He was in the sixth grade. He was extremely frustrated and felt that there was no resolution to his situation. This was unusual for him; it was rare to see him so upset and disillusioned. Seeing my little boy hurting, with his huge brown eyes looking at me, was so sad.

My heart broke. I was willing to do anything I could to relieve his pain. He felt that he was at the hands of a "bad" teacher who did not like him and was "out to get him." This was also strange because he liked school, was well liked and had no issues with his teachers in the past.

At that moment, I was jumping to all kinds of conclusions. I was not witnessing the situation. I was in it and immediately felt the teacher was guilty! As his protective mother, I merged with his frustration and offended feelings.

My son had an intense passion for basketball. Everything in his life revolved around playing basketball. Being at the hands of a "bad" teacher meant that if he did not receive good grades, he was in danger of not being able to play on the team.

The school year had just started, and in his mind he was doomed, finished at the hands of this very "bad" teacher who did not like him and was truly "out to get him." According to him, it was clear what was going to happen, and there was no way out. He was spinning around in a chair in my office, ranting and raving about his impending doom of what was to come of his situation. Again, it was very unusual to see my son being this dramatic.

My mind was racing with all my tools and the work I do, but at that moment I was a mother wanting to protect my son, and in my mind this teacher was guilty. Case closed!

At some point in the conversation, I took a deep breath and knew that I could not "save" my son or run to the school to make his case. But, at the same time, I wanted my son to know that I would defend him and that I believed him and I didn't wish to let him down.

Even though he kept telling me to do something and fix it, pleading, "Mom, I know you can fix this. Just talk to her, please Mom," I knew that running to the school was not the way to resolve this, but my heart was on the floor to see him struggle like this.

This was one of those parenting moments where I also wanted to stop the pain of what I was feeling and just fix it so it would be over. Only I knew that would be a short-term fix. The voice in my head confirmed that I should talk this out with my son and discover the tools for him to manage these kinds of situations. I had to find a way to witness my son in his frustration and put my feelings aside to allow us to work this out together.

A Moment Of Choice

So I took a deep breath and went to get some water. I took an emotional time-out. I remembered a memory of my son when he was about seven years old and playing football. I was never a real fan of this sport and the coach at the time did not help convince me otherwise. It was at a game when I heard the coach say something to my son that I felt was demeaning. Well, I went right up to that coach after the game and told him how I felt. We exchanged words. After that exchange, I went to my car where my son was waiting for me, and he said calmly, "Mom, if you ever do that again, I do not want you to come to my games. I can handle my coach." This memory flashed in my mind, reminding me that my son liked to handle his own situations, something that I had also encouraged. But lately we had some challenging life changes and I was more sensitive to protect him. So was this about him or me?

First I acknowledged his frustration. We spoke about how overwhelming this must be thinking that this teacher holds all the cards. I was careful not to make him wrong or to say that what he was feeling was not really what was happening.

First of all, who am I to challenge his story? I wished to understand. Challenging him would only make him want to convince me and reinforce something he does not wish for.

It is important that when we communicate with others, whether we feel they are right or wrong, that we respect the feelings they are sharing. Feelings are not right or wrong; they are simply your feelings. Feelings are defined based on the beholder.

At this point I had to acknowledge my feelings of wanting to fix this and not see him hurting. Taking a moment to do this allowed me to move out of my own way to be present in giving to him without my issues being in the way.

My son continued, "Mom, go and fix it. You can talk to her. You will know what to say." I shared with him that I would be willing to talk to his teacher after we had a conversation. He did not want to hear any of this. He wanted this fixed, NOW! I also wanted this fixed NOW so we could move on from this conversation, but I had to find patience.

Again, I showed compassion for what he was feeling and shared that I felt for him. He then took a deep breath as he saw I was not going to "fix" this; a conversation was his only hope.

This conversation took a lot of patience from both sides and I needed to remember to be conscious to move out of my own way because in my mind, I was thinking that this teacher was still guilty, and I wanted to defend my son. After I acknowledged his feelings and he got past trying to convince me to rush to his school, I asked him what he would like me to do. In his upset tone, he said, "I don't know. I already told you what I want!"

Logical Order To My Emotions

Okay, now I had to create a logical order to my emotions, an order to support the emotional outcome I wished for. First, what was in my power to help him in a way that would empower him? I asked him, "Would you like me to send her an email and request a conference so that we can all talk about this together, you included?" He agreed and I immediately wrote a note on my computer requesting a conference with her.

Then I asked him what he felt he could do to help the situation. Quite frustrated at my question, he explained to me that there was nothing he could do. He continued to explain that there was no hope for the situation. I chose to stay patient and acknowledged again how he felt.

And then I asked him again, "What if there was something you could do to help the situation, what could it be?" Instead of answering the question, he began to tell me all the problems that he saw with his teacher. "Mom, she just doesn't like teaching, and she doesn't like me. She doesn't like that I ask questions, and she doesn't give me attention when I ask questions. She does not like me. This is her first teaching job, and she worked in a company before this." Then he started to get into the drama of his experience again and started building a stronger case against the teacher.

I shared with him that I was listening to how he felt and that he might be correct in everything that he was saying. Nevertheless, his goal is to get a good grade in this class and play basketball. Regardless of the teacher's story, we had to find a way to accomplish his goal. I also took this moment to explain to him that there will be other situations like this one, whether with teachers or when he's doing business in the future. There are times when he will feel that someone is in his way of achieving his goal.

Then I said to him, "Let's just look at this like a basketball game and for just one moment, let's step away from what we think is going to happen. Do you want this story of what you think is going to happen to be your experience, or would you like the opportunity of getting a good grade and being able to play basketball?"

He gave me the rolling eyes as if to say that I knew the answer. I confirmed saying, "I know you want to play basketball and you wish to get a good grade. Then let's focus on finding a way to accomplish this."

I shared with him that I wasn't going to sit here and allow him to continue to reinforce what he says he does not want. This is his "Movie," and no person or situation has so much power over him. I understand it feels like he has no power, but this is not so. I shared with him some stories of when he accomplished other things that he felt were not possible. So instead of us taking this too seriously, even though it was feeling very serious for a moment, we decided to play with this experience as if it was a game. What if he approached it differently? Could he find a way to win this game? Well, now I was beginning to get my son's attention.

Let's Play

I said my famous words … "Let's play!" He did what most eleven-and-a-half year olds would do and again rolled his eyes at me and said, "Mom, you are not going to do your work with me!" I laughed and said again, "Let's play! What if you knew there was something that you could do on your part to support you having what you desire? Regardless of who she is or how she is feeling about you, let's put all that aside. I am talking about you. What can you do? What is in your control to improve the situation?"

I explained to him that he had a choice; the outcome he predicted or he could find a way to bring the story to his side of the game. I noticed that he shifted by the way he looked at me. I was also relieved that I had his attention and we were now in this game together.

I asked him again, "What do you feel you can do to support what you desire as your end result, leaving aside for a moment your personal feelings about this teacher? What can you do? What is in your power to control? What can you control now?"

He said, "I could start going to after-school tutoring classes." I agreed that this was a good idea. I asked him "How would that benefit the outcome you wish for?" He said, "She would see that I want to learn. Maybe she could get to know me differently. Maybe this would give me a chance to ask questions, and I would not feel so frustrated at not understanding all the material." Then we took a moment to discuss his frustration and feeling that the material was challenging. We spoke about the possibility that he may be projecting some of his frustration onto his teacher. We agreed that tutoring would also boost his confidence.

"Great, we have a game plan and by you boosting your confidence you are already ahead of the game!" I said, "You do that, and I will wait to hear when we can meet with the teacher."

I asked him to envision how it will feel to have the end result of what he wished for and to expect it to happen. As he tried to see and feel what it would feel like to have his end result, he got very frustrated. He let me know that he felt that this was not possible.

I asked him, "If your team is losing a game and you really, really want to win, does your coach huddle with the team and say, 'Team, keep doing that losing play again so we can win?' Would your coach ask you to keep doing the same play over and over and over again that was causing you to lose?" My son quickly interrupted me, "That would be really stupid Mom." I said, "You are correct, it is not very clever to do the same thing over and over that is causing you to have a losing game." He interjected, letting me know that the coach would call a time-out to regroup.

We shared that by stepping away from the game for just one moment, it would refocus the concentration of the team. Then my son said, "The coach would give us a new game plan for the next play." "Exactly!" I said. "With this new game plan he gives you, the team would be united in the vision of what you expect to happen, and be motivated to win! You have a few seconds to make that vision your play. To feel it, see it and play it."

I continued, "At this moment, what do you do as a player? You have to make this your game. At that moment of 'time out', you re-visualize how you are going to play differently. But in order to have that opportunity, you needed to step away from the game. Then you go in and start again by re-focusing on how you are going to look at the game. You do not waste your energy on what happened at the last play, you have to be disciplined to move straight into where you wish to be now."

So, basically my son had to make a choice: either he was going to go in with a new play with the same attitude, or he was going to take this new play and create a new attitude to have the possibility of a different outcome. So then I shared with him, "Now, let's take this back to the school. Before you walk into your classroom, knowing what you know right now, how does it make you feel?" I asked.

He admitted that he was not excited to go into class. He felt that he was going to class knowing that the teacher was going to pick on him. He said, "I already know that I am going to ask a question, and she is going to shoot me down. I already know that she doesn't like teaching. I already know all of this."

When You Shift Your Perception, You Shift Your Outcome

"Just for a moment, let's assume that all your points are valid." I continued, "But that is not the outcome you want, is it? Of course it isn't, so let's play with a different possibility."

I explained, "Before you walk into the classroom, you have already assumed that things are going to be the same, and you have no control. You were already expecting the outcome you said you did not want. Nevertheless, YOU are the master of this game, and you are the one that is in control of your 'Movie.'"

I kept going, "So now, before you even walk into the classroom, ask how do you want to feel? What do you have to lose by shifting the way you deal with it?"

He responded, "Mom, I want to feel like I have done really well in this class, and I want to get a really good grade. I want to learn something, and I want to feel excited about it. I actually like math."

"Great. Let's rock. So, before you walk into the classroom, what are you going to do?" I asked. He replied, "I don't know."

I shared, "Do you think that you could walk into the classroom with the same attitude as you did before we had this conversation and get the result you wish for? If you want a different result, you have to change your approach. If you want to win the game, you have to change your plan. So let's go over this again. Imagine you are ready to walk into her classroom.

You are now walking into her classroom feeling more confident because you are taking tutoring, you have been able to get answers to your questions and you know you are making the effort. You are not focused on her; you are focused on you. Now close your eyes and go over again how you feel walking into the classroom this way."

He was feeling better about the possibility of his result. We acknowledged that he had projected his outcome with his previous attitude. Now that he had a different expectation, he would have a different outcome. I asked him to go over this a few times and play in his imagination with how he expects to feel. To envision him Self walking into the door of his classroom feeling confident, knowing he has made a consistent effort. By feeling proud of himself, he naturally was going to project the best of himself.

He agreed that he felt better about going to class. Then I asked him how he felt about his teacher? Again, he had similar feelings but not as intense. I asked him how he would like to feel about his teacher, and he shared that he would like to feel good and hoped that she enjoyed teaching him.

I reminded him that we could not control the behaviors of others. The changes that he is making are for him to feel better about himself. Whatever he does may or may not change the way the teacher treats him. What he can control is the shift in his own attitude and his perspective of what he expects from her. Together, this will shift his judgment of her and the situation. This does not mean he is not correct in his assessment; it just means that it serves no purpose to strengthen what he does not wish for.

Then I asked him again if he would like to feel different about his teacher. He immediately said, "Of course mom! I don't feel good about not liking her, and I don't feel good about feeling that she doesn't like me."

Look For The Good

"Perfect," I said. "So let's play again." Now he was laughing with me. "From what I gather from our conversation, when you sit in your chair during class, you are waiting for a sign from your teacher that signals she is not thinking very good thoughts about you. You are looking for these signs to confirm that she doesn't like you. You wait to ask her a question and think she will shoot your answer down. Is this correct?" I asked.

"Yes," he said as he gave me a small smile.

"So you are listening to her and looking at her. You are waiting for her to basically humiliate you. Is this correct?" I asked again.

"Yes," he said.

I laughed and said, "This poor woman does not have a chance because you already have her marked. You have already judged this teacher; she is doomed. Even if she was nice to you, you wouldn't even trust her, or, maybe if she was nice, it would go unnoticed by you."

He smiled. I said, "Let's play another game like an experiment. Let's say you always get what you are looking for. Imagine that the way we focus our energy is the way we attract. Everything is energy and the way we focus is like grabbing this energy towards us."

He agreed. "So what if throughout your class you look for what you wish to find in your teacher. You wish to find goodness, kindness and respect in this teacher. So what do you feel you would have to do?" I asked. He said, "I am not sure. Be that to her."

I said, "Yes, be an example of what you expect from her." Then he started to defend himself saying he is a representation of those things in class. I shared that I was not challenging him on any of that. In this next week, I simply asked for him to be more conscious of his focus and behavior towards her no matter what she does. To be aware if he is "looking" to find her to be wrong or "looking" for the possibilities of the outcome he would like to have in her class. That even though she can be all the things he said, being an example of what you expect allows each to be responsible for themselves. And whatever happens, you feel good about you without judgment towards her or another.

Then I told him, "Play with this like a game — just play! The worst that could happen has already happened in your mind, so you have everything to gain by maneuvering this from another angle." So we went over this again in his imagination. I said, "Okay, you are walking in the door of the classroom and sitting in your chair. You feel a new possibility to have the outcome you wish for. You have shown up for things to be different. You feel good about how you are showing up."

Then I shared, "To retrain your focus when you look at your teacher in class, find three things you like about her." Of course I got the "look." I reassured him and said, "Even if it is the color of her shoes, her hair or something she said or did. Find three good things about her. Everyone has some good, play a game to go find it."

I explained to him that because his focus will shift, the energy would shift as well. Her energy will shift in another direction because he is no longer connecting to her with the old energy of finding what is wrong in her to justify his feeling.

In essence, everything that was being shared was about energy. Before he stepped into the room physically, his energy was already dictating the relationship. This is what we refer to your as your Vibrational Language. It goes ahead of your physical presence.

Projecting What You Expect

"Remember," I reminded him, "you will always find what you are looking for. Look for what is wrong, and you will find it. Look for the good, and you will find it. If you are looking for the good, good will follow. Looking for the good always makes us feel good about ourselves." So now he was clear. Thank goodness, he had his game plan and he was focused.

What happened after that was quite surprising to me. A few days passed and I had heard nothing from him about his progress or lack of, so I decided I would give this situation a week before I discussed it again. Of course, every time my son walked in the door from school, I wanted to ask for an update. This took discipline but I refrained. After a week, I still had not heard from his teacher, so I began to get worked up with judgment towards her and was convinced that my son said must be correct.

Attempting to be the calm and collective mom, I asked my son how things were going and he said, "Fine." Before he could go any further with the conversation, in a bit of a defensive tone, I said, "Can you believe that teacher has not responded to my email and it has been a week?" My son looked at me and said, "Mom, everything is fine. I spoke to her and told her she did not need to respond to your email." I had this blank stare on my face. I said "What?" He assured me everything was good and not to worry about it. Then he shared that she is actually pretty nice. It took everything I had not to go over every detail. He took responsibility of the situation, so I stepped back to appreciate this and trust how he chose to handle this. I could not empower him and then disempower him.

I decided to wait another week before I asked for more details. The next week came and he was doing even better. Wow, this was good. Time passed and after a few months we laughed at this story of how mad I was at this teacher. I had her judged for not responding to my email, and he was the one who told her not to respond to me. This was truly a lesson learned for me.

Perception Shifts The Outcome

We also smiled together as he was getting a "B" in the class and was still on the basketball team. After only a few months, I could wink at him with the "So ... Mom is not that crazy look" and confirm how his shift of perception shifted his outcome. The best part of this was that he was aware of the fact that his shift created the shift in the outcome.

I shared how extremely proud I was of him. It is challenging for us to change our minds when one feels so right. He chose to see it like a game, and now he has the habit of "looking for the good." The school year was about to be over, and he wanted to increase his grade. He said he went to this teacher to ask for extra credit, and he was so excited that he was the only one who got it! There was an end-of-the-year field trip and he actually chose this teacher as his chaperone. I thought this was so wonderful.

Wow, this relationship had come a long way, and they built a genuine respect for each other. The way this story transformed still chokes me up with emotion. Well, the teacher did end up going back to the corporate world after her first year working in education. My son was correct in thinking that she did not enjoy teaching that much, but that still did not make her a bad person. She had a huge impact on my son. He got an education from her that is far more valuable than any grade.

Now I do wish to clarify something. You can look for the good you wish in someone and the situation may not improve. Sometimes when we wish for good will in a situation with another it may not happen with that person; they will either move out of your way, or escalate their hurtful behavior. Whatever the end result with that person, you can be at peace with your behavior. You will also notice that they have little or no value in your world with the effect they have on you, if it is not a positive situation. With this approach and intention in looking for the good will, other opportunities that are good simply appear and good is found all around you and within others.

I would like to use this story as an opportunity to share the principles of Power Wishing® fundamentals that were used in action to achieve the desired results.

Here is a quick reference to the Power Wishing fundamentals:

- Acknowledge the situation in its present form.
- Acknowledge your feelings towards the situation.
- Acknowledge what you believe is going to happen in the present situation as it is.
- Ask your Self how you would like to feel about the situation.
- Ask your Self what is in your control right now to improve the situation, what can you do now.
- Connect with this situation as a "Movie," with the feeling of accomplishing what you can do now.
- Acknowledge your Self for being present and taking action.
- Acknowledge how you feel with the action you have taken to support your desired outcome.
- Ask for this as a possibility.
- Play with the situation and envision scenes, as you would like it to be with new possibilities.
- Keep going over the situation like a "Movie."

- Play, and then play some more, with the different possibilities you wish for.
- Play again with scenes like a "Movie" of this possibility.
- If fears show up, acknowledge them and create scenes of seeing the possibilities to resolve them.
- Next! Keep moving your Emotional Imagination forward into your present.
- Create scenes with your excitement of what you wish to happen.
- Go to another place and time in your life where you have felt this way, a place where you can reinforce your feelings with similar success.
- Anchor the end result with this feeling in every bit of your physical body and surroundings.
- Check in with what beliefs you have that are aligned with supporting this happening.
- Play with these scenes in your Emotional Imagination.
- See yourself playing out your day-to-day experience and how you feel.
- Envision how you respond, knowing you cannot control others.
- Go to this feeling as often as possible.
- In your day-to-day ... Witness. Look for what you are expecting.
- As you witness, respond with actions that are aligned with your possibility that you are creating.
- As you witness, know that a response could be no action or an action based on being aligned.
- Look for the good!
- Expect to find what you are looking for!
- Expect it and know that everything is supporting your desire with love.

Life Is Not By Luck – Good Choices Create Good Fortune

There is so much good vibration all around you.

Trust that good will happen for you and that there are good people who wish to share in the joy of goodness in your life.

As you look in the mirror, what do you find? YOU ... All the good in YOU! This is what is shaping your destiny ...

Look for the good and you will find it. Use words that reinforce your trust in who you are and express respect towards you.

Power Thoughts

Your Perspective = Your Reality

- My dreams are mine to live; this is why I have them.

- I expect to find what I am looking for in my life.

- The belief of what I believe I can expect makes the difference.

- When I shift my perception, I shift my outcome.

- My feelings are not right or wrong; they are simply my feelings.

- My life is not by luck; I make choices that create my good fortune.

- There is so much good vibration all around me and I feel it.

- The way I focus my energy is the way I attract.

- I know how to respond with actions that are aligned with my desires.

- Being an example of what I expect allows me to take responsibility for my Self.

Safe Emotional Love

You have a choice on how you choose to love another, and how you believe you should be loved. It is your choice and responsibility to be a high example of everything you believe in your Self and with others.

When you are authentic and choose to consciously be awake with your life as a Conscious Choice, your energy is clean and vibrant. When you live a life that is an authentic representation of who you are, you naturally wish to have relationships in your life that honor this, where the energy exchanged is uplifting.

Having said that, there is one very important component that I would like to share with you that I believe is so vital and non-negotiable as a part of your life of design and that is "safe emotional love." Among the many wonderful aspects of my work, if I had to narrow down and educate on only one of my subjects, it would be that of safe emotional love. This love is a vital part to the design of our lives.

I am deeply passionate about this subject, because I feel that there is such abuse towards others in the name of love, many that are obvious and some that are not. There is emotional abuse we do to ourselves and abuse projected by others in the name of love. If you have experienced emotionally safe relationships, you know that this is truly a gift that is beyond words.

Sharing Truth Respectfully

A safe relationship is also about feeling that you are safe in expressing yourself. If you're asked a question, you answer with who you are, not what you believe is expected from you. I remember something my teacher Frank would say, "If you lie to someone, it is because you hold him or her as an authority in your life." If I feel that I do not wish to share my truth with someone or feel the need to withhold information, at that moment I ask myself, "Why?" Do I see them as an authority over me? Do I believe there will be a "bad" consequence to sharing with them? Why do I not feel safe in sharing with them? Then I snap to who I am with today and within seconds I am aware of how I am placing them in my life and shift that right away by sharing my truth respectfully, or I acknowledge to my Self that there is an aspect of me that does not feel safe in sharing or I simple choose not to share at this time.

When you are untruthful to another, you hand over your power to them and you mislead them with who you really are. My teacher also used to say that, "Guilt is a form of manipulation." I remember hearing this in my first teachings with him at 14 years old and I thought this guy is crazy – guilt is an emotion I feel it, I thought about it for a moment, *what if* guilt is a form of manipulation? I started to be aware of when and why I would feel guilty. It usually was when I was not conforming to another's wishes and they blamed me for their feelings. I realized that, basically, it was a way to manipulate me to feel accountable to the other person.

Safe Love Is Sacred

The greatest gift we can give another is an honoring of the individual's Soul with a love that is without control, manipulation, guilt or conditional terms. Emotionally safe love is sacred.

When there is safe love, I find that there is no longer a necessity to be heard through negative actions to get attention. Through authentic communication, you grow as an individual and also collectively. You can agree to disagree without feeling belittled. You share your feelings based on how you feel, not by breaking down the other person. You add value to each other's life experiences and your children, partner or friends can trust that they can communicate with you without being "in trouble" or judged. When safe love is established in a family, the home becomes a sanctuary, "Heaven-on-Earth."

Being An Emotional Hostage

When your relationship ends up causing you more pain rather than acting as a buffer against distress, when you feel there is a hostile audience and unexpected discomforts may happen at any time, this is not safe love.

In this conversation we are having, when I share about a relationship, it can be defined as any relationship where you are relating with another.

A valuable aspect of safe love is consistency and predictability – following through on promises, keeping one's word and thus creating trust. When I experience or witness others say on a consistent basis they are going to do something and they do not, or if they act inconsistently with their emotions, or seem fine and then out of nowhere give a shocking reaction, I see this as manipulative and abusive.

When relationships are hostile, distrusting and angry, we do not feel the other has our best interests in mind and this does not feel safe. When in your relationship you feel real and genuine with each other, you live without the constant fear of the "other shoe dropping."

How can you feel a sense of peace where there is anxiety of what may happen? When sharing is more about responsibilities for the other and the relationship runs more like a business?

Being an "emotional hostage" in an unhealthy relationship will affect your health in a serious way. Since your brain can no longer justify your reasoning for being in this type of relationship, your nervous system takes over, which affects functions such as heart rate, perspiration, respiration, digestion, urination, desire for life, etc. The way I clearly see it, there is no gain in staying in hurtful relationships. You can reason all you wish, but when your body screams "NO MORE," then you cannot serve your Self or the ones you love, emotionally or physically.

When you feel safe, you are honored for your sensitivity, while in an unsafe relationship you protect your sensitivity by not sharing your Self or by being untruthful. Unsafe relationships are often emotionally abusive. Our society usually defines a picture of abuse as being physical, not verbal, emotional, economic or sexual. Sometimes it is very challenging to define if you are in an unsafe relationship when there is not physical abuse. Relationships that are unsafe are not limited to personal relationships; these also can include work-related relationships.

In a relationship that is NOT safe:
Judgment
Criticism
Ridicule and put-downs
Complaints
Rejection
Abandonment
Comparisons
Threats
Bullying
Aggressive behavior
Unpredictable or unstable behavior unspoken and covert rules
Unhealthy / inappropriate boundaries

In an unsafe relationship, YOU...

Spend a lot of energy thinking of ways to defend your actions even before you are approached in order to avoid conflict.

Consistently feel you are not good enough in their presence.

Worry about how the other will react and that is your base on how you make decisions.

Feel like you have no say when it comes to money, spending, purchases, and many other topics.

Feel confused around them with your judgment and constantly second-guess your Self.

Are held responsible for the other's happiness.

Blame your Self first when things happen.

Build a case against your Self first so you are prepared.

In an unsafe relationship, the other...

Implies that you are crazy and you believe you are the one who is crazy.

Is sarcastic or makes jokes that are hurtful put-downs, but when you share it hurts your feelings, says you are overly sensitive.

Does not suggest but expects you to be a specific way or dress a certain way (hair, nails, clothes, etc.)

Creates doubt about who you are and about others that you trust.

Will use children against you by threatening to get custody and take the kids away as a consequence to your behavior.

Places fault on you and implies that you made them angry.

Is most affectionate after a fight, wants you to forgive, forget and move on, usually without wishing to discuss it further and makes claims it won't happen again, they will change.

Sarcasm And Gossip Are Not A Part Of Safe Love

When I hear someone making sarcastic remarks and little jabs, acting as if they are just joking, I find this very hurtful. It is total unnecessary to tease someone and camouflage language in a way that is hurtful. I believe that what people say is their truth, whether they say it *joking* or not. Sarcasm to me is a cheap way to get one's point across instead of directly discussing something without hurtful, *joking* comments. Gossip is simply hurtful and manipulative.

Here is an excerpt from a story about Socrates on the issue with gossip:

In ancient Greece, Socrates was widely respected for his wisdom. One day, an acquaintance ran up to the great philosopher excitedly and asked, "Do you know what I just learned about your friend, Diogenes?"

"Hold on a minute," Socrates replied. "Before telling me anything, I would like you to pass a little test. It's called the Triple Filter Test."

"Triple Filter Test?"

"That's right," Socrates continued. "Before you talk to me about my friend, it might be a good idea to take a moment and filter what you're going to say. That's why I call it the triple filter test. The first filter is Truth. Have you made absolutely sure that what you are about to tell me is true?"

"No," the man said, "Actually, I just heard about it."

"All right," said Socrates, "So you don't really know if it's true or not. Now, let's try the second filter, the filter of Goodness. Is what you are about to tell me about Diogenes something good?"

"No, on the contrary … "

"So," Socrates continued. "You want to tell me something about Diogenes that may be bad, even though you're not certain it's true?"

The man shrugged, a little embarrassed.

Socrates continued, "You may still pass the test though, because there is a third filter, the filter of Usefulness. Is what you want to tell me about Diogenes going to be useful to me?"

"No, not really."

"Well," concluded Socrates, "If what you want to tell me is neither True, nor Good nor even Useful, why tell it to me or anyone at all?"

The Life Force Of Safe Love

In a safe relationship, you feel the other person is emotionally available and present. They are emotionally engaged and accessible. You treat each other as a priority. Even though the unexpected twists and turns may cause some emotional turmoil, everyone feels safe amongst challenges. You feel an openness of receptive energy to each other's sharing.

The energy in the relationship is free to flow and is not blocked by chaos or being guarded. Life has surprises but your relationships should not be limited with this.

Safe emotional love is your life force; it is life with a force of love that holds you and grounds you with roots to grow.

You feel respected, you feel heard, and you feel understood with validation. There is empathy for you and respect for your feelings.

Safe love is the hands of gentleness holding your Soul with love.

Safe emotional love is also being aware of another person's way of being and allowing the discovering of each other.

You do not define each other based on conditions. There is an aliveness and safety when your Authentic Self is present and you do not fear the loss of the relationship for being your Self.

Excitement, growth and security replace anxiety and fear.

In an emotionally safe relationship:

You know what it feels like to feel free to be your Authentic Self without feeling judged.

You know what it feels like to express authentically without a "bad" consequence.

You know what it feels like to set healthy boundaries.

You know what it feels like to say "No" without any guilt.

You know what it feels like to love yourself and feel supported for who you are.

You know what it feels like to change your mind without doubting your Self.

You know what it feels like to take care of yourself because you are honored for this.

You know what is feels like to be forgiven when you have hurt the other.

You know what it feels like to feel lovable.

You know what it feels like to receive love without feeling you have to "work" for it.

You know what it feels like to be in love without conditions.

You know what it feels like to feel appreciated.

You know what it feels like to feel safe.

Who do you feel emotionally safe with? Create safe emotional relationships and have these relationships in your life by valuing others as you wish to be valued.

Habits That Reinforce Safe Love

There are habits that support you in having safe love in your life, as well as providing a supportive space of safe love for others. When you know these habits support and honor your relationships in this way, there is not a necessity for more processing or understanding. You simply do them! You know what you know about what feels "right" in a relationship and an instinctive discipline takes over.

Healthy emotional bonds and intimacy naturally grow out of creating emotionally safe relationships. When we are in a safe emotional relationship, we feel loved without conditions; therefore, we freely love without conditions.

Even though as an individual we can feel secure, when we share with another through safe love, there is a feeling of security in knowing that the world is safer and sweeter because of this love.

Best In Me = The Best In You

Activate the best in you and then you have the best opportunity to activate this in another. By being the best example of what you expect, you create opportunity for others to be the best they can be. It is not our place to break them down and tell them what they should fix or how to live. This does not mean that you cannot share and discuss with a partner, family member and others your concerns about a habit or situation that you witness. It is totally understandable to share your feelings with someone. At times our sharing is because we wish that we felt better around them or about the situation. It is healthy to share, but have awareness if you are sharing for yourself to feel better or for their wellbeing without having any expectations for them to change.

All too often I have witnessed others attempting to change another so they can feel better about themselves. We create a pattern of wanting to control others to suit our needs or ideas of how we believe things should be. Again, usually it's so we feel better around them. If this were not the case, then why would there be such negative consequences in relationships when another makes a choice? If sharing with another were strictly for their wellbeing, and the opportunity to mutually enhance the relationship, then wouldn't there be more tolerance towards our differences?

It is liberating to release the need to control or change others. Many times releasing this behavior gives you the opportunity to really know someone for who they are without your projections of who you think they are or not. It is like saying, "You really do not know Bill Rodriquez; you only know the idea you have formed of him." Again, this does not mean that you do not address characteristics of a partner or situations that you feel are challenging. It simply means that you are sharing for your own desire to express your perspective and they can choose how they wish to receive what you are expressing.

It is also healthy to have boundaries to support the best in any relationship. This is different from wanting them to change something they may love about themselves to suit your own needs. By the way, if they do change something about themselves because they want to please you and it is not authentic for them, this can begin to build resentment. At a later point, if not addressed, this can become a negative cycle of bitter feelings and deep resentment.

So, if you feel you have a tendency to control and do not like the relationships this is creating, then create wishes to shift this behavior. If you wish to be a clearer communicator, then maybe see how shifting the way you communicate can enhance the relationships you love and those who surround you.

Let us remind each other that we are enough with the best that we can be at that moment. Building a relationship from this perspective is solid. We are always enough and it is beautiful to accept people as they are, as we would appreciate the same response.

Create wishes to enhance what you acknowledge about what you love about your Self and strengthen trusting yourself from a place within your inner Self. These emotions can be used to shift or to transform your relationships without focusing on the outcome. Enhancing what you love is far more powerful as a dominant force to generate the attraction of what you wish to expect from those around you.

Replace the feelings of lack you perceive in another with positive feelings of what you love about your Self. This can be done from a healthy energy of reinventing yourself because you are excited to enhance part of your being that brings you joy. This energy becomes a Vibrational Language that enhances you and your surroundings.

Building Safe Relationships

Make sure you honor your relationships by being an emotionally safe person, especially with children. Be the example of this trust and of the way you would like children or others to be with you.

When I was in third grade, my parents divorced and it was an emotionally painful time. I went to a Catholic school and my teacher who was a nun used to sit with me at lunchtime under my favorite tree and I would tell her all my eight-year-old pains. I believed we shared a safe relationship and to me, she represented the sacred values of God. I would tell her everything. She was my only real confidante and when she spoke I believed as an innocent child I could hear the echo of God; I completely trusted her. I remember looking forward to sharing with her at lunchtime. It took me a few years to realize that it was this nun who would tell all our conversations to my father, and this is why he would get upset at me when I would come home from school. When I would ask him how did he know certain things about my feelings about the divorce, he would say a "little birdie told me."

As far as I am concerned, whatever reasons my teacher used to justify sharing with my father are not valid. First of all, she gave her interpretation of my conversations, but more importantly she told me she would not share our private conversation and this led me to trust her. I felt this nun betrayed me, and my father felt betrayed by the conversations we had about him as well. He took it personally, when it was just about a little eight-year-old girl who was hurting inside. We are so tender when we are vulnerable, and when that is not honored, especially with a child's innocent trust, this can be very painful.

How can a child learn to feel safe if the ones who said they would keep them safe betray them? When a child learns early on that there are unsafe relationships in their world with those they trust, this is scary for them. It is such a powerful gift to give safe love to a child and witness them blossom.

Being Present

Before judging a child's behavior, I often suggest that the adult reflect on how they are setting the child up to succeed in their presence.

Do you listen without interruptions? Are you genuinely interested in them? Are you turning to your cell phones at the dinner table? Are you on your computer more times than you are being present with a child? Instead of turning to each other and being present in our communication and feelings, oftentimes technology replaces conversations and we lose the opportunity to understand and share about ourselves.

At a very young age, children receive a lot of external information. All day long they observe the media, TV and cultural behaviors that they are exposed to. They form all kinds of belief systems that may or may not be genuinely true for them or your family. They are informed to think through TV, computer, music and the school systems, many times without really having a choice. We expect them to be able to deal with peer pressure and make the "right" choices. How can they when the messaging that is reinforced support them NOT to think for themselves?

As the need to be constantly entertained or distracted has grown, DVD players often replace conversations shared together in the car. I find that as a culture we are forgetting how to entertain each other and share that which we are with our experiences. We live in such a fast-paced society where some of the ways we may share with others may seem like a waste of time, like going to the supermarket together, taking a drive or doing errands. Just doing mindless things with each other or children is beneficial to your relationship. You enjoy each other differently. Not everything has to have an end goal to it.

We are such a technological society, expecting instant gratification in so many areas of our lives and, when this does not occur, one may lose their patience with their loved ones or with opportunities for new relationships.

In a time where we are overloaded with words, texting, social media and email as a society, we find ourselves expressing most of our loving messages through technology. Typing is our main expression of love. Most hugs come through the mobile phone and a kiss is from i-chat on the computer.

What if we begin to value the expression of love by looking in the eyes of another? What if we express our love for no other reason than to share and communicate instead of having another assume that maybe you do not love them? What if we gave attention to holding hands as a way to provide comfort instead of an email to address the situation?

What if we made choices that support who we are and communicate them clearly so that feelings are felt again and love becomes a household word that feels good?

Sometimes just sitting together at dinner or driving with each other to the store without the phone in your ear can make room for random but very valuable conversations. My son is good at just popping into my office or sitting down and having a conversation out of nowhere. Because he is not a big talker, I stop and listen. This is one of those moments where we are sharing and building.

For example, when a loved one or a child comes home and they are greeted by the one they love with a phone in their ear and are told "one moment ...," after several times, it can easily lead to the other person feeling invisible and devalued. People then create behaviors because of these beliefs. Often this is not done intentionally; it is a habit that we do not even notice.

This is not a judgment of what is good or bad; simply an observation of how present we are and why we may become numb to our own feelings and beliefs about who we are, along with the effects this can have on others. The good news is that there are always moments for new opportunities; the past does not have to own you, nor do beliefs that no longer serve you. Today is the day. You are awake and every moment is yours to own. Your beliefs, your life and your future – now!

Clear Messaging

Spending time with each other also supports everyone to feel safe in saying "no" and confident in giving clear messaging. It also supports us to know how to honor each other when making agreements.

For several years, I was a member of the Young President Organization (YPO). This organization is a powerful network of global CEOs. They held conferences where we as CEOs received education and networked with each other and many great world leaders. In one of the conferences I attended, I heard a lecturer give a simple story about raising boys. At the time, my son was a baby so this was interesting to me. Nevertheless, this is also an example about clear messaging.

Chocolate Cake

The story began that one day little Sammy was doing something that he was asked to stop several times. His mother said, "Sammy, if you do not stop, you will not be able to have your favorite chocolate cake for dessert tonight." Sammy continued doing what he was doing, choosing not to listen to his mom. After a few warnings, his mom said, "Sammy, you will not have your favorite chocolate cake for dessert tonight." That was that.

Well, Sammy and his parents were all are sitting around the dinner table and this night in particular Sammy's father had invited some very important clients to dinner. Now it was time for the chocolate cake and actually it was Sammy's favorite. Everybody was enjoying this wonderful chocolate cake, and Sammy asked if he could have some and the mom said nicely, "Sammy, you know why you cannot have the cake." Tears began to slowly well up in Sammy's eyes and the mom looked at her husband and said, "I said no chocolate cake tonight."

Now the husband gave "the look" to the wife because they had guests at the house, and he certainly did not want to make a scene in front of these very important clients. The wife gave "the look" back, basically saying, "I said no."

This chocolate cake was so delicious that the guests asked for more. The mom walked around the table with this delicious chocolate cake and Sammy was just staring at her, asking again and again if he could please, please, please, please have some chocolate cake. He was promising he would listen next time. The mom again said no and the husband gave her "the look" as if she was embarrassing him. Sammy said over and over again with tears, "I promise I won't do it again, I promise I will listen better next time" and the mom looked at the husband and the husband looked at the mom. There were more tears from Sammy, and the guests were in complete silence. The mother started to defend her Self politely and went over how many times she gave Sammy warnings, how he completely chose not to listen knowing the consequence – no chocolate cake.

But the pressure was on. The mom felt she was getting looks from the guests, the husband was not being very supportive and Sammy was crying at the table. So the mom turned to Sammy and said, "OK, you can have chocolate cake." The gentleman client turned to Sammy's mother compassionately and said, "You realize that you just taught your boy that 'no' does not mean 'no' especially from a woman."

When we reflect on what this may mean, it can be chilling. For me this really hit home as I was raising my son and teaching him about respect. I realized that for me to change my "no" to "yes," it was important to clarify and to come to a new agreement or understanding and most important not give mixed messaging, especially when pressured. After a few times of doing this, we can create a pattern that no does not mean no when we are under pressure.

When we change a "no" under pressure or manipulation, this is not healthy for anyone. It confuses the message of communication. This is a simple story about a mother and her son but in reality it can be about any relationship. When you say "No," do you change your "No" because of pressure or because you wish to? Pay attention to when you change your "No" to a "Yes" or vice versa. If you wish to change your mind, then change it, but be aware of why you are doing this. Is it in the heat of the moment where you feel pressured out of fear, or is it because it feels *right* to you to change your mind?

Honor Agreements

You are responsible to each other and not for each other. This means that in a safe relationship, you honor agreements you have made to each other, and if you feel you need to change the agreement, discuss this beforehand if possible. If we are in a relationship where we feel responsible for someone else, for their feelings and actions, this leads to lack of accountability on the other person's part and resentments will likely arise. In a safe relationship, one takes responsibility for themselves and honors the commitments they have made based on their values.

We shared about taking inventory of your beliefs to see if your beliefs are up-to-date. I would invite you to do the same with the agreements you have with those closest to you. See if they are still valid for the relationship. Be accurate with each other; if you say something, mean it. This makes others feel visible in the relationship.

This is your life ... yours! The more peaceful and happy you are, the more you will feel love for your Self, and the more love you have to give to the ones you love. Taking care of your Self is not selfish; it's being responsible. If you are well, then you can take better care of others. When you take care of your energy, you are not depleted! Taking care of your energy means honoring your Self with the transparency of who you are.

You honor others by releasing the energy of trying to control them or their life's circumstances. When you live a life with clarity of who you are and what your values are, your energy has rhythm that flows in alignment with your genuine Self. When you live this way, you build from healthy emotions as your anchor.

You deplete your energy when using it to manage chaos and rejuvenate your energy by being authentic.

Be mindful that you do not make too many agreements to set your relationships up for disappointment. Simply be sure that the agreements you do make you can keep. If you have to change them, make new agreements before you break them. If you share in the relationship that you have an intention to do something for each other, it is important to honor your word or change it.

One of the values I stress with my children is accountability. We are each responsible for ourselves and responsible to each other with the agreements we make. A simple example of this with my children is in reference to school. I was not the type of parent to police them with their homework. I would share with them that I have my responsibilities to care for our home and they have their responsibilities to care for their grades. We agreed. I would make agreements with my children before a situation would occur so they knew what to expect – no surprises. We agreed that on Fridays I would check their homework report from school and if there was any missing homework, they were not allowed to go out on the weekend, and if it happened more than once that month, their electronics use would be suspended.

Most of the time, my children would own up to their choices and proactively tell me that they did not do their homework. They preferred whatever they chose over the consequences, no drama, no negotiating; pure accountability. It created ease in our home with situations that can be dramatic and disappointing. It is nerve-racking, especially for children, not to know what to expect from their parents or in their home life.

Yes, there are many things that you cannot predict, but for the ones that you can, make agreements ahead of time. This takes away any unnecessary anxiety.

Safe With Your Wounds

Being raised in an environment where I did not know what to expect, as well as suddenly losing those I have loved, has made me more sensitive in certain areas than most. My point here is that when you are in a safe relationship, the other person does not treat certain sensitivities as a weakness or try to get you to "toughen up." They honor this piece of you and everyone works together to create security, not because you are insecure but because they wish to support your healing. We each have the good, the bad, the joy and the pain that creates our emotional picture.

In a safe relationship, if one asks for something that supports them to feel secure from another, even if this is not the other's sensitivity, there is a loving consciousness to not add more to wounds that may not be healed yet. For example, because of sudden unexpected things that have happened in my life, I like to be communicated with and feel at ease when loved ones touch base with me. I still have a bit of panic when I cannot reach a loved one if they are traveling or if they usually call and then all of the sudden they do not call and I cannot reach them. For some people this is not a big deal; then again, they did not have the same experiences I had. The ones closest to me understand this and it is a way that they support our relationship, as I do for them in other ways.

Then of course with consistency my trust grows and I am not as vulnerable. My husband used to say "Sometimes people try to toughen you up on things, when they should really learn to soften up." I appreciated that because giving *hard love* is not necessarily the way to always get someone to grow: gentleness and kindness can be far more effective at times. Are there simple things you can do to support your relationship to feel safer? Are there things that you desire for your Self to feel at ease with the weaknesses you are strengthening?

Intimate Sharing

When we are in a relationship, whether friendship or love, we share many things with each other, and some of these conversations are sacred and shared with trust. I strongly feel that safe love means that these intimate and private understandings of another's personal details should never be shared outside of this relationship.

In a safe relationship, no matter what happens, even if the relationship is over, this type of truthful sharing is always to be held sacred and not used against the other. It pains me when I have witnessed, either personally or with clients, that intimate trust being betrayed. It creates so much pain when we share our vulnerability in a relationship and then we are deceived and intimate details are used to hurt one another. Strive for a safe environment where you give each other permission to be yourselves, allowing each other to feel safe to honor each other as individuals and also as a partnership. A relationship of safe love is one where sharing is held sacred no matter what.

Home Is A Safe Zone

We all need to have safe spaces to be nurtured, where we feel we will not have unexpected surprises. To be supported for who we are and to be safe when we are not who we really are at that moment. Home is one of these places that should be a safe space, a sacred space for sharing.

Having dinner with your family is a time to share and catch up. It is a time where everyone can feel comfortable that the conversation will be light, sharing in a positive way and knowing that bad news or criticism will not be a part of the conversation. Then everyone can look forward to knowing this family time is where sharing is positive.

We all have heard bad news at one time or another and usually we remember where that news was given to us. Do your best to give bad news outside your home. This way one does not create a sense of fear of the unknown when coming home because they may not know what to expect. It is like when you receive a phone call in the middle of the night with bad news; it is challenging if another call comes late at night not to assume it will be bad. It takes a while to relax each time the phone rings. There is nothing worse than coming home and being shocked with some news that would have been better to discuss elsewhere. Keep your home an emotionally safe place where you can regroup and recharge for the outside world. It is your sanctuary, your paradise in this world.

Connect with Joy

It does take emotional discipline to be aware of connecting with others through non-drama and joy instead of making time for each other because of a crisis. Discussing situations when there isn't a crisis avoids a lot of drama and unproductive energy. Having discipline to be aware to share with more joy than drama builds in trusting your relationships in times that there is the possibility of drama. When we are able to release drama, this enables us to clearly see what really needs to be resolved at the core of the situation.

Sometimes we may feel the impulse to share when we feel intense in our anger or pain, but this heated moment may not be the best time to share perspectives that might help to reach an understanding. More time may be needed before people can express themselves clearly and calmly. With my Latino blood and my Leo sensitivity along with my Capricorn ascendants, I usually wish to share and resolve things immediately, especially if I feel I am being bullied or misrepresented. I can say, like many of us, I am not always patient at this, but with awareness we grow and this is a part of life.

With experience, I have grown to know that when we listen clearly to each other at times when there isn't an emotional charge, we have a far better chance of hearing each other. Trust that you can play out your emotions in your imagination to create more of an understanding of how you would like to respond before creating drama. Sometimes drama is there because we are not sure of what to do. Play in your Emotional Imagination so you can find the answers you wish for with clarity and joy.

Take a moment to reflect on these questions:
When there is a situation that is hurtful to you, when do you share about it, when you have had enough or before this?
Are your relationships built with crisis or joy as the main focus?
In your relationships, when do you receive the most attention from each other – in crisis or in joy?
Do you make a point of sharing and acknowledging joyful moments in conversations?
Do you spend time finding ways to build with each other through conversations that are positive?
Do you share mutual interests that create a healthy loving bond?

People usually make extra time to share when there is a crisis – be aware you create special time to share about joy. Share without crisis or drama so the base of your relationship is built with positive attributes. Be spontaneous with sharing how you value those in your life.

Build your relationships' emotional immune system, meaning, "boost up" what you love about each other. People, especially our loved ones, can feel hurt when they feel taken for granted and this can cause major heartache. Take time to share with your significant other, friends, family and children to say thank you for being so wonderful in your life.

Do not take your loved ones for granted! Let them know that even with the things that you feel are expected of them, you notice and deeply appreciate them. Otherwise, at times our loved ones can feel the need to act out to receive our attention. This is especially true with our children and partners.

I thank my children often for calling me when they are out, receiving good grades, for staying out of trouble, etc. Yes, this is my expectation of them as their parent but I wish for them to know that I am aware of how they contribute to our healthy relationship and do not take this for granted.

One day my daughter turned to me out of nowhere and said, "Mom, you are a good YOU." It made me feel seen and acknowledged in such a good way. It reminded me that thanking those closest to us for being so wonderful and for supporting us in ways that may be taken for granted in daily life feels so good.

Emotions Are Natural

Being emotional is natural; suppressing and denying your emotions is not.

What you will find in giving yourself permission to acknowledge your feelings is that you are not overly dramatic, sensitive or emotional. As you express yourself, you will find the balance to what honors you and others.

It can be very challenging to find answers and manifest your desires when you suppress and ignore your emotions, or allow others to define your emotions for you.

When you shift your emotions, you may also change your mind, and then change your mind again, and others may do the same. This is totally OK and healthy. Asking yourself questions and answering them to discover how you feel gives structure and understanding to your beliefs.

If you do not know the answer to your own questions, are you able to be patient, or do you allow another to give you answers in place of your own?
What belief is the foundation of what you are expecting to receive and is this your belief or another's?

Remember, you are an Amazing Soul exploring the journey of the truth of who you are as the reflection of the life you desire. When you are happy and you know it, soak it in. When things feel *right,* they are for you and that is what you listen to. From there you will have more answers that take you to more truths.

My life, my work, is about sharing all day long. I especially love a good long conversation with my friends about life, feelings and everyone's favorite topic … LOVE! I will say I have highly opinionated friends from all walks of life who share with me clearly, but we have the space and love for each other to agree to disagree.

As I write this, I laugh. My friends were instrumental in the creation of my book. They challenged me, made edits, and we had long discussions over dinner and wine. It was an expanding collaboration that was respectful and many times enlightening. We all celebrate the finishing of my book, but my highlight of this accomplishment is the celebration of the loving friendships in my life. This is truly a treasure.

One thing that has supported our friendships is that we take time to get to know each other and do not assume. If we assume, we assume the best.

We are respectful about giving advice, especially since many of us are artists in one form or another, intellects but all sensitive. I also come from a big family, and as I am the oldest of seven siblings, I understand when there are a lot of opinions in a group. I am respectful towards the way I give advice and so are my friends. We have discernment with what is imposing our opinions and what is sharing with each other.

Joy, More Joy

Do you often imagine sharing more joy and love with those close to you? It is fun to daydream ways to share more good feelings with those you love and imagine experiences that match this. Use Power Wishing™ to manifest more of what you desire in the relationships with your loved ones. Before you know it, connecting with joy will be a part of your normal day, and unnecessary chaos will no longer be needed to stay connected to each other.

Love As We Define It

Life is precious, not because of when we are going to take our last breath but because we have so many opportunities to love. Take every opportunity to choose love and to share connecting to the goodness with those around you.

Do your best to do everything possible to live your definition of love as a way of life versus as a reaction to your life ending. Express your definition of love in your daily life.

Your definition of love is powerful; it is the expression of the best of you to share with others and is the foundation of all you create.

POWER THOUGHTS

Safe Love

- ○ I honor emotionally safe love as sacred.

- ○ Safe emotional love is a vital part of my healthy relationships.

- ○ I am conscious to share more joy in my relationships.

- ○ I follow through on my promises, creating trust with others.

- ○ I live my definition of love as a way of life.

- ○ I find my Self daydreaming of wonderful ways to share with my loved ones.

- ○ I honor my loved ones and frequently let them know in various ways.

- ○ My home is a safe sacred space that I enjoy.

- ○ Taking care of my Self is not selfish; it's being responsible.

- ○ Being emotional is natural; emotionally shocking others is not natural.

Love Heals

"Where there is love there is life." – Mahatma Gandhi

There Is So Much Love For You

Love is like a warm blanket that comforts and nurtures your Soul. Love surrounds you in many different forms and love is expanding around you as well as within you. Love is different for every Amazing Soul and can be defined in many ways. Love is the base of all creation; it created you. It exists in all of creation because it is the very root and foundation for all the energies in the Universe.

Love is an experience that is felt, it is the experience that creates all other experiences. Love is what creates the experience of discovering others and our Selves. And through the experience of love we define our lives. Love is an energy force that inspires all things. The feeling of lack of love or being full of love is a force that motivates us in different ways.

There are many ways to define love. Love is always evolving and defining itself in our lives based on life experiences. We are constantly discovering and redefining parts of our life based on love. Each of us finds our *own* experiences of love and this feeling keeps us motivated to connect with other Amazing Souls. When you connect with others with love in your heart, no matter how it is defined, it is the best expression of the Light you carry within.

My mother's husband was a special Soul. One night shortly after he passed away, I had a very vivid dream of him and I can still remember it clearly more than 15 years later as it had a profound effect on me. There were many details in this dream, but the message of this night vision was simple. He showed me what happens when one dies. He showed me that one reviews their life, like a movie on a screen. There is no judgment towards this movie from an outside source, like God. He showed me that you review your life and there are things you can feel proud of and ones that you sincerely review and have a feeling of how you would have done it differently. Even if there were experiences of regret towards love, it is our handling of this experience that matters most.

It was clear from him and in my dream that we ask ourselves only one question as we are reviewing our life. He said to me very clearly, we are judged on one thing and one thing only, that is it.

Did I create this with love?
It is about your intention more than the result.

Love is an experience to cherish. As I shared, we all define love differently. Love is not about staying or leaving someone; it is how we engage with the situation. This also includes love for our Selves. Again, this is not about perfection but about our evolution in our growth with love as we continue to define this in our lives.

When you choose to lead a life connected to love, it inspires life in you and this inspires others, which creates alignment with All There Is and the prosperity you desire.

Since we continue to desire to have experiences of Love throughout our life, we will continue to redefine, expand and experience love. This is the beauty of exploring a life of love.

"Once you are in union with your Soul, your love becomes not a relationship but a shadow of you." – Osho

Love Is The Light That You Are

Every Soul is responsible for themselves and the choices they make with love. We will experience hurt, anger and feelings that do not feel good in the name of love; we may even do things that are a reaction of this. Perfection is not the goal, growth is. We all have reactions based on blame, resentment or waiting for people to be a certain way before one can be happy. The goal is not to allow this to override hope, faith, love, love for your Self, and love for your life.

We can do our best to be patient with our loved ones, and those we are getting to know better. Seeds of love always grow. If we attempt to control the way they should grow, then are we expressing genuine loving? When we allow the seeds of love to grow because we have planted them with love without conditions, that love grows in ways that we cannot imagine and the seeds spread to experiences that continue to expand our definition of love.

Trust that love is more powerful than your fears and insecurities. Even if at the time an Amazing Soul does not return the love you feel you deserve, be your expression of love, even if you feel the loss of this Soul. Sometimes Amazing Souls do not see the growth of the seeds of love that has been given to another. When they do not see them they may react feeling rejected and stop expressing love to that person. Choose to give love because one never knows when, where or with whom your seeds will grow.

Your Love Creates

All feelings are choices and choices create life experiences. Unfortunately, many Amazing Souls allow the experiences of their life to dictate their feelings instead of understanding that their feelings create their life experiences.

One may fall "asleep" to trusting themselves, to honoring their dreams with the belief of the power of love to heal anything and create everything. This creates fear, which creates more unhappy circumstances to appear in their lives. All Amazing Souls have the choice to end this cycle, and that choice is love. The choice is self-love.

When genuine love is exchanged there is an acceptance of one another with love that is not conditional, even when it may not appear this way in the physical at the time. Know this truth, because your Soul does.

I truly believe that there is so much love and goodness for you everywhere. When we love ourselves differently, we recognize love differently. As you continue to accept and love your Self more and more, you feel the love of the "seen" and "unseen" world that is always present, waiting for you to recognize it. With this recognition, you are reminded that you are never alone in your journey of love.

Nothing, I repeat nothing, can separate loved ones, not a body, not a Universe, nothing. Love is an energy that knows no time, space or circumstances. It transcends everything.

Loving Energy Is Always Connected To You

As I have shared, I refer to Source Energy; some may call this energy God, G-D, Creator, Jesus, Holy Spirit, Adonai or Elohim or simply as Pure Expansive Love. This Source Energy is Absolute Love for you. It is a pure Love without conditions that is present for all the victories you ask for.

This Loving Energy is here to provide you with love to remind you of the Amazing Soul that you are and to love thyself.

This Loving Energy is here to assist you with the formula "Ask and you shall receive." When you ask to receive, this is given without you needing to feel compromised, selfish or guilty. There is no judgment, no preconceived idea of what you are supposed to be or do, no punishment or testing of you. Those emotions are human and so foreign to this Loving Energy that is the partner of your Soul to expand in you, co-creating what you believe. There is love, only love, and this Loving Energy wishes to reinforce the love.

Your life is a reflection of what you desire, and what you believe is possible with this desire. God or the Universe cannot give you what you do not believe is possible. When I feel I am consciously connecting with Source Energy as Love, then I feel a support system that is expanding my expectation.

One night with my family at the dinner table we were giving thanks for our meal. As usual, I closed my eyes and felt in my heart gratitude for our meal and for sharing with my loved ones. I also blessed the hands that made this food and asked that this food be cleansed with love for the best connection to our bodies. When I was finished my son asked, "Mom, who are you praying to?" I loved this question because for me this Love is not in any form; how would I explain this if I could not language this in a form. I just said, "I am not praying to something, I am praying to a connection of Infinite Love, that I believe expands my prayer." In what I have shared with you it is obvious that I am accepting of each one's belief of spirituality because I truly believe many people arrive at the same place of beliefs in different ways with and without religion. To me, there can be different names for what I call Divine Love. What I value is a human being's expression of this in their life through love and kindness.

Expect The Unexpected Love

Though there may be experiences that we have in life that do not seem good, please remember these negative experiences were not designed to be "bad" towards you. Sometimes at the moment it is challenging to find the positive. What I am sharing is that if we believe that good happens for us and we trust this, then the challenging experience will create an expansion for more positive experiences in our life. We may or may not understand why things happen the way they do; what is vital is that we have faith in our trust. Trust that this will lead to positive experiences that serve us in the best way.

The formula of "Like Attracts Like" has a few exclusions. Not every experience is a mirror of you. If you have experienced abuse, this does not mean you are an abuser. It may present knowledge for you to realize an aspect of your Self through this experience, an emotional opportunity to expand your Self. Maybe that experience brought you an understanding of compassion or to know how to have healthy boundaries.

When the father of my children died a short time ago, we received beautiful loving support from various source. We also didn't receive love from places we thought for sure we would and this was disappointing. What surprised us the most was in the many ways where we least expected to receive love in the most unexpected ways and from the most unexpected people. This was something that connected us to expanding our belief of what was possible, and feeling love in miraculous ways even in sadness.

I often say that love is love and where this comes from is where it is supposed to be from. I find this to be very true in my life. I feel at times, especially when we feel in need of love and comfort, we might limit the possibilities of love by placing a box where we believe it can only come from and from those we feel it has to be from. Staying open to love in unexpected ways will exceed your expectations of the capacity of love from others and also create space for Divine Love.

Your Life Defined

I understand that at times it can seem too challenging to embrace the thought that some of the challenging experiences you have had are, in some way, a guide to steer you towards to what you are asking for.

If you were able to witness life experiences from the perspective of trusting and knowing that there is only goodness for you, and that experiences only support the opportunities you have asked for – would your outlook shift on the way you witness your life or define good or bad?

Even though there is a strong knowing within my Self that this is true for me, at times when I have been deeply hurt by an experience, I remember that it was challenging to hear words of encouragement. Many had the intention to support me and would share kindly with sayings like, "Good will come from this" or "It was meant to happen" or "When one door closes another one opens," or "It could be worse," etc. At the time, it felt like these sayings did not help and I felt that I could not validate my hurt with positive expressions. I looked at this advice as some psychoanalysis talk to "get me over it" and accept my situation without my feelings. Then as I was in that space of not feeling very positive, the "Mental Courtroom" would appear in my head as if to say that if I did not believe "more good" will come from this or be positive, then I would be penalized or more of the same would come again because I was not appreciating other aspects of my life. No, this is not true.

Going through a process of healing and not being able to see the good at the moment does not make you unappreciative; it just means you are going through your process towards healing. Sometimes we feel hurt but we cannot process the hurt. This does not mean we do not value our blessings – it simply means we are hurt. But processing hurt may not be immediate.

Sometimes people have this notion that when they are upset or in emotional pain, they should be able to shift this feeling to joy in a moment's notice. Give your Self permission to be able to feel your feelings of being upset for a moment in time. These feelings are valid. You will shift them gradually with patience and accept how you feel *in* the moment. If you need support from professionals, get it. Take care of your Emotional Self, "Ask" for the strength and wisdom to heal your heart and reach out to others.

Life Experiences Support Our Growth

There is a process to your feelings. Being in your feelings does not mean you are creating drama or being a victim: it means you are feeling what you are feeling. Drama is when you blame others to avoid your feelings and talk about your pain in a way that is hurtful towards others.

If you ignore the process of feeling your emotions, I believe you will recreate experiences to feel those feelings again. You will encounter the same feeling over and over again so that you can process it for good and no longer repeat the pattern. Having a hurtful experience and resolving it emotionally is mighty. It is also an empowering experience to know you release fearing it happening to you again. Acknowledge your Self for doing your very best and when moments get challenging close your eyes and take a breath and think of a time when you felt loved or had joy. This will support your emotional energy to have another direction.

Loving Energy does not have conditions towards giving and serving us with love. We are the ones who place these conditions, defined with our expectations. Why are there pain, illness, and loss, as we would never say that we have asked for this? Why do we sometimes hurt in a way that feels so painful, as if this pain goes through every bit of our core? How can we believe that there is a connection at all times to this Loving Energy and that it is here to love and serve us if we feel deep pain and loss? There are experiences in our lives that we may not have explanations for. Nevertheless, it is not about whether this Source Energy loves us or not; this is about life experiences that support our growth. Not everything that happens always has an explanation we can understand, but we can do our best to emotionally respond to these experiences with the best of who we are.

Forgiveness Is About Honoring Yourself

One way to resolve hurt is through forgiveness, a gift of Divine Love. This beautiful act is so important to the nourishment of the Soul as forgiveness is so powerful on so many levels.

When you hold resentment toward another, you are bound to that person or condition by an emotional link that is stronger than steel. Forgiveness is the only way to dissolve that link and get free.

Genuine Forgiveness, *from the heart*, is a release of energy that no longer serves you. What does this mean? When you feel the hurt and pain of unexpected betrayals or deep loss, it is felt *energetically* as an emotional weight. One may try to break down this energy "logically," questioning, "Why?" But, many times there is no logical answer to why. What's logical about someone saying that they love you with all their heart and Soul and then betraying you?

At times, there are seemingly no answers that will help you arrive at a place of forgiveness to heal your pain. When we *do not* forgive, we carry a heavy burden of energy in our heart and Soul, which affects us physically, mentally and emotionally.

If I choose to forgive another, I wish to release the pain with all my heart – sincerely, cleanly and completely. When you have truly given someone forgiveness, you will know; you *feel* it. Do your best not to wait for answers in order to free your Self; some things you may not understand, at least for now. Time and space may be needed to process your pain.

"As I walked out the door toward the gate that would lead to my freedom, I knew if I didn't leave my bitterness and hatred behind, I'd still be in prison." – Nelson Mandela

I had the great honor of meeting Nelson Mandela in February of 1995 in South Africa. In my view, he was a living example of forgiveness in a way that supported the entire world to reflect on their definition of forgiveness. Regardless of your belief towards the personal or political beliefs he held, he did create awareness towards the subject of forgiveness. I was very fortunate to share with him. Though his eyesight was poor, his eyes held a deep connection and you felt present with him. As we exchanged words, I remember looking at him and feeling this presence of peace – a presence that is created from choosing to forgive and leaving behind what no longer serves you to have room for more peace and what does serve your definition of your life.

Forgiveness Is Self-Love

Forgiveness does not mean that you forget what has happened to you, but rather that what happened will not have the same charge or control over you. Forgiveness is not approval of what someone else has done; it is not about agreeing or accepting their behavior.

With forgiveness you are saying, "I love my life. I choose to be alive and I do not allow the hurt to be my choice of a life." Forgiveness simply enables you to no longer be affected by the hurt. People who love you will get more of you and the person who hurt you will get less of you.

Everyone has their own "Movie" and their perspective may have nothing to do with you. People will perceive what they wish. Therefore, do not base your decision of forgiveness on another's opinion or approval.

Forgiveness is a release of your pain, a release of the negative energy that is blocking your possibilities. It frees you to have other opportunities and blessings. When you truly forgive and release, there is a renewing of life that could only come through forgiveness. Yes, there was great pain in what caused your hurt, but there will also be great blessings through forgiveness. Forgiveness is for YOU!

Forgiveness Is A Conscious Choice

Forgiveness is about taking back the ownership of your life, choosing to drive in the direction you wish to steer your life and not allowing the one who hurt you to be the driver. When you forgive consciously, you are not allowing the pain you feel to take over your world or to be a reflection of the way you see your world.

Lighten Your Soul

I remember that my grandmother, my mom's mother, was a very spiritual woman. She was cool and had a way about giving her opinion as if she was dropping a seed in the ground; you could grow from her comment or leave it there.

Before she left her physical body, she did something I will never forget. The ambulance came to take her to the hospital and she knew that her physical life was ending. She asked to have one moment to herself before they put her in the ambulance; the medical team honored this. She took a moment by herself to ask for forgiveness from others; she forgave them, and most valuable, she forgave herself. I cannot imagine that my sweet grandma would have any issues with forgiveness, but she wanted to make sure she crossed over with clean, pure intentions of love. She consciously reflected and left with peace.

I always remember this story; her consciousness and love for herself and others touched my heart deeply. I believe that when you forgive, you lighten your Soul *and* that of the one you are forgiving. You leave it to another consciousness to make whatever judgments or consequences between that person and their God. It is not our place to police another, nor is any of us in any position to judge. I have also witnessed that the way people define God or choose their belief of religion creates tremendous hurt between families, friends, communities and countries. Many times I find that this is ironic as our spiritual and religious path should be of love and Light and not create deep hurt.

The Time for Forgiveness is NOW!

With great clarity, I remember a flight that I took several years ago. My brother was leaving on a second tour in the military and the whole family traveled to say goodbye to him; this was always so difficult. I had decided to take an earlier flight to get back home to my two small children and, though I had a strange feeling about the flight, I just thought it was my usual caution of flying. I am quite particular of where I sit on a plane, and on this flight I was given an option to change my seat but I felt I had to keep the seat I had.

The flight seemed smooth and on time, which was good; I had an additional flight to take before I finally made it home. As we were getting close to landing, the pilot made an announcement that the wheels of the plane were not able to come down and that he was going to circle to burn as much fuel as he could. He promised that he would give us updates. Time went by so slowly, but he eventually updated us, saying that we would have to make an emergency landing. It's amazing, how some memories and their feelings do not leave you. As I am writing this, tears fill my eyes.

I can remember that moment thinking of my children and my love for them. There was silence and then people started to cry. I thought of my grandmother and what she did right before she knew she was going to leave her physical life. I thought of my Cuban grandfather and how he never recovered from the loss of his son in Vietnam; I know a huge part of him died with him.

I am a strong believer in prayer and I believe that my intentions, with love, can shift just about anything. The pilot came on again and we were told the procedures of the emergency landing. Tears started to roll down my face. I was not ready to die. I felt my love for my children and my family, and I began to ask for forgiveness. I prayed with all my heart and Soul that I receive forgiveness and release all those that had hurt me and I asked to be released through forgiveness with all those I had hurt. I asked with such sincerity for peace in all our hearts.

My children, my husband at the time, each of my family members and all others who came to mind – I placed each of their faces, one at a time, in my imagination and told them that I loved them. I asked to be forgiven and forgave whatever needed to be cleared for peace.

In the midst of all this, people continued crying. It seemed like an eternity, circling, waiting to see what could happen and we braced ourselves for the worst. For that moment I resigned that I was going to die.

I noticed the lady next to me was a lady of faith. Then, it dawned on me why I was not motivated to change my seat. She was praying, fervently, completely anchored in her knowing, faith and her belief in prayer. I looked at her and grabbed her hand and said that I was not willing to die yet and she agreed she was not either. We knew intuitively the power of prayer united with another and that our prayer would be heard. I told her that I believed with all my heart and Soul that through our desire to live, and with our love for those in our lives, we could make those wheels come down! With tears in our eyes, we decided to pray together. We prayed out loud and, as we were praying, flashes of my children went through my mind.

As tears streamed down my face and with all my might, I said, "I am not ready to die or leave my children, bring those wheels down, NOW!" I have no idea how long this lasted but it felt like forever and at the same time it all happened so fast. Magically, I was so clear that I was not going to die. I began to see all the life I still wanted to live; I was full of life.

Then the pilot announced that two of the four wheels had come down, that we had a better chance of landing safely. The lady next to me looked at me and we smiled! Then I said, "All four must come down!" Again we prayed! I am not sure what happened next; I was so connected to my deep state of prayer and to the conviction of my expectation. Just then, I realized we were ready to land! The landing felt like a scene out of a movie; there was foam on the runway, emergency vehicles everywhere. It was such an intense and surreal scene.

When we finally landed, everyone clapped and cheered in relief. It was apparent they did not expect for us to make it, but we had made it. We were alive! We walked outside the plane and there was staff clapping and cheering as they walked us into a room to give us personal care. I questioned if it was our prayers and those of others that created this "miracle." Then again, did it really matter how or why my prayer was answered?

WOW! So many years later, I still have these tears as I remember that moment. I remember the lady next to me so vividly. She knew with all her heart that we could make a difference. Our desire for life and belief in our definition of Source Energy was so strong; we pulled on that with all our might to partner with our prayer.

Following the landing, I was still numb and in a state of mini-shock, but I had to get myself together to take the next flight. My son at the time was about seven years old and dreamed of being a basketball star. That summer he enrolled in the Miami Heat basketball camp and that day they were playing in the Miami Arena with some of the Miami Heat players. He was so excited and all I wanted was to be there with him.

As I walked to my next gate everything felt like it was moving in slow motion. With a heightened sense, I observed how some people weren't connecting with each other and others were very present. I kept saying to myself, "I want to be more present; I wish to give more attention to my world." I arrived at my gate for the next flight and suddenly felt a sense of fear. As I was ready to board, I started to cry. I felt like I could not move; I felt paralyzed. I had flashes of my children, of saying goodbye to my brother (the one I named my son after). It was all so surreal.

I panicked! The man at the gate just looked at me with the kindest of eyes and did not need to say a word. It was as if time stood still with his patience and all was understood. I boarded the flight.

Finally I arrived in Miami; time still felt like it was moving so slowly, it was as if I was watching a movie in slow motion. Again, I noticed the lack in how others were connecting with each other and I wanted to scream so loud, "Don't miss an opportunity to love! Look at your loved ones! Be alive! The time is NOW!"

I did make it on time to see my son at the arena. With a huge smile, I watched his big brown eyes look at his life with wonder and excitement. I could not really explain my experience; it felt so layered and deep. For me, the experience was not about fear but about love and my desire to really live life. I can say that from that moment on, my life had more color in it; my desire grew to share the color in my world with others and be an example for others to see the color in their world.

After that experience, I made a point to be even more proactive as I look at my life and the way I forgive. I can say that sometimes forgiveness comes easy, and sometimes the hurt is too painful. Although I wish for the pain to go away, I may not be fully ready. Nevertheless, I trust that simply with my intention of desire to forgive, I have more room for love and the healing process has already begun.

The Law of Forgiveness

Many things have happened to all of us over the course of our lives that have surprised us in different ways, and at times some were not so positive.

The past few years for me had felt overwhelming as these challenging experiences happened at the same time. I feel that genuine forgiveness has its stages, as does the processing of a death. It is a distinct process; at first it is disbelief, then anger, deep hurt, sadness and mourning all expressed in different ways.

Personally, if I am experiencing this, I create discipline for my Self to avoid exposing my Self to even more hurt. This could be by choosing to not discuss the situation in conversation or by fueling rumors, or it could be by setting boundaries to refrain from communicating with the person until I feel clearer. This supports me to step back and isolate the situation of hurt to that experience and work on my healing. Eventually, I am then able to witness the situation *and* the person to see how I wish to move forward and how I have grown through the experience.

"FORGIVE: The conscious, continuous process of giving up resentment and the desire to punish; to stop being angry; to let go of power and control over others." – Frank Natalie

Forgiveness is a state of being ... a high state of consciousness, which you become and from which you operate. Consciously and unconsciously you no longer wish to add to another's pain, or to be connected to another by holding onto wanting them to feel your pain; you just let go of justifying the need to prove them wrong and there is a release of blame or hurt.

I learned many things from my first formal awareness teacher Frank Natalie, but the greatest was forgiveness. Even at 14 years old I could not completely process forgiveness the way I do today, but one thing I do remember was this feeling that by forgiving, I could be free from the pain owning me.

I offer to you a special prayer that was created with love in my heart to support others in their forgiveness, so that peace and harmony replace the hurt in your Soul. With my work, I truly wish to share tools for you to manifest the blessings you wish to have. With this Forgiveness Prayer, which I say often, to support my intention of genuine forgiveness, I have witnessed so many people experience healing as a result.

Forgiveness Expands Love

The Law of Forgiveness comes from the prayer "Our Father" wherein it is said, "... and forgive us our trespasses as we forgive those who trespass against us ..." It is Universal Law that when you forgive and "Ask" for forgiveness in return, the emotional charge of the situation is neutralized. Again, forgiving another does not mean you are validating their actions towards you; it simply expands the space in your energy to release the emotional charge that may be blocking you from creating more abundance. Through forgiveness, you also release your Self from participating in the judgment of another.

The *Forgiveness Prayer* was created to expand love and release the energy of hurt, blame or resentment. It has been a way for me to let go of having to understand the "whys" and to create my true intention of love, peace and acceptance by getting out of my own way.

The *Forgiveness Prayer* is a language of energy, a powerful tool that formulates a release, allowing you to move energy and heal. It supports your own healing and clears you with the other person that you are forgiving through this prayer.

Collectively, we all benefit from forgiveness. When you choose peace in your life, more peace is felt in the world. With forgiveness, the Universal Computer hears your heartfelt intention without the charge of pain being your main voice; it hears the voice of love from your Soul. This is defined as you make the "Ask" of forgiveness and you claim more love and goodness in *your* world.

I invite you to use this special prayer, created in memory of my teacher and dear friend Roberta Herzog, to release others as well as your Self, from being in an energetic place that serves no one. Repeat this prayer for as many people as you wish. However, my suggestion is that you focus on only one person at a time. This is also effective for anyone with whom you wish to experience harmony and healing.

When you meditate with this prayer, be gentle with your Self and release any regret. Without shame, acknowledge your growth of choosing a willingness to move forward, even if at this time you do not have all the answers to your questions.

Forgive those who asked you to change who you are or your path in life. Maybe you saw this as rejection of your Soul; perhaps they thought they knew your Soul. Next! You know what is best for you.

Allow yourself to be seen with gentleness and authenticity; know that this is your Soul's foundation as you release all fight and struggle. Release the fight to prove and defend your Self and blame another. Trust that all is well, with plenty of unexpected goodness crossing your path.

Give what you wish to receive from others. Begin to feel the love that surrounds you from the "seen" and the "unseen."

There is so much love for you; look for it and "Ask" to recognize it as it is ever-present and waiting for you. "'Ask' and you do receive."

The Forgiveness Prayer

When you rise in the morning and before retiring at night, sit quietly with your eyes closed and picture in your mind's eye the Soul you wish to forgive, while smiling and *feeling* happy.

Then say the following prayer out loud to this Soul:
"_____, (Say the name of the Soul here), I forgive you for everything you've ever said or done to me in thought, word or deed that has caused me pain in this or any other time, on all levels and all space and time. You are free and I am free!"

And "_____, I ask that you forgive me for everything that I have ever said or done to you in thought, word or deed that has caused you pain in this or any other time, on all levels and all space and time. You are free and I am free!"

"Thank you, God/Creator/Universe (choose what is a match for you), for this opportunity to forgive _____ and to forgive myself."

You will "know" when to cease saying this prayer, possibly after a few days to 2 weeks. Nevertheless, listen to your heart and you will know the best timing for your Self. When you experience some shift in your attitude towards this Soul, a sense of release may come in the form of crying, laughter, a feeling of wellbeing, etc. You may also experience the Soul's attitude change towards you. You will know when you can think of this person or see this person and you are more neutral and you do not feel pulled to their energy. You will find yourself freed from pain while becoming happier, healthier and feeling more peace in mind, body and spirit.

Love is always the greatest power of healing, the greatest power in this existence that we have. Love is the existence of the definition of God by any name in the physical, and forgiveness is one of the attributes of this love. How many stories do you know of miracles because of love? Love that has given life where there was no life felt, and it has given hope when there was no hope and it has created miracles as normal experiences.

What Do Children Think Of Love?

I love being around children, they bring what we complicate down to basics. The sky is blue, the grass is green; they hear the bird sing and a hug really matters to them. The world is magical and they are sensitive because they connect with presence to their desires and feelings.

Children have this innocence towards what we have made complicated. As adults we tend to overthink what is natural, which is to embrace others and love.

Here are a few quotes from some children on love:

"When someone loves you, the way they say your name is different. You just know that your name is safe in their mouth." – Billy, age 4

"Love is when a girl puts on perfume and a boy puts on shaving cologne and they go out and smell each other." – Karl, age 5

"Love is what makes you smile when you're tired." – Terri, age 4

"Love is when you go out to eat and give somebody most of your french fries without making them give you any of theirs." – Chrissy, age 6

"Love is when my mommy makes coffee for my daddy and she takes a sip before giving it to him, to make sure the taste is OK." – Danny, age 7

"Love is what's in the room with you at Christmas if you stop opening presents and listen." – Bobby, age 7

"If you want to learn to love better, you should start with a friend who you hate." – Nikka, age 6

"Love is when you tell a guy you like his shirt, then he wears it everyday." – Noelle, age 7

"Love is when your puppy licks your face even after you left him alone all day." – Mary Ann, age 4

"I know my older sister loves me because she gives me all her old clothes and has to go out and buy new ones." – Lauren, age 4

"When you love somebody, your eyelashes go up and down and little stars come out of you." – Karen, age 7

Love Is....
Love is being generous, not just giving gifts
Love is forgiving, not holding grudges
Love is laughter, not arguing and meanness
Love is hugs and kisses, no hitting or hurting
Love keeps you warm; it is never cold
Love is kindness, not being cruel
Love is caring, always showing its heart
Where there is love, there is peace
– My daughter wrote this at age 11

Power Thoughts

Love Heals

- ○ Love is always evolving and defining itself in my life.

- ○ Love is the base of all creation; it created me.

- ○ Forgiveness is an act of self-love.

- ○ I love my life and I do not allow pain to dictate my life.

- ○ Forgiveness is an honoring of my Self.

- ○ I am open to love in unexpected ways that will exceed my expectations of love.

- ○ Forgiveness is a release of my pain and energy that is blocking my possibilities.

- ○ I believe and trust there is so much love and goodness for me everywhere.

- ○ Every Soul is responsible for the choices they make with love.

- ○ The planted seeds of my growth always grow in the best way.

Kindness: The Soul's Gratitude of Being

Kindness ... It is the most beautiful act humankind can share of love in the physical. Kindness is a deep feeling that is beyond words. Kindness is a pure form of love.

To me, the act of Kindness is the action of love without conditions, the closest feeling of wholeness of our pure Self to another.

Kindness is a powerful force to shift pain into a memory healed with love.

Kindness and sharing are very important attributes to Power Wishing™; without it, your manifesting will be limited, for all-powerful manifestations are created with the energy of love as the base. Sharing multiplies and expands love and blessings.

At times we may feel we cannot share because we will not have enough for ourselves. While this logically may seem like a good rationale at times where we feel we have little to offer, I hope to shift this perception completely. We can always share something and what we share with the goodness of our heart is plentiful.

Kindness Is Love in Action

Your *intention* of sharing is the base of your giving. Have you noticed that one's act of kindness given with pure intent and without agenda can shift a person's perspective on life or a feeling about himself or herself forever? The energy of kindness is magical, as it can transform any situation.

Kindness is a powerful gift. Kindness is a beautiful, vibrant energy to share. Kindness transcends beliefs. Kindness heals. Kindness is best in its natural form when it is shared with a pure heart and is unexpected!

"When I was young, I used to admire intelligent people; as I grow older, I admire kind people." – Abraham Heschel

When in Doubt Choose Kindness

We are a society of differences and contrasts, which gives us the opportunity to make choices. Sometimes we can be in situations where we are not sure what choice to make or how to act. Being a high example of what you expect from others is the best choice.

Everyone has different beliefs towards their life that creates who they are and the experiences they have. I've felt you can tell a lot about a person based on how they share kindness. I have met many different people from various cultures and economic backgrounds, and the degree of kindness that is expressed is because of who they are, not because of what they have. Kindness comes from within and it is a moment for you to represent yourself and your love in action. Kindness is a choice and a sacred gift to share with others. When others are not as kind with you, then you can bless them on their way, as their choice to be this way is not a reflection of you.

We never know what another is going through. Perhaps they are at a challenging time in their life and they have trouble receiving and so they reject the very thing they wish for. People wake up to being ready to receive love at various times in their life experience.

Kindness Is An Act Of Peace

Sometimes we need a moment to slow down and be present in our life and take opportunities to be kind. Slowing down is not being slow; it is like savoring an amazing bottle of wine and enjoying it. In the enjoyment, you acknowledge what you appreciate, what you value and how kind others are to you and you to them. In this savoring, your appreciation is the voice of your prayer for more of this and more of that happens ... it has to; you always get what you are looking for.

One day, I was having breakfast with my daughter in a really cool restaurant in Miami. My daughter seemed preoccupied. The bombing at the Boston marathon had happened the day before and this was disturbing to her, as it was to most of us.

She looked around at the people and then asked me if what happened there would be a way of life everywhere. I told her, "Maybe." I did not choose to reassure her about how she is always protected and all will be good for her. I allowed her to share her concerns of moving to London for university and about the travels she wishes to experience. She expressed her panic, her fears and then the conversation shifted. She asked if I thought there would ever be world peace?" I replied, "How can there be a possibility of world peace when we are not even kind to the ones closest to us or the people we see every day?"

I shared with her that world peace is created by human beings, not by policy or rules. She looked at me and said, "Yeah, you're right." When we shared this way, a relief came over her, as if she had control over her space and could make a difference with her actions. We reaffirmed our belief that we expect goodness in our lives and our surroundings.

Kindness With Boundaries

The painful awareness I have had in this experience of life is the truth that there are mean people. Some people are just mean, period. I cannot change a mean person with my kindness or love, nor can I allow a mean person to change me. They too are having their own experience and choosing to share with others in a way I define as not-so-nice way. This has been a huge awakening for me and so hurtful. I always wish to believe the best in others and think that the love we share will bring out the best but sometimes it brings out abuse and hurt that has nothing to do with us.

Some people have more vested in staying mean than in shifting that behavior. My daughter has helped me make peace with this; she does not waste her energy with mean people and has very clear boundaries around this. This has been a growing experience for me. Sometimes you need to know your boundaries with others and honor this as a respect for your Self. Though I may have my own personal boundaries, I can still hold space with my own kindness. Kindness to me is a form of appreciation for my blessings and an acknowledgment of all that I have that I love, which is separate from the way others choose to behave.

Kindness As An Expectation

It can deeply hurt our feelings when kindness is not returned the way we expect, especially from someone we love. We may feel irritated, annoyed and angry that an offering of love felt invisible. Do yourself a favor and release the need to expect this from others. Release reactions of self-righteous judgment towards others based on your perception of the "differences" you are witnessing. Let it go. We are not here to be in other people's business or to figure out their mind or why they do what they do.

How they define kindness and what drives them to be kind is their business, as is their life. Why merge with energy that depletes you and is exhausting? Some people are takers and see kindness as a weakness. Oh well ... that's their "Movie," not yours ... NEXT!

I am sure many of us have been kind in our lives and at the time it seemed to have gone unnoticed. Perhaps someone did not acknowledge us or there have been times when we did not acknowledge someone else's act of kindness. Sometimes when we are at a different time and place in our lives we appreciate things differently.

Healthy Kindness

Kindness shared purely without expectations and agenda is where there is an uplifting to the Souls. If you have expectations towards receiving based on your kindness, have clarity about this and know this truth. And sometimes we may not know how to receive without feeling we are expected to do something in return. Other times we give kindness out of insecurity of losing a relationship or we are kind out of a habit to be polite. This all OK, but if this is the case, please understand that these are not examples of the healthy kindness I am defining here.

It is healthy to have boundaries with your kindness. As you continue to honor yourself more and have clarity on how you feel, you will understand the intention of why you do what you do.

I believe that giving the energy of kindness to the world helps circulate love and goodness in the world. My grandmother had a saying that she crafted in a framed needlepoint, "Give the best to the world and the best will come back to you."

My point is give people an opportunity to feel love through the action of kindness without judgment towards them, and without any expectation. If you are going to give kindness, then give it because it feels good to you.

Simple Kindness

A friend of mine got into a very bad accident and I was in the emergency room with the family. The doctor came out and said that he probably only had a five percent chance to live, but they were attempting their best to save him in surgery. My heart dropped when I saw the look on the face of his parents. It was all so shocking. I offered to leave the hospital to pick up some clothes for the family.

This hospital is not in a very good part of town, so usually I am quite alert when driving in that area. After I left the hospital, I came to a red light and stopped. The shock of what I just witnessed at the hospital was more overwhelming than I had realized and I started to get lost in my thoughts. I did not notice that the light turned green, then red and then green again. I had not moved. I finally continued my drive on this second green light and I remember thinking to myself how much I appreciated people being patient and not honking their horn. I feel if at that moment they had honked their horn like crazy, I would have felt such panic.

I apologized in my heart to those that waited behind me and then gave thanks for their kindness. It made me appreciate that moment and possibly what others are going through when I may mistakenly judge them on the road.

I learned something powerful in that moment, as I can at times be an impatient driver. Since that experience, I have more patience when driving. Whenever I am feeling impatient, I remember what that moment meant to me. Total strangers offered me kindness when I needed it. It sounds so basic but it was quite valuable at that moment. Even the simple experience of driving can give us an opportunity to be kind. You never know what news someone has just heard. You never know so many things about people's personal world.

The bottom line is whether you know what someone is going through or not, does it really matter? Can we just give the benefit of the doubt, rather than thinking the worst? What does matter is the choice we make when we are given the opportunity at that moment. Kindness teaches others what they may have forgotten in a nice way that is easily received and enhances the other.

Kindness Can Change The Course Of Your Life

Sometimes, when I conduct my seminars I will ask the participants to share what act of kindness had a profound effect on them. The stories I hear have been amazing. Interestingly, these stories usually give an insightful window into the vision of who they are today. Some have shared that a simple act of kindness they received influenced the career they have now.

One woman who is a registered nurse at a large hospital shared that when she was nine years old, her mother passed away. In that moment, when her mother left her physical, a nurse came to her and just held her. Even with her own family around, this woman felt the nurturing love of this nurse in a moment of such despair and this experience inspired her to become a nurse later in her life. This story was so moving to the entire group of participants that she shared with. Most of her colleagues had not even known that she lost her mother when she was still a child. It was a beautiful story of the power of healing with simple kindness. I can attest that I have experienced great kindness from my teachers, and this has motivated me to contribute to our schools.

An exchange of a smile can have a huge effect on someone's day. Kindness does not have to be a monumental experience in order for it to matter. Never underestimate the simplicity of kindness as a monumental experience for someone.

Take a moment to reflect on your kindness to others:

How did it feel to share kindness?
Did you share kindness from your heart spontaneously?
Did you expect something in return when you shared?
Did you give without having an agenda?
Are you aware of what are you feeling when you extend kindness?
What are you thinking as you share kindness?
Is kindness a part of your every day?
Do you enjoy being kind?
Do you give kindness to those closest to you and in your daily life like you would to a stranger?
Do you believe that kindness should come from the one you give it to or do you feel that what goes around comes around?
Are you comfortable receiving kindness?
What feelings or thoughts are active in your awareness when you receive kindness?

Unexpected Giving – Unexpected Life Change

I found this story on the Internet and it touched my heart.

"A *Cab Ride I'll Never Forget*"[9]

Twenty years ago, I drove a cab for a living. One night I took a fare at 2:30 AM. When I arrived to collect, the building was dark except for a single light in a ground floor window. Under these circumstances, many drivers would just honk once.

But I had seen too many impoverished people who depended on taxis as their only means of transportation. Unless a situation smelled of danger, I always went to the door. This passenger might be someone who needs my assistance, I reasoned to myself.

So I walked to the door and knocked. "Just a minute," answered a frail, elderly voice. I could hear something being dragged across the floor. After a long pause, the door opened.

A small woman in her 80s stood before for me. She was wearing a print dress and a pillbox hat with a veil pinned on it, like someone out of a 1940's movie. By her side was a small nylon suitcase. The apartment looked as if no one had lived in it for years. All the furniture was covered with sheets. There were no clocks on the walls, no knick-knacks or utensils on the counters. In the corner was a cardboard box filled with photos and glassware.

"Would you carry my bag out to the car?" she said. I took the suitcase to the cab and then returned to assist the woman. She took my arm and we walked slowly toward the curb. She kept thanking me for my kindness. "It's nothing," I told her. "I just try to treat my passengers the way I would want my mother treated."

"Oh, you're such a good man," she said. When we got in the cab, she gave me an address, and then asked, "Could you drive through downtown?" "It's not the shortest way," I answered quickly. "Oh, I don't mind," she said "I'm in no hurry. I'm on my way to a hospice."

I looked in the rear-view mirror. Her eyes were glistening. "I don't have any family left," she continued. "The doctor says I don't have very long." I quietly reached over and shut off the meter. "What route would you like me to take?" I asked.

---

[9] Original story by Kent Nerburn: www.kindspring.org

For the next two hours, we drove through the city. She showed me the building where she had once worked as an elevator operator.

We drove through the neighborhood where she and her husband had lived when they were newlyweds. She had me pull up in front of a furniture warehouse that had once been a ballroom where she had gone dancing as a girl. Sometimes she'd ask me to slow in front of a particular building or corner and would sit staring into the darkness, saying nothing.

As the first hint of sun was creasing the horizon, she suddenly said, "I'm tired. Let's go now." We drove in silence to the address she had given me. It was a low building, like a small convalescent home, with a driveway that passed under a portico. Two orderlies came out to the cab as soon as we pulled up. They were solicitous and intent, watching her every move. They must have been expecting her.

I opened the trunk and took the small suitcase to the door. The woman was already seated in a wheelchair. "How much do I owe you?" she asked, reaching into her purse. "Nothing," I said. "You have to make a living," she answered. "Oh, there are other passengers," I responded.

Almost without thinking, I bent and gave her a hug. She held onto me tightly. Our hug ended with her remark, "You gave an old woman a little moment of joy." After a slight pause, she added, "Thank you." I squeezed her hand, and then walked into the dim morning light. Behind me, a door shut. It was the sound of the closing of a life.

I didn't pick up any more passengers that shift. I drove aimlessly lost in thought. For the rest of that day, I could hardly talk. What if that woman had gotten an angry driver, or one who was impatient to end his shift? What if I had refused to take the run, or had honked once, then driven away? On a quick review, I don't think that I have done anything more important in my life.

We're conditioned to think that our lives revolve around great moments. But great moments often catch us unaware, and what others may consider a small one can change everything.

Sharing Gratitude Has Value

To me, kindness should be as natural as breathing. In our home, kindness is the most important character value. This is non-negotiable. I am grateful that kindness is expressed with respect and honored with my children. Having kindness as a base in any environment also supports healthy conversations when there are differences. Sharing with kindness is the best way to get out of your own way and remember all that you have and all that you can continue to hope for.

I remember when my children were younger, a way to say thank you to their teachers at the end of year was to make bookmarkers. When they got a bit older, I shared the idea of writing handwritten notes. They were at an age where they felt this was a bit embarrassing for them. They tried to convince me that a gift was better, but this is where I pulled the "I am the mom card" and said the card was important and we can also give a gift. So they wrote the cards and hand-delivered them to school. I got a stare as they walked out the door to remind me that I was embarrassing them. But then they started to receive thank you notes back from the teachers, sharing how they felt about receiving their notes, or a teacher would stop them to say thank you for the note. They would come home gushing, telling me every detail. I chose not to say, "You see!" with humor even though I wanted to.

Instead, I reinforced how proud I was of them. They also learned that they could not assume that someone knows that they are appreciated. They witnessed that sharing a thank you card made a difference for everyone. Now as teenagers they are aware that sharing their gratitude with others verbally and in writing has value.

Kindness Is Always Good

One afternoon my son sold an iPad on eBay to a mother who bought it for her son's birthday, the mother requested that he send it right away, as this was a special gift. He asked, "Mom, do you think I should send a happy birthday wish and a thank you note with the iPad?" WOW! I thought that was so thoughtful and it touched my heart that he did so.

For about a month after he sold the iPad, we attempted to get the money from Pay Pal. We thought the money was in the account, and there was an issue with the account. Unfortunately, the whole thing was a scam and we were given fake receipts of PayPal payments, and my son was not given the money.

I felt for him because he was planning to use that money for something special, and trusted the process. Where I felt quite disappointed was the fact that these people played on kindness in their messages to him and I did not want him to be tarnished towards being kind to others.

I shared this with him and he said, "Mom that's their problem, not mine. I did what I thought was good. They have the problem, not me."

What a relief! I was grateful that he took that so well and in seconds had clear perspective of this unfortunate situation. These things happen, and again things like this cannot change who we are. The little bits of kindness, especially those that are done anonymously, are very powerful. Acts of kindness remind others that there is still goodness in the world around them. *To give kindness, just because, is reason enough.*

Take a moment to reflect:

If there was one person you could think of right now that you could let them know you appreciate them, who would that be?
Do you share with others that you appreciate them?
Do you let them know clearly? How?
How could you say thank you? How good would this feel to you?
When was the last time you wrote a handwritten note?

The "Luck" Of Kindness

When giving with the sincere desire to give because it feels good, do you think you create luck in your life? When something good happens, I will often hear the person comment that they were just lucky. When I hear this, I ask them if the luck they felt was attracting the right people who were kind to them, and they usually say yes. My next question to them would be, "Is this *luck* or is it the *luck* you have created through your intentions and actions?"

Like many of you, if I find something that is lost, I return it or find the owner. Why? Because I feel it is the *right* thing to do. It is not mine to keep. Also, I would like the same consideration from someone if this happened to me.

Recently, I flew from Miami to London. We had just arrived and I was tired and a bit disoriented, especially after learning that we had accidentally given the hotel our arrival date for the following day and they were fully booked. Though the people at the hotel were so gracious, the hotel was completely full. It was an unusually sunny day, so I decided to go outside for a moment and I placed my purse right in front of me as I went to fix my jacket.

In that second, a man with a beer in his hand who looked like he lived on the streets came close to me and pointed at my purse. He got very close to me and I could smell him. He looked me in the eyes and said,

"I could take this from you right now and you would not know it!" He pointed to my purse and said, "Pick up your purse now and do not leave it like that again." I just stared at him, as the thought of losing everything on the first day of my three-week trip flashed in front of me: I imagined having my passports, money, jewelry and computer stolen, along with no hotel room. I looked straight at him with a bit of panic and said, "Thank you, thank you so much."

As he walked away down the street, he kept looking back at me making these hand signals. I was still frozen as I said every thank you prayer I knew.

Now, was that luck? I walked back inside the hotel and I think my face was pale. They must have thought I looked this way because there were no rooms available and so they began comforting me. They said they found us a room down the street. I told them that I was just going to sit in the lobby for a while and wait there. I sat on the sofa in a state of gratitude and just listened to myself. I felt I needed to just chill and regroup at that moment, so I did. After about an hour, a smiling happy gentleman from the front desk said, "You will not believe what just happened? Someone just cancelled and the room is an upgrade." *Luck?* I feel that just sitting in that sofa and being in a state of appreciation allowing things to flow brought the *luck* to find me.

Gracious Giving

If you commit to giving to another, I feel it is so important on so many levels to do so without the other person feeling like a beggar for what you said you were going to do. If you have an agenda in giving to a person or an organization, this is your choice and should be shared up front. No judgment, I simply remind you to make it clear and do not have anyone ask twice for what you said you were going to give.

It is so degrading for someone to have to beg for what has been promised to him or her. Sometimes people shrug off whether what they promised is a big deal or not. You truly do not know what your promise means to another or how this affects them.

I believe in serving our communities and those that may be in challenging circumstances. I believe that this is a way to bless others and myself. In giving service and sharing with others you are saying you acknowledge them and you value them or your community.

Sharing Kindness

When I was having different people tour the inner-city school, to see if they wished to participate in supporting it, I remember people would say how wonderful it was what I was doing. Yes, it did take time, commitment, courage, and belief but thankfully I was not alone in this ... there were so many incredible people working together.

I would share with others that these children were giving me a gift. They gave me the opportunity to fill my Soul, enrich myself and reminded me of basic love. They strengthen what I value about kindness. They were innocent in their sharing and receiving. This was refreshing to me. I felt I was the one that truly received with a sense of purpose that felt so alive and present.

When I would show people the schools and where I felt they could add value as a community, I did not ask for money; I simply created awareness. I shined a light on the opportunity for them to make a choice and share because they felt a connection to something that moved them, and then the money and resources followed genuinely.

I believe sharing kindness out of pity, because there is a lack and you may feel sorry for the person or situation, is not necessarily the highest exchange of kindness. But when there is an act of kindness shared because you are reminded and remind others of great possibilities and you want to support this vision, this is beautiful. It doesn't come from a place where you feel "bad" for others but because you see in them what they at the moment may have forgotten to see in themselves. You show them through your sharing of kindness at that moment as an opportunity for them to see and awaken their greatness.

When you share, you give acknowledgment to the people who contribute in your life. Serving others is a beautiful honor in a relationship. I feel it is an honor to serve my family and my community. Be conscious to take time to honor those who serve you. Acknowledge them. Serve others by being an enhancer in their lives; that wherever you go because of your presence you made life better for those around you. Kindness and sharing is a way for me to actively say "thank you for all my blessings." When you share, you are also acknowledging what you have plenty of and create plenty more of that.

Choose to share kindness as compassionate empowerment, a choice that enhances another because you see in them at that moment what they may not see for themselves.

Kindness Is A Virtue

Cherishing your Self through kind thoughts is self-love. Treat your body with appreciation. Treat yourself with the kindness you would like to receive from others. When people know what I do, they start to share conversations about all kinds of things that they may not normally talk about. Sometimes out of nowhere they will say, you know I am not that spiritual. I answer, "Really?" They reaffirm this and give me answers about their definition of God and religion as I listen and then I ask, "Are you kind?" They say, "Yes!" and I reply, "Well, that is spiritual to me!"

"This is my simple religion. There is no need for temples; no need for complicated philosophy. Our own brain, our own heart is our temple; the philosophy is kindness." – H.H Dalai Lama

It is moving when people who are in need of kindness are the ones who give it. There was a story I enjoyed reading about a woman who was eight months pregnant who was unemployed. She was with her small daughter and found an envelope with $4,000 of cash inside it. She turned it in to the police even though it would have been legal to keep it. She said that they certainly could have used the money, but she had taught her daughter to be honest. Plus returning it was worth it to her to have a clear conscience and set a good example for her daughter. A few days later, a lady in her seventies claimed the money and gave a thank you card with a small reward to the woman who found the money.

Boston homeless man Glen James found a bag containing more than $42,000 in cash and traveler's checks. He clearly could have kept the money, but instead he turned it in saying, "There's no way I could have kept even a penny of that money, there's just no way." A complete stranger who lives hundreds of miles away in Virginia was so moved by the story that he started an online fundraising drive that's raised over $140,000 for him. Now, the homeless man is able to afford his own home.

In both cases, the act of kindness was because they believed it was an important value for *them.* They could have kept the money, and they both were having financial hardships, but their virtues of being honest and kind were far more powerful. The powerful part of this story is that they were kind and did what was right for them based on their own beliefs and this blessed everyone. They shared kindness and virtue without agenda. I truly believe that blessings will come to those who share in kindness in so many unexpected ways.

Opportunities To Be Kind

"Too often we underestimate the power of a touch, a smile, a kind word, a listening ear, an honest compliment, or the smallest act of caring, all of which have the potential to turn a life around." – Leo Buscaglia

Life has enough challenges. Choose Kindness. Give a smile, acknowledge the person in your building who cleans the bathrooms, say thank you to the person at the toll, wait two extra seconds in line as someone looks for change, be especially kind to your loved ones.

I find that sometimes those closest to us can be overlooked to receive the kindness they deserve from us. Maybe one feels they will always be there. Be aware to give to those closest to you and that you are not more concerned with strangers than your own. I honor kindness in every form and valuing this with those closest to you is a gift that stays forever in their heart and soul.

When we give to another, no matter what our riches, it is that we give with the heart that matters the most and which beholds the gift to the giver. Whatever you praise and bless, you magnify. Kindness is a voice of praise.

POWER THOUGHTS

Kindness

- o Kindness is a healing gift that I possess and share.

- o Kindness is the action of love without conditions, sharing the wholeness of my pure Self.

- o Kindness is a powerful force to shift pain into a memory healed with love.

- o I share kindness to those closest to me and in my home as a priority.

- o Kindness comes from within, a moment for me to represent love in action.

- o Kindness always matters.

- o The simplicity of my kindness can be a monumental experience for someone.

- o Kindness heals.

- o Sharing and receiving kindness is the Loving Energy that fuels our daily lives.

- o My kindness is a reflection of my inner peace.

Soul Support

If you have ever sat down to do a puzzle, you know that you naturally create a system for solving it. I love jigsaw puzzles and ever since I was a little girl, I can sit for hours on end doing puzzles. Once, when I started one of the hardest puzzles I have ever done, I spread out all the pieces and immediately felt overwhelmed and asked myself, "Where do I start?" First, I imagined it completed like the picture on the box and then I worked backwards to create the system to support that picture. I started with the border pieces and then grouped by color, then category, then one by one I started to create a match. I stayed consistent and kept working at it until all the pieces fit together. I created a system and my brain processed this flow as a pattern and eventually every piece was put together to match the picture. Human behavior has its patterns, some healthy and some less so.

It is very exciting to witness your dreams appear in front of your eyes. It feels magical when you find the love you have been wishing for or the dream job or home. Life feels so blissful as if you are floating on a cloud and everything is flowing in perfect order. You feel this total certainty of trust with this experience and are confident that more will follow. Then at some moment, you begin to witness that with this flow there are changes that may have to take place, where you may need to shift your habits or your physical space or make changes in your relationships. You are in that state of bliss; where you have clarity and everything feels in sync and these shifts or changes seem so effortless and easy. Sometimes you have had these behaviors or relationships for a very long time and even though it is time to shift them, you feel so positive.

So why is it that sometimes we have certain fears that start to take over? Why do we sabotage this positive flow to stick to habits or an old lifestyle?

When you interrupt an unhealthy human behavior, there will be some resistance. Either or both parties may feel vulnerable in this disruption. We can become attached to the consistency of a habit, relationship, a job, etc.

Unhealthy habits and emotions can feel comfortable when they are what we are familiar with. But "what if" we knew what we would feel like experiencing comfort with our new vision?

What if you trusted that a new state of being would actually feel more comfortable, because it is in sync with the truth of your Soul with joy. Understand that the fears and worry that get in our way are basically beliefs that created bad habits to keep us in a certain place in our life.

When you create new habits towards releasing what does not serve you to move forward, a fog has been cleared in your intuition and you have clarity that easily guides you. It's like the sky opened up with more shining stars. When *you know you know* – this is your wisdom and you trust this.

Why do people choose to go against their knowing and allow life to pass them by as they stay in regret or illness or blame towards others? Why is this? We could answer this with a list of reasons. What is important is why would you?

When your Soul has woken up either to love or passion in your life, it feels like a calling. It is also accompanied by a physical feeling, an energy that goes through your body and that awakens you with recognition. When you feel that *calling of your Soul*, own it. I see it like this: there is an "Ahh-Soulful" moment. You feel it and you know it. Actually, there is a sense of disbelief that it is even in front of your eyes. It could be that love or opportunity you have been wishing for ... and there it is! WOW. This is a moment of choice and I would grab it and never let it go. There is a tremendous support to make all your desires come true.

A Soulful Awakened Life

Let's get back to basics. We all love, think, have habits, a routine – we are always doing these things. If you are doing them already, why not gear them in the direction that is a system of supporting the dream that has appeared in your life? Do you realize the energy it takes to stay in something that does not serve you? That energy is draining, resistant and creates struggle in the simplest things in your life; your life flow is cut off. But many people stay in this lack of energy flow because it is what they know, and they come up with all these logical reasons as to why they need to stay in a situation they no longer want.

The dream that appeared in your life may or may not have logic; but there is logic in living a *soulful awakened life*. So let's see about the logic to this. A dream has appeared in your life and yes it takes energy to strengthen it but you are already using energy to stay in something you no longer wish for. Why not use the energy you are using to stay in something you *do* desire? It makes no logical sense to use your resources of energy to stay where your energy is being depleted. The reason most do this is out of fear and with fear comes more fear.

"What if" what you feared was resolved and it no longer existed? Instead of buying into fear as being the lead role in your "Movie," play with directing a "Movie" without this fear. Or ask your Self "What would I wish for to replace this fear? Or "How may this fear have served me?" Get comfortable within your self to vision what it could be like to live your wish. For example, one wishes to leave a relationship that they are miserable in. I ask them, "What do you fear?" The usual answer is they fear they would be alone. I share with them that if they knew that a wonderful loving partner was waiting for them would they handle their decision differently? And always it is a big "YES, of course!" I ask them to use their Emotional Imagination to feel a loving partner, and this adds more value to feel comfortable with being alone. I suggest playing out "Movies" of feeling confident and doing things that feel good without feeling the fear of being alone. The partner will naturally show up in a healthy way when the partner is not used to mask the fear the person has. When you play with resolving your fears, and create "Movies" of life as you wish, you create freedom and attract your desires clearly.

Fear does not create; it dissipates. Love, dreaming, and being awake to your life and emotions is what creates the magic you wish for in life – always. Do not let your life pass you by. Free your Self from your own self-inflicted bondage and free others that you have kept there by not wishing to move forward based on your own fears.

A part of my passion for awakening Amazing Souls comes from working with those dying and witnessing the desire they have to leave this life without regret. Assisting the dying and seeing their families begging for more time with their loved ones and wishing to resolve any challenges and regrets can be heart-wrenching. Yes, they say hindsight is always 20/20, but in reality many times we are living aware of our fears and choices we know we must make.

Use Power Wishing™ to break down your fears to face them. Once you face them you will see them no different than when one faces a bully only to watch them shrivel in front of your eyes because you no longer fear them. The formulas of Power Wishing are simple and the tools that I have suggested will support you to create the results you desire. What may be challenging for many is to keep the consistency of your new pattern of shifting your beliefs about your Self and trust that life continues to unfold magically. To trust the *real* YOU is so powerful.

Your Shadow Self or false personality of survival is not solid and will attempt to convince you that it is true. Your false Self is in essence a reaction to life, whereas the genuine YOU is a pure connection to your essence, responding to a flow of life that is happening for YOU.

You are setting a new pattern based on the choice you have made to support the expectation of your desires. I find that just when people are ready to have what they desire, they tend to go back into an old pattern out of fear, or in Power Wishing terms, due to not strengthening the anchoring of their emotional vision. They find and feel the old habit to be safe and more comfortable, though this type of behavior leads to feeling stuck.

Sometimes you stay in this suck place and just never move forward again. You shut the door to the voice of your Soul and drift back to sleep, numb to your Authentic Self. How do you push through this feeling of being stuck? How do you keep the flow that you desire as your new pattern? As I have mentioned before, some things are just about discipline. Stay consistent with behaviors and surround yourself with environments that serve you.

Consistency Is Key

When I was about 20 years old, I was selling wholesale jewelry to US stores from a manufacturer in Spain. The representative came from Spain to support me in my sales. We were in Los Angeles and I shared with him that even though we were selling high-end goods, we needed to have them in low-profile presentations because we might get mugged; to me this is common street sense. He felt differently. We were crossing a street and within seconds we were mugged and all my samples for the next season were stolen and this was when I would finally turn a profit. Within minutes not only did my whole life flash in front of me but also my unpaid bills. I had no clue what I was going to do, because the samples alone at that time took a few months to make, and I would miss an entire season of sales. I was devastated.

I returned home to my very small two-bedroom apartment and had to rent out a room to a student to help with the rent. One day she was on her way to a Super-Bowl party and asked if I wished to go. There was only one thing I wished for and that was to stay in bed and not get out, ever. But I decided to go even though I was not in a great mood.

When we were at this party, the women were talking about shoes with a woman that sold them in her apartment. I love shoes. Let me repeat – I love shoes. I got distracted in the conversation and forgot about not having money and went to see her shoes. They were great! I was in heaven. I was distracted into such a good emotional space that I forgot my *problems*. I saw a pair of shoes I loved, that I still wear today. I pulled out $40 dollars that I should have used towards my bills and bought them, and I gave that money without a care in the world.

It so happened that the woman who owned these shoes and I hit it off. We began to talk, and she shared how she was going out of town the following week. One thing led to another in our conversation and we discussed how I would take her inventory while she was gone and attempt to sell her shoes. Years later, we laughed at this conversation because she did not know me for more than a few hours and she was giving me all her shoes, her whole business investment. It made no logical sense.

I packed up her shoes and decided I was going to attempt to sell them in my small apartment. I made flyers and placed them everywhere. The day came that I was going to sell these shoes. To my disappointment only one person came and he was a male friend of mine who owned a clothing store, but he was not in need of women's shoes. I was not too happy at the fact that I had high hopes and did not make one sale, but the advice he gave me was what ended up making me more money than any sales I could have had that day.

He said, "Be consistent, the strength of your consistency in whatever you choose will win. Just stay consistent in whatever you are aspiring. Because one day others will give up and you will pass them by and succeed." Stay consistent in your behaviors; do not settle for laziness towards your thoughts and habits.

I did that. Every day I continued to push my sales, and eventually the woman and I opened a store and became the best of friends, memories I still cherish. The rest, as they say, is history.

Believe In Your Soul's Voice, Not Your Mind's Doubts

When you feel your Self getting stuck, say to yourself … "NEXT!" … and keep moving. If you are in a situation you don't like, see how it is serving you. Either shift it or leave it if necessary.

We often desire to create discipline for things such as working out or limiting our sweet tooth. Have the discipline to focus on encouraging the things that you desire more of and would like to enhance. Create habits that support your Soul and Spirit. Release on all levels being sloppy with the design of your life and do not allow habits to form that do not support you. I understand this can be challenging at times, but if you make a discipline to push through that challenge in the flash of that moment, just imagine what you could do! Imagine that in handling those moments your life does not feel like one big challenge and because of this you avoided living to live a life that is less than what you desire. Be your number one fan as you persist and move through your resistance, and before you know it, your new habit will click and become a natural part of your life. What is natural to your Soul will eventually be easier than resisting your Self.

Let me stop here for a moment and explain my definition of discipline. I view discipline as a support, not a hard-core, painful decision. To me, discipline is empowering because it supports me to have what I wish for. It may require me to make some changes that at first but I feel so grateful to know what changes to make that will lead me closer to my wish being granted. Maybe, my discipline comes from working for myself or knowing how I feel when I miss an opportunity or knowing how good it feels to wake up and witness the world I have created. Or possibly, I have discipline because it just makes sense. Having discipline that serves your goals is practical.

Taking accountability and showing up is a huge part of creating discipline and focus in your life. By being accountable, you avoid unnecessary chaos and release expending excess energy on rationalizing and circling around the truth. Just do it! Take any excuses for not showing up and shift them to an action of showing up.

Support Zone

You must make choices to move forward with your dream to be a solid reality. You must also protect your dream. You must create an environment to support yourself. The same way you would not surround a newborn baby with people that have the flu or have a refrigerator full of sweets if you wish to shift the weight of your body.

Now, we may not be able to trade in our family or fire our boss, but we can create a supportive "zone." Surround yourself with people, places and experiences that are in alignment with your dreams and that support your best Self. This zone supports your energy when there may be areas in life that are depleting you; *your support zone replenishes you.*

Who are the friends who support you with this way of thinking? Where do you go to feed your dreams? Where does your Soul get inspiration? How do you feed and nurture your Soul? Nurturing your Soul is a discipline that is also non-negotiable. *Your spiritual health creates all your wealth.*

Toxic-Free Zone

Your surrounding environment has a collective consciousness. When you hang around toxic people, they feed off your energy. Toxic people can be anyone from naysayers, gossipers and bullies to abusive partners or addicts. If you hang around these types of people because you feel sorry for them, please remember ... you cannot save anyone unless they wish to save themselves. Do your best to release the habit of hanging out in atmospheres that do not stimulate you positively.

It's exhausting when we use our emotional energy attempting to influence those who do not have good intentions. Whatever you do, and however "good" and loving you might be, you will not shift how others choose to be. They will shift when they feel like it and it will not be a reflection on you whether they do or do not.

Also, release from speaking negatively about those people you are not able to "trade in." Stop reaffirming what you say you do not wish for. Focus instead on reinforcing the positive aspects of your world that you wish to enhance. Chose to elevate those around you. I am sure you know what it feels like to make a positive difference in someone's life and this feels so much better than the alternative.

The conversations you have with yourself – that "Mental Courtroom" in your head that goes back and forth on topics and ideas – this should also be a toxic-free zone. Be aware to have positive inner dialogues with your Self, ones that are constructive.

If you are not your number one fan, then how can you expect anyone else to be? Be kind to your Self. Release the need to beat your Self up with thoughts and break your Self down with worry. STOP IT! Just stop; it serves nothing.

You are not a victim of your environment; you are the creator of it. Make choices that honor this. You are responsible for creating a clean environment within. There is everything to gain with this.

You must take responsibility for your energy because your energy IS your life and your health. *At the end of the day or better yet, at the end of your life, it is you that has to be at peace with who you are.*

Build your emotional immune system.

"As you simplify your life, the laws of the Universe will be simpler; solitude will not be solitude, poverty will not be poverty, nor weakness, weakness."
– Henry David Thoreau

Keep it simple! Keep it simple! If it feels *right* for you, it is *right*. Simplify your life by being your Authentic Self. Utilizing Power Wishing as a way of life will simplify the perceived complications created by not being who you truly are, your false personality. Be You! Your life is based on your beliefs.

Eliminate clutter – both physical and emotional – to create a supportive space.

Release in your life what you are a slave to; make more room for what supports you. This includes people, places, things and wasted time. Release what does not serve you, as if you have shed an old skin. Release those around you who continue to resist you. Embrace those who embrace you. You are a master of your emotional life. Your life is your design based on what you know to be true for you.

Schedule Soul support for your Soul.

Clear your calendar of unnecessary obligations. Create a schedule for your Self and pencil in appointments for things that make you happy. Schedule playtime, have time to be spontaneous. If you need support to create clarity for your dreams ... collage it ... write it ... make time to script your "Movie." Simply listen to your feelings and trust they are on your side ... create rituals and habits that support you. Be less serious and have more fun.

Embrace spirit within and around you.

I can pretty much guarantee that your cell phone, the newspaper and the TV will not connect you closer to your Authentic Voice or the wonderful gifts that are waiting for you to receive. Take time to be with your Self, take walks in nature, and take time to consciously connect to Source Energy, God, Creator – however you define this for your Self. But define it and connect consciously, as this love is an important support.

Slow down.

When you are upset, tired, or feeling impatient ... take a break. Disconnecting does not mean rejecting. A disconnect can be a moment to gain clarity and recharge yourself. Disconnecting does not mean you are a failure or you are giving up. You just require a quiet moment to your Self without anyone's energy, influence or needs around you.

All feelings are good because each emotion tells you something.

Feelings are the connection to your core truth; they are your wisdom and guide. Resist the habit of creating numbness in your life by avoiding what is hurting your feelings. *Running from a situation or quitting something that is challenging is not the same as choosing to avoid exposing your Self to experiences that are hurtful and counterproductive to you.* Know the difference and act accordingly, establish healthy boundaries to honor your Self and set your Self up for success.

Value your feelings.

Everyone has their own "Movie" and their perspective may have nothing to do with you. People will perceive what they wish. Therefore, do not base your decisions on another's opinion or approval. *When someone does not validate your feelings, this does not mean your feelings are not valid; it simply means this person has not validated them.*

Witness your "Movie."

Be present to witness what you have created in your life – enjoy it and honor your creation. By witnessing you can also move out of your own way and allow your Self to respond to enhancing your life, your way.

Choose the influences around you.

TV and media create powerful points of reference in your imagination. Be aware of what images and experiences you are taking in, even through movies. Use media as a way to enhance the ideas you wish to manifest. It is your choice how you allow it to influence the choices you make. Support media influences that support your wishes.

Be consistent.

Changing a pattern takes consistency. Do your best to stay consistent with behaviors that serve your desires. I find that right when people are ready to have what they wish, many tend to go back to comfortable habits that do not support this. Either because they fear that the goodness that awaits them is not real, or they see other people's resistance towards what they wish for. This can create a frustrating pattern of feeling stuck. The truth is that feeling stuck is just a part of an energetic shift that you are feeling. All will balance out. Remember, other people were used to you being a certain way.

Stay consistent with your focus on the shifts that you are choosing to make, and others will be supportive or will adapt or move out of your way. You will bring others into the experience that will support the life you wish to choose. Believe in your Self, your values, your character and all your goodness. Have gratitude for your Self and shift your focus away from your doubts and fears. Be consistent to move out of your way and own fears, as these are just veils that conceal the "good" that awaits you.

Choose Soul support surroundings.

Examine relationships that are toxic and ask your Self, "How are they serving me?" Conserve your energy for experiences you wish to have. There is little need to attend events or be in relationships that are not a match for you. Each and every day pay attention to opportunities that enhance your wellbeing and activate more of your genuine Self. Find people you admire and respect and mirror their best qualities.

Add value to others simply because of your presence.

Inspire greatness in others by acknowledging the greatness you see in them. Treasure and celebrate your loved ones by sharing what you love about each other. Let us remind each other that we are enough. Building a relationship from this perspective is solid. We are always enough and it is beautiful to accept people as they are, as we would appreciate the same response. Connect with others through joy and admiration. Be the expression of the gift that you are, a gift to yourself and a contribution to others. Love another by being true to your Self.

Sharing is an act that benefits you.

Give to others; share your resources and make the world a better place by being one that gives. The beauty of giving without agenda is that the world is a better place and you are even better for it. As you circulate your resources, whether through time or money, you create more of what you are sharing as you bring hope to others. You are the main benefactor.

Bless your past and take with you what serves you NOW.

Your past does not own you. Release your focus on the negative experiences and the habit of repeating them over and over again in your mind. When you do this, you are re-living them and reactivating them in the present moment. Why do you want to repeat a "Movie" of what you do not wish for? Why bring the past that no longer serves you to your future? *The past does not own you, your belief of your past does and this owns your future.*

Divine Love blesses your future.

Source Energy is not interested in your past, but interested in who you are now. Today is the day. This is the moment you can be free from your past that no longer serves you and blesses your future. There are always new moments for new opportunities. It is what you choose to do with your experience towards the direction of what you believe and expect for your reality. Today is the day, you are awake and every moment is yours to own. Own the blessing of your life as your definition of wishes granted.

There is magic to just saying "NEXT!"

When you get stuck ... simply say to yourself "Next" and keep moving forward. "Next" means that things are what they are and you chose not to give more energy to a situation that you may never understand or is not productive on any level. Saying "Next," is commanding your Vibrational Language to let this go, not because it is not important or valuable, but because right now there is not a solution and you choose to move forward. Next! Onward!

Just start somewhere.

You know enough to start now – 99% of everything is showing up, and this is how you know the next step. There is nothing for you to go back and live over, or fix, or feel regret about now. Every part of your life has unfolded just right. Feel empowered with your own deep personal knowing of your love for your Self and others. Take action, as action creates your prayers answered in the physical. Praying without action is like reading a book about swimming but never getting into the water. You will never know the experience of swimming unless you get into that water. Now knowing all that you know from where you now stand, take the next step. The answers will come forth to you, with each step you take. Go forth in joy, and get on with having a life reflecting your dreams. You can only get it *right,* with love as your base for all things possible.

Honor your Self.

Many illnesses are due to emotional congestion causing you to be a prisoner in your own body. Remember the "PBI Disorder" – too much information and no action. The "BBB Syndrome" – cure this syndrome by treating every "but" in your vocabulary. Every excuse is giving reason for your prayer not to be answered, treat that reason. Evil only has the reality you give it. When you speak of evil or think of evil, you have given it power. Nothing can scare you – if you do not give it power.

Your life is not to be sacrificed.

It is not your duty to do anything that sacrifices your own integrity or your own spiritual integrity. If you feel you are sacrificing anything for anyone, or your life is a sacrifice for any cause, then this is not a core value but an excuse not to show up for your Self and to allow another or a cause to take power over you. Your life is a choice; make a choice, not a sacrifice.

Do not tolerate anything less than ...

Refuse to tolerate anything except harmonious love in your life. Shift your beliefs of your ability to shift your circumstances and they will no longer be the same. Blessings are your Divine birthright. Accepting less than your birthright is because of bad habits within your imagination. You can become your own master or your own prisoner.

Our will is the will of Divine Love.

Divine Love is powerful to expand all that you are and all that you believe is possible and more. The rest is an illusion of fear. You bring to your Self what you believe and you *will* this by your Vibrational Language®: the Love that surrounds you gives what you expect.

Self-inflicted struggle is not the opportunity for more Light; it is the self-destruction of your Light. The abundance that you are rejecting is not a rejection of Source Energy. It is ridiculous to ever say that evil or suffering could ever be that of the *will* of a *God*; this is a human creation. You are an Amazing Divine Soul, loved beyond what you can imagine.

Release your worries to Divine Love.

As an Amazing Soul, your natural state is Love. Therefore, Love banishes fear, and peace is the Earth you step upon. Release on all levels fear of people, circumstances or of your own perceived limitations, for this is being in an unnatural state and is ignoring your Divineness. Nothing, no one has power apart from the power we give it by believing in it. Your Divinity is always connected with Divine Love. Know this and be filled with peace.

Live in harmony.

Living in harmony with your Self creates synergy with the world around you. You are healthy because you are happy, not because you are healthy. Seek and you shall find, ask and you shall receive, knock and the door shall be opened. Imagine being consciously awake as you seek. Ask and knock at the door of life with the virtues that honor your Divinity in partnership with Divine Love. Imagine what you will find and receive with all the possibilities open to you. Miracles are only miracles because we have low expectations of who we truly are. When you honor your true Self and your partnership with Divine Love as an awakened state, miracles that have always been present are now seen and become your normal way of life.

Claim it!

Claim what you desire. Stay quiet in prayer with your desire until it is realized. Hold the space of love for it to grow by not permitting any interference. Give thanks for what you have asked for and claim this feeling as a present experience now. Pray with another who holds your truth, and you multiply the prayers of each other. The Divine wisdom of Love is yours. This wisdom guides you and you feel this consciousness with every breath you breathe. You are supplied with all you desire as you know your Divinity and ask with consciousness of love connected with Source Energy.

Allow Divine Love to resolve for you.

Release resentment or condemning of another – when you hold resentment towards anyone, you are bonded to that person by a cosmic link, a real mental chain. You are tied to the very thing you say you resent. Release the need to defend and react; do not live as if you are being attacked. Connect with the wisdom of your character. There is Divine justice and allow this to take care of matters. You are not the judge of another.

Forgive.

Forgiveness is a release of your pain, a release of the negative energy that is hindering your possibilities. It frees you to have other opportunities and blessings. When you truly forgive and release, there is a renewing of life that could only come through forgiveness. Yes, there was agony in what caused your hurt, but there will also be great blessings through forgiveness. You send out thoughts of peace, love and healing to the whole Universe for all are equal to you and deserving of love. Freely forgive all those who have done you harm and let them go. They are free and you are free.

Keep it simple.

Prayer is simple, direct and spontaneous. Do not complicate your prayer with the intellect. Pray the simple prayer with your heart and Soul. You are a sacred prayer that is answered. Pray. Believe. Expect.

Prayer for another is also a prayer for you.

Pray for another what you would pray for your Self, speak towards another as you would speak to your Self, act towards another as you would act towards your Self. Though we may seem separate, we are all connected.

Honor others.

Honor others for the love they share with you from their perspective. Honor your definition of love. Release others who do not love you the way you wish … or accept them. Bless those in your life by being your definition of love.

Pray with love, love without conditions.

Close your eyes, connect with your heart and shower yourself with love. Love without conditions, as this is pure love. Feel this as white Light and have this fill every bit of your cellular body.

Breathe with knowing that love heals all.

If you have a situation that you do not know how to resolve, turn it over to Divine Love to resolve for you and show you guidance for this. Give thanks for this resolution.

When you love someone and feel hurt or have hurt another, shower your Self and them with love without conditions or expectation. Sometimes our pain takes us past an understanding to know how to heal or love. Allow Divine Love to be the force that heals with you.

If you have a loved one and desire to help them or are worried about them, the prayers of worry for another send an unconscious message to the one you are praying for as if there is lack in them. This is not your intent. Allow love that has no conditions to be what activates them to love themselves and to be the force that heals their lack and releases you from your worry. Allow this love to pour through every cell of your loved one's body. Pray that they receive this love and recognize their greatness.

Love inspires and heals all.

Your expression of love is YOU. Be the expression of love that inspires you, honors you and others. Build on what you love about yourself and the world around you.

Own your life with praise.

Claim your life by praising it! Every time you praise something, every time you appreciate something, every time you feel good about something, you are commanding more of what you love. You are giving a clear message of expectation. When you are in this allowing all good things will flow for you ... it is the reflection of your expectation answered.

Be an inspiration to your Self.

Inspire your Self with the life you aspire to live. Live an inspired life. Be interesting to yourself. Look for the good! You find what you are looking for by looking for the good *will*. Smile, feel joy and laughter, as there are many opportunities to feel the life you know is possible. Stay focused on what brings you joy. Yes, being happy does matter!

Praise your blessings.

Praise your life. Praise every experience and everyone. What you praise you raise. If something that you wish for comes easily for you, celebrate this! Release all resistance to things that come easily for you and to you. Give thanks!

Yes, yes I am blessed.

Do not miss the opportunity for love and kindness; this is an action of gratitude for our blessings.

You matter.

The world awaits you. Contribute to the world by being who you truly are. *Your presence here matters.* You are a unique Amazing Soul whose existence is greatly valued and cherished. Let others truly experience the Amazing Soul that you are by celebrating your Authentic Self. Know with total certainty that you are significant and a blessing.

YOU

You have the ability to awaken the life that you know exists in your Soul. YOU are a unique and a powerful manifester.

You create your self-fulfilled prophecy. So be it!

Know That You Are Loved

Know that within you there is great love. Know that within others there is great love. Know there is great love for you everywhere. Smile in this knowing, with peace the understanding that we are all loved.

Honor each other with safe love. You know what it feels like to love from a place of gentle authenticity and to be loved this way. Trust that sharing your authentic love with another creates a partnership that goes beyond this time and place.

You know how to honor another Soul by sharing gentle truth when answering a question. You trust that the gentle truth that is shared is an honoring of your Souls and will influence more than the present outcome. This honoring transcends beyond time and space with a love that is eternal and an integrity that is sacred.

You know what it feels like to speak to your Self as you wish for another to speak to you. You know how to speak to others as you wish to be spoken to.

You know how to love another as you wish to be loved. You know what it feels like to love yourself as you wish to be loved.

You feel love and excitement as you plant your seeds of the possibilities you wish to manifest with the prayer of your "Ask." As you feel the gift of your powerful Emotional Imagination activating the growth of your seeds with your free will, you are joyful.

You know what it feels like to have total certainty that the soil of Source Energy receives this with Absolute Love, nourishing your seeds to give you the fruits of your "Ask" with ease.

You know what it feels like to plant your seeds with your Emotional Imagination. You know that the seeds you plant of feelings that feel good to you are what you expect to receive from your desire. And Source Energy provides for you.

You have total certainty of knowing that Source Energy loves you and provides the fertile soil for you to co-create *together.* You know what it feels like to trust this, as you allow this Love to be an active partner with you. You know how to release doubts and fears of your "Ask" as you acknowledge this partnership, which nourishes the co-creation of the fruits of your desire beyond what you expect.

You feel so grounded in knowing that you are a blessing. You know what it feels like to be blessed with your "Movie" of life and its journey of feelings as you honor and feel empowered by expressing *who you are* based on your best Emotional Self.

You feel peaceful knowing with total certainty that struggle, pain and lack are shifted to a prayer of abundance, wellbeing and peace. You easily use your imagination to ignite emotions that are noble to your heart and Soul. You know how to "check in" with your Emotional Self, feeling free to ask your Self real questions and feel your genuine answers. You reflect and answer with the awareness that you may be asked to go outside of your comfort zone and you feel confident in doing so.

You simply continue to make choices that are consistent in being aligned with who you genuinely are and you feel excited about what you are expecting.

You *Stage Your Day*. You *Stage Your Night*. You live knowing how to be proactive in creating your stage of life.

You know how to release worry and if you go a bit off alignment, it's OK. You know what if feels like to make another choice and move forward. Next!

You feel such joy inside you as you play! Play with creating experiences that feel good as a match to your desires!

You are alive in your life. You continue to feel full inside with the knowing that there is so much love for you ... so much love holding you as you continue to embrace the magnificence of experiencing life as an Amazing Soul.

You feel your life as a continuous journey, an ever-evolving story full of unique experiences that explore who you are as you discover others and enhance your Self and your relationships.

You feel this electricity of excitement as your prayers are answered. This feels so good and joyful to you. You choose the characters in your "Movie" that support your script, and you know how to honor your choices and honor the "Movies" of others in such a relaxed way.

You recognize the life force of your heart and embrace this with excitement. You feel your heart recognizes those who surround you as they love and embrace you for who you are. You celebrate, as you create environments that reflect the vision you hold about your Self.

You define your life by the way you define your Self. Your life is the definition of you! You trust this. You live this. You feel Love expanding this with you.

You are living the possibility of the dreams that you love and hold precious and dear, as they are your reality. You believe in great love and feel this in your life. You feel such gratitude for the strength and vitality to experience your dreams at this time.

You bless your life, you bless your circumstances, you bless others, and you praise all your possibilities and multiply these with love. You know what if feels like to love and embrace what you have created in your life and *know* that YOU have created it. You honor this with a smile, as you are excited to create more of what you love in your life that is an exciting journey!

You fully understand and allow the Love that embraces you to live your dreams. Later is NOW and you know how to take action towards this.

You love yourself, you love your life, and you love your world and you are so loved.

You feel peace and tranquility for all is well. You are blessed and miracles of your blessings are experiences as your life.

You continue to enhance the presence of being all that you love, feeling loved, lovable and supported for all that you are. You expand your vision of life with possibilities that were once dreams but now unfold as your life.

You continue to receive blessings with ease as you rejoice and praise your life experience as the YOU that you truly are!

With love and blessings for your wishes granted,

Anne Louise

Acknowledgments

I first would like to acknowledge God's presence in my life, my "Source Energy" that I am consciously connected to as Energy of love that fuels every aspect of my being and my life. Thank you.

My children Sophia and Andrew, My life with both of you is the best gift I could ever ask for. Sharing our life experiences is always magnificent. You both are unique beautiful Souls that share with kindness and values that only continue to bring joy and lots of laughter to every part of me. I am so fortunate to have children like you, as is the world! We are one. Thank you for all the patience and love that you give to support what I love, knowing that I love being your mom most of all.

Dad, Thank you for sharing great books with me that inspired my imagination and set the foundation for my expansive studies. You directed me to redefine success and reinforced me to accept my differences as an added value to who I am. Thank you for your knowledge, commitment and love. Adrianna, you are so special and are always there for us as an angel. Thank you.

Mom, Thank you for genuinely encouraging my work through all the years, sharing my work with others, helping me organize my workshops and edits. I deeply appreciate your insight to introduce me to my first awareness teacher, Frank Natale, at age 14. Thank you for your kindness, understanding and love.

Michael, Jennifer, Louie, Andrew, Gracie & Brian, my six heartfelt siblings, I love you all and I love your families! I appreciate each of you individually for the way that you hold my children and me dear to your heart.
I value the great experiences we have shared together as siblings and friends. I love witnessing all of us live our passion for life. Thank you to each and every one of you for adding such love to my life.

Christina Nicodemou, What a magnificent journey! Thank you for believing, for trusting in me and for expanding the gift of my work to others. I appreciate you and I honor your commitment to living the experiences of this work and sharing it with the lives of so many. This book was completed with your enthusiasm, commitment and loving Light. We made it, again. I have so much love for you and your family, especially sweet baby Kai Valentinos ... a beautiful manifestation of a powerful wish that brings this work to life in the form of great love.

Elaine, you are always there for me no matter what idea I have. Even if it were to go to the moon, we would make it there together. Thank you for reminding me of the best of me. I am so grateful and appreciative of the solid friendship we have shared for over thirty years and for your loving support in my life. I love you and your family dearly. Thank you for being you.

Christina High, Thank you for the hours of endless conversations of life and love and everything in between. Thank you for your belief in all that I believe is possible. I cherish our special soulful friendship, you are a true Earth Angel and I love you and your family.

Ruth & Peter, I love you both. I am very grateful for your love and commitment with my family and for all your support of my work. Thank you for giving generously in all ways with such Light and especially for my second home in New York. Ruth, your amazing support of this book is so valued with your editing skills and commitment. Thank you for your devoted friendship.

Tere, thank you for our journey of sisterhood and for honoring who I am and what I believe in with such love and commitment. I love you, my nieces and Javier dearly.

Natacha, I love you and I am deeply grateful for all we continue to share. With your depth of love and understanding, your presence always reminds me that everything will be good.

Tania & Glen, Thank you for always being there for my children and me. For making sure that I am always *covered* and for reminding me that everything is going to be just "fine." You are always right ... always. I am grateful for the anchor you are in my life. Love you both and your family!

Nai, thank you for the love and belief you have with all that I believe. Thank you for being next to me. I love you and your family.

Dan, Thank you for my website and the countless hours you spend making sure it is perfect as a labor of love you have for my work and our friendship. Thank goodness you appeared to be our angel and made sure this happened. With appreciation and love.

Ingrid, Thank you for your contribution to the vision I held for this book. I am grateful with love for your friendship and for all the ways in which you support my work with encouragement, care and loving detail.

Kasia & Patryk, Thank you for valuing my work and patiently holding the vision of my published book. Your time, presence and knowledge are appreciated with love. I am grateful for the opportunity to partner with you both on the journey of sharing my series of books with the world.

Dr. Christina King, with love for the Amazing Soul that you are. I deeply appreciate your trust, the support you have given me to bring the Amazing Soul to readers. I still hear your laughter.

Suzanne, thank you for all your support and dedication to this work, and the gift of Alicia. I love you.

Alicia, your editing skills transformed my word to be heard with grace and ease. Thank you.

Celia, thank you for your talent that transformed the book cover to another level.

Luisa, Angie & Connie, thank you for never saying no and always sharing your support with so much love!

Fula & Fred, Thank you so much for being present in creating clarity and the foundation for my children and me to move forward with a solid foundation. You gave us Light at a time where there was loss and hurt. You continue to embrace us, bringing us of peace. We deeply appreciate your commitment to our wellbeing. I am grateful, as are my children. We love you.

Raque & Jaime, Your beacon of Light, your kindness and care filled our hearts with hope at our time of loss. You have loved us in ways that healed our grief and continue to share in ways that bring joy. I am grateful, as are my children. Thank you with so much love and admiration.

Steven, Tatiana, Sandra & Cocho, thank you for love & commitment towards the well being of my children's future, reminding them that they are visible and you believe in them.

To my dearest grandparents, Mamin, Papin, Grandma & Grandpa, The love of my grandparents gave me freedom to fly and still does.
Uncle Louie, who is still so present as he was when I was a child and continues to be, Thank you for your commitment to our family.

To my extended family of soul sisters, This book is a part of my life's work; nevertheless, our many conversations of experiences with joy, loss, pain, the witnessing of our lives, the birth of our children, the love stories, the soul contracts are all a part of this work. I am grateful for each of you and all the opportunities we have to share the pure love that holds us in the place of prayer for the possibilities that we wish for each other and ourselves. We consistently remind each other of what we love about each other and share what we believe in each other when we have forgotten ourselves. We laugh together and keep taking chances, knowing we are at each other's side! Thank you. Thank you. Thank you ... for your love and trust. I have so much love for you all.

To my community of Amazing Souls and Power Wishers, Thank you for taking the time to share yourselves. I deeply appreciate your letters and your stories, which inspire me to continue to share this work and write these books. Thank you! Thank you with all my heart and soul for being a part of my wish granted with the publishing of this book! At the base of this book is LOVE. Love for oneself, for others and for the unexpected surprises of life ... There is great love that surrounds us all. I thank you for sharing your hearts and honor you with love.

Special thanks to those who took the time to read my manuscript and offer feedback about the book so it can give the best of me. It means the world to me!

To my teachers ... those in the "seen" and "unseen" who believed in me and pushed me beyond what I knew existed within me, Thank you for holding the space for me to enhance my gifts and for seeing the best in me. I deeply appreciate, with love and admiration, your commitment and vision.

To the "Unseen" world of those beautiful Souls that continue to show me and utilize me to illustrate to others that love does transcend in the non-physical ... to share the love and life that exists beyond the veil of this existence, Thank you for your trust. I am grateful to be a vehicle to bring peace to the hearts and souls of others.

Simple Results ©

Inspiration. Enhancement. Success.

A sample of Simple Results courses:

POWER WISHING ®
ADVANCED POWER WISHING®
VISUALIZATION TECHNOLOGY®
EMOTIONAL IMAGINATION®
LANGUAGE YOUR LIFE®
CHARACTER LEGACY
BUSINESS LEADERSHIP
VIBRATIONAL LANGUAGE®

"Character is not a mood; it is the foundation of who you are."

To reserve Anne Louise Carricarte as a speaker
or host a Simple Results workshop with your organization,
please contact our team at:

info@SimpleResults.net

www.SimpleResults.net